New Swan Shakespeare   ADVANCED SERIES

GENERAL EDITOR   Bernard Lott M.A. Ph.D.

Antony
and
Cleopatra

WILLIAM SHAKESPEARE

Antony and Cleopatra

Edited by John Ingledew M.A.

Longman

Longman Group Ltd, London
Associated Companies, branches and representatives throughout the world

First published 1971
Second impression 1974
ISBN 0 582 52743 0

Phototypeset by Oliver Burridge Filmsetting Ltd, Crawley, Sussex
Printed in Great Britain by Lowe & Brydone (Printers) Ltd,
 Thetford, Norolk.

Contents

Acknowledgements We are grateful to the following for permission to reproduce copyright material:

Faber & Faber Ltd. for extracts from Chapter 5 'Antony and Cleopatra: A Shakespearian Adjustment' from *Elizabethan and Jacobean Poets* by John F. Danby; Macmillan & Co. Ltd., St. Martin's Press Inc. and The Macmillan Company of Canada for an extract from *Oxford Lectures on Poetry 1909* by A. C. Bradley; Methuen & Co. Ltd. and Thomas Y. Crowell Co. Inc. for an extract from *A Shakespeare Encyclopaedia* by Oscar J. Campbell and Edward G. Quinn (published in America under the title *The Reader's Encyclopedia of Shakespeare*) copyright © 1966 by Thomas Y. Crowell Co. Inc.; Staples Press Ltd. for an extract from *Shakespeare and the Popular Dramatic Tradition* by S. L. Bethell.

We have been unable to trace the American copyright holder of *Shakespeare and the Popular Dramatic Tradition* by S. L. Bethell, and would appreciate any information that would enable us to do so.

The illustrations are reproduced by courtesy of the following:

The Harry Beard Theatre Collection, Cambridge for page xi a and b;
The Chichester Theatre and John Timbers for pages xiii bottom, xliii a;
The Glyptothek, Munich for page xxvii d;
C. Walter Hodges for page lxi;
The Louvre, Paris for page xxvii b;
The Raymond Mander and Joe Mitchenson Theatre Collection for page xxv;
The Mansell Collection for pages xliii b, lv;
The Radio Times Hulton Picture Library for pages xi c and d, xiii a and b.

The map on pages cvi and cvii is by Hanni Bailey.

GENERAL EDITOR's Foreword

THE AIM of the edition of *Antony and Cleopatra* in the *New Swan Shakespeare Advanced Series* is to ensure that the reader fully understands and appreciates the play itself. To this end it pays unusual attention to explanation of the text. A large number of points that other editions take for granted or touch upon inconclusively are now treated at length, and besides dealing with such matters as archaic language and allusions to customs no longer current, the notes explain briefly certain rare words still alive in modern English which happen to occur in the play (e.g. *reneges, wassail*). Help is also given with complicated syntactical constructions and with patterns of imagery which may not be obvious at first sight. The content of the play, its historical, social and philosophical bases, and the conventions implied in the way characters react to one another may be strange to many readers; these matters too are treated in detail. Nevertheless the total extent of the notes on the left-hand pages is not very great. There are two reasons why the notes can be comparatively short and yet comprehensive. First, the language of the explanations is simple and direct. Second, in other editions much space has frequently been given to alternative readings of the text of the play, and to various conjectures about what difficult passages really mean. The present edition omits nearly all speculation of this kind. Where the meaning is doubtful, it does not give numerous alternative explanations; instead, the editor has chosen the one which seems to him to fit the context most satisfactorily; if *one* possible alternative definitely serves to make the meaning clearer, this is added. Reference is made to the readings of the original text, the First Folio of 1623, only where a helpful explanation of the passage is to be had.

Some background knowledge is essential to a full understanding of the play. Certain passages can be explained only in the light of some aspect or other of the 'world view' of Shakespeare's day, or by some piece of information about the ancient world in which the action supposedly takes place, or about Shakespeare's view of this ancient world. Some of these things will be unknown to many readers, especially those who are not very familar with the English background to Shakespeare's plays. Such information is given briefly so as to clarify the meaning of the passage in question, but no attempt has been made to give a far-reaching account of the whole subject. Readers who are completely familiar with the English background will occasionally be able to ignore notes of this type, but others may find them useful, since they will remove difficulties rooted not in the use of the language but in the Shakespearian ethos.

At the back of the book there is an index which glosses and gives the location of all the difficult or unusual words in the text. By reference to the location in the text the student will find a note which will in most instances expand the brief equivalent given in the glossary. The index will also help him to trace passages in the play: if he remembers a key word likely to be included in the index, he can look it up and find there a line reference in the text. In this way the glossarial index is also an index to the notes.

Elaborate criticism of the play is not given, although some passages of literary criticism relating to it are reproduced, and further sources are indicated in the bibliography. A study of these sources can, however, wait until the play is thoroughly known and appreciated for its own sake.

The Introduction to *Antony and Cleopatra* differs in one way from the introductions to other plays in the series: it includes a considerable extract from North's translation of Plutarch's *Life of Marcus Antonius*. The departure is justified by Shakespeare's dependence on this source for his historical facts and our interest in the way the poet-dramatist adapted the material to make a great play. This is not vital to an understanding of the play although it will certainly help us to appreciate the genius of Shakespeare himself.

Otherwise all the help offered, in the form of notes, glosses and introduction, has only this end in view: that the student should understand the play, since the only way to full enjoyment of the play is full understanding of what it means.

Introduction

Meaning and purpose in Antony and Cleopatra

In *Antony and Cleopatra*, written about 1606, Shakespeare takes up the events of Roman history at the point where he left them some six or seven years before in *Julius Caesar*. Since there are numerous references in *Antony and Cleopatra* to people and events in *Julius Caesar* it may be helpful to recapitulate briefly the plot of the earlier play. *Julius Caesar* opens in the year 44 B.C. shortly after Caesar returns in triumph to Rome, having crushed Pompey and his forces at the Battle of Pharsalus in 48 B.C. Cassius, jealous of Caesar, attempts to incite Brutus against him. Brutus is torn between his affection for Caesar and fear of his ambition, which he thinks will lead to a loss of republican freedom and the establishment of a tyranny by Caesar. He decides to join Cassius and other disaffected Romans in a conspiracy, and together they murder Caesar in the Capitol, though at Brutus's request they spare Caesar's friend Antony. After the death of Caesar, Brutus explains to the Roman crowd the motives that led him to take part in the killing; he then leaves the scene, foolishly allowing Antony to address the crowd. Antony subtly provokes the mob to fury against the conspirators, who are forced to flee from Rome. Antony joins forces with Octavius, Caesar's grand-nephew, and Lepidus to form a coalition of three known as the Triumvirate, and they pursue the conspirators to Macedonia. Brutus, encamped at Sardis, is visited by Caesar's ghost who informs him that he will see him the next day at Philippi, and it is here that Brutus and Cassius are defeated by the forces of the Triumvirate and take their own lives. The triumvirs then divide the Roman world between them. *Antony and Cleopatra* opens with Antony in Egypt and the other two triumvirs in Italy.

Despite the continuity of historical events we soon perceive that there is very little connection between the character of Antony in the two plays. Shakespeare makes a fresh start, as it were, so that the young, brilliant and single-minded political opportunist of *Julius Caesar* is transformed, in *Antony and Cleopatra*, into a middle-aged pleasure seeker, a great man in decline.

In its meaning, structure and characterization *Antony and Cleopatra* is a much more complicated play than *Julius Caesar,* and has given rise to a bewildering variety of interpretations, most of which tend to run to extremes, either of denunciation or of glorification of the lovers. Often these seem to be the result of preconceived ideas about the morality of the lovers. While both responses can find supporting evidence from the play, their advocates omit a good deal that is there in the play in order to sustain their argument. Our critical approach, however, must be to take all the events, in the order in which the dramatist unfolds them to us, relating each event in the sequence to what has gone before. If the dramatist is doing his work well, character and action will be so interwoven that what happens will influence and change his characters and thus shape subsequent events. Our final appreciation will be determined by the whole action, though of course the dramatist relies heavily on the ending – the catastrophe or denouement – to convey the ultimate impression and meaning he intends. Our response to people and events in drama, while related to our response to life, is different in all kinds of subtle ways. We are more indulgent in literature than in real life to vicious but attractive characters, like Falstaff in *Henry IV*, for example; we are more moved by tragic events. This is because dramatic art is not life, but a simplification and selection from it, so that paradoxically, while we may remain detached spectators, we are more simply and directly involved in the drama without all the distractions and complications and qualifications of real life. We have to accept that most plays create their own world, and it is within the limits of the play's world that we have to judge its people and events. Most playgoers make these adjustments instinctively, accepting for the duration of the play the existence, for example, of magic and monster in *The Tempest*, fairies in *A Midsummer Night's Dream* or the Ghost in *Hamlet*. The meaning of a Shakespearian play is the impression that the playgoer carries away with him from the theatre, and this is an amalgam made up of the intellectual significance of the words spoken, the acting performance, which is largely dictated by the words of the text, and the tone or atmosphere generated by the imagery and the rhythmic and melodic effects of the poetry.

Like all Shakespeare's plays, *Antony and Cleopatra* is shaped by the dramatic conventions of the time, and by the current thought and outlook of the age. We can learn a good deal from external evidence of this kind, and even more from the internal evidence of the play itself, about Shakespeare's purposes in the play.

In the first place, we would hardly expect that Shakespeare, whose development as a dramatist was towards a deepening awareness of the complexity and mystery of life, should late in his career, after writing plays as profound as *Hamlet, Othello, Lear* and *Macbeth,* present us with a play which demanded a simple response such as the straightforward denunciation or glorification of a pair of lovers. We would not expect denunciation to be the response required by Shakespeare, whose Sonnets record the poet's entanglement with the so-called Dark Lady, which in many ways parallels Antony's passion for

Cleopatra as portrayed by

a) *Harriet Faucit 1813.*

b) *Isabella Glyn 1849.*

c) *Lily Langtree 1890.*

d) *Sarah Bernhardt at the beginning of this century.*

Cleopatra. Like Antony, who loved her while believing that she had been a 'boggler ever', the poet tells us

> When my love swears that she is made of truth
> I do believe her, though I know she lies.
>
> (Sonnet 138)

'Vilest things / Become themselves' in Cleopatra, 'whom everything becomes'; so too with the Dark Lady, of whom Shakespeare asks

> Whence hast thou this becoming of things ill,
> That, in the very refuse of thy deeds
> There is such strength and warrantise of skill
> That, in my mind, thy worst all best exceeds?
>
> (Sonnet 150)

Antony accuses Cleopatra of being 'triple-turned', that is, of having been unfaithful to three lovers; the poet accuses the Dark Lady of 'two oaths' breach', and is equally powerless to overcome his passion. It would be unwise to press the parallels too far, but it is unlikely that any man, having been harrowed as the poet was in this affair, could present a similar situation unsympathetically in the play.

Another piece of external evidence that tends to preclude a simple rejection of Cleopatra is the connection between her and Queen Elizabeth, which this extract from a modern historian, with no thought of Cleopatra in mind, makes clear:

> England's Elizabeth was, Englishmen agreed, a phoenix, singular in her kind, incommensurable by any general standard. In that they were more right than they knew. There has never been anything in history like the forty-five-year-long love affair between Elizabeth Tudor and the people of England. . . .
>
> From the first she courted them, posed for them, cajoled them. It was for them she made herself beautiful and a little remote, and surrounded by a glittering court; for them she made herself suddenly affable and familiar and beguiling. . . . With sure instinct she composed herself into a picture of what they wanted her to be, as a lover must. She was proud and imperious often (a queen should be like a queen) and she did not forget sometimes to make them jealous and uneasy. She varied her caresses with slaps, and at times she could receive their well-meant advice with chill scorn, warning them not to meddle with the affairs of princes . . . and producing all the sudden tempest of a lover's quarrel to follow it with sunshine equally overwhelming. In a word she was careful never to bore them but equally careful to assure them . . . that

*Antony
as portrayed by*

*a) Beerbohm Tree
1907.*

*b) Frank Benson in
the 1920's.*

b

a

*A more recent
portrayal of Antony
and Cleopatra:
John Clements and
Margaret Leighton
in 1969.*

she loved them better than anything else. How much art there was in her conduct, and how much nature, a mere historian cannot be expected to say . . .*

The habit of analogizing, of tracing parallels between the great figures of the past and the present, was strongly rooted in the Elizabethans,† who would naturally make connections and comparisons between these two great queens. In 1606, when Shakespeare was writing his play, the early promise of James I's reign had withered, and disillusioned Englishmen were thinking more and more nostalgically of the spacious days of Good Queen Bess, conveniently forgetting her shortcomings. Shakespeare himself had been in trouble with the authorities when his *Richard II* was performed in London's streets and theatres in 1601 as part of the bid by the Earl of Essex to win popular support for his attempt to usurp the throne. Elizabeth was in no doubt about the analogies: "I am Richard. Know ye not that?" she asked William Lambarde, her keeper of the Tower, while Essex, she knew, saw himself in the role of Bolingbroke, the usurper. It is interesting, too, that Shakespeare's contemporary, Fulke Greville, who wrote a play on Antony and Cleopatra, prudently burned it because, as he said,

> Many members in that creature [the play] – by the opinion of those eyes who saw it – having some childish wantonness in them apt to be construed or strained to a personating of vices in the present governors and government.

Another aspect of sixteenth century thought which is relevant to our understanding of the play is the renaissance conception of the 'great man' or hero. For the ancient Romans, Julius Caesar and Antony were pre-eminent examples of the heroic in their possession of the quality of *virtus,* that is, male force and energy, the Roman ideal of masculinity. Military prowess, courage in battle, magnanimity and a single-minded devotion to one's honour and fame were essential ingredients of the classical hero, who was often self-assertive, boastful and cruel, and so at odds with the Christian conception of male perfection, which demanded contrary qualities like humility, prudence and love. In renaissance literature and life, so strongly influenced by classical ideals, we find a tension between these two conflicting ideas of the hero. Some preferred the classical ideal, and many strove to synthesize the two. Several of the great men of Shakespeare's time, like the Earl of Leicester, Sir Philip Sidney, Sir Walter Raleigh and the Earl of Oxford, displayed in their

---

*   Garret Mattingly, *The Defeat of the Spanish Armada* (1959), pp. 25, 27.

†   Although Elizabeth died in 1603, the adjective 'Elizabethan' is used in this edition, as normally, to refer also to that part of Shakespeare's life and work which fell within the reign of her successor, James I.

lives elements of the classical ideal of the heroic. In drama it found expression in Marlowe's *Tamburlaine*, Chapman's *Bussy D'Ambois*, and in several plays about Julius Caesar, while the tension between the two ideals can be seen in Shakespeare's *Coriolanus*. The fact that the Latin word *virtus* was often translated by the English word 'virtue' has led frequently to confusion, since for the modern reader the English word carries connotations of moral virtue not included in the meaning of *virtus*. For the ancient world the possession of *virtus* offset, or made unimportant, moral blemishes in the hero. Plutarch, Shakespeare's source for his play, was aware of Antony's moral failings but excuses them in view of Antony's heroic qualities, which make him finally an object of admiration beyond praise or blame. This attitude is reflected in the play, and must be allowed for in our judgement of Antony. We find him boasting of his descent from Hercules who was the great type of the hero for the ancient world, though he was in many ways an immoral man. Antony, too, is obsessed with his honour and reputation, as we see in his meeting with Octavius in Rome:

> The honour is sacred which he talks on now,
> Supposing that I lacked it.
>
> (II.ii.89)

> but mine honesty
> Shall not make poor my greatness, nor my power
> Work without it.
>
> (II.ii.96)

To Octavia he explains

> If I lose mine honour,
> I lose myself.
>
> (III.iv.22)

and after his flight from Actium he is filled with shame at his dishonour:

> I have offended reputation;
> A most unnoble swerving.
>
> (III.xi.49)

So closely is his honour identified with himself that after his loss of honour he experiences a sense of the disintegration of his whole personality:

> Here I am; Antony,
> Yet cannot hold this visible shape.
>
> (IV.xiv.13)

His great rage when he finds Thidias kissing Cleopatra's hand (III.xiii), and

later when he believes that she has betrayed him (IV.xii) is another manifestation of the heroic ideal; in fact, on this latter occasion Antony prays that his
rage may be truly Herculean:

> teach me
> Alcides, thou mine ancestor, thy rage.

(IV.xii.43)

Cleopatra appears to admire and be in awe of Antony most when he is
displaying one or another of the attributes of the hero, and they are in
important element in the attraction he holds for many other characters in the
play.

Modern sensibility tends to be distrustful of the great man, and hostile to
the martial virtues and to the hero generally, and we have to make an effort
to appreciate that Antony's concern with his ancestry, honour and reputation,
and his anger, were all evidence of his heroic nature for the sixteenth-century
playgoer.

By the time Shakespeare came to dramatize the story of Antony and
Cleopatra it was one of the world's great love stories, and its appeal lay
largely in its uniqueness. It had to some degree been mythologized and had
acquired some of the aura of mystery that attaches to myth. The two extreme
views already mentioned are found as far back as the medieval versions of
the story. While Dante places Cleopatra in the second circle of hell in his
Divine Comedy, Chaucer cites her in his *Legend of Good Women* as an example
of the faithful wife who follows her husband even in death. The same
division of opinion is evident in renaissance versions of the story, which
depicted Cleopatra as the unfortunate victim of love, or presented her as a
wicked enchantress and siren whose seductive magic bewitched not only
Antony, but also Julius Caesar, 'the foremost man of all this world', and
Pompey the Younger, before him. The main characters are more fully discussed on pp xxxv–xliii; we should just note here that Shakespeare took
over and emphasised the unique, superlative and inimitable aspects of his
two main characters. He takes pains to show the truth of Antony's assertion

> I bind,
> On pain of punishment, the world to weet
> We stand up peerless.

(I.i.38)

and this should warn us against attempts to see them as Everyman and Every-
woman, typical representatives of mankind, whose story embodies moral
lessons for universal application.

How then did Shakespeare approach the story, and what did he want us
to think of it? A close look at the structure and method of exposition of the

first few scenes may be helpful in answering this question. The play opens with Philo lamenting to his fellow-Roman, Demetrius, the deterioration of Antony from 'the triple pillar of the world' into 'a strumpet's fool'. In performance the names of these Romans is never mentioned, which gives them something of a representative, choric role. We are struck by the strength of Philo's feeling about Antony, conveyed in the powerful metaphor and exaggerated speech:

> those his goodly eyes
> That o'er the files and musters of the war
> Have glowed like plated Mars, now bend, now turn
> The office and devotion of their view
> Upon a tawny front. His captain's heart,
> Which in the scuffles of great fights hath burst
> The buckles on his breast, reneges all temper,
> And is become the bellows and the fan
> To cool a gipsy's lust.

(I.i.2)

This is a portrait of the conventional epic hero in action, before love, that enemy of heroic action and the single-minded pursuit of honour, corrupted him.

Philo's attack is followed at once by the entry of Antony, Cleopatra and her train in oriental magnificence. When they speak we are struck by the disparity between what we now see and hear and what Philo has led us to expect. We are suprised by Cleopatra's quarrelsomeness, her attempt to annoy Antony by suggesting that he is at the beck and call of his wife Fulvia and the command of the young Octavius. Antony's powerful speech, 'Let Rome in Tiber melt', instead of illustrating the degeneracy suggested by Philo, has a heroic ring about it, and his expression of contempt for worldly things, 'kingdoms are clay', commands our assent. As we perceive that there is powerful feeling behind Antony's speech too, we begin to question the trustworthiness of Philo's view of the situation.

Our next glimpse of Cleopatra, in I.ii, surprises us. The seemingly confident and mocking queen of I.i is replaced here by an anxious woman, disturbed because a Roman thought has struck Antony and interrupted his desire for mirth (I.ii.75). Her hold on him is seen to be much less certain than their first appearance had suggested. We get a further surprise later in the scene when Antony, reversing all he has earlier said about the boundlessness of his love, decides to break away from this cunning and enchanting queen and return to Rome. His admission of his 'dotage' echoes Philo's words, and we are forced to question the nature and reality of Antony's love. In I.iii Cleopatra uses every weapon in her armoury to hold Antony in Egypt – scorn, anger, sarcasm, pretended fainting – but without success. Ironically, her heartfelt cry as she realizes her failure

> O, my oblivion is a very Antony,
> And I am all forgotten.
>
> (I.iii.91)

which impresses us as her first expression of real feeling for Antony, is taken by him as a piece of play-acting, 'idleness itself', so that we are at once doubtful about how well Antony understands her. Antony's contempt provokes her final speech of the scene:

>   'Tis sweating labour
> To bear such idleness so near the heart
> As Cleopatra this. But sir, forgive me,
> Since my becomings kill me when they do not
> Eye well to you. Your honour calls you hence;
> Therefore be deaf to my unpitied folly,
> And all the gods go with you!
>
> (I.iii.94)

Here again we have a sense of sincere feeling, and for the first time in Cleopatra, a dignity and majesty of bearing.

These opening scenes, then, are full of contrasts, contradictions and surprises, and as they proceed the situation grows in complexity, so that we are forced to suspend judgement between the two major viewpoints of Rome and Egypt until we know more about the situation. This technique, prohibiting snap judgements, is employed throughout the whole movement of the play. As the conflicting evidence for both sides mounts up, we see increasingly clearly that simple condemnation or apotheosis of the lovers is inadequate and untenable.

Shakespeare employs various other methods to enforce this suspension of judgement. Firstly, the play is remarkable for the amount of ambiguity it contains, found mainly in the characterization of Cleopatra and Octavius. Cleopatra is such a consummate actress that often we are unsure whether she is acting a part or not, while Octavius, a superlative politician, frequently expresses himself ambiguously or contrives to say one thing and imply another, and guards his speech carefully, conscious of the effect of his words on his listeners. Secondly, there is a pervasive use of irony which constantly surprises us with the unexpected. One kind of irony is created by the fact that we, the audience, are given a knowledge of events hidden from the characters of the play. We know more about Antony and his feeling for Cleopatra than she does, more about Cleopatra then he does, and we see the incompleteness of many of the opinions of them voiced by the other characters. For example, we know, as Antony does not, of the force of

Cleopatra's passion for him from her musings in his absence in I.v and from her assault on the Messenger in II.v. We know, as Cleopatra does not, that his marriage to Octavia is simply a political move, and we know, as neither of them does, from the prophecies of Enobarbus, of the certainty of Antony's return to Cleopatra. This superior vantage point that we enjoy, through the ironic detachment it effects, distances us from the protagonists and prevents the close identification that is aimed at in the more conventional type of tragedy centred upon a single character. Our sympathy tends to be intellectual rather than emotional: we know why they act as they do, but we do not feel as they do. Cleopatra's great hymn of praise to Antony after his death in v.ii describes an Antony, real to her, but one whom we have not seen in the action of the play. Another indication that this ironic distancing was Shakespeare's deliberate intention is the fact that this is the least 'interior' of his tragedies, making singularly little use of soliloquy, the device that takes us directly into the mind of the character, making close identification possible.

Irony of situation, too, is common. Enobarbus, who wins our trust and respect as the champion of common sense, pursues what seems a rational course of action in deserting Antony, but in doing so loses his self-respect and is finally killed by the emotion which he has scorned. Similarly, Antony, apparently doing the right thing in leaving Cleopatra and returning to his duty in Rome, appears curiously second-rate beside Octavius. Paradoxically, we see Antony's greatness only when he is in opposition to Rome. Such ironies as these invalidate the assumption that the moral of the play is the preference of reason over passion. This is reinforced too by our awareness that however admirable and essential to ordered social and political life the Roman qualities of duty, self-discipline and austerity are, there is little joy, laughter or openness in the Roman way of life. Octavius can command a loyal following, but not of the same warm human quality as that of Eros for Antony, or Charmian and Iras for Cleopatra. Antony feasts his soldiers out of true liberality and affection for them; Octavius does so as a politic gesture and because he has plenty and 'they have earned the waste'. While Octavius loves his sister he is quite prepared to sacrifice her as a pawn in his political game, and we cannot imagine him laying down his life for her or anyone. The vitality of the Alexandrian world fascinates more Romans than Antony: Maecenas and Agrippa are eager to hear all about his life there, Pompey delights in gossip about it and Lepidus is curious about its wonders.

To say that moral condemnation of the lovers is not Shakespeare's intention is not to say that there is no concern with morality in the play. Shakespeare does not, of course, present pagan Rome as a Christian community, but he and his fellow Elizabethans read history with a contemporary eye. Their interest was not intellectual and antiquarian, striving at an accurate reproduction of the past, as with the modern historian, but didactic – an attempt to derive lessons from the past for application in the present and future. The ethical tone of the play is thus the normal Christian one of Elizabethan society. Far from banishing moral considerations, Shakespeare introduces one at the beginning of the play with Philo's reference to Antony as 'the bellows and the fan/To cool a gipsy's lust', and as if to give visual stress to this reference to lust, the third of the Seven Deadly Sins, we have at once the entry of Cleopatra 'with eunuchs fanning her'. Cleopatra's first words, 'If it be love indeed', question the nature of Antony's passion. Is it lust or love? The question is forced on our attention, and there are numerous terms running through the play, such as 'strumpet', 'trull', 'whore', 'loose-wived', 'cuckold', 'adulterous', 'libertine', 'amorous surfeiter', 'lascivious wassails', 'blemish', 'fault', 'filth', 'viciousness', 'chastity' and 'sin' which would inevitably have moral connotations for an Elizabethan audience, as indeed for us today. Shakespeare goes out of his way to stress the illicit nature of Antony's love for Cleopatra, and his infidelity to Fulvia. In the three opening scenes Fulvia is mentioned seventeen times. Both messengers refer to her as 'Fulvia thy wife', and Cleopatra asks 'Why did he marry Fulvia, and not love her?' and 'What, says the married woman you may go?' and 'Why should I think you can be mine and true . . . Who have been false to Fulvia?' In one respect the moral code of the play differs from that of Shakespeare's age: in the suicide of the lovers, which in the world of the play is not viewed as sinful (a question which Cleopatra debates with herself at IV.xv.80), but rather as an admirable affirmation of love. This, however, was a common dramatic convention even in plays set in a Christian context, such as *Romeo and Juliet* and *Othello*.

The tendency of some critics to underplay the moral content of the play usually accompanies the attempt to aggrandise Antony. This weakens the drama by simplifying Antony's choice into a simple contest between love and politics. In fact, the dilemma and subsequent tragedy are very much heightened by the fact that the moral element is part of the struggle. Antony's departure from Egypt is not just a matter of political expediency, but also a praiseworthy moral effort to break 'these strong Egyptian fetters' and 'the poisoned hours [which] had bound me/From mine own knowledge'. Shakespeare, of course, does not give undue prominence to Antony's immorality, since to dwell on it too insistently would be to make sympathy for the lovers hard to attain.

Similar attempts to glide over or explain away repellent actions in the heroine also have a way of weakening the play. To take one example, it has been suggested that Cleopatra's dishonesty in holding back half her treasure from Caesar in v.ii is a stratagem prearranged with her treasurer Seleucus, so that when he exposes her lie to Caesar it will deceive Caesar into thinking that she wants to go on living, whereas she has already determined on suicide.

The argument against this theory is that there is not a word in the text to support it. Had Shakespeare intended such an important dramatic effect he would have made it quite plain, as he easily might, by a few interchanged words between Cleopatra and Seleucus before Caesar's entry, or in an aside after it. This interpretation also raises such questions as why, if Cleopatra is bent on suicide, she sends her messenger to find out what Caesar intends to do with her, a question which she pursues in v.ii with Dolabella. It is only when Dolabella returns to confirm her fears that Octavius intends to display her in his triumphal march through Rome that she finally summons up the courage to face death and orders the asps to be brought to her. We have to accept the unpalatable fact of Cleopatra's cowardice which Shakespeare stresses throughout the play, and which explains what would otherwise be her unnecessary delay in taking her life between iv.xv and v.ii. She is afraid to die while there is any hope of life on acceptable terms. Her physical fear is shown earlier in her flight from Actium, for which she abjectly begs Antony's pardon for her 'fearful sails'. She is afraid to approach Antony and later panics at his accusation of betrayal and rushes to the refuge of her monument. Her refusal to open the gate even to the dying Antony is another example of it:

> I dare not, dear.
> Dear my lord, pardon: I dare not,
> Lest I be taken.

(iv.xv.22)

Fear is so great at this point that it swamps her love. Finally Octavius reveals

> her physician tells me
> She hath pursued conclusions infinite
> Of easy ways to die.

(v.ii.350)

The words 'infinite' and 'easy' underline her timorousness and remind us of her welcome of the worm that 'pains not'.

Cleopatra's loss of nobility in cheating over the treasure does not, in fact, damage the play as some have argued. Firstly, her behaviour is consistent with all that we know of her; secondly, her frailty in this matter wins our sympathy, for she is humiliatingly caught out in a lie at a moment when everything is at its blackest for her, while Caesar by contrast is on top of the world; thirdly, it throws her final access of nobility into greater relief when it does come later in the scene, by stressing the strong attraction that life still has for her and the great effort of courage required in her to give it up; and fourthly, her final victory over Caesar is all the more satisfying after her setback over the treasure.

The imperfections in Antony and Cleopatra and in their relationship have
to be accepted by us as Shakespeare presents them. The relationship is
assailed and questioned in many ways so that we remain in doubt about it
until the final scene. The Roman disapproval among both Antony's followers
and enemies, the strong accent on sensual pleasure, Cleopatra's boasting of
her past loves, the bewildering evidence of wiles, tantrums and deceptions,
her ambiguous behaviour with Thidias, Antony's assertion of unbounded love
followed by his desertion of her, his own doubts and charges of betrayal, all
sustain the uncertainty to the end of the play. The widespread use of imagery
of change, oscillation and the dualism of life with its two faces, like Antony
himself who is 'one way like a Gorgon' the other way 'a Mars', contributes
to the atmosphere of doubt and ambiguity.

Curiosity and interest are maintained by our awareness that the lovers'
knowledge of each other is incomplete. They understand in each other those
qualities and traits that they themselves possess; those qualities that they do
not share they tend to misunderstand. Cleopatra knows that Antony values
his Roman sense of honour, but she does not begin to understand his sense
of shame at his 'most unnatural swerving'. She has to ask Enobarbus whether
she or Antony was at fault in fleeing from Actium. When he bids farewell to
his servants she is out of her depth at the emotions evoked and asks 'What
does he mean?' On his side, Antony does not understand that her flirtatious
behaviour with Thidias is as natural to her and as harmless as breathing, so
that she is puzzled and hurt by his charges of betrayal, and exclaims, 'Not
know me yet?' (III.xiii.157). Very late in the play he is still in doubt:

> Whose heart I thought I had, for she had mine.
>
> (IV.xiv.16)

He assumes, we notice, that she knew of the totality of his love:

> Egypt, thou knew'st too well
> My heart was to thy rudder tied by th'strings,
> And thou shouldst tow me after. O'er my spirit
> Thy full supremacy thou knew'st.
>
> (III.xi.56)

It is pathetic and ironic that Cleopatra did not know this. Her jealousy, her
repellent violence and many of her exasperating deceptions are much less
culpable in our eyes because we see that they spring from her insecurity, so
clearly reflected in her pitiful 'All may be well enough' (III.iii.46). It is one
of the major ironies of a highly ironic play that Antony should stigmatize her
as a 'triple-turned whore' when the charge is less true of her than of him. She
has had three lovers in succession (and none like Antony, she leads us to
believe) but has betrayed none of them. Antony, on the other hand, has

deserted Fulvia for Cleopatra, Cleopatra for Octavia and Octavia for Cleopatra. We can hardly blame her for not knowing her 'full supremacy' over his spirit. We have heard him reveal that he made the marriage with Octavia for his peace and that he will return to Egypt, but she does not know this.

The love is illicit and flawed, but it is real and is refined by time and suffering, as their mutual knowledge grows, filling in the areas of misunderstanding. Antony's flight from Actium and his unhesitating suicide when he hears that she is dead convince Cleopatra of his love for her, and ennoble hers for him. We see this in her moving epitaph beginning 'Noblest of men, woo't die' (IV.xv.59). But her love is still subject to her timidity and her hankering for life. The final and greatest statement of it is her rhapsody beginning, 'His face was as the heavens' (v.ii.79–92), and this follows her conquest of her fear. As late as IV.xv.27 she could speak of Octavia as Antony's 'wife', but there is a significant change in her last moments of life:

> Husband, I come.
> Now to that name my courage prove my title!
> I am fire and air; my other elements
> I give to baser life.

(v.ii.283)

She who has borne Antony children leaves life with the exquisite

> Peace, peace!
> Dost thou not see my baby at my breast,
> That sucks the nurse asleep?

(v.ii.304)

There can be no doubt, from the treacherous and immoral nature of the political world that destroys them, from the moving dramatic climaxes such as the grief of Antony's servants, the heartbreak of Enobarbus, the suicides of Eros, Charmian and Iras, and from the exaltation and dignity of the deaths of Antony and Cleopatra, that Shakespeare, far from asking us to denounce them as moral reprobates, seeks our imaginative sympathy for their passing. Their love has a positive value in its warmth and spontaneity of personal feeling, which in its turn attracts devotion from others, qualities lamentably absent in the world of politics where personal feelings are subordinated to expediency. We see also that many of the faults of the lovers, such as jealousy, anger and cruelty, paradoxically denote an unrestrained love, and are in a sense the excesses of virtues.

Shakespeare does not sentimentalize, however. We do not always see in the lovers what they see in each other. We are aware that in vainly seeking the infinite in the finite, they idealize their love and each other; this is in the nature of love and lovers, and produces its effect of pathos and poignancy.

We are meant to carry in solution in our minds a simultaneous awareness of the grave faults of the lovers: their wilful choice of self and the destruction and suffering it causes others, and the negative irresponsibility of their rejection of their social and political duties. They attain a personal peace, but it is Caesar who fashions the universal peace, without which civilization and the personal values that the lovers affirm would scarcely be possible.

Shakespeare sets out to capture our interest and attention with his dramatization of the story of two exceptional but humanly frail characters. He neither glorifies nor condemns them. He is not saying that life is inevitably like this, nor is he saying that love is better than politics, or the reverse. The play is not a statement about how life ought to be lived, embodying neat moral formulae. As the title suggests, it is the story of a relationship, and not, like the earlier great tragedies, *Hamlet, Othello, Lear* and *Macbeth* the exploration of the dilemma of a single character threatened by powerful forces of evil both inside and outside himself. There is no evil character or cosmic force in *Antony and Cleopatra*. The fate of the lovers is freely chosen, and in every way their own responsibility. The tragedy is not of the kind postulated by Aristotle, producing a catharsis (or harmonizing of the emotions) through pity and terror. The pity is here, though not the terror that we find in the four great tragedies mentioned above, but Shakespeare never intended that it should be. He takes this well-known story, and says in effect, 'It happened like this.' The play fascinates and moves us by its truth to the paradoxes and complexities of human nature, and to the sadness and mystery of life. We should not try to force it into the familiar category of tragedy; it is *sui generis*, a play of its own kind, making, as we might expect, since it deals with two exceptional and singular characters, its own unique appeal and effect. Perhaps the last word should be given to Caesar, who always says the right thing:

> No grave upon the earth shall clip in it
> A pair so famous.

(v.ii.355)

The text of Antony and Cleopatra

Reference is made in the Introduction and Notes to the First Folio. A folio is simply a book made up of sheets which have been folded once, giving two leaves, or four pages. The First Folio, published in 1623, seven years after Shakespeare's death, was the first collected edition of his plays, printing many of them, including *Antony and Cleopatra,* for the first time. It is thus our sole authority for the text of the play, which seems to have been printed from Shakespeare's own manuscript, or from a good transcript of it. There

340

THE TRAGEDIE OF
Anthonie, and Cleopatra.

Actus Primus. Scæna Prima.

Enter Demetrius and Philo.

Philo.

Ay, but this dotage of our Generals
Ore-flowes the measure : those his goodly eyes
That o're the Files and Musters of the Warre,
Haue glow'd like plated Mars :
Now bend, now turne
The Office and Deuotion of their view
Vpon a Tawny Front. His Captaines heart,
Which in the scuffles of great Fights hath burst
The Buckles on his brest, reneages all temper,
And is become the Bellowes and the Fan
To coole a Gypfies Lust.

Flourish. Enter Anthony, Cleopatra, her Ladies, the Traine, with Eunuchs fanning her

Looke where they come :
Take but good note, and you shall see in him
(The triple Pillar of the world) transform'd
Into a Strumpets Foole. Behold and see.

Cleo. If it be Loue indeed, tell me how much.

Ant. There's beggery in the loue that can be reckon'd

Cleo. Ile set a bourne how farre to be belou'd.

Ant. Then must thou needes finde out new Heauen, new Earth.

Enter a Messenger.

Mes. Newes (my good Lord) from Rome.

Ant. Grates me, the summe.

Cleo. Nay heare them Anthony.
Fuluia perchance is angry : Or who knowes,
If the scarse-bearded Cæsar haue not sent
His powrefull Mandate to you, Do this, or this
Take in that Kingdome, and Infranchise that :
Perform't, or else we damne thee.

Ant. How, my Loue ?

Cleo. Perchance? Nay, and most like :
You must not stay heere longer, your dismission
Is come from Cæsar, therefore heare it Anthony.
Where's Fuluias Processe? (Cæsars I would say) both?
Call in the Messengers : As I am Egypts Queene,
Thou blushest Anthony, and that blood of thine
Is Cæsars homager : else so thy cheeke payes shame,
When shrill-tongu'd Fuluia scolds. The Messengers.

Ant. Let Rome in Tyber melt, and the wide Arch
Of the raing'd Empire fall : Heere is my space,
Kingdomes are clay : Our dungie earth alike

Feeds Beast as Man ; the Noblenesse of life
Is to do thus : when such a mutuall paire,
And such a twaine can doo't, in which I binde
One paine of punishment, the world to weete
We stand vp Peerelesse.

Cleo. Excellent falshood :
Why did he marry Fuluia, and not loue her?
Ile seeme the Foole I am not. Anthony will be himselfe.

Ant. But stirr'd by Cleopatra.
Now for the loue of Loue, and her soft houres,
Let's not confound the time with Conference harsh;
There's not a minute of our liues should stretch
Without some pleasure now. What sport to night ?

Cleo. Heare the Ambassadors.

Ant. Fye wrangling Queene :
Whom euery thing becomes, to chide, to laugh,
To weepe : who euery passion fully striues
To make it selfe (in Thee) faire, and admir'd.
No Messenger but thine, and all alone, to night
Wee'l wander through the streets, and note
The qualities of people. Come my Queene,
Last night you did desire it. Speake not to vs.

Exeunt with the Traine.

Dem. Is Cæsar with Anthonius priz'd so slight ?

Philo. Sir sometimes when he is not Anthony,
He comes too short of that great Property
Which still should go with Anthony.

Dem. I am full sorry, that hee approues the common
Lyer, who thus speakes of him at Rome ; but I will hope
of better deeds to morrow. Rest you happy.

Exeunt

Enter Enobarbus, Lamprius, a Soothsayer, Rannius, Lucillius, Charmian, Iras, Mardian the Eunuch, and Alexas.

Char. L. Alexas, sweet Alexas, most any thing Alexas,
almost most absolute Alexas, where's the Soothsayer
that you prais'd so to th' Queene ? Oh that I knewe this
Husband, which you say, must change his Hornes with
Garlands.

Alex. Soothsayer.

Sooth. Your will ?

Char. Is this the Man ? Is't you sir that know things ?

Sooth. In Natures infinite booke of Secrecie, a little I
can read.

Alex. Shew him your hand.

Enob. Bring in the Banket quickly, Wine enough.

Cleopa

The first page of Antony and Cleopatra from the First Folio (1623).

are many printer's errors in the First Folio text, but most of them are obvious and can easily be corrected. A handful have given trouble and have led to various suggested emendations. These are mentioned briefly in the Notes.

Shakespeare's use of his source-material

Shakespeare's main source for *Antony and Cleopatra* was Plutarch's *Life of Marcus Antonius,* one of his *Parallel Lives of the Greeks and Romans.* Plutarch, a Greek writing in the first century A.D. when Greece was under Roman domination, was close to the events he was describing; his grandfather Lampryas, he tells us, related to him stories of Antony's life in Alexandria told him by Philotas, a doctor who lived there at the time. Plutarch was an immensely popular and influential writer with readers in the sixteenth century, when his original Greek was translated into Latin and then into the vernacular languages. It was the French translation in 1559 by Jacques Amyot, Bishop of Auxerre, which Sir Thomas North translated into English in 1579, and this was the version Shakespeare used in writing *Julius Caesar, Antony and Cleopatra* and *Coriolanus.*

Plutarch explains that his intention was

> not to write histories but only lives. For the noblest deeds do not always show men's virtues and vices; but oftentimes a light occasion, a word or some sport makes men's natural dispositions and manners appear more plain than the famous battles won.

His primary interest, then, is not history but biography, and his probing into the motives of human behaviour and into the minutiae of personality was the secret of his fascination for renaissance readers. His analytic approach to character and his attempt to get behind human action to its causes – one of the dramatist's chief concerns – were unusual among ancient classical writers. As Amyot, discussing the difference between history and biography, explains to his readers,

> Yet doth the one respect more the things, and the other the persons: the one is more common, and the other the more private: the one concerneth more the things that are without the man, and the other the things that proceed from within: the one the events, the other the consultations.

Most Roman historians are overtly propagandist; they see with Roman eyes, and are influenced by their political ideology, republican or imperialist, so that their work suffers a consequent simplification or distortion, and their presentation of character a loss of roundness and inwardness. As a Greek,

Contemporary portraits of the
main characters in Antony and
Cleopatra.

a

a) Cleopatra from an
   Alexandrian coin.

b) A basalt head of Octavia.

b

d

c) Antony from a Roman coin,
   on the reverse of which
   is the head of Octavia.

c

d) A marble bust of Octavius
   Caesar.

Plutarch is free from these limitations; his interest in great men is much more judicial and impartial. His approach is summed up in this quotation from Euripides:

> The good and bad cannot be kept apart
> But there is some commingling.

Any dramatist using Plutarch as a source-book finds a balance of good and bad qualities built into his characters. In place of the immaculate hero and the deep-dyed villain of myth or melodrama, Plutarch gives us fallible human beings, and this feature of his biographies is reflected in Shakespeare's play, adding in large measure to its strength and interest, and also to its complexity.

Elizabethan dramatists felt free to take certain liberties with the facts of history. While faithfully reproducing the broad sweep of historical events, they would interpret character freely, and omit, alter or add to their source material according to their dramatic needs and purposes. Shakespeare was no exception. We find him bringing together in one scene events widely separated in time, cutting out detail irrelevant or inimical to his interpretation of his protagonists. The events of *Antony and Cleopatra* which appear to follow swiftly and continuously, were in reality spread over a period of ten years. His main problem, of course, was to transform prose narrative into poetic drama, and this required careful selection and adaptation of material in order to produce the compression and fluency demanded of dramatic action. We find characters developed in ways not hinted at by Plutarch: Enobarbus, about whom Plutarch tells us almost nothing, is an example of this. Elsewhere, in an effort to turn reported facts into immediate dialogue, Shakespeare invents characters like Silius, Iras, Mardian, Varrius, Demetrius and Philo. Their speeches, however, are frequently based on Plutarchan material. Demetrius and Philo, for example, represent the common Roman view of Antony's activities in Alexandria, so often referred to by Plutarch. Since Antony is in the last phase of his life when the play opens, Shakespeare omits details of his early life unless these have a bearing on his interpretation of the later Antony. For example, he puts into Caesar's mouth admiring praise of Antony's fortitude after his defeat at Modena many years before, in order to establish Antony's former Roman virtue, and accent his deterioration to his present debauched life. Again, Enobarbus's description of the first meeting of Antony and Cleopatra on the River Cydnus is necessary if we are to understand the central situation of the play, the power of Cleopatra and the fascination she held for Antony.

It is sometimes asserted that the poetic quality of Plutarch's prose made Shakespeare's task of turning narrative prose into poetic drama an easy one, and the passage cited in support is the Cydnus meeting. In fairness to Shakespeare this view needs challenging. Firstly, to sustain it, we would have to argue that the poetic qualities in Plutarch somehow survived translation from Greek into Latin, and thence into French and English. Secondly, we find that the Cydnus passage in Plutarch is a glorious exception, an uncharacteristic 'purple patch'. Thirdly, the passage, though colourful, is also prosaic in many respects. Shakespeare had to work to create great poetry from it. As rendered by North, Plutarch is often racy and vigorous, but quite as often tortuous and wordy, with long meandering sentences, heavy antithetical clauses and piled-up adjectives and nouns. Amyot, apologizing for his own jerky style, blames it on 'Plutarch's peculiar manner of inditing, which is rather sharp, learned and short, than plain, polished and easy'. Montaigne congratulates Amyot on having

> so successfully-happy been able to explain an author so close and thorny and unfold a writer so mysterious and entangled.

It is not, then, *how* Plutarch wrote, but rather *what* he wrote that attracted Shakespeare's age.

One unquestionably appealing feature of Plutarch for the dramatist was his power of creating telling dialogue. The speech in Plutarch between Charmian and the guard, just before her death, illustrates this:

> One of the soldiers, seeing her, angrily said unto her:
> 'Is that well done, Charmion?'
> 'Very well,' said she again, 'and meet for a princess descended from the race of so many noble kings.'
> She said no more, but fell down dead hard by the bed.

Given such a highly-charged and succinct account – ready-made drama, as it were – Shakespeare had no need or desire to alter it, and so in the play we have:

> GUARD   What work is here, Charmian? Is this well done?
> CHARMIAN   It is well done, and fitting for a princess
> Descended of so many royal kings.
> Ah, soldier!   [*She dies* (v.ii.321)

We see here the close verbal dependence upon North's language and word-order, more marked than in any other use of source-material in all Shakespeare's plays. There is the minimum of change necessary to turn the prose into blank verse.

Where Shakespeare finds metaphor in North's Plutarch he usually retains it. Plutarch, for example, tells us that Pompey so ruled the seas 'that none durst peep out with a sail'; Shakespeare repeats the metaphor in his 'No vessel can peep forth'. Generally, however, metaphor is sparse in Plutarch, and most of the metaphor of the play, one of its greatest achievements, is

Shakespeare's own. Indeed it is fair to say that on the whole Shakespeare follows Plutarch most closely in his least dramatic passages, in expository details such as the movement and composition of armies, lists of kings, and accounts of battles. This can be seen in the following passage:

> The second news, as bad as the first: that Labienus conquered all Asia with the army of the Parthians, from the river of Euphrates and from Syria unto the countries of Lydia and Ionia.

which in the play becomes:

> Labienus –
> This is stiff news – hath with his Parthian force
> Extended Asia; from Eúphrates
> His conquering banner shook, from Syria
> To Lydia, and to Ionia.
>
> (I.ii.90)

Where the purpose, as here, is simply to fill in necessary expository detail economically, with no attempt at creating emotional response, Shakespeare does some straightforward borrowing, though even here we should notice his characteristic injection of a metaphor, the shaking of the banner, which creates a picture seen in the mind. Other examples of this kind of dependence are the accounts of the troubles aroused in Italy by Lucius and Fulvia, and of Ventidius's campaign.

A more typical use of Plutarch is Shakespeare's habit of taking over and expanding a hint from him. Plutarch tells how Cleopatra mocked Antony's prowess as a fisherman by having a diver fix a dried saltfish to his hook under the water. In the play Charmian relates this anecdote, but what leads her to do so is the preceding speech which Shakespeare, prompted by the saltfish story in Plutarch, has invented for Cleopatra:

> Give me mine angle; we'll to th'river there,
> My music playing far off. I will betray
> Tawny-finned fishes: my bended hook shall pierce
> Their slimy jaws, and as I draw them up,
> I'll think them every one an Antony,
> And say, 'Ah ha! y'are caught.'
>
> (II.v.10)

In this way Shakespeare works up a story in Plutarch to reveal Cleopatra's wit, flirtatiousness and playfulness, creating dramatically something of the 'infinite variety' that captivated Antony. Often an idea prosaically expressed in Plutarch becomes memorable after it has passed through the forge of the dramatist's creative imagination. Plutarch's 'when she was but a young

thing and knew not what the world meant' becomes a striking and characteristic expression in Cleopatra's mouth:

> My salad days,
> When I was green in judgement, cold in blood.

(I.v.73)

Here it is the metaphor, the wit and compression which lend distinction.

A close comparison of play with source-book affords illuminating insight
into the creative process. Plutarch tells us baldly:

> When Cleopatra landed, Antonius sent to invite her to supper to him.
> But she sent him word again, he should do better rather to come and
> sup with her. Antonius therefore, to show himself courteous unto her
> at her arrival, was contented to obey her, and went to supper to her.

As Enobarbus tells it

> Upon her landing, Antony sent to her,
> Invited her to supper. She replied,
> It should be better he became her guest,
> Which she entreated. Our courteous Antony,
> Whom ne'er the word of 'No' woman heard speak,
> Being barbered ten times o'er, goes to the feast,
> And, for his ordinary, pays his heart
> For what his eyes eat only.

(II.ii.222)

What gives the passage dramatic life is Shakespeare's additions. The detail
that no woman ever heard the word 'No' from Antony, while exposing a
weakness, cleverly captures sympathy for him at the same time. The detail of
his repeated barbering creates the picture of a nervous Antony, no match for
the allurements of Cleopatra. We are reminded of the image of the fish caught
on her hook and are in no way surprised to learn that the meeting cost him
his heart. We should note too that the speech is part of the characterization of
Enobarbus. He mocks Antony's weakness and helplessness, but his words
simultaneously suggest his affection and sympathy for Antony. The use of
Plutarch here neatly illustrates Shakespeare's power of doing several things
at a time.

The transmutation of narrative description into dramatic situation is nowhere better seen than in Shakespeare's adaptation of the Cydnus passage, in
which Enobarbus with considerable relish, recreates the meeting of Antony
and Cleopatra for the benefit of the eager Agrippa and Maecenas, whose
attitude is a mixture of official Roman disapproval of Egyptian luxury, and
unofficial curiosity and admiration at Cleopatra's magnetism and splendour.

Plutarch's 'her barge . . . the poop whereof was of gold' becomes

> The barge she sat in, like a burnished throne
> Burned on the water: the poop was beaten gold.
>
> (II.ii.194)

The throne image introduces the idea of majesty, enhanced by the reference to gold, the 'royal' metal, and linked up with the supreme element of 'fire' through the words 'burned' and 'burnished'. Cleopatra at her death explicitly claims to be all 'fire and air', unmixed with baser elements. Plutarch's prosaic description has become a vibrant picture; the ship, apparently of solid gold, is a blazing image, which the sun, another symbol of royalty, causes to be reflected by the water. The key words are picked out by the alliterated 'b' sounds, and by the assonance of 'burned' and 'burnished'. Plutarch's 'the sails of purple, and the oars of silver' becomes

> Purple the sails, and so perfumèd that
> The winds were love-sick with them; the oars were silver
> Which to the tune of flutes kept stroke, and made
> The water which they beat to follow faster,
> As amorous of their strokes.
>
> (II.ii.196)

By inverting 'the sails of purple' to 'purple the sails' Shakespeare takes the emphasis off sails and puts it on the colour, important here since it is the royal colour and so meshes with the other images of majesty. He further stresses it by inverting the normal iambic foot at the beginning of the line to a trochaic one, so that 'purple' stands out both metrically and rhythmically, as well as in the word order.

Plutarch speaks of the savour of perfumes emanating from the barge; Shakespeare particularizes this by inventing perfumed sails which attract the winds to follow them. As almost always, Shakespeare's imagery is concrete, based on his sensory experience, and also unique in seeing connections between things that escape the ordinary person's eye. Having watched the wind billowing out the sails of a ship – a sight he would have frequently seen on London's Thames – his imagination perceives a connection between this experience and love. The winds amorously pursuing the sails prefigure the imminent magnetizing of Antony by Cleopatra. The image of this love-chase is reinforced in the next lines in which the water follows faster as if amorous of the strokes of the oars. Plutarch's catalogue of musical instruments, which would interrupt the thought and could only with difficulty be fitted into a fluent verse pattern, is reduced to just the flute. Again, Shakespeare's metaphor starts with something seen, the hollow depression made by the pull of the oar through the water, and the resultant rush of the water to fill it, and again he makes a connection between this sight and the love motif, in which Cleopatra is doing all she can to attract Antony. Plutarch's 'And now for the person of herself' is contracted to 'For her own person', and the phrase 'It beggared all description' is added. Shakespeare cleverly avoids having to describe her, while at the same time creating an impression of surpassing beauty, so great that however splendid the description might have been, it would have been as far short of the reality as a beggar is in relation to another man.

By turning Plutarch's passive 'she was laid' to the active 'she did lie' Shakespeare makes Cleopatra the active mistress of events rather than the passive instrument; she stage-manages the whole scene. Whereas Plutarch narrates simply that Cleopatra was dressed as Venus commonly is in paintings, Shakespeare turns this into a superlative tribute by telling us that she was more beautiful than the painted Venus whose artists make her more beautiful than she could have been in nature. Plutarch's 'fair' boys become Shakespeare's 'dimpled' ones; again the vague and generalized adjective is replaced by a specific one, which makes us see a particular facial feature of the children

> With divers-coloured fans, whose wind did seem
> To glow the delicate cheeks which they did cool,
> And what they undid did.
>
> (II.ii.206)

This is Shakespeare's rich remoulding of Plutarch's 'with the which they fanned wind upon her'. We are invited to see through the apparent paradox, signalled by that word 'seem', of the cheeks, while being cooled by the wind of the fans, at the same time made to glow. This, we know, is what happens to coals which are fanned, but not to human beings, and we deduce that Cleopatra's cheeks glow despite the fanning because of her emotional excitement at her forthcoming meeting with Antony. The juxtaposition of the opposites 'undid did' suggests also the backward and forward movement of the fans.

At this point Agrippa's interruption 'O rare for Antony' serves the double function of breaking up what might otherwise be too long and rich a speech which could become monotonous, and of voicing and guiding the audience's response. Enobarbus descends from this climax, to talk next of Cleopatra's companions on the barge, working up to the second climax of the effect of all this upon Antony. Whereas Plutarch in rather schoolmasterly fashion explains that the Nereides 'are the mermaids of the waters' Shakespeare more tactfully explains without seeming to do so, by putting the phrase in apposition:

> Her gentlewomen, like the Nereides,
> So many mermaids, tended her i' th'eyes,
> And made their bends adornings.
>
> (II.ii.209)

Cleopatra is placed firmly in the centre of the picture with her women ministering to her, their sinuous movements suggesting the ornamental frame around a portrait. The tackle which becomes 'silken' in the play – another touch making this barge unique among ships – is handled by 'flower-soft hands', another metaphor from the concrete tactile experience of the velvet bloom on the petals of flowers. Plutarch's rather obvious and vague adjectives in 'a wonderful passing sweet savour of perfumes' are sharpened to 'A strange invisible perfume'. The invisible yet powerful presence of perfume parallels the invisible and mysterious attraction of Cleopatra for Antony. Plutarch tells how the wharf-side was 'pestered with innumerable multitudes of people. Some of them followed the barge all alongst the river's side', others ran 'one after another to see her'. As Enobarbus describes it

> A strange invisible perfume hits the sense
> Of the adjacent wharfs. The city cast
> Her people out upon her.

(II.ii.215)

The personification of the city and the violent verbs of motion, 'hit' and 'cast', point up the power of Cleopatra's magnetism. There is no straggling of people following their inclinations, as in Plutarch, but rather action ('hits') followed by total and seemingly helpless reaction ('cast out'). Cleopatra draws everyone to her so that Antony, in the middle of giving audience, is left suddenly alone, with nothing to do but whistle to keep his courage up. The disparity between the majesty suggested by 'enthroned', and the helpless ordinariness suggested by 'whistling' humorously accentuates Cleopatra's triumph over him. It is so complete that if the air had been free to create a vacuum, it too would have gone to see Cleopatra, and Antony would not even have been able to whistle.

We can thus see that in such a passage as the above, where there is close dependence upon Plutarch, Shakespeare is constantly at work, shaping and enriching his source material to fit dramatic situation and character. Plutarch offers a framework of events, guiding-lines in character relationships, illustrative anecdote and dialogue snatches, detachment, integrity and common sense. Nevertheless, it should be stressed that three-quarters of the play ranks as independent composition, and it is a fair generalization to say that this is the better part of the play. The most powerful emotional and dramatic effects are obtained where Plutarch gives least help and where Shakespeare is relying on his own inventive powers. The impact of the first act, for example, owes much to the fact that four of its five scenes are set in Alexandria, and for these Shakespeare took very little from Plutarch. Act III, on the other hand, normally regarded as the least satisfactory part of the play, is heavily indebted to Plutarch. The comic incidents, such as the Charmian-

Soothsayer exchanges in i.ii, the drinking scene in ii.vii, and the Clown in v.ii, are wholly Shakespeare's as are most of the scenes developing the relationship between Antony and Cleopatra, the emotional climaxes of Enobarbus's death, Cleopatra's great hymn of praise to the dead Antony, and Cleopatra's own death.

Shakespeare's interpretation and adaptation of the characters he found in Plutarch is discussed below. It is enough to note here that the changes he makes are those of an experienced dramatic craftsman, directed towards shaping Plutarch's amorphous material into a closely integrated and fluent dramatic unity.

Apart from the major debt to Plutarch occasional minor echoes of other writers have been found. There are a few details incorporated from Appian's *The Civil Wars*, while *The Tragedy of Cleopatra* by Samuel Daniel furnishes one or two verbal borrowings, and it is probable that Shakespeare was familiar with some of the many European plays about Antony and Cleopatra, or translations of them, such as the Countess of Pembroke's *Antonius*. In none of these cases is there evidence of significant dependence.

The principle characters in Antony and Cleopatra

Antony and Cleopatra is one of Shakespeare's longest plays and has a larger cast than any other. The four major parts comprise two-thirds of the play: Antony has 25 per cent of the lines, Cleopatra 20 per cent, Caesar 12 per cent and Enobarbus 10 per cent. The remaining third is spread thinly between 45 characters, none of whom has more than 4 per cent, and most of whom have much less. These figures show clearly that Shakespeare's interest was focused upon the figures of Antony and Cleopatra who between them are given almost half the play. The only other parts of any size are those of Caesar, who functions chiefly as a foil and centre of opposition to Antony and his way of life, and Enobarbus, important because of his relationship with the lovers and his informed comments upon them. The great number of small parts gives us the sense of a bustling, crowded world, and of the panoramic sweep of the action.

ANTONY is in many ways different from Plutarch's figure, and the changes are all directed towards the creation of a sympathetic tragic hero. Shakespeare omits all detail of his dissolute youth, his cruelties, bribery and extortion, his susceptibility to flattery, his tyrannical desire to 'deprive his countrymen of their liberty', and Plutarch's view that he 'slew himself cowardly and miserably'. He cuts out Plutarch's report that kings, friends and servants deserted him before the battle of Actium; that the man to whom Cleopatra gave the suit of golden armour (Scarus in the play) at once defected to Caesar; that Antony commanded the killing of Pompey, instead of deploring it, as in the play; that Fulvia 'ruled Antony at home and abroad' (since a henpecked husband is not a heroic figure); that his infatuation for Cleopatra cost the lives of thousands of his soldiers, and much more which would have been destructive to his purpose.

Shakespeare uses poetic means to magnify Antony's stature. Numerous images link him with the gods and the god-like. Philo likens his gaze to that of Mars, god of war, and describes him as a triple pillar of the world; Lepidus sees him as 'the Jupiter of men' and as 'the Arabian bird', the unique phoenix; to Enobarbus he is a 'mine of bounty'; to Caesar's soldier 'a Jove'; to Cleopatra he is a 'Herculean Roman', 'the greatest soldier of the World', 'heavenly mingled', 'infinite virtue', 'the day of the world' (i.e. the sun), her 'man of men' and 'lord of lords'. Like a Colossus, 'His legs bestrid the ocean, his reared arm / Crested the world'. Antony himself, with the boast characteristic of the classical hero, calls himself 'the greatest prince o' th'world / The noblest', and refers to his descent from Hercules. 'A rarer spirit', says Agrippa, 'never / Did steer humanity.'

Antony is great too in his frailties. 'His taints and honours / Waged equal with him' as Maecenas puts it, and his faults seem all the more distressing because of his greatness. Many of the terms used about him – 'the bellows and the fan / To cool a gipsy's lust', 'th'adulterous Antony', 'a doting mallard', 'the old ruffian' – demean him. Ventidius reveals Antony's jealousy of successful subordinates. His treatment of Octavia is painful, and his cruelty to Thidias is not redeemed by any later confession of its shamefulness, as is Cleopatra's attack on the messenger. But if Shakespeare does not spare Antony, we should notice that Antony does not spare himself, and this is one subtle means by which the dramatist secures respect for him. It is wrong to say, as has been said, that Antony has no moral sense. He admits his broken vows, his drunkenness and slavery to 'poisoned hours' of pleasure which 'bound me up / From mine own knowledge', and he plays the penitent with Caesar as far as his notion of honour will let him. We cannot agree with Bradley, who in general writes so well on Antony, that he leaves Cleopatra 'only because he knows he will return'. In soliloquy (and it is a dramatic convention that soliloquy is always trustworthy) Antony speaks of making a complete break. 'These strong Egyptian fetters I must break' (I.ii.107), and 'I must from this enchanting Queen break off'. He fails, but this was not his intention. In Plutarch there are strong suggestions that Antony was literally bewitched by Cleopatra and deceived by her. Shakespeare is careful to assure us that Antony is not deceived by her, but that he knows her for what she is; the tensions which this knowledge set up in his mind, and the moral struggle it gives rise to greatly enrich his characterization.

The essence of Antony's nature is revealed in his advice to Caesar at Pompey's banquet, 'Be a child o' th'time', and Caear's answer 'Possess it' succinctly underlines his nature and the difference between the two men, as well as pointing ominously to the outcome when two such men clash. There is something childlike in Antony's habit of living in the present, of taking the easiest way out of present difficulties. Just as 'Things that are past are done' with him (I.ii.88), so things that lie in the future do not exist for him. He is unwilling, or constitutionally unable, to face up to the future implications of his actions in the present. Significantly he silences Enobarbus when he prophesies what will happen after Pompey is disposed of (II.ii.107). Living in the present he can agree to the marriage with Octavia (possibly hoping that it will overcome his desire to return to Cleopatra) and declare

> May I never
> To this good purpose, that so fairly shows,
> Dream of impediment!

(II.ii.148)

and in the next scene reveal his intention of returning to Cleopatra, having just assured Octavia of his intended reform. Having decided to return to Egypt, he can then go off to Athens with Octavia, and take offence when Caesar reveals his distrust. Antony is a child of the time, in that he means what he says at the time, and suits his behaviour to the occasion – an opportunism which is one of the few links with the character of Antony in *Julius Caesar*. He seems unaware of his inconsistencies in his respect.

Shakespeare, then, sets himself a formidable task in having to make a tragic hero out of such a deeply-flawed man, but slowly and surely he does it. There is no miraculous conversion of Antony; he gropes forward, with occasional backslidings, to a larger measure of self-realization. Much of the hostile comment occurs early in the play; later, the accent is more on his finer qualities. We see that the Roman view of him, while true, is inadequate.

Antony's redemption is partly effected by a series of emotional climaxes of ascending strength, such as his moving Cleopatra to tears (III.xi), then his servants and Enobarbus (IV.ii), the desertion of Enobarbus and Antony's generous reaction to it (IV.v), the death of Enobarbus (IV.ix), Antony's unquestioning suicide when he hears that Cleopatra is dead, Eros's loyal suicide, and Antony's magnanimity in uttering no word of reproach when the cruel irony of Cleopatra's deception is made known to him (IV.xiv), his concern for her welfare and his pathetic belief that she will not have the courage to follow him in death, and his death itself (IV.xv).

Partly, too, we see that his frailties are inextricably bound up with his virtues. His shameful flight from Actium occurs because of the totality of his love, and his fury with Thidias is similarly motivated. Lepidus introduces the idea that Antony's faults are

> hereditary
> Rather than purchased; what he cannot change
> Than what he chooses.

(I.iv.13)

This may be 'too indulgent', as Caesar says, but together with the unfavourable and inescapable prophecy of the soothsayer and the sense of Antony's fettered helplessness in his love for Cleopatra, it does tend to lighten Antony's culpability by suggesting an inevitability in events beyond his control. Antony's desertion of Octavia was a damning fact in the story which Shakespeare had somehow to incorporate without arousing our total contempt for Antony. He omits mention of the fact that Octavia had borne him two children and was expecting a third when he left her, and that he later had her evicted from his house in Rome, since this would have destroyed all respect for Antony. He also invents a number of provocative acts by Caesar to justify Antony's rift in Act III and through Octavia's devotion to her brother, softens the blows of Antony's desertion of her. Our consciousness of the incompatible temperaments of Antony and Octavia prevents the rupture attaining tragic proportions. The reiterated contrast between Antony's age and Caesar's youth is another means of winning support for Antony. It is a strong element in his suffering and shame that he, a grizzled soldier of great experience, should be beaten by the 'boy' Caesar, a 'novice' in war.

At his first appearance Antony declares that 'kingdoms are clay' and that for him Rome can melt in Tiber, since the nobleness of life lies in love, but hardly has he said it when 'a Roman thought' strikes him, and he is showing a considerable interest in kingdoms. His story is largely the process by which he comes to be convinced of the truth of his words, a process in which he who had 'With half the bulk o' th'world played as he pleased / Making and marring fortunes', and giving 'a kingdom for a mirth' loses everything, and even seems to lose himself

> Here I am, Antony,
> Yet cannot hold this visible shape.

(IV.xiv.13)

Kings, allies, friends and servants melt away. His loss of command is excruciatingly painful to him. As Charmian puts it

> The soul and body rive not more in parting
> Than greatness going off.

(IV.xiii.5)

Yet he learns to accept his stripping:

> Fall not a tear, I say; one of them rates
> All that is won and lost.

(III.xi.69)

Antony, reduced to himself, is at his greatest, and the full Caesar seems empty by comparison.

Antony is the central figure of the play. Despite the fact that he leaves the stage in Act IV, he has the largest part in the play, and dominates the action for the final Act. He is the inspiration, constantly present in her thoughts and actions, of Cleopatra, on whom the play focuses in the last Act. The moral and political dilemma, the choice between duty and pleasure, and the great burden of the subsequent suffering, are his.

CLEOPATRA, as Plutarch presents her, is an inscrutable creature, and Shakespeare, well aware of the dramatic appeal of mystery, had no desire to simplify or explain her away. We can list many of her undoubted qualities – on the one side, her vanity, sensuality, violence, cruelty, bawdiness, cowardice; on the other, her beauty, wit, vitality and intelligence – but her character is something more than the total of all her qualities. Its essence is indefinable, and this is one reason for her perennial fascination.

Shakespeare's determination to retain her mystery emerges in many ways. Firstly, the opinions of her expressed by other characters run from one extreme to the other: she is a strumpet, a lustful gipsy, a trull, a ribaudred nag, a boggler ever, a whore, a false soul, a right gipsy, a lass unparalleled, a most triumphant lady, royal wench, great fairy, a wonderful piece of work, a rare Egyptian, and much more.

Secondly, Shakespeare deliberately creates around her bewildering paradoxes and polarities, setting normal standards of judgement on their head. The passions (in the bad sense of the word) make themselves in her 'fair and admired'; whatever she does 'becomes' her; she makes defect perfection; when she is wanton the priests bless her; instead of satisfying appetite she increases it; even fans which normally cool, seem to heat her; age cannot wither her. Cleopatra combines both human and divine; to fix the limits of Antony's love for her would require 'new heaven, new earth'; she 'o'erpictures' Venus; none of her parts 'but is a race of heaven'; she is a priestess of Isis, the moon goddess.

Thirdly, Shakespeare took over the common belief that she was a sorceress. 'Witch', 'spell', 'charm', 'enchanting Queen' are words used to describe her, but Shakespeare carefully avoids making it clear whether or not they are well founded.

Fourthly, her speech and action frequently raise doubt by their ambiguity. Did she really betray Antony at Actium? What were her intentions in the

Thidias incident? Had she 'packed cards' with Caesar when her fleet surrendered? Does she love Antony? There are answers to many of the questions that arise, but Shakespeare holds most of them back to increase suspense. He employs a retrospective technique in which, late in the play, we are given answers to questions raised earlier, so that we have frequently to revise earlier opinions. This is a mark of Shakespeare's mature work and enhances dramatic interest.

The infinite variety of Cleopatra, then, makes finite judgement singularly difficult. Her uniqueness is indisputable.

Cleopatra has many faults, but in her defence it should be said that she is often represented as worse than she is. Plutarch did not like her, and describes her love as 'a pestilent plague', 'the last and extremest mischief of all other'; 'if any spark of goodness or hope of rising were left him, Cleopatra quenched it straight and made it worse than before.' This was not how Shakespeare saw her, and he improves her in many ways. Historically she made preparations for flight before the battle of Actium, and planned after it to transfer her fleet from the Mediterranean to the Red Sea without any concern for Antony; she tried out her poisons on prisoners, watching the effects on them; she opposed Antony's sending Enobarbus's treasure to him; and when Caesar arrived she blamed her conduct on her fear of Antony. To have retained this material would have destroyed Cleopatra as tragic heroine. Shakespeare, we observe, transfers this last detail to Caesar:

> THIDIAS He knows that you embraced not Antony
> As you did love, but as you feared him.
>
> CLEOPATRA   O!
> THIDIAS The scars upon your honour, therefore, he
> Does pity as constrainèd blemishes,
> Not as deserved.
>
> CLEOPATRA   He is a god, and knows
> What is most right. Mine honour was not yielded,
> But conquered merely.
>
> (III.xiii.56)

Her acting must be such as to be capable of the construction that Enobarbus puts upon it, namely that she is deserting Antony, but we are surely meant to see her exclamations as deeply ironic. When Thidias comes she insists that everyone should hear what he has to say, which is hardly to be expected if she is planning treachery:

> CLEOPATRA   Caesar's will?
> THIDIAS Hear it apart.
> CLEOPATRA   None but friends. Say boldly.
>
> (III.xiii.46)

It is Thidias, at the end of the interview, who begs a kiss, and Cleopatra, being Cleopatra, gives him her hand. All that she has done is acknowledge her defeat by Caesar; there is no hint of betraying Antony in all that is said. Ironically again, when the fleet surrenders, it is Antony who suspects her. Diomedes assures him that his suspicion of her collusion with Caesar 'never shall be found' (IV.xiv.121), and this is confirmed by the subsequent meeting between Cleopatra and Caesar.

A good deal that is deplorable in her behaviour, such as her violence towards the messenger, can be seen to spring from frustrated love, uncertainty and fear. It is worth noting that Queen Elizabeth's well-known temper, so frequently displayed to terrified messengers of all ranks, won the admiration of many Englishmen as royally spirited behaviour in no way unbecoming in a queen, so that perhaps the Elizabethans would have taken a different view of Cleopatra's displays of fury.

Associated with the unpredictable behaviour which springs from Cleopatra's fear is her mutability of temperament, stressed in the play through her connection with the moon, the symbol of inconstancy. Caesar reports that

> She
> In th'habiliments of the goddess Isis
> That day appeared, and oft before gave audience,
> As 'tis reported, so.
>
> (III.vi.16)

Isis was represented visually as a cow, so that it may be no accident that in her most startling inconstancy Cleopatra, fleeing from Actium, was, according to Scarus, 'like a cow in June'. Antony remarks when he sees her behaviour with Thidias that she is no longer Cleopatra:

> Alack, our terrene moon
> Is now eclipsed.
>
> (III.xii.153)

Cleopatra changes and learns, partly from Antony – and we see this in the way in her last moments she echoes things that he has earlier said –, partly from her loss of him, and partly from her own fear. Without him she finds the world 'darkling', 'no better than a sty', and sees as he has said that 'All's but naught' (IV.xv.78). She decides that suicide is no sin, and learns more readily than Antony did the vanity of material possessions.

> My desolation does begin to make
> A better life. 'Tis paltry to be Caesar:
> Not being Fortune, he's but Fortune's knave,
> A minister of her will. And it is great
> To do that thing that ends all other deeds,
> Which shackles accidents and bolts up change.
>
> (v.ii.1)

This new insight, however, which the verb 'does begin' denotes, is a difficult thing to translate into practice, and Cleopatra is not yet ready to do the thing that 'bolts up change'. She has a courage of her own, displayed when physical fear is not involved, as we see in her behaviour in arming Antony with a gaiety she does not feel in IV.iv, but it is the confrontation with Caesar that gives her the necessary physical courage as she triumphantly asserts

> My resolution's placed, and I have nothing
> Of woman in me: now from head to foot
> I am marble-constant; now the fleeting moon
> No planet is of mine.
>
> (v.ii.238)

The repetition of the word 'now' accentuates the change in her. She has overcome the moon element in herself. It is characteristic of Cleopatra that she should Egyptianize even the 'high Roman fashion', seeking an easy way to die, sensuous and pleasurable. As with Antony, Shakespeare gives us no incredible conversion. She has her own life-style and sustains it to the end. Hauling up Antony is 'sport' (one of his words); in joining Antony she prepares for another meeting like her first one with him on the River Cydnus; she is jealous that Iras may reach Antony first and steal the kiss it is her heaven to have

> The stroke of death is as a lover's pinch
> Which hurts, and is desired.
>
> (v.ii.291)

This marvellous consistency, even in her inconsistencies, is one of the triumphs of her characterization. Caesar sums it up neatly:

> Bravest at the last,
> She levelled at our purposes, and being royal
> Took her own way.
>
> (v.ii.331)

Shakespeare heightens her nature in the final scenes through dramatic and poetic intensification; her lyricism, the devotion of her maids, her newly acquired tenderness, the pathos of the narrowing down of her world until she is 'confined in all she has, her monument', the death-in-life imagery in which Antony goes to join her, his bride, and she her husband, and even Caesar's remark that 'she looks like sleep,/As she would catch another Antony', all achieve their end of capturing compassion and wonder. Again, we mustn't sentimentalize, but hold in balance in our mind all that we know of Cleopatra. In the fields of the blest, 'where souls do couch on flowers', we can be sure she will be the same Cleopatra as always.

*a) Cleopatra's habit of identifying herself with Isis
is shown in this modern interpretation by
Margaret Leighton in 1969, where her throne is
decorated by the disk and horns of the goddess (see b).*

*b) An Egyptian bronze figure of the goddess Isis
and her son, Horus.*

OCTAVIUS CAESAR is an absorbing study of the political man. We see how different Shakespeare's conception of him was from Plutarch's when we recall that historically he was a handsome man 'somewhat given to women and play', who enjoyed sports and fishing, who 'always spake words to move laughter', was learned, eloquent and superstitious. Shakespeare seems to have taken one hint from Plutarch, however:

> But peradventure we are too curious searching out his private life: yet that may sometimes discover great personages more than their public actions in which they are more careful to frame their countenances, and do counterfeit most.

In earlier plays like *Henry IV,* Parts 1 and 2, *Henry V* and *Julius Caesar,* Shakespeare had explored the nature of the political man, showing how public life demanded the possession and exercise of qualities which we deplore in our private lives, and conversely, the suppression of many attractive human qualities. His age was one when violence and lawlessness were near the surface of life, where self-assertion was the recognized road to success, and where there was a constant threat of civil insurrection and intrigue. The time demanded a tough, single-minded ruler, willing to suppress personal interests to the larger public good, and prepared to use Machiavellian methods to outsmart dissident and rebellious elements. Octavius is a man of this mould; he does a good deal of 'framing of countenance' and 'counterfeiting'.

Octavius is a master of ambiguity. He has no private life in the play; all his appearances are in public and he is very much concerned to make the correct public impression, to do and say the right thing. We can accept very little of what he says at face value, since many of his speeches have a hidden political purpose behind them, and are often intended by him to be capable of more than one interpretation. Antony is puzzled by his use of the word 'practised' and asks him 'How intend you, "practised"?' Caesar replies, 'You may be pleased to catch at mine intent/By what did here befall me' (II.ii.46). It is not always easy to 'catch at' Caesar's 'intent'. When the triumvirs urge Pompey to accept their proposals Caesar adds

> And what may follow,
> To try a larger fortune.
>
> (II.vi.33)

which is at once a promise of fortune if Pompey accepts and a threat hinting at his destruction if he does not. The same menace lies behind his parting words as Antony leaves for Athens with Octavia:

> You take from me a great part of myself:
> Use me well in't.
>
> (III.ii.24)

With political foresight Octavius plans each step towards his goal of world domination. He is lucky that Antony breaks from Cleopatra when he does, since he needs Antony's soldiership for his first objective, the control of Pompey. Octavius has little hope (or desire) of lasting peace with Antony

> for't cannot be
> We shall remain in friendship, our conditions
> So differing in their acts.
>
> (II.ii.116)

but he brilliantly manipulates Antony when they meet, clinching the occasion with the political marriage to Octavia. This gives him a political initiative since any maltreatment of her by Antony can be used as a justification for the war with Antony which he foresees as necessary. Meanwhile, with Antony out of the way in Athens, he is free to proceed piecemeal with his plans: firstly the destruction of Pompey, which belies his assertion earlier that Antony will never be able to charge him with breaking his oath; then the removal of Lepidus. Historically Antony was a party to both acts; in the play he is made innocent of them, and thus given solid grounds for his anger with Caesar. When Antony protests, Caesar tells his followers

> I have told him Lepidus was grown too cruel.
>
> (III.vi.32)

The 'I have told him' suggests a fabricated excuse; we cannot believe the mild-mannered Lepidus could be capable of cruelty. When the expected desertion of Octavia occurs, Caesar uses it as his pretext for war, 'seeking an honest colour to make war with Antony' as Plutarch puts it. After the defeat of Antony he concedes that the world was not big enough for both of them, that Antony was like a disease in his body which he had to lance:

> I must perforce
> Have shown to thee such a declining day,
> Or look on thine: we could not stall together
> In the whole world.
>
> (v.i.37)

In Plutarch Caesar sheds tears alone in his tent at the news of Antony's death. In the play he receives the news and sheds tears in public, so that they are at once suspect in this world where so many tears are like the crocodile's, insincere. His lament over Antony does not seem to square with what we have seen of their relationship:

> But yet let me lament
> With tears as sovereign as the blood of hearts . . .
> The arm of mine own body, and the heart
> Where mine his thoughts did kindle.
>
> (v.i.40)

We remember his 'old ruffian' a little earlier, and doubt his sincerity. Just as he is mounting to a rhetorical climax business intrudes and is given priority:

>   Hear me, good friends –
>
> *Enter an* EGYPTIAN
>
> But I will tell you at some meeter season:
> The business of this man looks out of him.
> We'll hear him what he says.

(v.i.49)

Such incidents reveal the essence of his character. His desire to convince his followers of his own rectitude reveals the shrewd politician:

>   Go with me to my tent, where you shall see
>   How hardly I was drawn into this war,
>   How calm and gentle I proceeded still
>   In all my writings. Go with me, and see
>   What I can show in this.

(v.i.73)

Like Antony and Cleopatra, Caesar has a strong sense of dignity and decorum, of what is fitting to his position, and it is this sense which is affronted by Octavia's unheralded return to Rome like a 'market-maid':

>   You come not
> Like Caesar's sister.

(III.vi.42)

and it is in character that part of his complaint should be that her arrival 'prevented/The ostentation of our love (III.vi.51). Unlike Antony and Cleopatra, however, he lacks the common touch. He shudders at the thought of Antony rubbing shoulders with knaves that smell of sweat and he is contemptuous of the servility and inconstancy of the mob. We are not surprised to learn that he is feared rather than loved, and cannot imagine him establishing any warm personal relationship with his subordinates as Antony and Cleopatra do. This aloofness, however, is possibly necessary in Shakespeare's view to the political leader.

Octavius more than offsets his military inferiority to Antony by the superb efficiency that marks all his actions. He is always one move ahead. When Maecenas says that the Romans should be told of Antony's accusations (III.vi.19) Caesar tells him that they have already been informed; when Agrippa says that Antony should be answered, Caesar replies, 'Tis done already' (III.vi.31). He outwits Antony's spies over his troop movements, crosses the Ionian Sea and captures Toryne with a speed that Antony finds 'impossible' and Canidius 'beyond belief'. His own intelligence service is impeccable. He knows of Antony's defection before Octavia. 'I have eyes upon him / And his affairs come to me on the wind' (III.vi.62).

One of the great dramatic moments of the play is the meeting of Caesar and Cleopatra, the two masters of guile, in v.ii. The first round goes to Caesar with his humiliating pretence to be unable to distinguish Cleopatra from her maids:

> Which is the Queen of Egypt?
>
> > (line 112)

Cleopatra quickly ripostes, suggesting that events have been brought about by the gods, not by Caesar

> > Sir, the gods
> Will have it thus.
>
> > (line 115)

When Proculeius had earlier prevented Cleopatra's suicide he begged her to

> > Let the world see
> His nobleness well acted, which your death
> Will never let come forth.
>
> > (line 44)

From what we have seen and heard of Caesar we would expect the nobleness to be 'acted' and, of course, 'well acted'. We see the 'acting' when Caesar now tells her

> For we intend so to dispose you as
> Yourself shall give us counsel.
>
> > (line 186)

since he has formerly revealed (v.i.65) that he intends to use her in his triumph, and the deception is underlined when Dolabella enters just after Caesar's exit to confirm that this is his hidden purpose. Cleopatra, who perceives that he 'words' her, wins the last round, however, after the intervening humiliation over her treasure, by frustrating Caesar's political intentions through her death – the only character to outwit him.

It would be mistaken to regard Caesar as totally repellent. However we may deplore his use of his sister as a political pawn, we recognize that he is warmly attached to her. Plutarch tells us that 'it was predestined that the government of all the world should fall into Octavius Caesar's hands', an idea reflected in the play. Caesar tells Octavia

> Be you not troubled with the time, which drives
> O'er your content these strong necessities,
> But let determined things to destiny
> Hold unbewailed their way. Welcome to Rome;
> Nothing more dear to me. You are abused
> Beyond the mark of thought, and the high gods,
> To do you justice, makes his ministers
> Of us and those that love you.

(III.vi.83)

He laments at Antony's death that

> our stars,
> Unreconcilable, should divide
> Our equalness to this.

(v.i.46)

The soothsayer's prohecy that Caesar's fortune would outshine Antony's the portents reported by Scarus (IV.xii.3) and the references to destiny, necessity, the stars, and predetermined events have the effect of making events appear inevitable, and Caesar the agent of the gods. He is the 'universal landlord', the bringer of 'The time of universal peace' in which 'the three-nooked world/Shall bear the olive freely'(IV.vi.5).

Although Caesar usually has one eye on his audience, there seems to be genuine admiration in his eulogy of Antony's fortitude at Modena (I.iv.56) and his epitaph over Cleopatra's body. Yet he would not be Caesar if he did not end on a note of ambiguity:

> and their story is
> No less in pity than his glory which
> Brought them to be lamented.

(v.ii.357)

He seems to be praising both Antony and himself.

The general coldness of Caesar and the questionable morality of some of his methods are a powerful means of focusing our interest and preference on the lovers, but we cannot fail to see that though he is 'ass unpolicied' to Cleopatra, he is the necessary prelude to the 'universal peace'; the *Pax Romana* which he established could not have been achieved by an Antony.

ENOBARBUS performs several functions, not the least being that of a kind of Greek chorus figure, giving the audience essential background information about events and characters (as in his description of the first meeting of Antony and Cleopatra and his reminiscences about life in Alexandria for the benefit of Agrippa and Maecenas); commenting on and interpreting the action (such as the reconciliation of Pompey and the triumvirs, and Antony's marriage to Octavia), and forecasting future developments. He is also used as a foil to Antony, shaping our attitude to him at crucial points, and as a guide to several other characters through his remarks on them. Shakespeare brings together and expresses through Enobarbus a great deal of narrative detail and critical comment scattered haphazardly through the pages of Plutarch, yet skilfully contrives to create a coherent and interesting character. He is virtually Shakespeare's own creation; all Plutarch tells us is that a Domitius Ahenobarbus deserted Antony at Actium, had his treasure sent to him by Antony and died of a fever.

To fulfil these functions Enobarbus has quickly to be established as a like-able and trustworthy character, and the dramatist loses no time in doing this. We learn early in the action that Enobarbus is a realist who sees things clearly as they are, a voice of common sense who expresses his opinions bluntly, a good mixer, equally at home in the company of a Caesar or a servant. He is the professional soldier – tough, humorous, a hard drinker, bawdy-tongued, willing to enjoy what pleasures his military life offers, but sub-ordinating them to the demands of his profession. Granville-Barker is surely wrong in seeing him as a misogynist. It is true he shows his dislike of Fulvia, but then so does everyone else. He mixes happily in the company of Cleopatra's maids, and though he sees through many of Cleopatra's coquetries he admires her unique qualities. Like all other pleasures, women must be set aside when duty calls:

> Under a compelling occasion let women die. It were pity to cast them away for nothing, though between them and a great cause they should be esteemed nothing.
>
> (I.ii.128)

As well as expressing his own attitude, it is a shrewd warning to Antony, whose dilemma is precisely that he is torn between a woman and 'a great cause'. Nevertheless he tells Antony that not to have seen Cleopatra would be to have missed 'a wonderful piece of work'.

When Antony informs him of his decision to leave Egypt in I.ii, Enobarbus attempts to stiffen Antony's resolution by warning him to expect a masterly display of histrionics – which is what we get. This illustrates his prophetic function, seen also in the forecast that Antony will return to Cleopatra (II.ii.236, II.vi.121), that the marriage with Octavia will lead to greater dissension (II.vi.123), that Cleopatra's presence at Actium will be disastrous for Antony (III.vii.8), that Caesar and Antony will fight when Pompey is removed (II.ii.107, III.v.13), that Caesar will reject Antony's challenge to single combat (III.xiii.29), and that Thidias will be whipped (III.xiii.88). This function serves the dual purpose of indicating the future action, and, through the accuracy of his forecasts, of establishing our dependence on Enobarbus's views as objective assessments of the situation.

Enobarbus's uncompromising honesty is seen in his contempt for Lepidus's time-serving and flattery. He has no intention of entreating Antony to 'soft and gentle speech' as Lepidus requests (II.ii.3) but rather 'To answer like himself'. He points out the hollowness of the pretended friendship between Antony and Caesar

> Or if you borrow one another's love for the instant, you may, when you hear no more words of Pompey, return it again: you shall have time to wrangle in when you have nothing else to do.
>
> (II.ii.107)

Shakespeare is here doing several things at once: revealing Enobarbus's character, pointing out to us the reality behind the appearances of the scene, and pointing to future events. When Antony silences Enobarbus, he remarks, 'That truth should be silent I had almost forgot' – a biting comment on the diplomacy of the triumvirs.

As soon as this meeting is over, Enobarbus is used to fill in the background events with his famous Cydnus description. It is often objected that this speech is too imaginative and poetic for a blunt character like Enobarbus. It would be a sufficient answer to this to say that whether we today like it or not, it was an accepted and common convention of Elizabethan drama to put expository material into the mouths of characters whom it did not fit. But is this the case here? To begin with, the description has a solid substratum of fact which we would expect, and can accept as true from Enobarbus. The situation is dramatic in that he makes the most of his opportunity to impress his friends with an account of his experiences. Enobarbus uses metaphors which are highly concrete, rooted firmly in the solid world of sensory experience, but it is his perceptiveness that sees the connections between the facts he reports and their significance (as in the metaphors of the water following the oars, and the winds lovesick with the sails), and this activity is wholly in keeping with his character as displayed throughout the play. It is of course naïve to suppose that a commonsensical soldier is incapable of flights of fancy. Enobarbus is an intelligent and imaginative man. He sees, for example, as none of the negotiators does (with the probable exception of Caesar) that it is precisely the qualities they all admire in Octavia which will ensure the shipwreck of the marriage to one who 'himself is not so'.

We see elsewhere his terse epigrammatic power, displaying the same kind of metaphorical conceit in his scathing mockery of Lepidus's flattery of his fellow triumvirs

> They are his shards, and he their beetle.
>
> (III.ii.20)

and his witty pointedness

> Hoo! Hearts, tongues, figures, scribes, bards, poets cannot
> Think, speak, cast, write, sing, number – hoo! –
> His love to Antony.
>
> (III.ii.16)

His suspicion of Caesar's tears when taking leave of Octavia reveals a similar quickness of wit and invention:

> ENOBARBUS Will Caesar weep?
>   AGRIPPA He has a cloud in's face.
> ENOBARBUS He were the worse for that were he a horse;
>   So is he being a man.
>
> (III.ii.50)

A man who expresses himself like this is no rough commonplace soldier, as he is often played by the actor.

Enobarbus turns his deflating power against pretence wherever he finds it. Antony's tears over Brutus at Philippi were also false, he implies. That year 'he was troubled with a rheum' and

> What willingly he did confound he wailed.
>
> (III.ii.58)

This mockery serves the important dramatic function of preventing any deep audience involvement in the separation. The comic quality drives out any hint of the tragic mood.

Enobarbus's professionalism is seen in his disapproval of woman's interference in military matters (III.vii) and more particularly in his shock at Antony's flight which moves him for the first time in the play. He decides to remain loyal to Antony though he see that it is 'good night indeed' (III.x.29), and this commends him to us, the more so because it forces him to neglect the guiding principle of his life, his reason:

> I'll yet follow
> The wounded chance of Antony, though my reason
> Sits in the wind against me.
>
> (III.x.34)

He cannot understand how Antony could have put a woman before his soldiership:

> The itch of his affection should not then
> Have nicked his captainship at such a point

(III.xiii.7)

and he asks Cleopatra, 'What though you fled . . . why should he follow?' (III.xiii.4). The question shows the limitations of Enobarbus's understanding. Rationally he is right, but he lacks an understanding of the emotional nature of his master. In his flight and in his challenge to Caesar, Antony followed his emotion rather than his reason, and there is rich irony in Enobarbus's blaming Antony for this weakness when he himself has just allowed emotion to guide his own decision. The fact that Enobarbus does not desert Antony at Actium as he did historically makes him a more admirable character.

Enobarbus is guilty of one major misreading of the situation, and it is an error that makes for high drama, namely his interpretation of Cleopatra's offer of her hand to Thidias to kiss as an act of treachery.

> Sir, sir, thou art so leaky
> That we must leave thee to thy sinking, for
> Thy dearest quit thee.

(III.xiii.63)

Since he has decided to find some way to leave Antony, the plural 'we' inculpates himself, and it is possibly his sense of guilt at this decision that prompts him to try to share it by including Cleopatra in it. Ironically it is Enobarbus and not Cleopatra who deserts the sinking Antony. It is a subtle psychological stroke that Enobarbus's error of judgement and his deplorable action in fetching Antony should only have been possible when he was not being true to himself. He had just revealed in soliloquy that

> Mine honesty and I begin to square.

(III.xiii.41)

It is deeply ironic, too, that Enobarbus, having made the rational decision to leave one who persists in irrational behaviour, is placed at the mercy of his emotions. The sight of Antony taking farewell of his servants makes him 'onion-eyed'. When we see him next (IV.vi) he is a broken man

> I have done ill
> Of which I do accuse myself so sorely
> That I will joy no more.

(IV.vi.18)

The arrival of his treasure, a gesture of love from Antony, intensifies his anguish. We are reminded of his answer when Cleopatra had asked what they should do – 'Think, and die' (III.xiii.l) – when he now resolves to take his life 'If swift thought break it not . . . but thought will do't, I feel' (IV.vi.34). Ironically the 'thought' that breaks his heart is emotional, not rational, a sense of his turpitude to this 'mine of bounty', Antony. His prayer that posterity should remember him as a 'master-leaver and a fugitive' powerfully aids in building up our sympathy for Antony. Enobarbus had said of Antony

> A diminution in our captain's brain
> Restored his heart.   (III.xiii.198)

The same is true of Enobarbus. His death is emotion's revenge on reason.

The characterization of Enobarbus is a fine example of Shakespeare's skill in integrating character with dramatic function.

LEPIDUS has a very small part of forty-eight lines, which reflects his slightness, and he disappears from the scene in III.ii. He is presented as a semi-comic figure, ludicrous in his fulsome flatteries of Caesar and Antony, for which he is made fun of by Agrippa and Enobarbus, a fussy, pacific figure, mocked by the servants preparing Pompey's feast as one out of his depth in great affairs. When the servant carries him out on his back, helplessly drunk, we have a visual symbol of his exit from the political world for which he has not the stamina.

OCTAVIA has an even smaller part. She is a virtuous, passive and rather pathetic figure, shamelessly used by both her brother and Antony for political reasons, but Shakespeare is careful to make her a rather shadowy creature to avoid arousing too much audience sympathy for her.

The theatre of Shakespeare's day

To know something of the theatre for which Shakespeare wrote, of its conventions, possibilities and limitations, so different from the modern theatre, is to have a deeper understanding of the nature and meaning of the plays themselves.

The earliest permanent theatres in Elizabethan times reflected many of the structural features of the inn-yards and the bull-baiting and bear-baiting arenas of the time. Like them they were three-storeyed, and round, octagonal or square, the buildings surrounding an open-air auditorium on all sides. An 'apron' stage, or 'platform', projected forward from one wall with the audience sitting or standing around three sides of it. Between the building of the first of these theatres, The Theatre, in 1576, and the closing of the theatres by the Cromwellians in 1642, we know of the existence of nine public theatres in London. Their life-span was short, and only three or four were in operation at any one time during this period. In the latter part of his career Shakespeare was writing plays for performances in the private theatres, which were smaller, roofed theatres catering for a more sophisticated audience, but *Antony and Cleopatra* was written for performance at The Globe the public theatre owned by Shakespeare's acting company, the King's Men, and built in 1599 (see Visscher's view of London, p.lv).

The extant building contract for the erection of the Fortune Theatre in 1600 provides much useful detail about Elizabethan theatres. The Fortune was a square theatre, measuring 80 feet on the outside, with an auditorium 55 feet square on the inside. The stage jutted forward halfway, 27 feet 6 inches, and was 43 feet wide, thus leaving a narrow gap of 6 feet on either side where the audience could stand. A significant feature of these theatres was their smallness. Although they could hold some 2500 people, no member of the audience could be more than 25 yards from the furthest player, while the great majority were very much nearer. This created an intimacy between player and spectator which had a powerful influence on the construction of the plays. The soliloquy and the aside, two common conventions in Elizabethan drama were credibly employed with a stage on which the actor could go right forward with audience on three sides of him and confide or whisper his thoughts to them. This is difficult on the average modern stage, in which the audience, sitting in darkness, look from a distance into a kind of lighted room, cut off from them by the proscenium arch or frame around the stage.

We should notice, too, the largeness of the stage itself, occupying almost half the area of the theatre. It made possible scenes in which groups or individuals could be so far apart that they could realistically be represented as not hearing or seeing each other. We have an example in IV.xiv, after Antony's abortive attempt to kill himself:

DIOMEDES   Where's Antony?
DECRETAS There, Diomed, there.
DIOMEDES   Lives he? Wilt thou
                 Not answer man?
ANTONY   Art thou there, Diomed?
                                                    (IV.xiv.112)

The stage was raised some four feet above ground level, so that both the groundlings or 'penny stinkards' standing on the flat auditorium and those paying more and sitting in the surrounding galleries could see and hear more easily. Wooden panelling stretching around the front and sides of the stage prevented the audience from seeing beneath the stage and created an enclosed 'underground' area successfully exploited by many dramatists. Since the

A view of London in the early 17th century showing St. Paul s Cathedral and the theatres on the South Bank (from an engraving by Visscher 1616).

main stage was uncurtained it was important for the dramatist to ensure that it was cleared naturally, within the action of the play, of bodies or stage properties, The death of Antony, for example, was acted on the main stage, and iv.xiv ends with the stage direction (in the First Folio), 'Exit bearing Antony', in order that the stage should be clear for Caesar's entry in the following scene. So also in ii.vii the First Folio stage direction 'Enter two or three servants with a banket (i.e. banquet)', shows how stage furniture such as tables and stools would be brought in naturally within the action of the play. They would similarly be cleared by the servants when the banquet was over. Where this could not be done on the outer stage the action would usually take place in the inner stage (known variously as the study, the discovery-space, or the enclosure), a recessed room in the centre of the wall at the back of the stage. It had curtains, and presented the dramatist with a valuable opportunity to extend the dimensions of his play by varying the setting, presenting scenes in small places, like a bedroom, a cave, a study or cell. This inner stage had entrances at the sides and back, so that when the curtain was closed stage properties could be moved on and off unseen. In this way the acting was not held up as it so often is today. The common alternation of strongly contrasting scenes in Elizabethan plays – outdoor or public scenes often followed by indoor and private ones – is explained by the existence of the inner stage, and the upper stage situated above it, with a light railing or balustrade along the front of it. This too had a curtain set a few feet back from the railing, so that when closed it created a narrow passage or terrace, and when opened provided another room for indoor scenes. Many scenes set on city walls or battlements, or in upper rooms or towers would be acted on the upper stage, which was built at a height of about seven feet and thus enabled the actors (who in Elizabethan times were much shorter than modern man – about 5 feet 2 inches on the average) to jump safely from the upper stage as they have to in some of the history plays for example, to the main stage below. The upper stage would be used for iv.xv where the First Folio stage directions reads, 'Enter Cleopatra and her maids aloft', and it would be the upper stage to which they later heave up Antony.

Jutting out over part of the main stage was a roof known as the 'shadow', 'heavens' or 'canopy', supported by two large pillars, one at each forward corner. An eyewitness tells us that these were wooden, but so skilfully painted that they could not be distinguished from marble. They were useful in dividing up the stage for scenes in which separate groups operated, and in providing hiding places for the many spying and eavesdropping scenes in Elizabethan drama. The underside of the 'heavens' was magnificently painted or sculptured with representations of the sun, moon, stars, signs of the zodiac and other heavenly bodies, and this doubtless accounts for the many invitations by the actor for his audience to behold the heavenly bodies.

When Julius Caesar declares

> The skies are painted with unnumbered sparks,
> They are all fire, and every one doth shine.
>
> (*Julius Caesar* III.i.63)

the audience is being asked to admire the sparkling new 'heavens' of the Globe, completed just a few months before. Enobarbus, addressing the moon just before his death in IV.ix, possibly drew the attention of his audience to this feature of the Globe with a hand gesture.

On either side of the curtain of the inner stage in the back wall was a door, and these doors were the normal means of entering and leaving the main stage. They would wherever possible be used symbolically to suggest the different hinterlands behind them, thus assisting the audience in understanding where the scene was set. The First Folio stage direction for II.vi reads:

Flourish. Enter POMPEY *at one door, with drum and trumpet; at another* CAESAR, LEPIDUS, ANTONY, ENOBARBUS, MAECENAS, AGRIPPA, MENAS *with soldiers marching*.

The martial music, the marching soldiers and the crowded stage as these opposing forces meet in mid-stage make a strong visual impression of hostility and of violence imminent if reconciliation does not follow. In III.x the doors are used to suggest opposing camps beyond, where

> CANIDIUS *marcheth with his land army one way over the stage, and* TAURUS, *the lieutenant of* CAESAR *the other way. After their going in, is heard the noise of a sea-fight.*

This, with the following eye-witness accounts of the fighting, is the nearest Shakespeare can get to representing a sea-battle.

Signboards were sometimes used to denote setting, but this crude practice, mocked by Sir Philip Sydney, seems to have early fallen out of use. The normal method of indicating locality is for one of the characters to tell us where we are, as when Touchstone in *As You Like It* remarks 'Now am I in Arden'. Very often location is unimportant and unmentioned by the dramatist, though we usually know whether we are indoors or not. In V.i the scene begins out of doors, that is, on the main stage; at the end of it Caesar invites his followers to go with him to his tent, so that they would leave through the curtain of the inner stage. Often the end of one scene will indicate where a subsequent scene is set, as in II.iii where Ventidius receives his commission for Parthia, which is where he is when we see him next in III.ii. The short scene II.iv shows the triumvirs' preparations to meet Pompey at Mount Misenum, so that when they meet in II.vi we know without explanation where we are. The dramatist's frequent need to tell his audience where they are, what time of day it is, or what time has passed, is the occasion of much of the finest poetry in the drama of the time, though there happens to be little of this verbal scene painting or time-setting in *Antony and Cleopatra*.

Above the upper stage, in the third and top storey of the theatre, was the musicians' gallery and sound-effects room. It was from here that a trumpet would sound to indicate that a performance was about to begin, and a flag was run up to indicate that a play was in progress. Elizabethans were great music lovers, a fact which explains the prevalence of songs in the plays. Music in *Antony and Cleopatra* is limited to the mysterious music that heralded the departure of Hercules from Antony (IV.iii), for which some of the musicians would have to be in the gallery, others below the stage, since the music is heard both in the air and under the earth, and to Pompey's feast in II.vii, where Enobarbus calls for loud music from the musicians who would be on-stage with the other actors.

Other features which extended the possibilities of Elizabethan staging were the trapdoors, of which there would be one or more on the main stage and possibly one in the inner stage, through which devils, ghosts and other spirits from the nether world would enter; and one in the heavens from which gods and other aerial spirits might descend. It is believed that in some theatres there were windows above the two doors in the back wall.

Performances in the public theatres were in daylight, usually in the afternoons. Burning torches would be carried to suggest darkness in night scenes, as, probably, in IV.ix which begins with the sentry telling us that 'the night/ Is shiny'. More realistic effects were obtained in the private theatres where the room could be darkened, or performances given after dark.

There was little or no use of stage scenery of the modern kind, confining the stage to a fixed location, but stage properties, that is, movable articles of stage furniture, such as tables, chairs, walls, banks of earth or flowers, gates, wells, and trees, were quite widely used. When Antony says in IV.xii 'Where yond pine does stand / I shall discover all' it is probable that he would climb a property tree (widely used in Elizabethan plays, and apparently a solid and realistic property) to get a better view of the naval battle. When he returns, his bitter lament, '*this* pine is barked' (referring to himself) would have much more impact if the audience can see the tree with which he compares himself. A bed or litter would be needed for Caesar's order in v.ii after Cleopatra's death, 'Take up her bed'.

The physical features of the theatre were a fruitful source of imagery for the playwright. When Antony, dejected and ashamed after his flight from Actium, declares

> Hark, the land bids me tread no more upon't;
> It is ashamed to bear me.
>
> (III.xi.1)

he alludes to the reverberations of his heavy tread over the hollow wooden boards of the stage, so that Shakespeare neatly uses the sound that the audience can hear as a symbol of Antony's mood of dejection, underlined by his later observation to Cleopatra, 'Love, I am full of lead' (III.xi.73).

When Cleopatra suggests that Antony is dissembling in I.iii she uses the actor's art as a symbol of deception:

> Good now, play one scene
> Of excellent dissembling, and let it look
> Like perfect honour.   (I.iii.78)

This particular image of an appearance which is not the reality comes aptly from one who is such a consummate actress herself. Later, Cleopatra voices her fear that her life will be dramatically enacted in years to come:

> The quick comedians
> Extemporally will stage us, and present
> Our Alexandrian revels: Antony
> Shall be brought drunken forth, and I shall see
> Some squeaking Cleopatra boy my greatness
> I' th'posture of a whore.   (V.ii.216)

She refers to the custom of boy actors taking the parts of women in Shakespeare's day. Grounded at school in the art of rhetoric, in which Elizabethan acting was firmly rooted, these boys were accomplished actors. Shakespeare could give these lines to his boy-Cleopatra confident that he would not demean the part in the way Cleopatra feared. Normally the boys' parts were short, to ease the physical and mental strain on the boys, but the part of Cleopatra with 630 lines was an exception; it is the longest woman's role in all Shakespeare's plays. Because boys took these parts, dramatists were careful to avoid close physical intimacy as far as possible, especially in love scenes. The relationship would be suggested indirectly, as in Enobarbus's descriptions and comments, or Cleopatra's reminiscing, and through the evocative power of imagery and poetic effects generally. Granville-Barker, pointing out that Shakespeare is careful not to show Antony's return to Cleopatra on stage, remarks 'how carefully Shakespeare avoids writing any scene which a boy could not act without unpleasantness or in fear of ridicule', and also that Antony and Cleopatra are never alone on-stage together.

The use of boy actors was short-term: as soon as their voices broke and their beards grew they could no longer be used for women's parts. This explains the almost total absence of particularized description of women in the plays, for if the dramatist described one of his heroines as tall, fair and blue-eyed, he might have a boy to fit the description one week, but not the next. We notice that beyond a reference or two to Cleopatra's dark skin, and her own reference to her wrinkles (which could be an imaginary feature, designed to win sympathy for her), her appearance is not itemized, and it is in generalized terms like 'For her own person, / It beggared all description' that her beauty is established. The servant's description of Octavia is similarly vague, and is not to be taken as a true account of her anyway.

Elizabethan acting companies were small. They would be lucky to have nine or ten male actors, three or four boys, and half a dozen supernumeraries to take small or mute parts, such as those of soldiers, attendants, messengers. Doubtless stage hands and musicians, when not required to provide music, would be pressed into service for a play with a large cast like *Antony and Cleopatra* which has forty-nine speaking parts. The dramatist was thus severely circumscribed when representing crowd scenes, and would have had to exploit his limited company carefully to suggest large numbers. Battles would be staged representationally, with small isolated encounters suggesting the larger pattern of events. In II.vii, for example, Agrippa and a few of Caesar's soldiers, whom he orders to retire, rush in one door as if pursued, and out the other, quickly followed by Antony and Scarus in obvious pursuit, so that in ten lines we have a victory enacted on-stage. Adroit use of smoke, fireworks, trumpets and drums, all helped to create the illusion of large-scale conflict. Realism was attempted in the matter of blood-shedding, with the use of concealed pigs' bladders containing blood, property heads and limbs, and real entrails brought reeking from the nearest slaughter-house.

The structure of Elizabethan plays, the way the dramatist unfolded his story, was certainly influenced by the limited number of actors available. With fifteen to twenty actors, and forty-nine speaking parts, duplication was necessary, and Shakespeare had to structure his play to make this possible. We find that several characters who appear early in the play fade out and are not seen again. Philo and Demetrius make only one appearance, in I.i., and so are available for parts like those of Agrippa and Maecenas who first appear in Act II. Pompey, Menas, Menecrates and Lepidus disappear halfway, so that actors taking these parts would be free to take those which appear only at the end of the play, such as Dolabella, Proculeius or the Clown. Alexas is off-stage between III.iii and IV.ii (a gap of eight scenes) and could take the part of Canidius who appears only in III.vii and III.x.

Frequently the text makes explicit the movement, gesture and facial expression that Shakespeare required. When Cleopatra advances on Seleucus we have a clear idea of how Shakespeare envisaged the action:

> What, goest thou back? Thou shalt
> Go back, I warrant thee; but I'll catch thine eyes
> Though they had wings.

(V.ii.155)

The same is true of Agrippa's remark that Caesar 'has a cloud in's face' (III.ii.51), or Caesar's instruction to Cleopatra, 'Arise, you shall not kneel' (v.ii.114). Where the acting directions are not built into the text they are often supplemented by stage directions such as, 'she strikes him down' (II.v.61), 'She drags him up and down' (II.v.64), 'Menas whispers to Pompey' (II.vii.34), 'Enter Cleopatra led by Charmian and Eros' (III.xi.24) which establishes a visual impression of Cleopatra's apprehension, 'Enobarbus places them hand in hand' (II.vii.105), an ironic appearance of amity which we know is not real, 'They place themselves in every corner of the stage' (IV.iii.7), and 'They heave Antony up to Cleopatra' (IV.xv.37).

Period accuracy was not attempted in the costuming. As in *Julius Caesar*, the Romans would be dressed in doublet and hose. The Roman mob is described as wearing 'greasy aprons', Enobarbus wears a hat, and Cleopatra orders Charmian to cut her lace, and refers to her tires and mantles. All this is contemporary Elizabethan clothing and the armour Cleopatra and Eros buckle on Antony would be contemporary also. This use of sixteenth-century costuming reflected the way they looked at history as a storehouse of lessons for immediate application to the present. Very large sums were spent on costumes, which had to be the genuine article for the kings, queens, noblemen and warriors who crowded the Elizabethan stage, if they were to

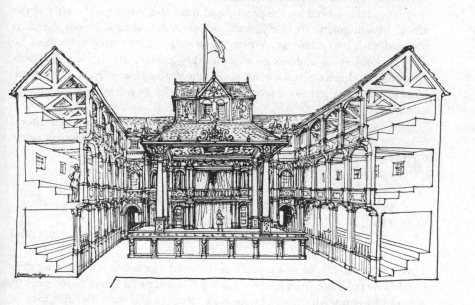

A reconstruction of the Fortune Theatre in 1600 from C. Walter Hodges' 'The Globe Restored' (Oxford).

avoid the censure of a demanding and vocal audience who would not put up with the kind of inferior imitations that can be hidden today by distance from the stage and the use of modern lighting techniques. This lavishness was part of a general attempt to create in the theatre an exotic and splendid world which Londoners were denied in their daily lives. There are numerous contemporary tributes to the magnificence of the Elizabethan theatre.

The multiple stage of the Elizabethan theatre, with its various levels and depths – apron stage, inner stage, upper stage, trapdoors, and movable properties – was an extremely flexible instrument admirably adapted to the telling of a story swiftly and uninterruptedly, and Elizabethan dramatists learned to exploit it to the full.

Language and verse in the play

Shakespeare's use of language is remarkable in many ways and demands the careful attention of the reader. Firstly, he uses an enormously rich and varied vocabulary, greater than that of any other writer. In the second place he often loads his words with more meanings than one, particularly in his verse lines.

Whereas prose is normally straightforward, expressing one unequivocal meaning, verse often deliberately sets out to do many things at one time, and the poetic dramatist is more given than other poets to using language in this way since he is forced by the pressure of time, the 'two hours' traffic of the stage', into linguistic economy, compression and intensity. Words are often charged with two meanings. When Caesar calls Antony his 'competitor' he wants his hearers to understand it as meaning 'partner' (which was one of its meanings in the sixteenth century), but he really means 'rival', as we the audience perceive. The one word, then, does a lot of work in characterizing Caesar.

Often words and phrases are not to be understood from their literal meaning, but from the context in which they occur. When Cleopatra calms Charmian with the words (quoted earlier, p.xxiii)

> Peace, peace!
> Dost thou not see my baby at my breast,
> That sucks the nurse asleep?
>
> (v.ii.304)

a prose equivalent, 'Be quiet, can't you see the asp is painlessly killing me', would lose the better part of the meaning. The repeated word 'peace' reveals a new Cleopatra who has relinquished struggle and accepted the idea of death. The mother-child image establishes a tender Cleopatra all the more impressive because of the contrast with the earlier Cleopatra we have seen, and the final word 'sleep' suggests that death is not a finality but the prelude to a new meeting with Antony. The whole passage generates a sympathy which the prose version is incapable of doing.

The significance of words is often incomplete without reference back to earlier parts of the play. The Guard's words to Cleopatra in v.ii 'He brings you figs', are simple enough, but are loaded with irony and foreboding since he is unwittingly introducing not just the Clown but Death also, and our mind is forced back to the previous mention of figs by Charmian when the Soothsayer tells her she will outlive her mistress, 'O excellent! I love long life better than figs' (I.ii.30). The figs herald death, and she does outlive Cleopatra, by a few seconds. There are many other examples of meaning working retrospectively in this way in the play.

The staple of Shakespeare's verse is the iambic pentameter, that is, a line made up of five iamic feet (an iambic foot consisting of two syllables, the first unstressed, the second stressed, with the stress falling on those syllables which are accented in normal speech) as in the following lines:

> Ănd gól|děn Phóe|bŭs něv|ěr bé|běhéld
>
> Ŏf eyés|ăgáin|sŏ róyal!|Yoŭr crówn's|ăwrý;

> (v.ii.313)

The stressed syllables are marked ´, the unstressed ones ˘ and each foot is divided from the next by the vertical stroke |. The great majority of the lines follow this basic pattern. In such lines as

> Lĕt nót|thĕ píece|ŏf vír|tŭe whích|ĭs sét|
>
> Bĕtwíxt|ŭs, ás|thĕ cém|ĕnt ŏf|oŭr lóve|

> (III.ii.28)

we have an example in *cement* of a word differently sounded in the sixteenth century from today. The stress was on the first syllable, and the line is a regular iambic pentameter. Other examples of apparent irregularity are cases where elision, that is, the suppression of a syllable, is necessary to preserve regularity, as in

> Thĕ béds|i' th'Eást|ăre sóft,|ănd thánks|tŏ yóu

> (II.vi.50)

The words *in the east*, properly three syllables, have to be truncated as the spelling in the text (taken from the First Folio) indicates, to make two syllables as the metre requires. One other freedom open to the Elizabethan poet was to sound a final -*ed* in verbs and adjectives which was not sounded in normal speech. We have this in

    The bus|iness she|hath broach|èd in|the state|

                                               (I.ii.159)

where the sounded -*ed* gives the line its ten syllables, and so makes it a regular iambic pentameter.

From time to time the dramatist will vary the metre to avoid monotony, or for special dramatic or poetic effects. For example, in the line

    Purple|the sails|and so|perfum|èd that|

                                               (II.ii.196)

the first foot is trochaic (having a stressed syllable followed by an unstressed one). Thus the word *Purple,* by reversing the normal rhythmical pattern, draws attention to itself, which is what Shakespeare wanted, since this is the royal colour, and Cleopatra's majesty is the theme of the passage in which this line occurs.

Further variety and flexibility are attained by the occasional use of lines longer or shorter than ten syllables, and by variations in the position of the caesura, the pause which the sense of the words dictates within many of the lines.

This is illustrated in the following lines, where the caesura is marked by the double vertical lines ||:

    There's not a minute of our lives||should stretch

                                   (I.i.46)

    Fulvia thy wife||first came into the field

                                   (I.ii.80)

    The hand could pluck her back||that shoved her on

                                   (I.ii.118)

In using blank verse, Shakepeare was taking over the form handed down by his predecessors who had by trial and error discovered it to be the best medium for conveying dramatic purpose in a memorable and succinct way. Shakespeare's achievement lay in exploiting this medium until he had made it a refined instrument of great flexibility, capable of containing multiple meanings compactly and of communicating subtle shades and nuances of meaning. We see the compactness in such phrases as 'flower-soft hands', 'fearful sails', 'your considerate stone', 'loose-wived', 'triple pillar', 'ebbed man', 'kingdoms are clay'. Some, like 'beggared all description' have passed into the common currency of the language, but all of them would require many more words in prose to convey their meanings and would be much less memorable.

Images which in isolation have only a single meaning can acquire various levels of meaning when repeated or woven into a pattern running throughout a play. The dramatist may use this reiterated imagery to convey meaning, shape the audience's response, or create a special tone or atmosphere. In *Antony and Cleopatra* images of abundance, fertility, luxury and languor abound in the Egyptian scenes, and these are contrasted with images of asceticism, war, business, coldness in the Roman scenes. The imagery, then, characterizes and differentiates the two ways of life, the two scales of value, of Rome and Egypt.

We find, too, clusters of connected images, such as the sun-serpent-Nile group in the Egyptian scenes. The sun, 'the fire that quickens Nilus' slime', mysteriously generates life, including, among other creatures, the serpent, the royal symbol of the Egyptian rulers, and we learn that Antony's phrase for Cleopatra is 'serpent of old Nile'. We are thus aware of the ambivalence in the later conversation between Lepidus and Antony:

LEPIDUS Y'have strange serpents there?
ANTONY Ay, Lepidus.
LEPIDUS Your serpent of Egypt is bred now of your mud by the operation of your sun.

(II.vii.22)

The aspic, we are told, has the slime of the river upon it, which it 'leaves/ Upon the caves of Nile', so that there is an aptness in the fact that Cleopatra's end should be closely associated with her origins. The sun is of course another symbol of royalty, so that Cleopatra in the earthly order as Queen is a counterpart of the sun in the heavenly order. She is 'with Phoebus' amorous pinches black', Phoebus being the sun-god, and when Antony hears of her death he sees it as sunset; for him 'the long day's task is done', and 'the torch is out'. This image-group, however, is used equivocally in the play, since the serpent is also associated with poison and satanic temptation, the sun connotes heat, intemperance and lust, and the Nile generates flies and gnats that consume the body. Each fresh occurrence of these associated images compels us to relate it to former ones, so that a rich texture of ambiguity, complexity and subtlety is woven around Cleopatra and Egypt and their effect on Antony.

The same two-edged quality of the imagery is found in the food and drink imagery. From one point of view it indicates generosity, abundance and enjoyment; from another, surfeit, waste, corruption.

Another noteworthy group of images is that which establishes the cosmic or universal dimensions of the play. These include images of sun, moon, stars and the heavens generally. The word 'world' occurring over forty times suggests a conscious attempt by the dramatist to impress on us the magnitude of the issues with which the play deals.

The many images concerned with tying and untying, knitting together, and the patching of clothes, help to create the atmosphere of uncertainty and mutability that is so basic to the themes of the play. Allied to this are the numerous images taken from the actor's art of 'dissembling', which underline that the appearance is often not the reality in the world of the play.

Less than 8 per cent of the play is in prose, and the high percentage of verse reflects the exalted and formal level of events and personages, since verse is almost always used in public scenes involving high-ranking characters. What prose there is, is used in three main ways: firstly, to denote the speech of characters low in the social scale; secondly, for speech among those of higher rank in their more relaxed and unofficial moments; and thirdly, for comic scenes.

Examples of the first are the speeches of Cleopatra's maids when off duty in I.ii, of the servants preparing the banquet in Pompey's galley in II.vii, and of the Clown in v.ii. Of the second use of prose we have an example in II.ii when the triumvirs have left the stage after their reconciliation and Enobarbus, Maecenas and Agrippa relax, chatting about Egypt after the formality of state affairs, though we should notice that Enobarbus returns to blank verse for the Cydnus speech, since this deals with royalty and high events. A further example is the commentary by Enobarbus and Menas after the meeting of Pompey and the triumvirs, and a third in III.v, also a choric scene, in which Eros and Enobarbus amplify and comment on Caesar's actions complained of by Antony to Octavia in blank verse in the preceding scene, though at the end of III.v they revert to blank verse again, possibly to give weight to Enobarbus's prophecy that Caesar and Antony will soon be fighting it out for world supremacy like two dogs over a bone.

These two uses of prose sometimes shade into one another. Messengers and servants like Charmian and Iras always speak verse in the presence of their superiors, and the soldiers on guard in IV.iii speak verse, which underlines that they are on duty and thus behaving formally. In the fortune-telling scene (I.ii) the Soothsayer speaks in verse, which gives authority to his words and marks his gravity off from the jocularity of the maids.

We find Enobarbus lapsing into prose when speaking privately to Antony about Cleopatra and Fulvia in I.ii. This cleverly shows the closeness of the relationship between them. At the same time Enobarbus's comments are satiric and bawdy in tone, so that in substance and manner they are better suited to prose than verse.

The use of prose for comic scenes is found in the fortune-telling (I.ii), the interlude between Cleopatra and the Clown (v.ii), the comments of Enobarbus on women (I.ii) and interestingly in the banquet scene (II.vii) where Lepidus when drunk speaks prose, suggesting his lack of ability to control his tongue and his loss of dignity. Antony speaks prose while teasing him, but nowhere else in the play, while Caesar and Cleopatra fittingly speak verse throughout.

One other significant use of prose is the three lines in which Enobarbus interrupts the deliberations of Caesar and Antony with his prophetic debunking:

> Or if you borrow one another's love for the instant, you may, when you hear no more words of Pompey, return it again: you shall have time to wrangle in when you have nothing else to do.

(II.ii.107)

When Antony silences him he remarks, 'That truth should be silent I had almost forgot.' This prose irruption in a formal verse scene strongly suggests that verse here, the language of diplomacy, is a rhetorical cloak to hide the true meaning of the words spoken, while prose voices the truth.

Rhyme is very little used. Apart from the rhyme in the short song sung at Pompey's feast, there are only 13 couplets, mostly insignificant and possibly accidental. There are six scenes, including the last, which end with a couplet, a common convention which gives finality, as in Cleopatra's injunction to her maids at the end of IV.xv

> Come, we have no friend,
> But resolution, and the briefest end.

Language difficulties

The basis of Shakespeare's language is the common speech of his time, but many of its words have dropped out of use. Archaisms of this kind in *Antony and Cleopatra,* like *anticked, burgonet* and *cantle,* will send us to the notes on the facing page or, if they occur again, to the Glossary. Neologisms, that is, words Shakespeare coined for the first time, abound, and many of them have also dropped out of use, like *disponge, dislimn, discandy,* or were never in general use. A further difficulty, more dangerous because often unrecognized, is the large number of words which have survived to the present day but with different meanings from those they had in Shakespeare's time. Examples of this are *avoid* (meaning: go away), *clip* (embrace), *extended* (seized), *friend* (lover), *formal* (ordinary), and *admiral* (flagship).

The modern reader, unless he is familiar with the Authorized Version of the Bible (1611), may at first have a little difficulty in interpreting certain grammatical forms which are not a part of the English of today. The most important of these are considered here.

TENSES. Modern English uses continuous or progressive tenses more than the English of Shakespeare's time:

> They cast their caps up and carouse together   (IV.xii.12)

where we should perhaps expect 'They *are throwing* their caps up and *are drinking* together.'

DO, DID etc. In Shakespeare's English the auxiliary *do* was often used where modern English does not use a compound tense:

> Each heart in Rome does love and pity you.
>
> (III.vi.93)

(Modern: 'Every heart in Rome loves and pities you.')

> Antony,
> Enthroned i' th' market-place, did sit alone
>
> (II.ii.217)

('sat' or 'was sitting').

On the other hand, where today we use *do* to form the negative, Shakespearian English did not always do so:

> We looked not for Mark Antony here.
>
> (II.vi.105)

('We did not expect to find Mark Antony here.')

-ETH, -TH. This present tense ending is associated with 3rd person singular subjects, but is not invariably used with such subjects. The form is illustrated by *hath* in the following quotation, but notice also that the archaic verb *reneges* has the modern -s ending.

> His captain's heart,
> Which in the scuffles of great fights hath burst
> The buckle on his breast, reneges all temper.
>
> (I.i.6)

THOU, THEE, THY etc. These correspond to the modern *you, your* etc. but even in Shakespeare's time the distinction between singular *thou* and plural *you* was disappearing. The verb forms associated with *thou* as subject have the ending -*est* –

> Thou teachest like a fool.
>
> (I.iii.10)

– but there are exceptions, as we might expect, for the very common verbs: 'Thou *art* a soldier only' (II.ii.111); 'thou *shouldst* know' (I.iii.40); 'every hour . . . *shalt* thou have report' (I.iv.35); 'Thou *didst* drink' (I.iv.61). As the last example shows, the inflexion is not applied only to the present tense; the lines preceding it have other past tense examples in 'thou slew'st' (*slewest* = you killed) and 'thou fought'st against'.

A few passages of literary criticism relating to Antony and Cleopatra

The aim of the following selections is to present varied viewpoints on the play by distinguished critics.

(a) This passage from *Samuel Johnson* is a characteristic example of eighteenth century criticism. Johnson was uneasy about the moral tone of the play, but praised its structure and frequent scene changes, two points which many subsequent critics have found fault with.

> This play keeps curiosity always busy, and the passions always interested. The continual hurry of the action, the variety of incidents, and the quick succession of one personage to another, call the mind forward without intermission from the first act to the last. But the power of delighting is derived principally from the frequent changes of the scene; for, except the feminine arts, some of which are too low, which distinguish Cleopatra, no character is very strongly discriminated. Upton [an eighteenth century critic], who did not easily miss what he desired to find, has discovered that the language of Antony is, with great skill and learning, made pompous and superb, according to his real practice. But I think his diction not distinguishable from that of others: the most tumid speech in the play is that which Caesar makes to Octavia.
>
> The events of which the principal are described according to history, are produced without any art of connection or care of disposition.
>
> Samuel Johnson: *Preface to Shakespeare*, 1765

(b) From *Coleridge* we have an example of early Romantic criticism:

> The highest praise, or rather form of praise, of this play, which I can offer in my own mind, is the doubt which the perusal always occasions in me, whether the *Antony and Cleopatra* is not, in all exhibitions of a giant power in its strength and vigour of maturity, a formidable rival of *Macbeth*, *Lear*, *Hamlet* and *Othello*. *Feliciter audax* is the motto for its style comparatively with that of Shakespeare's other works, even as it is the general motto of all his works compared with those of other poets. Be it remembered, too, that this happy valiancy of style is but the representative and result of all the material excellencies so expressed.
>
> This play should be perused in mental contrast with *Romeo and Juliet*; – as the love of passion and appetite as opposed to the love of affection and instinct. But the art displayed in the character of Cleopatra is profound; in this, especially, that the sense of criminality in her passion is lessened by our insight into its depth and energy, at the very moment that we cannot but perceive that the passion itself springs out of the habitual craving of a licentious nature, and that it is supported

and reinforced by voluntary stimulus and sought-for associations, instead of blossoming out of spontaneous emotion.

Of all Shakespeare's historical plays, *Antony and Cleopatra* is by far the most wonderful. There is not one in which he has followed history so minutely, and yet there are few in which he impresses the notion of angelic strength so much; – perhaps none in which he impresses it more strongly. This is greatly owing to the manner in which the fiery force is sustained throughout, and to the numerous momentary flashes of nature counteracting the historical abstraction. As a wonderful specimen of the way in which Shakespeare lives up to the very end of this play, read the last part of the concluding scene.

S. T. Coleridge: 'Notes on Antony and Cleopatra'
from Essays and Lectures on Shakespeare, 1808

(c) *Hazlitt* exemplifies the nineteenth century's growing interest in and concentration upon character, and particularly that of Cleopatra.

This is a very noble play. . . . It presents a fine picture of Roman pride and Eastern magnificence: and in the struggle between the two, the empire of the world seems suspended like

> the swan's down feather,
> That stands upon the swell at full of tide
> And neither way inclines.

The characters breathe, move, and live. Shakespeare does not stand reasoning on what his characters would do or say, but at once *becomes* them, and speaks and acts for them. He does not present us with groups of stage puppets or poetical machines making set speeches of ostensible motives, but he brings living men and women on the scene, who speak and act from real feelings, according to the ebbs and flows of passion, without the least tincture of the pedantry of logic or rhetoric. Nothing is made out by inference and analogy, by climax and antithesis, but everything takes place just as it would have done in reality, according to the occasion. The character of Cleopatra is a master-piece. . . . The Egyptian is voluptuous, ostentatious, conscious, boastful of her charms, haughty, tyrannical, fickle. Her luxurious pomp and gorgeous extravagance are displayed in all their force and lustre, as well as the irregular grandeur of the soul of Mark Antony. . . .

She has great and unpardonable faults, but the beauty of her death almost redeems them. She learns from the depth of despair the strength of her affections. She keeps her queen-like state in the last disgrace, and her sense of the pleasurable in the last moments of her life. She tastes a luxury in death.

William Hazlitt: Characters of Shakespeare's Plays, 1817

(d) In the detailed psychological analysis of *A. C. Bradley* we have the late Romantic focus upon character at its best.

It is curious to notice . . . how often the first epithets used in reference to *Antony and Cleopatra* are 'wonderful' and 'astonishing'. And the main source of the feeling thus expressed seems to be the 'angelic strength' or 'fiery force' of which Coleridge wrote. The first of these two phrases is, I think, the more entirely happy. Except perhaps towards the close, one is not so conscious of fiery force as in certain other tragedies; but one is astonished at the apparent ease with which extraordinary effects are produced . . . .

In the first three Acts of our play . . . people converse, discuss, accuse one another, excuse themselves, mock, describe, drink together, arrange a marriage, meet and part; but they do not kill, do not even tremble or weep. We see hardly one violent movement; until the battle of Actium is over we witness scarcely any vehement passion; and that battle, as it is a naval action, we do not see. Even later, Enobarbus, when he dies, simply dies; he does not kill himself. We hear wonderful talk; but it is not talk, like that of Macbeth and Lady Macbeth, or that of Othello and Iago, at which we hold our breath. The scenes that we remember first are those that portray Cleopatra; Cleopatra coquetting, tormenting, beguiling her lover to stay; Cleopatra left with her women and longing for him; Cleopatra receiving the news of his marriage; Cleopatra questioning the messenger about Octavia's personal appearance. But this is to say that the scenes we remember first are the least indispensable to the plot. One at least is not essential to it at all. And this, the astonishing scene where she storms at the messenger, strikes him, and draws her dagger on him, is the one passage in the first half of the drama that contains either an explosion of passion or an exciting bodily action. Nor is this all. The first half of the play, though it forebodes tragedy, is not decisively tragic in tone. Certainly the Cleopatra scenes are not so. We read them, and we should witness them, in delighted wonder and even with amusement. The only scene that can vie with them, that of the revel on Pompey's ship, though full of menace, is in great part humorous. Enobarbus, in this part of the play, is always humorous. Even later, when the tragic tone is deepening, the whipping of Thyreus [i.e. Thidias] in spite of Antony's rage, moves mirth. A play of which all this can truly be said may well be as masterly as *Othello* or *Macbeth,* and more delightful; but, in the greater part of its course, it cannot possibly excite the same emotions. It makes no attempt to do so; and to regard it as though it made this attempt is to miss its specific character and the intention of its author. . . .

But, if he had chosen, he might easily have heightened the tone and tension in another way. He might have made the story of Antony's attempt to break his bondage, and the story of his relapse, extremely exciting, by portraying with all his force the severity of the struggle and the magnitude of the fatal step. . . .

But he does no such thing till the catastrophe is near. Antony breaks away from Cleopatra without any strenuous conflict. No serious doubt of his return is permitted to agitate us. We are almost assured of it through the impression made on us by Octavius, through occasional glimpses into Antony's mind, through the absence of any doubt in Enobarbus, through scenes in Alexandria which display Cleopatra and display her irresistible. And, finally, the downward turn itself, the fatal step of Antony's return, is shown without the slightest emphasis. Nay, it is not shown, it is only reported; and not a line portrays any inward struggle preceding it. On this side also, then, the drama makes no attempt to rival the other tragedies; and it was essential to its own peculiar character and its most transcendent effects that this attempt should not be made, but that Antony's passion should be represented as a force which he could hardly even desire to resist. By the very scheme of the work, therefore, tragic impressions of any great volume or depth were reserved for the last stage of the conflict; while the main interest, down to the battle of Actium, was directed to matters exceedingly interesting and even, in the wider sense, dramatic, but not overtly either terrible or piteous; on the one hand, to the political aspect of the story; on the other, to the personal causes which helped to make the issue inevitable. . . .

We turn for relief from the political game to those who are sure to lose it; to those who love some human being better than a prize, to Eros and Charmian and Iras; to Enobarbus, whom the world corrupts, but who has a heart that can break with shame; to the lovers, who seem to us to find in death something better than their victor's life.

This presentation of the outward conflict has two results. First, it blunts our feeling of the greatness of Antony's fall from prosperity. . . . Our deeper sympathies are focused rather on Antony's heart, on the inward fall to which the enchantment of passion leads him, and the inward recovery which succeeds it. And the second result is this. The greatness of Antony and Cleopatra in their fall is so much heightened by contrast with the world they lose and the conqueror who wins it, that the positive element in the final tragic impression, the element of reconciliation, is strongly emphasized. The peculiar effect of the drama depends partly, as we have seen, on the absence of decidedly tragic scenes and events in its first half; but it depends quite as much on this emphasis. In any Shakespearean tragedy we watch some elect spirit colliding, partly through its error and defect, with a superhuman power which bears it down; and yet we feel that this spirit, even in the error and defect, rises by its greatness into ideal union with the power that overwhelms it. In some tragedies this latter feeling is relatively weak. In *Antony and Cleopatra* it is unusually strong; stronger with some readers at least, than the fear and grief and pity with which they contemplate the tragic error and the advance of doom. . . .

Though we hear nothing from Shakespeare of the cruelty of Plutarch's Antony, or of the misery caused by his boundless profusion, we do not feel the hero of the tragedy to be a man of the noblest type, like Brutus, Hamlet, or Othello. He seeks power merely for himself, and uses it for his own pleasure. He is in some respects unscrupulous; and, while it would be unjust to regard his marriage exactly as if it were one in private life, we resent his treatment of Octavia, whose character Shakespeare was obliged to leave a mere sketch, lest our feeling for the hero and heroine should be too much chilled. Yet, for all this, we sympathize warmly with Antony, are greatly drawn to him, and are inclined to regard him as a noble nature half spoiled by his time.

It is a large, open, generous, expansive nature, quite free from envy, capable of great magnanimity, even of entire devotion. Antony is unreserved, naturally straightforward, we may almost say simple. He can admit faults, accept advice and even reproof, take a jest against himself with good-humour. He is courteous (to Lepidus, for example, whom Octavius treats with cold contempt); and, though he can be exceedingly dignified, he seems to prefer a blunt though sympathetic plainness, which is one cause of the attachment of his soldiers. He has none of the faults of the brooder, the sentimentalist, or the man of principle; his nature tends to splendid action and lusty enjoyment. But he is neither a mere soldier nor a mere sensualist. He has imagination, the temper of an artist who revels in abundant and rejoicing appetites, feasts his senses on the glow and richness of life, flings himself into its mirth and revelry, yet feels the poetry in all this, and is able also to put it by and be more than content with the hardships of adventure. Such a man could never have sought a crown by a murder like Macbeth's, or, like Brutus, have killed on principle the man who loved him, or have lost the world for a Cressida. . . .

The first of living soldiers, an able politician, a most persuasive orator, Antony nevertheless was not born to rule the world. He enjoys being a great man, but he has not the love of rule for rule's sake. . . .

When he meets Cleopatra he finds his Absolute. She satisfies, nay glorifies, his whole being. She intoxicates his senses. Her wiles, her taunts, her furies and meltings, her laughter and tears, bewitch him all alike. She loves what he loves, and she surpasses him. She can drink him to his bed, out-jest his practical jokes, out-act the best actress who ever amused him, out-dazzle his own magnificence. She is his playfellow, and yet a great queen. Angling in the river, playing billiards, flourishing the sword he used at Philippi, hopping forty paces in a public street, she remains an enchantress. Her spirit is made of wind and flame, and the poet in him worships her no less than the man. He is under no illusion about her, knows all her faults, sees through her wiles, believes her capable of betraying him. It makes no difference. She is his heart's desire made perfect. To love her is what he was born for. What have the gods in heaven to say against it? To imagine heaven is to imagine her; to die is to rejoin her. To deny that this is love is the madness of morality. He gives her every atom of his heart. She destroys him.

Shakespeare has paid Cleopatra a unique compliment. The hero dies in the fourth Act, and the whole of the fifth is devoted to the heroine. In that Act she becomes unquestionably a tragic character, but, it appears to me, not till then. . . . What raises Cleopatra at last into pure tragedy is, in part, that which some critics have denied her, her love for Antony.

Many unpleasant things can be said of Cleopatra; and the more that are said the more wonderful she appears. The exercise of sexual attraction is the element of her life; and she has developed nature into a consummate art. When she cannot exert it on the present lover she imagines its effects on him in absence. Longing for the living, she remembers with pride and joy the dead; and the part which the furious Antony holds up to her as a picture of shame is, for her, glory. She cannot see an ambassador, scarcely even a messenger, without desiring to bewitch him. Her mind is saturated with this element. If she is dark, it is because the sun himself has been amorous of her. Even when death is close at hand she imagines his touch as a lover's. She embraces him that she may overtake Iras and gain Antony's first kiss in the other world.

She lives for feeling. Her feelings are, so to speak, sacred, and pain must not come near her. She has tried numberless experiments to discover the easiest way to die. Her body is exquisitely sensitive, and her emotions marvellously swift. They are really so; but she exaggerates them so much, and exhibits them so continually for effect, that some readers fancy them merely feigned. They are all-important, and everybody must attend to them. She announces to her women that she is pale, or sick and sullen; they must lead her to her chamber but must not speak to her. She is as strong and supple as a leopard, can drink down a master of revelry, can raise her lover's helpless heavy body from the ground into her tower with the aid only of two women; yet, when he is sitting apart sunk in shame, she must be supported into his presence, she cannot stand, her head droops, she will die (it is the opinion of Eros) unless he comforts her. When she hears of his marriage and has discharged her rage, she bids her women bear her away; she faints; at least she would faint, but that she remembers various questions she wants put to the Messenger about Octavia. Enobarbus has seen her die twenty times upon far poorer moment than the news that Antony is going to Rome.

A. C. Bradley: Oxford Lectures on Poetry, 1909

(e) *S. L. Bethell* argues in theological terms that the play is an affirmation of the sensual, intuitive life of spontaneous affection symbolized in Cleopatra set against the life of reason and worldly wisdom embodied in Caesar.

Caesar incarnates the practical reason, or worldly wisdom, with which are closely linked the notions of restrictive morality and political order (Stoicism and the Roman law). Antony has a foot in both worlds: I have already contrasted him with Caesar, but there are also points of comparison. He is a Roman and has his share of Roman fortitude; he has mortified the flesh for military glory; and if Caesar will sacrifice his sister for political ends, Antony will sacrifice her, Cleopatra, and himself in the same cause, at least until the lure of Egypt proves too strong. Antony's position is central, for the choice between Egypt and Rome is for him to make. It is Cleopatra who stands opposite Caesar, incarnating 'intuition', the life of the spontaneous affections, with which are linked the notions of expansive morality and aesthetic order (it is the positive affections which transcend her 'baser life' [v.ii.286] while the dignity of sense experience is vindicated poetically in Enobarbus's great description of the barge incident). . . .

Antony chose Egypt, intuition, the life of the spontaneous affections, with its moral and aesthetic corollaries; of all which Cleopatra is the focus and symbol. Shakespeare does not satisfy the psychologists with his character of Cleopatra; but he does not attempt a character in the sense of Trollope, or George Eliot, or even Dickens. In Cleopatra he presents the mystery of woman, the mystery of sensuality, an exploration of the hidden energies of life, and a suggestion of its goal. Intuition or spontaneous feeling is opposed to practical wisdom, generosity to prudence, love to duty, the private affections to public service; and the former in each instance is preferred. Not that the Roman values are entirely repudiated: there is a case for Caesar, 'Fortune's knave' (v.ii.3) though he be. But the Egyptian values are affirmative; the

Roman, negative or restrictive: the good life may be built upon the Egyptian, but not upon the Roman. It is a way of saying that the strong sinner may enter heaven before the prudential legislator. In *Antony and Cleopatra* the strong sinners meet their purgatory here. They do not desire or seek it; it is forced upon them from without – grace which visits them in the guise of defeat. Changes of character inexplicable by psychological determinism are readily explained if we perceive that Shakespeare is applying theological categories. Earthly defeat is the providential instrument of eternal triumph: it comes undesired, but when it comes, is freely accepted, and so converted into a process of necessary cleansing. Antony's purgatory lies in military failure and a bungled suicide prompted by the false report of Cleopatra's death; Cleopatra's in surviving Antony, and in the thought of a Roman triumph. In the end the better Roman qualities are needed to transmute the Egyptian into eternal validity. . . .

In *Lear*, Shakespeare struggled with the problem of evil; in *Macbeth*, with the problem of sin in a Christian universe. In *Antony and Cleopatra*, he returns to the old problem: what are the positive bases of the good life? He finds them in the affections, and the affections as rooted deep in the sensual nature. Of these Cleopatra is the symbol, sensual even in death; for, paradoxically, it is these Egyptian values which must survive death. Caesar, the worldly wise, is 'ass unpolicied!' (v.ii.304) However shocking to the Nordic man, this position is theologically orthodox. Caesar's sins are deeper-seated and more deliberate than the sins of Antony and Cleopatra, and his heart is entirely set on the passing world. There is significance in Cleopatra's greeting to Antony after his short-lived victory:

> Lord of lords!
> O infinite virtue, com'st thou smiling from
> The world's great snare uncaught?
>
> (IV.viii.16)

She is his god, and not his evil genius, rescuing him from an undue preoccupation with the world, which is a snare and a delusion (cf. the Psalmist's frequent use of the 'snare' metaphor, e.g. Bible, *Psalms* 141:10). Nevertheless the Egyptian values need a Roman purgatory to fit them for survival; they are cleansed through adversity, of the taint of selfishness. Antony kills himself in order to rejoin Cleopatra whom he believes to be dead; Cleopatra looks forward in the same way to their future reunion. Purged of selfish fear, the element of self-giving inherent in the sensual nature is revealed in its eternal significance, while Caesar, on the other hand, has no such selfless hold upon eternity.

This is one way of poetically stating the resurrection of the body:

> she looks like sleep,
> As she would catch another Antony
> In her strong toil of grace

(v.ii.342)

Perhaps here, as elsewhere, the word 'grace' may have a tinge of theological significance.

S. L. Bethell: *Shakespeare and the Popular Dramatic Tradition,* 1944

(f) *John F. Danby* takes an anti-romantic view of the play with no redemptive quality in the love theme. The play presents the opposition of the World and the Flesh, both inadequate values, lacking a third term, the spiritual quality.

Not enough weight has been given in recent assessments of the play to the ambiguity which invests everything in Egypt equally with all things in Rome. Yet this ambiguity is central to Shakespeare's experience in the play. If it is wrong to see the 'mutual pair' as a strumpet and her fool, it is also wrong to see them as a Phoenix and a Turtle. . . .

There is something deliquescent in the reality behind the play. It is a deliquescence to the full display of which each judgement, each aspect pointed to, and each character, is necessary, always provided that no single one of these is taken as final. The proportion of comment and judgement on the central characters is higher in *Antony and Cleopatra* than anywhere else in Shakespeare. This further underlines its uniqueness and the difficulties of coming by an adequate final assessment. Antony and Cleopatra are presented in three ways. There is what is said about them; there is what they say themselves; there is what they do. Each of these might correspond to a different 'level' of response. Each is in tension against the others. Each makes its continuous and insistent claim on the spectator for judgement in his own right. The pigments vividly opposed to each other on the canvas have to mix in the spectator's eye.

Underlying, however, the bewildering oscillations of scene, the overlapping and pleating of different times and places, the co-presence of opposed judgments, the innumerable opportunities for radical choice to intervene, there is, I think, a deliberate logic. It is this which gives the play its compact unity of effect and makes its movement a sign of angelic strength rather than a symptom of febrility. It is the logic of a peculiarly Shakespearian dialectic. Opposites are juxtaposed, mingled, married; then from the very union which seems to promise strength dissolution flows. It is the process of this dialectic – the central process of the play – which we must trace if we wish to arrive anywhere near Shakespeare's meaning. . . .

The outstanding achievement of the first scene is the way in which it begins with the soldiers' condemnation and returns us at the end to the same thing – allowing for this side eighteen lines out of the sixty-two. Yet at the end we are no longer satisfied as to the adequacy of what Demetrius and Philo say. Not that what they say has been disproved by what we have seen of Antony and Cleopatra. They are and they remain a strumpet and her fool. To have any judgment at all is to choose, apparently, either the judgment of the soldiers at the beginning of the scene or the lovers' own self-assessment that immediately follows it. (Coleridge chose the former; Dr. Sitwell and Mr. Wilson Knight take the latter.) To entertain either judgment, however, is not enough. The deliquescent truth is neither in them nor between them, but contains both. *Antony and Cleopatra* is Shakespeare's critique of judgment. . . .

The first three scenes show how pervasive is that quality in technique and vision which we have called the Shakespearian 'dialectic'. It comes out in single images, it can permeate whole speeches, it governs the build-up inside each scene, it explains the way one scene is related to another. The word 'dialectic', of course, is unfortunately post-Hegelian. The thing we wish to point to, however, in using the word, is Shakespearian. In *Antony and Cleopatra* Shakespeare needs the opposites that merge, unite, and fall apart. They enable him to handle the reality he is writing about – the vast containing opposites of Rome and Egypt, the World and the Flesh. . . .

Cleopatra has been loved by recent commentators not wisely but too well. As Caesar impersonates the World, she, of course, incarnates the Flesh. Part of Shakespeare's sleight of hand in the play – his trickery with our normal standards and powers of judgment – is to construct an account of the human universe consisting of only these two terms. . . . Shakespeare gives Cleopatra everything of which he is capable except his final and absolute approval. . . .

The earlier criticism of *Antony and Cleopatra* tended to stress the downfall of the soldier in the middle-aged infatuate. More recent criticism has seen the play as the epiphany of the soldier in the lover, and the reassurance of all concerned that death is not the end. In the view that has been put forward here neither of these is right. The meaning of *Antony and Cleopatra* is in the Shakespearian 'dialectic' – in the deliquescent reality that expresses itself through the contraries. . . .

The Roman condemnation of the lovers is obviously inadequate. The sentimental reaction in their favour is equally mistaken. There is no so-called 'love-romanticism' in the play. The flesh has its glory and passion, its witchery. Love in *Antony and Cleopatra* is both these. The love of Antony and Cleopatra, however, is not asserted as a 'final value'. The whole tenor of the play, in fact, moves in an opposite direction. Egypt is the Egypt of the biblical glosses: exile from the spirit, thralldom to the fleshpots, diminution of human kindness. To go further still in sentimentality and claim that there is a 'redemption' motif in Antony and Cleopatra's love is an even more violent error. To the Shakespeare who wrote *King Lear* it would surely smack of blasphemy. The fourth and fifth acts of *Antony and Cleopatra* are not epiphanies. They are the ends moved to by that process whereby things rot themselves with motion – unhappy and bedizened and sordid, streaked with the mean, the ignoble, the contemptible. Shakespeare may have his plays in which redemption is a theme (and I think he has), but *Antony and Cleopatra* is not one of them.

Antony and Cleopatra is an account of things in terms of the World and the Flesh, Rome and Egypt, the two great contraries that maintain and destroy each other, considered apart from any third sphere which might stand over against them. How is it related to the plays of the 'great period', the period which comes to an end with *King Lear*?

The clue is given, I think, in the missing third term. *Antony and Cleopatra* is the deliberate construction of a world without a Cordelia, Shakespeare's symbol for a reality that transcends the political and the personal and

> redeems nature from the general curse
> Which twain have brought her to.
>
> (*King Lear*, IV.vi.209)
>
> John F. Danby: *Poets on Fortune's Hill*, 1952

(g) *O. J. Campbell* sees the play in Aristotelian terms as one in which the tragic hero Antony through his slavery to passion becomes a victim of *hubris*.

As *Romeo and Juliet* exalts first love, so *Antony and Cleopatra* presents with a slight touch of satire, middle-aged love. For the idealism and headlong rashness of *Romeo and Juliet*, *Antony and Cleopatra* substitutes all the ways of civilized passion in which both principals are adepts. Their glorifying of their own emotions becomes an obsession. Antony becomes a victim of *hubris* [i.e. insolent pride or feeling of security], for he is so obsessed by Cleopatra and her arts of seduction that he almost arrogantly ignores the threat they offer to his military operations and public duties.

Antony, like Shakespeare's other tragic protagonists, is a slave of one of the passions. The lovers' sacrifice of everything else in life to their mutual captivation never renders them despicable. Bernard Shaw's comment that in *Antony and Cleopatra* Shakespeare turns 'hogs into heroes' since the modern equivalent of the pair 'can be found in every public house' is nonsense. . . .

In the early part of the play Cleopatra is little more than a royal courtesan, devising new ways to attract, hold, and influence Antony. Being an Egyptian, she was to Elizabethan audiences a cousin to the gypsies, and, like them, adept at conjuring. It is the infinite variety in her practice of the art of love that makes it like the work of a magician. Her swift and fascinating changes of mood are not so much calculated as instinctive, a coquette's compulsion to attract. 'She is cunning past man's thought,' exclaims Antony. As he falls deeper and deeper under her spell, he finds his personality disintegrating. To Eros he says in rueful surprise,

> Here I am Antony/Yet cannot hold this visible shape, my knave.
> (IV.xiv.13)

At this point in the story Cleopatra's influence on Antony has become in no way ennobling, but destructive of all the martial virtues that have made him a hero.

Although in the last two acts she continues to dally with Antony's infatuation, the false news of her death that she sends her lover is the supreme example of her juggling with his love. His death in her arms purges her love of its trickery, but not completely of its parade. In preparation for her suicide, she orders her women to array her in all her royal splendor, partly to do Antony honor when she meets him in Elysium, but partly that all those who may chance to see her dead body – Octavius in particular – will wonder at her queenly beauty. She does not take her life in the high Roman fashion, but 'pursues conclusions infinite of easy ways to die', so that her suicide, like other events in her life, is a sensuous experience. She imagines the asp that stings her to death to be a baby 'that sucks the nurse asleep'. Her death is a coda to Antony's tragedy. It does not ennoble her; it merely offers her a transcendent opportunity of exhibiting the artful self-indulgent creature that she has always been. Her death is not, like Antony's, heroic. She is merely a lovely object that Antony's fall topples to ruin with him.

The theme of the action may be said to be the ancient one of the hero's choice of love over empire. The basic structure of the drama is that of a chronicle history, but it is one that serves as the setting of a hero's slavery to one of the passions.

O. J. Campbell: A Shakespeare Encyclopaedia, 1966

Extracts from Plutarch's Life of Marcus Antonius

He had a noble presence and showed a countenance of one of a noble house. He had a goodly thick beard, a broad forehead, crook-nosed; and there appeared such a manly look in his countenance as is commonly seen in Hercules' pictures, stamped or graven in metal. Now it had been a speech of old time that the family of the Antonii were descended from one Anton, the son of Hercules, whereof the family took name. This opinion did Antonius seek to confirm in all his doings, not only resembling him in the likeness of his body, as we have said before, but also in the wearing of his garments. . . .

But besides all this, that which most procured his rising and advancement was his liberality, who gave all to the soldiers and kept nothing for himself. And when he was grown to great credit [renown], then was his authority and power also very great, the which notwithstanding himself [he] did overthrow by a thousand other faults he had. . . .

But the very same night Antonius had a strange dream, who [he] thought that lightning fell upon him and burnt his right hand. Shortly after word was brought him that Caesar lay in wait to kill him. Caesar cleared himself unto him and told him there was no such matter. But he could not make Antonius believe the contrary. Whereupon they became further enemies than ever they were; insomuch that both of them made friends of either side to gather together all the old soldiers through Italy, that were dispersed in divers towns, and made them large promises, and sought also to win the legions on their side, which were already in arms. . . .

Cicero . . . sent Hircius and Pansa, then Consuls, to drive Antonius out of Italy. These two Consuls together with Caesar, who also had an army, went against Antonius that besieged the city of Modena, and there overthrew him in battle. But both the Consuls were slain there.

Antonius, flying upon [fleeing after] this overthrow, fell into great misery all at once; but the chiefest want of all other, and that pinched him most, was famine. Howbeit he was of such a strong nature that by patience he would overcome any adversity; and the heavier fortune lay upon him, the more constant showed he himself. . . . And therefore it was a wonderful example to the soldiers to see Antonius, that was brought up in all fineness and superfluity, so easily to drink puddle water and to eat wild fruits and roots. And moreover it is reported that, even as they passed the Alps, they did eat the barks of trees and such beasts as never man tasted of their flesh before. . . .

So Octavius Caesar would not lean to [make friends with] Cicero, when he saw that his whole travail and endeavour was only to restore the commonwealth to her former liberty. Therefore he sent certain of his friends to Antonius, to make them friends again. And thereupon all three met together (to wit, Caesar, Antonius, and Lepidus) in an island environed round about with a little river; and there remained three days together. Now, as touching all other matters, they were easily agreed and did divide all the Empire of Rome between them, as if it had been their own inheritance. . . .

Now the government of these Triumviri grew odious and hateful to the Romans, for divers respects. But they most blamed Antonius, because he, being elder than Caesar and of more power and force than Lepidus, gave himself again to his former riot and excess when he left to deal in the affairs of the commonwealth. But, setting aside the ill name he had for his insolency, he was yet much more hated in respect of the house he dwelt in, the which was the house of Pompey the Great, a man as famous for his temperance, modesty, and civil life, as for his three Triumphs. For it grieved them to see the gates commonly shut against the captains, magistrates of the city, and also ambassadors of strange nations, which were sometimes thrust from the gate with violence; and that the house within was full of tumblers, antic dancers, jugglers, players, jesters, and drunkards, quaffing and guzzling, and that on them he spent and bestowed the most part of his money he got by all kind of possible extortions, bribery, and policy. . . .

Antonius being thus inclined, the last and extremest mischief of all other (to wit, the love of Cleopatra) lighted on him, who did waken and stir up many vices yet hidden in him, and were never seen to any; and, if any spark of goodness or hope of rising were left him, Cleopatra quenched it straight and made it worse than before.

The manner how he fell in love with her was this. Antonius, going to make war with the Parthians, sent to command Cleopatra to appear personally before him when he came into Cilicia, to answer unto such accusations as were laid against her, being this: that she had aided Cassius and Brutus in their war against him. The messenger sent unto Cleopatra to make this summons unto her was called Dellius; who when he had throughly considered her beauty, the excellent grace and sweetness of her tongue, he nothing mistrusted [did not believe] that Antonius would do any hurt to so noble a lady, but rather assured himself that within few days she should be in great favour with him. Thereupon he did her great honour and persuaded her to come into Cilicia as honourably furnished as she could possible, and bade her not to be afraid at all of Antonius, for he was a more courteous lord than any that she had ever seen.

Cleopatra, on the other side, believing Dellius' words and guessing by the former access and credit she had with Julius Caesar and Gnaeus Pompey, the son of Pompey the Great, only for her beauty, she began to have good hope that she might more easily win Antonius. For Caesar and Pompey knew her when she was but a young thing, and knew not then what the world meant. But now she went to Antonius at the age when a woman's beauty is at the prime, and she also of best judgement. So she furnished herself with a world of gifts, store of gold and silver, and of riches and other sumptuous ornaments, as is credible enough she might bring from so great a house and from so wealthy and rich a realm as Egypt was. But yet she carried nothing with her wherein she trusted more than in herself and in the charms and enchantment of her passing [exceptional] beauty and grace.

Therefore when she was sent unto by divers letters, both from Antonius himself and also from his friends, she made so light of it and mocked Antonius so much that she disdained to set forward otherwise but to take her barge in the river of Cydnus, the poop whereof was of gold, the sails of purple, and the oars of silver, which kept stroke in rowing after the sound of the music of flutes, howboys [oboes], citherns, viols, and such other instruments as they played upon in the barge. And now for the person of herself: she was laid under a pavilion of cloth of gold of tissue, apparelled and attired like the goddess Venus commonly drawn in picture; and hard by her, on either hand of her, pretty fair boys apparelled as painters do set forth god Cupid, with little fans in their hands, with the which they fanned wind upon her. Her ladies and gentlewomen also, the fairest of them were apparelled like the nymphs Nereides (which are the mermaids of the waters) and like the Graces, some steering the helm, others tending the tackle and ropes of the barge, out of the which there came a wonderful passing sweet savour of perfumes, that perfumed the wharf's side, pestered with innumerable multitudes of people. Some of them followed the barge all alongst the river's side; others also ran out of the city to see her coming in; so that in the end there ran such multitudes of people one after another to see her that Antonius was left post-alone [completely alone] in the market-place in his imperial seat to give audience. And there went a rumour in the people's mouths that the goddess Venus was come to play with the god Bacchus, for the general good of all Asia.

When Cleopatra landed, Antonius sent to invite her to supper to him. But she sent him word again, he should do better rather to come and sup with her. Antonius therefore, to show himself courteous unto her at her arrival, was contented to obey her, and went to supper to her; where he found such passing sumptuous fare, that no tongue can express it. But, amongst all other things, he most wondered at the infinite number of lights and torches hanged on the top of the house, giving light in every place, so artificially set and ordered by devices, some round, some square, that it was the rarest thing to behold that eye could discern or that ever books could mention. The next night, Antonius feasting her contended to pass her in magnificence and fineness; but she overcame him in both. So that he himself began to scorn the gross service of his house, in respect of Cleopatra's sumptuousness and fineness. And, when Cleopatra found Antonius' jests and slents [sarcastic remarks] to be but gross and soldierlike in plain manner, she gave it him finely and without fear taunted him throughly.

Now her beauty, as it is reported, was not so passing as unmatchable of other women, nor yet such as upon present view did enamour men with her; but so sweet was her company and conversation that a man could not possibly but be taken. And, besides her beauty, the good grace she had to talk and discourse, her courteous nature that tempered her words and deeds, was a spur that pricked to the quick. Furthermore, besides all these, her voice and words were marvellous pleasant; for her tongue was an instrument of music to divers sports and pastimes, the which she easily turned to any language that pleased her. . . .

Now Antonius was so ravished with the love of Cleopatra that though his wife Fulvia had great wars and much ado with Caesar for his affairs, and that the army of the Parthians (the which the king's lieutenants had given to the only leading of Labienus) was now assembled in Mesopotamia ready to invade Syria; yet, as though all this had nothing touched him, he yielded himself to go with Cleopatra into Alexandria, where he spent and lost in childish sports (as a man might say) and idle pastimes the most precious thing a man can spend, as Antiphon saith: and that is, time.

For they made an order between them which they called *Amimetobion* (as much to say, 'no life comparable and matchable with it'), one feasting each other by turns, and in cost exceeding all measure and reason. And, for proof hereof, I have heard my grandfather Lampryas report that one Philotas a physician, born in the city of Amphissa, told him that he was at that present time in Alexandria and studied physic; and that, having acquaintance with one of Antonius' cooks, he took him with him to Antonius' house (being a young man desirous to see things), to show him the wonderful sumptuous charge and preparation of one only supper. When he was in the kitchen and saw a world of diversities of meats and, amongst others, eight wild boars roasted whole, he began to wonder at it and said: 'Sure you have a great number of guests to supper.' The cook fell a-laughing and answered him: 'No,' quoth he, 'not many guests, nor above twelve in all.' . . .

But now again to Cleopatra. Plato writeth that there are four kinds of flattery; but Cleopatra divided it into many kinds. For she, were it in sport or in matters of earnest, still devised sundry new delights to have Antonius at commandment, never leaving him night nor day, nor once letting him go out of her sight. For she would play at dice with him, drink with him, and hunt commonly with him, and also be with him when he went to any exercise or activity of body. And sometime also when he would go up and down the city disguised like a slave in the night, and would peer into poor men's windows and their shops, and scold and brawl with them within the house, Cleopatra would be also in a chambermaid's array, and amble up and down the streets with him, so that oftentimes Antonius bare away both mocks and blows. Now, though most men misliked this manner, yet the Alexandrians were commonly glad of this jollity and liked it well, saying very gallantly and wisely that Antonius showed them a comical face, to wit, a merry countenance; and the Romans a tragical face, to say, a grim look. . . .

On a time he went to angle for fish; and when he could take none he was as angry as could be, because Cleopatra stood by. Wherefore he secretly commanded the fishermen that when he cast in his line they should straight dive under the water and put a fish on his hook which they had taken before; and so snatched up his angling rod and brought up fish twice or thrice. Cleopatra found it straight; yet she seemed not to see it, but wondered at his excellent fishing. But when she was alone by herself among her own people, she told them how it was and bade them the next morning to be on the water to see the fishing. . . . Antonius then threw in his line; and Cleopatra straight commanded one of her men to dive under water before Antonius' men and put some old salt fish upon his bait. . . . When he had hung the fish on his hook, Antonius, thinking he had taken a fish indeed, snatched up his line presently. Then they all fell a-laughing. . . .

Now Antonius delighting in these fond [foolish] and childish pastimes, very ill news were brought him from two places. The first from Rome: that his brother Lucius and Fulvia his wife fell out first between themselves, and afterwards fell to open war with Caesar, and had brought all to nought, that they were both driven to fly out of Italy. The second news, as bad as the first: that Labienus conquered all Asia with the army of the Parthians, from the river of Euphrates and from Syria unto the countries of Lydia and Ionia. Then began Antonius with much ado a little to rouse himself, as if he had been wakened out of a deep sleep and, as a man may say, coming out of a great drunkenness. So first of all he bent himself against the Parthians, and went as far as the country of Phoenicia. . . . He was informed that his wife Fulvia was the only cause of this war; who being of a peevish, crooked, and troublesome nature, had purposely raised this uproar in Italy, in hope thereby to withdraw him from Cleopatra.

But by good fortune his wife Fulvia, going to meet with Antonius, sickened by the way, and died in the city of Sicyon. And therefore Octavius Caesar and he were the easilier made friends together. For when Antonius landed in Italy, and that men saw Caesar asked nothing of him, and that Antonius on the other side laid all the fault and burden on his wife Fulvia, the friends of both parties would not suffer them to unrip any old matters, and to prove or defend who had the wrong or right, and who was the first procurer of this war, fearing to make matters worse between them; but they made them friends together. . . . This seemed to be a sound counsel, but yet it was to be confirmed with a straiter [firmer] bond, which fortune offered thus. There was Octavia the eldest sister of Caesar - not by one mother, for she came of Ancharia, and Caesar himself afterwards of Accia. It is reported that he dearly loved his sister Octavia; for indeed she was a noble lady, and left the widow of her first husband Caius Marcellus, who died not long before; and it seemed also that Antonius had been widower ever since the death of his wife Fulvia. For he denied not that he kept Cleopatra; but so did he not confess that he had her as his wife; and so with reason did he defend the love he bare unto this Egyptian Cleopatra.

Thereupon every man did set forward this marriage, hoping thereby that this lady Octavia, having an excellent grace, wisdom, and honesty joined unto so rare a beauty, that when she were with Antonius (he loving her as so worthy a lady deserveth) she should be a good mean to keep good love and amity betwixt her brother and him. So, when Caesar and he had made the match between them, they both went to Rome . . . and so the marriage proceeded accordingly.

Sextus Pompeius at that time kept [remained] in Sicilia, and so made many an inroad into Italy with a great number of pinnaces and other pirates' ships, of the which were captains two notable pirates, Menas and Menecrates, who so scoured all the sea thereabouts that none durst peep out with a sail. Furthermore, Sextus Pompeius had dealt very friendly with Antonius, for he had courteously received his mother when she fled out of Italy with Fulvia; and therefore they thought good to make peace with him. So they met all three together by the mount of Misena, upon a hill that runneth far into the sea, Pompey having his ships riding hard by at anchor, and Antonius and Caesar their armies upon the shore side, directly over against him.

Now after they had agreed that Sextus Pompeius should have Sicilia and Sardinia, with this condition, that he should rid the sea of all thieves and pirates and make it safe for passengers, and withal that he should send a certain [an agreed amount] of wheat to Rome, one of them did feast another, and drew cuts who should begin. It was Pompcius' chance to invite them first. Whereupon Antonius asked him: 'And where shall we sup?' 'There', said Pompey, and showed him his admiral galley which had six banks of oars. 'That', said he, 'is my father's house they have left me.' He spake it to taunt Antonius, because he had his father's house, that was Pompey the Great. So he cast anchors enow into the sea to make his galley fast, and then built a bridge of wood to convey them to his galley from the head to Mount Misena; and there he welcomed them, and made them great cheer.

Now in the midst of the feast, when they fell to be merry with Antonius' love unto Cleopatra, Menas the pirate came to Pompey and, whispering in his ear, said unto him: 'Shall I cut the gables of the anchors, and make thee lord not only of Sicilia and Sardinia, but of the whole Empire of Rome besides?' Pompey, having paused awhile upon it, at length answered him: 'Thou shouldst have done it and never have told it me; but now we must content us with that we have. As for myself, I was never taught to break my faith nor to be counted a traitor. . . .'

With Antonius there was a soothsayer or astronomer of Egypt, that could cast a figure [calculate a horoscope] and judge of men's nativities, to tell them what should happen to them. He, either to please Cleopatra or else for that he found it so by his art, told Antonius plainly that his fortune, which of itself was excellent good and very great, was altogether blemished and obscured by Caesar's fortune; and therefore he counselled him utterly to leave his company and to get him as far from him as he could. 'For thy Demon,' said he, '(that is to say, the good angel and spirit that keepeth [protects] thee) is afraid of his, and, being courageous and high when he is alone, becometh fearful and timorous when he cometh near unto the other.' Howsoever it was, the events ensuing proved the Egyptian's words true. For is said that as often as they two drew cuts for pastime who should have anything, or whether they played at dice, Antonius always lost. Oftentimes when they were disposed to see cock-fight, or quails that were taught to fight one with another, Caesar's cocks or quails did ever overcome; the which spited Antonius in his mind, although he made outward no show of it; and therefore he believed the Egyptian the better.

In fine [in short], he recommended the affairs of his house unto Caesar, and went out of Italy with Octavia his wife, whom he carried into

Greece, after he had had a daughter by her. . . . In the meantime, Ventidius once again overcame Pacorus . . . at which battle was slain a great number of the Parthians, and among them Pacorus the King's own son slain. This noble exploit, as famous as ever any was, was a full revenge to the Romans of the shame and loss they had received before by the death of Marcus Crassus. And he made the Parthians fly, and glad to keep themselves within the confines and territories of Mesopotamia and Media, after they had thrice together been overcome in several battles. Howbeit Ventidius durst not undertake to follow them any farther, fearing lest he should have gotten Antonius' displeasure by it. . . . And yet, to say truly, he did so well quit himself in all his enterprises, that he confirmed that which was spoken of Antonius and Caesar: to wit, that they were always more fortunate when they made war by their lieutenants than by themselves. For Sossius, one of Antonius' lieutenants in Syria, did notable good service. . . .

But Antonius, notwithstanding, grew to be marvellously offended with Caesar, upon certain reports that had been brought to him. And so took sea to go towards Italy with three hundred sail. And, because those of Brundusium would not receive his army into their haven, he went farther unto Tarentum. There his wife Octavia, that came out of Greece with him, besought him to send her unto her brother; the which he did. Octavia at that time was great with child, and moreover had a second daughter by him; and yet she put herself in journey, and met with her brother Octavius Caesar by the way, who brought his two chief friends, Maecenas and Agrippa, with him. She took them aside and, will all the instance she could possible, entreated them they would not suffer her, that was the happiest woman of the world, to become now the most wretched and unfortunatest creature of all other. 'For now', said she, 'every man's eyes do gaze on me, that am the sister of one of the Emperors and wife of the other. And if the worst counsel take place (which the gods forbid!) and that they grow to wars, for yourselves it is uncertain to which of them two the gods have assigned the victory or overthrow. But for me, on which side soever victory fall, my state can be but most miserable still.'

These words of Octavia so softened Caesar's heart that he went quickly unto Tarentum. But it was a noble sight for them that were present, to see so great an army by land not to stir, and so many ships afloat in the road quietly and safe; and furthermore, the meeting and kindness of friends, lovingly embracing one another. . . . After they had taken leave of each other, Caesar went immediately to make war with Sextus Pompeius, to get Sicilia into his hands. Antonius also, leaving his wife Octavia and little children begotten of her with Caesar, and his other children which he had by Fulvia, he went directly into Asia.

Then began this pestilent plague and mischief of Cleopatra's love – which had slept a long time, and seemed to have been utterly forgotten, and that Antonius had given place to better counsel – again to kindle and to be in force, so soon as Antonius came near unto Syria. And in the end, 'the horse of the mind', as Plato termeth it, that is so hard of rein (I mean the unreined lust of concupiscence), did put out of Antonius' head all honest and commendable thoughts. For he sent Fonteius Capito to bring Cleopatra into Syria. Unto whom, to welcome her, he gave no trifling things. But unto that she had already he added the provinces of Phoenicia, those of the nethermost Syria, the isle of Cyprus, and a great part of Sicilia, and that country of Jewry where the true balm is, and that part of Arabia where the Nabatheians do dwell, which stretcheth out towards the Ocean.

These great gifts much misliked [displeased] the Romans. But now, though Antonius did easily give away great seigniories, realms, and mighty nations unto some private men, and that also he took from other kings their lawful realms (as from Antigonus King of the Jews, whom he openly beheaded, where never king before had suffered like death), yet all this did not so much offend the Romans as the un- measurable honours which he did unto Cleopatra. . . . Octavia his wife, whom he had left at Rome, would needs take sea to come unto him. Her brother Octavius Caesar was willing unto it, not for his respect at all (as most authors do report), as for that he might have an honest colour [excuse] to make war with Antonius if he did misuse her and not esteem of her as she ought to be. But, when she was come to Athens, she received letters from Antonius willing her to stay there until his coming, and did advertise her of his journey and determination; the which though it grieved her much and that she knew it was but an excuse, yet by her letters to him of answer she asked him whether he would have those things sent unto him which she had brought him. . . .

Cleopatra knowing that Octavia would have Antonius from her and fearing also that, if with her virtue and honest behaviour (besides the great power of her brother Caesar) she did add thereunto her modest kind love to please her husband, that she would then be too strong for her and in the end win him away, she subtilly seemed to languish for the love of Antonius, pining her body for lack of meat. Furthermore, she every way so framed her countenance that, when Antonius came to see her, she cast her eyes upon him like a woman ravished for joy. Straight again, when he went from her, she fell a-weeping and blub- bering, looked ruefully of the matter, and still found the means that Antonius should oftentimes find her weeping; and then, when he came suddenly upon her, she made as though she dried her eyes, and turned her face away, as if she were unwilling that he should see her weep. All these tricks she used, Antonius being in readiness to go into Syria to speak with the King of Medes. . . .

When Octavia was returned to Rome from Athens, Caesar commanded her to go out of Antonius' house and to dwell by herself, because he had abused her. Octavia answered him again that she would not forsake her husband's house and that, if he had no other occasion to make war with him, she prayed him then to take no thought for her. 'For', said she, 'it were too shameful a thing that two so famous captains should bring in civil wars among the Romans, the one for the love of a woman and the other for the jealousy betwixt one another.' . . .

But yet the greatest cause of their malice unto him [Antony] was for the division of lands he made amongst his children in the city of Alexandria. And, to confess a troth, it was too arrogant and insolent a part, and done (as a man would say) in derision and contempt of the Romans. For he assembled all the people in the show-place where young men do exercise themselves; and there upon a high tribunal silvered he set two chairs of gold, the one for himself and the other for Cleopatra, and lower chairs for his children. Then he openly published before the assembly that, first of all, he did establish Cleopatra Queen of Egypt, of Cyprus, of Lydia, and of the lower Syria, and, at that time also, Caesarion King of the same realms. (This Caesarion was supposed to be the son of Julius Caesar, who had left Cleopatra great with child.) Secondly he called the sons he had by her 'the Kings of Kings': and gave Alexander for his portion, Armenia, Media, and Parthia (when he had conquered the country); and unto Ptolemy for his portion, Phoenicia, Syria, and Cilicia. . . . Now, for Cleopatra, she did not only wear at that time, but at all other times else when she came abroad, the apparel of the goddess Isis, and so gave audience unto all her subjects as a new Isis.

Octavius Caesar reporting all these things unto the Senate and oftentimes accusing him to the whole people and assembly in Rome, he thereby stirred up all the Romans against him. Antonius on the other side sent to Rome likewise to accuse him; and the chiefest points of his accusations he charged him with were these: first, that having spoiled [plundered] Sextus Pompeius in Sicilia he did not give him his part of the isle; secondly, that he did detain in his hands the ships he lent him to make that war; thirdly, that having put Lepidus their companion and triumvirate out of his part of the Empire and having deprived him of all honours, he retained for himself the lands and revenues thereof which had been assigned unto him for his part; and

last of all, that he had in manner divided all Italy amongst his own
soldiers and had left no part of it for his soldiers. Octavius Caesar
answered him again that, for Lepidus, he had indeed deposed him and
taken his part of the Empire from him, because he did over-cruelly use
his authority; and secondly, for the conquests he had made by force of
arms, he was contented Antonius should have his part of them, so that
he would likewise let him have his part of Armenia. . . .

So Antonius through the persuasions of Domitius, commanded
Cleopatra to return again into Egypt, and there to understand the
success [learn the result] of this war. But Cleopatra fearing lest Antonius
should again be made friends with Octavius Caesar by the means of his
wife Octavia, she so plied Canidius with money, and filled his purse,
that he became her spokesman unto Antonius, and told him there was
no reason to send her from this war, who defrayed so great a charge
[she who bore such great expenses]. . . . These fair persuasions won
him; for it was predestined that the government of all the world should
fall into Octavius Caesar's hands. . . . Afterwards he [Antony] sent to
Rome to put his wife Octavia out of his house, who, as it was reported,
went out of his house with all Antonius' children (saving the eldest of
them he had by Fulvia, who was with his father), bewailing and lamenting her cursed hap that had brought her to this, that she was accompted
one of the chiefest causes of this civil war. The Romans did pity her, but
much more Antonius, and those specially that had seen Cleopatra, who
neither excelled Octavia in beauty, nor yet in young years. . . .

Now after that Caesar had made sufficient preparation, he proclaimed open war against Cleopatra, and made the people to abolish
the power and empire of Antonius because he had before given it up
unto a woman. And Caesar said furthermore that Antonius was not
master of himself, but that Cleopatra had brought him beside himself
by her charms and amorous poisons, and that they that should make
war with them should be Mardian the eunuch, Photinus, and Iras, a
woman of Cleopatra's bed-chamber that frizzled her hair and dressed
her head, Charmion, the which were those that ruled all the affairs of
Antonius' empire. Before this war, as it is reported, many signs and
wonders fell out. . . . The admiral galley of Cleopatra was called
Antoniad, in the which there chanced a marvellous ill sign. Swallows
had bred under the poop of her ship; and there came others after them
that drove away the first and plucked down their nests.

Now when all things were ready and that they drew near to fight,
it was found that Antonius had no less than five hundred good ships of
war, among which there were many galleys that had eight and ten
banks of oars, the which were sumptuously furnished, not so meet for

fight as for triumph, a hundred thousand footmen and twelve thousand horsemen; and had with him to aid him these kings and subjects following: Bocchus King of Libya, Tarcondemus King of High Cilicia, Archelaus King of Cappadocia, Philadelphus King of Paphlagonia, Mithridates King of Comagena, and Adallas King of Thracia; all which were there every man in person. The residue that were absent sent their armies; as Polemon King of Pont, Manchus King of Arabia, Herodes King of Jewry; and furthermore, Amyntas King of Lycaonia and of the Galatians; and, besides all these, he had all the aid the King of Medes sent unto him. . . .

Now Antonius was made so subject to a woman's will that, though he was a great deal the stronger by land, yet for Cleopatra's sake he would needs have this battle tried by sea; though he saw before his eyes that, for lack of watermen, his captains did prest by force all sorts of men out of Greece that they could take up in the field, as travellers, muleteers, reapers, harvest men, and young boys, and yet could they not sufficiently furnish his galleys; so that the most part of them were empty, and could scant row, because they lacked watermen enow. . . .

So Octavius Caesar sent unto Antonius to will him to delay no more time, but to come on with his army into Italy; and that for his own part he would give him safe harbour, to land without any trouble and that he would withdraw his army from the sea as far as one horse could run, until he had put his army ashore and had lodged his men. Antonius on the other side bravely sent him word again, and challenged the combat of him man to man, though he were the elder; and that if he refused him so, he would then fight a battle with him in the fields of Pharsalia, as Julius Caesar and Pompey had done before.

Now, whilst Antonius rode at anchor, lying idly in harbour at the head of Actium. . . . Caesar had quickly passed the sea Ionium and taken a place called Toryne, before Antonius understood that he had taken ship. Then began his men to be afraid, because his army by land was left behind. But Cleopatra making light of it: 'And what danger, I pray you,' said she, 'if Caesar keep at Toryne?' . . .

Furthermore he [Antony] dealt very friendly and courteously with Domitius, and against Cleopatra's mind [wishes]. For, he being sick of an ague when he went and took a little boat to go unto Caesar's camp, Antonius was very sorry for it, but yet he sent after him all his carriage, train and men; and the same Domitius, as though he gave him to understand that he repented his open treason, he died immediately after. There were certain kings also that forsook him, and turned on Caesar's side; as Amyntas and Deiotarus.

Furthermore his fleet and navy that was unfortunate in all things and unready for service compelled him to change his mind and to hazard battle by land. And Canidius also, who had charge of his army by land, when time came to follow Antonius' determination, he turned him clean contrary, and counselled him to send Cleopatra back again, and himself to retire into Macedon, to fight there on the mainland. And furthermore told him that . . . it should be no shame nor dishonour to him to let Caesar have the sea, because himself and his men both had been well practised and exercised in battles by sea, in the war of Sicilia against Sextus Pompeius; but rather that he should do against all reason, he having so great skill and experience of battles by land as he had, if he should not employ the force and valiantness of so many lusty armed footmen as he had ready, but would weaken his army by dividing them into ships. But now, notwithstanding all these good persuasions, Cleopatra forced him to put all to the hazard of battle by sea; considering with herself how she might fly and provide for her safety, not to help him to win the victory, but to fly more easily after the battle lost. . . .

So, when Antonius had determined to fight by sea, he set all the other ships on fire but three-score ships of Egypt, and reserved only but the best and greatest galleys, from three banks unto ten banks of oars. Into them he put two-and-twenty thousand fighting men, with two thousand darters and slingers. Now, as he was setting his men in order of battle, there was a captain (and a valiant man that had served Antonius in many battles and conflicts and had all his body hacked and cut) who, as Antonius passed by him, cried out unto him and said: 'O noble Emperor, how cometh it to pass that you trust to these vile brittle ships? What, do you mistrust these wounds of mine and this sword? Let the Egyptians and Phoenicians fight by sea, and set us on the mainland, where we use to conquer, or to be slain on our feet.'

Antonius passed by him and said never a word, but only beckoned to him with his hand and head, as though he willed him to be of good courage, although indeed he had no great courage himself. . . . For the armies by land Canidius was general of Antonius' side, and Taurus of Caesar's side. . . .

Howbeit the battle was yet of even hand, and the victory doubtful, being indifferent to both; when suddenly they saw the three-score ships of Cleopatra busy about their yard-masts, and hoising [hoisting] sail to fly. So they fled through the midst of them that were in fight, for they had been placed behind the great ships, and did marvellously disorder the other ships. For the enemies themselves wondered much to see them sail in that sort with full sail towards Peloponnesus. There

Antonius showed plainly that he had not only lost the courage and heart of an Emperor but also of a valiant man, and that he was not his own man, proving that true which an old man spake in mirth: that the soul of a lover lived in another body, and not in his own. He was so carried away with the vain love of this woman, as if he had been glued unto her and that she could not have removed without moving of him also. For, when he saw Cleopatra's ship under sail, he forgot, forsook and betrayed them that fought for him, and embarked upon a galley with five banks of oars, to follow her that was already begun to overthrow him, and would in the end be his utter destruction. When she knew his galley afar off, she lift up a sign in the poop of her ship, and so Antonius coming to it was plucked up where Cleopatra was; howbeit he saw her not at his first coming, nor she him, but went and sat down alone in the prow of his ship, and said never a word, clapping his head between both his hands. . . . And so lived three days alone, without speaking to any man. But, when he arrived at the head of Taenarus, there Cleopatra's women first brought Antonius and Cleopatra to speak together and afterwards to sup and lie together. . . .

Then Antonius sent unto Canidius to return with his army into Asia by Macedon. Now for himself, he determined to cross over into Afric; and took one of his carects or hulks loaden with gold and silver and other rich carriage, and gave it unto his friends, commanding them to depart and to seek to save themselves. They answered him weeping that they would neither do it nor yet forsake him. Then Antonius very courteously and lovingly did comfort them, and prayed them to depart; and wrote unto Theophilus, governor of Corinth, that he would see them safe and help to hide them in some secret place until they had made their way and peace with Caesar. . . .

Many plainly saw Antonius fly, and yet could very hardly believe it, that he, that had nineteen legions whole by land and twelve thousand horsemen upon the sea side, would so have forsaken them, and have fled so cowardly. . . . And yet his soldiers still wished for him, and ever hoped that he would come by some means or other unto them. Furthermore they showed themselves so valiant and faithful unto him that after they certainly knew he was fled they kept themselves whole together seven days. In the end Canidius, Antonius' lieutenant, flying by night and forsaking his camp, when they saw themselves thus destitute of their heads and leaders they yielded themselves unto the stronger. . . .

Canidius himself came to bring him news that he had lost all his army by land at Actium. On the other side he was advertised also that Herodes King of Jewry, who had also certain legions and bands with him, was revolted [had deserted] unto Caesar, and all the other kings in like manner; so that, saving those that were about him, he had none left him. . . .

Indeed, they did break their first order they had set down, which they call *Amimetobion* (as much to say 'no life comparable'), and did set up another, which they called *Synapothanumenon* (signifying 'the order and agreement of those that will die together'), the which in exceeding sumptuousness and cost was not inferior to the first. . . .

Cleopatra in the meantime was very careful in gathering all sorts of poisons together, to destroy men. Now, to make proof of those poisons which made men die with least pain, she tried it upon condemned men in prison. For, when she saw the poisons that were sudden and vehement and brought speedy death with grievous torments, and, in contrary manner, that such as were more mild and gentle had not that quick speed and force to make one die suddenly, she afterwards went about to prove the stinging of snakes and adders, and made some to be applied unto men in her sight, some in one sort and some in another. So, when she had daily made divers and sundry proofs, she found none of them all she had proved so fit as the biting of an aspic, the which causeth only a heaviness of the head, without swounding [fainting] or complaining and bringeth a great desire also to sleep, with a little sweat in the face, and so by little and little taketh away the senses and vital powers, no living creature perceiving that the patients feel any pain. . . .

This notwithstanding, they sent ambassadors unto Octavius Caesar in Asia, Cleopatra requesting the realm of Egypt for their children, and Antonius praying that he might be suffered to live at Athens like a private man, if Caesar would not let him remain in Egypt. And, because they had no other men of estimation about them (for that some were fled, and, those that remained, they did not greatly trust them), they were enforced to send Euphronius the schoolmaster of their children. . . . Furthermore, Caesar would not grant unto Antonius' requests. But, for Cleopatra, he made her answer that he would deny her nothing reasonable, so that she would either put Antonius to death or drive him out of her country. Therewithal he sent Thyreus one of his men unto her, a very wise and discreet man, who, bringing letters of credit from a young lord unto a noble lady, and that besides greatly liked her beauty, might easily by his eloquence have persuaded her. He was longer in talk with her than any man else was, and the Queen herself also did him great honour; insomuch as he made Antonius jealous of him. Whereupon Antonius caused him to be taken and well-favouredly whipped, and so sent him unto Caesar; and bade him tell him that he made him angry with him, because he showed himself proud and disdainful towards him, and now specially when he was easy to be angered, by reason of his present misery. 'To be short, if this mislike thee,' said he, 'thou hast Hipparchus one of my enfranchised bondmen with thee. Hang him if thou wilt, or whip him at thy pleasure, that we may cry quittance.'

From thenceforth Cleopatra, to clear herself of the suspicion he had of her, she made more of him than ever she did. For first of all, where she did solemnize the day of her birth very meanly and sparingly, fit for her present misfortune, she now in contrary manner did keep it with such solemnity, that she exceeded all measure of sumptuousness and magnificence, so that the guests that were bidden to the feasts and came poor, went away rich. . . .

When the city of Pelusium was taken, there ran a rumour in the city that Seleucus, by Cleopatra's consent, had surrendered the same. But, to clear herself that she did not, Cleopatra brought Seleucus' wife and children unto Antonius, to be revenged of them at his pleasure. Furthermore Cleopatra had long before made many sumptuous tombs and monuments, as well for excellency of workmanship as for height and greatness of building, joining hard to the Temple of Isis. Thither she caused to be brought all the treasure and precious things she had of the ancient Kings her predecessors: as gold, silver, emeralds, pearls, ebony, ivory, and cinnamon; and besides all that, a marvellous number of torches, faggots, and flax.

So Octavius Caesar being afraid to lose such a treasure and mass of riches, and that this woman for spite would set it afire, and burn it every whit, he always sent some one or other unto her from him, to put her in good comfort, whilst he in the meantime drew near the city with his army.

So Caesar came, and pitched his camp hard by the city, in the place where they run and manage their horses. Antonius made a sally upon him, and fought very valiantly, so that he drave Caesar's horsemen back, fighting with his men even into their camp. Then he came again to the palace greatly boasting of this victory, and sweetly kissed Cleopatra, armed as he was when he came from the fight, recommending one of his men of arms unto her, that had valiantly fought in this skirmish. Cleopatra to reward his manliness gave him an armour and head-piece of clean gold; howbeit the man at arms, when he had received this rich gift, stale away by night and went to Caesar.

Antonius sent again to challenge Caesar to fight with him hand to hand. Caesar answered him that he had many other ways to die than so. Then Antonius, seeing there was no way more honourable for him to die than fighting valiantly, he determined to set up his rest [stake everything], both by sea and land. So being at supper as it is reported, he commanded his officers and household servants, that waited on him at his board, that they should fill his cups full, and make as much of him as they could. 'For', said he, 'you know not whether you shall do so much for me tomorrow or not, or whether you shall serve another master; and it may be you shall see me no more, but a dead body.' This notwithstanding, perceiving that his friends and men fell a-weeping to hear him say so, to salve that he had spoken he added this more unto it: that he would not lead them to battle where he thought not rather safely to return with victory than valiantly to die with honour.

Furthermore, the self same night within little of midnight, when all the city was quiet, full of fear and sorrow, thinking what would be the issue and end of this war, it is said that suddenly they heard a marvellous sweet harmony of sundry sorts of instruments of music, with the cry of a multitude of people, as they had been dancing and had sung as they use in Bacchus' feasts, with movings and turnings after the manner of the Satyrs. And it seemed that this dance went through the city unto the gate that opened to the enemies, and that all the troop that made this noise they heard went out of the city at that gate. Now such as in reason sought the depth of the interpretation of this wonder thought that it was the god unto whom Antonius bare singular devotion to counterfeit and resemble him, that did forsake them.

The next morning by break of day he went to set those few footmen he had in order upon the hills adjoining unto the city; and there he stood to behold his galleys which departed from the haven and rowed against the galleys of his enemies; and so stood still, looking what exploit his soldiers in them would do. But when by force of rowing they were come near unto them, they first saluted Caesar's men, and then Caesar's men re-saluted them also, and of two armies made but one, and then did all together row toward the city. When Antonius saw that his men did forsake him and yielded unto Caesar, and that his footmen were broken and overthrown he then fled into the city, crying out that Cleopatra had betrayed him unto them with whom he had made war for her sake. Then she, being afraid of his fury, fled into the tomb which she had caused to be made; and there locked the doors unto her, and shut all the springs of the locks with great bolts; and in the meantime sent unto Antonius to tell him that she was dead. Antonius, believing it, said unto herself: 'What dost thou look for further, Antonius, sith spiteful fortune hath taken from thee the only joy thou hadst, for whom thou yet reservedst thy life?' When he had said these words, he went into a chamber and unarmed himself; and being naked said thus: 'O Cleopatra, it grieveth me not that I have lost thy company, for I will not be long from thee. But I am sorry that, having been so great a captain and Emperor, I am indeed condemned to be judged of less courage and noble mind than a woman.'

Now he had a man of his called Eros, whom he loved and trusted much and whom he had long before caused to swear unto him that he should kill him when he did command him; and then he willed him to keep his promise. His man drawing his sword lift it up as though he had meant to have stricken his master. But turning his head at one side, he thrust his sword into himself and fell down dead at his master's foot. Then said Antonius: 'O noble Eros, I thank thee for this; and it is valiantly done of thee, to show me what I should do to myself, which thou couldst not do for me.' Therewithal he took his sword and thrust it into his belly; and so fell down upon a little bed. The wound he had killed him not presently, for the blood stinted a little when he was laid; and when he came somewhat to himself again, he prayed them that were about him to dispatch him. But they all fled out of the chamber, and left him crying out and tormenting himself; until at last there came a secretary unto him called Diomedes, who was commanded to bring him into the tomb or monument where Cleopatra was.

When he heard that she was alive, he very earnestly prayed his men to carry his body thither; and so he was carried in his men's arms into the entry of the monument. Notwithstanding, Cleopatra would not open the gates, but came to the high windows, and cast out certain chains and ropes, in the which Antonius was trussed; and Cleopatra her own self, with two women only which she had suffered to come with her into these monuments, triced [hauled] Antonius up. They that were present to behold it said they never saw so pitiful a sight. For they plucked up poor Antonius, all bloody as he was and drawing on with pangs of death, who holding up his hands to Cleopatra raised up himself as well as he could. It was a hard thing for these women to do, to lift him up. But Cleopatra stooping down with her head, putting to all her strength to her uttermost power, did lift him up with much ado and never let go her hold, with the help of the women beneath that bade her be of good courage, and were as sorry to see her labour so, as she herself. So when she had gotten him in after that sort and laid him on a bed, she rent her garments upon him, clapping her breast and scratching her face and stomach. Then she dried up his blood that had berayed [disfigured] his face, and called him her lord, her husband, and Emperor, forgetting her own misery and calamity, for the pity and compassion she took of him.

Antony made her cease her lamenting, and called for wine, either because he was athirst, or else for that he thought thereby to hasten his death. When he had drunk, he earnestly prayed her and persuaded her that she would seek to save her life, if she could possible without reproach and dishonour; and that chiefly she should trust Proculeius above any man else about Caesar; and, as for himself, that she should not lament nor sorrow for the miserable change of his fortune at the end of his days; but rather that she should think him the more fortunate for the former triumphs and honours he had received, considering that while he lived he was the noblest and greatest prince of the world, and that now he was overcome not cowardly, but valiantly, a Roman by another Roman.

As Antonius gave the last gasp, Proculeius came that was sent from Caesar. For, after Antonius had thrust his sword in himself, as they carried him into the tombs and monuments of Cleopatra, one of his guard called Dercetaeus took his sword with the which he had stricken himself and hid it; then he secretly stale away, and brought Octavius Caesar the first news of his death, and showed him his sword that was bloodied. Caesar hearing these news straight withdrew himself into a secret place of his tent, and there burst out with tears, lamenting his hard and miserable fortune that had been his friend and brother-in-law, his equal in the Empire, and companion with him in sundry great exploits and battles. Then he called for all his friends, and showed them the letters Antonius had written to him, and his answers also sent him again, during their quarrel and strife; and how fiercely and proudly the other answered him to all just and reasonable matters he wrote unto him. After this he sent Proculeius, and commanded him to do what he could possible to get Cleopatra alive, fearing lest otherwise all the treasure would be lost; and furthermore, he thought that if he could take Cleopatra and bring her alive to Rome, she would marvellously beautify and set out his triumph.

But Cleopatra would never put herself into Proculeius' hands, although they spake together. For Proculeius came to the gates that were very thick and strong, and surely barred, but yet there were some cranews [cracks] through the which her voice might be heard. And so they without understood that Cleopatra demanded the kingdom of Egypt for her sons, and that Proculeius answered her that she should be of good cheer and not be afraid to refer all unto Caesar. After he had viewed the place very well, he came and reported her answer unto Caesar; who immediately sent Gallus to speak once again with her, and bade him purposely hold her with talk whilst Proculeius did set up a ladder against that high window by the which Antonius was triced up, and came down into the monument with two of his men, hard by the gate where Cleopatra stood to hear what Gallus said unto her.

One of her women which was shut up in her monuments with her saw Proculeius by chance as he came down, and shrieked out: 'O poor Cleopatra, thou art taken.' Then, when she saw Proculeius behind her as she came from the gate, she thought to have stabbed herself in with a short dagger she wore of purpose by her side. But Proculeius came suddenly upon her, and taking her by both the hands said unto her: 'Cleopatra, first thou shalt do thyself great wrong, and secondly unto Caesar, to deprive him of the occasion and opportunity openly to show his bounty and mercy, and to give his enemies cause to accuse the most courteous and noble prince that ever was, and to appeach him, as though he were a cruel and merciless man that were not to be trusted.' So even as he spake the word he took her dagger from her, and shook her clothes for fear of any poison hidden about her. . . .

Many princes, great kings, and captains did crave Antonius' body of Octavius Caesar, to give him honourable burial. But Caesar would never take it from Cleopatra who did sumptuously and royally bury him with her own hands, whom Caesar suffered to take as much as she would to bestow upon his funerals. Now she was altogether overcome with sorrow and passion of mind, for she had knocked her breast so pitifully, that she had martyred it and in divers places had raised ulcers and inflammations, so that she fell into a fever withal; whereof she was very glad, hoping thereby to have good colour [excuse] to abstain from meat, and that so she might have died easily without any trouble. . . . But Caesar mistrusted the matter by many conjectures he had, and therefore did put her in fear, and threatened her to put her children to shameful death. With these threats Cleopatra for fear yielded straight as she would have yielded unto strokes; and afterwards suffered herself to be cured and dieted as they listed [desired].

Shortly after, Caesar came himself in person to see her and to comfort her. Cleopatra being laid upon a little low bed in poor estate, when she saw Caesar come into her chamber, she suddenly rose up, naked in her smock, and fell down at his feet marvellously disfigured; both for that she had plucked her hair from her head, as also for that she had martyred all her face with her nails; and besides, her voice was small and trembling, her eyes sunk into her head with continual blubbering, and moreover they might see the most part of her stomach torn in sunder. To be short, her body was not much better than her mind. Yet her good grace and comeliness and the force of her beauty was not altogether defaced. But, notwithstanding this ugly and pitiful state of hers, yet she showed herself within [reflected her inner state of mind] by her outward looks and countenance. When Caesar had made her lie down again, and sat by her bed's side, Cleopatra began to clear and excuse herself for that she had done, laying all to the fear she had of Antonius. Caesar, in contrary manner, reproved her in every point. Then she suddenly altered her speech, and prayed him to pardon her, as though she were afraid to die and desirous to live. At length, she gave him a brief and memorial of all the ready money and treasure she had. But by chance there stood Seleucus by, one of her treasurers, who to seem a good servant came straight to Caesar to disprove Cleopatra, that she had not set in all but kept many things back of purpose. Cleopatra was in such a rage with him that she flew upon him, and took him by the hair of the head, and boxed him well-favouredly. Caesar fell a-laughing and parted the fray. 'Alas', said she, 'O Caesar, is not this a great shame and reproach, that thou having vouchsafed to take the pains to come unto me, and hast done me this honour, poor wretch and caitiff creature brought into this pitiful and miserable estate, and that mine own servants should come now to accuse me; though it may be I have reserved some jewels and trifles meet for women, but not for me, poor soul to set out myself withal, but meaning to give some pretty presents and gifts unto Octavia and Livia, that, they making means and intercession for me to thee, thou mightest yet extend thy favour and mercy upon me?' Caesar was glad to hear her say so, persuading himself thereby that she had yet a desire to save her life. So he made her answer that he did not only give her that to dispose of at her pleasure which she had kept back, but further promised to use her more honourably and bountifully than she would think for. And so he took his leave of her, supposing he had deceived her. But indeed he was deceived himself.

There was a young gentleman, Cornelius Dolabella, that was one of Caesar's very great familiars, and besides did bear no evil will unto Cleopatra. He sent her word secretly, as she had requested him, that Caesar determined to take his journey through Syria, and that within three days he would send her away before with her children. When this was told Cleopatra, she requested Caesar that it would please him to suffer her to offer the last oblations of the dead unto the soul of Antonius. This being granted her, she was carried to the place where his tomb was; and there, falling down on her knees, embracing the tomb with her women, the tears running down her cheeks, she began to speak in this sort: 'O my dear lord Antonius, not long sithence I buried thee here, being a free woman; and now I offer unto thee the funeral sprinklings and oblations, being captive and prisoner; and yet I am forbidden and kept from tearing and murdering this captive body of mine with blows, which they carefully guard and keep, only to triumph of thee. Look therefore henceforth for no other honours, offerings, nor sacrifices from me, for these are the last which Cleopatra can give thee, sith now they carry her away. Whilst we lived together, nothing could sever our companies. But now at our death I fear they will make us change our countries. For as thou being a Roman hast been buried in Egypt, even so wretched creature I, an Egyptian, shall be buried in Italy, which shall be all the good that I have received by thy country. If therefore the gods where thou art now have any power and authority, sith our gods here have forsaken us, suffer not thy true friend and lover to be carried away alive, that in me they triumph of thee. But receive me with thee, and let me be buried in one self tomb with thee. For though my griefs and miseries be infinite, yet none hath grieved me more, nor that I could less bear withal, than this small time which I have been driven to live alone without thee.'

Then, having ended these doleful plaints, and crowned the tomb with garlands and sundry nosegays, and marvellous lovingly embraced the same, she commanded they should prepare her bath; and when she had bathed and washed herself she fell to her meat, and was sumptuously served. Now whilst she was at dinner there came a countryman, and brought her a basket. The soldiers that warded [kept guard] at the gates asked him straight what he had in his basket. He opened the basket and took out the leaves that covered the figs, and showed them that they were figs he brought. They all of them marvelled to see so goodly figs. The countryman laughed to hear them, and bade them take some if they would. They believed he told them truly, and so bade him carry them in. After Cleopatra had dined, she sent a certain table [letter] written and sealed unto Caesar, and commanded them all to go out of the tombs where she was, but the two women. Then she shut the doors to her. Caesar, when he received this table and began to read her lamentation and petition, requesting him that he would let her be buried with Antonius, found straight what she meant, and thought to have gone thither himself; howbeit he sent one before in all haste that might be, to see what it was.

Her death was very sudden. For those whom Caesar sent unto her ran thither in all haste possible, and found the soldiers standing at the gate, mistrusting nothing, nor understanding of her death. But when they had opened the doors they found Cleopatra stark dead laid upon a bed of gold, attired and arrayed in her royal robes, and one of her two women, which was called Iras, dead at her feet; and her other woman called Charmion half dead and trembling, trimming the diadem which Cleopatra ware upon her head. One of the soldiers, seeing her, angrily said unto her: 'Is that well done, Charmion?' 'Very well,' said she again, 'and meet for a princess descended from the race of so many noble kings.' She said no more, but fell down dead hard by the bed.

Some report that this aspic was brought unto her in the basket with figs, and that she had commanded them to hide it under the fig leaves, that, when she should think to take out the figs, the aspic should bite her before she should see her; howbeit that, when she would have taken away the leaves for the figs, she perceived it, and said: 'Art thou here then?' And so, her arm being naked, she put it to the aspic to be bitten. Others say again, she kept it in a box, and that she did prick and thrust it with a spindle of gold, so that the aspic, being angered withal, leapt out with great fury, and bit her in the arm. Howbeit few can tell the truth. For they report also that she had hidden poison in a hollow razor which she carried in the hair on her head. And yet was there no mark seen of her body, or any sign discerned that she was poisoned; neither also did they find this serpent in her tomb. But it was reported only that there were seen certain fresh steps or tracks where it had gone, on the tomb side towards the sea and specially by the door side. Some say also that they found two little pretty bitings in her arm, scant to be discerned; the which it seemeth Caesar himself gave credit unto, because in his Triumph he carried Cleopatra's image, with an aspic biting of her arm. And thus goeth the report of her death.

Now Caesar, though he was marvellous sorry for the death of Cleopatra, yet he wondered at her noble mind and courage; and therefore commanded she should be nobly buried and laid by Antonius; and willed also that her two women should have honourable burial.

Bibliography

The original dates of publication are given. In many cases more recent editions have been published.

(1)   Criticism with special reference to *Antony and Cleopatra*.

Bethell, S. L.: *Shakespeare and the Popular Dramatic Tradition*, pp. 116–31, 1944.
Bradley, A. C.: *Oxford Lectures*, 1909. Contains a valuable essay on the play, pp. 279–308.
Brown, J. R.: *Shakespeare: Antony and Cleopatra, A Casebook*, 1968.
Cecil, Lord David: *Poets and Storytellers*, pp. 3–24, 1949.
Coleridge, S. T.: *Lectures upon Shakespeare and Some of the Old Dramatists*, 1849.
Danby, J. F.: *Poets on Fortune's Hill*, Faber, 1952. Contains an essay on the play.
Dickey, F. M.: *Not Wisely But Too Well: Shakespeare's Love Tragedies*, San Marino, 1957.
Granville-Barker, H.: *Prefaces to Shakespeare*, Second Series, 1930. Contains a chapter on the play.
Halliday, F. E.: *Shakespeare and his Critics*, 1949; reprint 1958.
Holloway, J.: *The Story of the Night*, pp. 99–120, 1963.
Knight, G. W.: *The Imperial Theme*, p. 376f, 1931, revised edition 1951.
Knights, L. C.: *Some Shakespearean Themes*, 1959.
MacCallum, M. W.: *Shakespeare's Roman Plays and their Background*, 1910.
Ridler, A.: *Shakespeare Criticism 1919–35*, O.U.P., 1936.
         Shakespeare Criticism 1919–60, O.U.P., 1963.
Riemer, A. P.: *A Reading of Shakespeare's Antony and Cleopatra*, 1968.
Schanzer, E.: *The Problem Plays of Shakespeare*, 1963.
Schücking, L. L.: *Character Problems in Shakespeare's Plays*, 1922.
Shakespeare Survey 10, Cambridge, 1956. Devoted to the Roman Plays.
Stewart, J. I. M.,: *Character and Motive in Shakespeare*, pp. 59–78, 1949.
Traversi, D. A.: *Shakespeare: The Roman Plays*, 1963.
Waith, E. M.: *The Herculean Hero*, 1962.

(2)   Shakespeare's Language and Imagery.

Charney, M.: *Shakespeare's Roman Plays: The Function of Imagery in the Drama*, pp. 79–141, Cambridge, Mass., 1961.
Clemen, W.: *The Development of Shakespeare's Imagery*, 1951.
Hulme, H.: *Explorations in Shakespeare's Language*, 1962.

Onions, C. T.: *A Shakespeare Glossary*, Oxford, 1911; 2nd, ed., rev., with addenda, 1953.
Spurgeon, C. F. E.: *Shakespeare's Imagery and What It Tells Us*, 1935.

(3)   Sources.

Bullough, G.: *Narrative and Dramatic Sources of Shakespeare*, Vol. 5, Routledge & Kegan Paul, 1964.
Muir, K.: *Shakespeare's Sources, Comedies and Tragedies*, Vol. 1, Methuen, 1957.
Spencer, T. J. B.: *Shakespeare's Plutarch*, Penguin, 1964.

(4)   The Age of Shakespeare. -

Craig, H.: *The Enchanted Glass: The Elizabethan Mind in Literature*, New York, 1936; Oxford, 1950.
Ford, B. (ed): *The Age of Shakespeare*, A Pelican Guide to English Literature, Vol. 2, Penguin, 1955.
Lee, S. and Onions, C. T. (editors): *Shakespeare's England: An Account of the Life and Manners of his Age*, Oxford, 2 vols., 1916.
Tillyard, E. M. W.: *The Elizabethan World Picture*, Chatto and Windus, 1943.
Wilson, J. D. (ed): *Life in Shakespeare's England*, C.U.P., Pelican, 1944.

(5)   The Elizabethan Theatre and Acting.

Adams, J. C.: *The Globe Playhouse: Design and Equipment*, Cambridge, U.S.A., 1942.
Beckerman, B.: *Shakespeare at the Globe 1599–1609*, Macmillan, New York 1962.
Coghill, N.: *Shakespeare's Professional Skills*, 1964.
Hodges, C. W.: *The Globe Restored: A Study of the Elizabethan Theatre*, Benn, 1953.
Joseph, B. L.: *Elizabethan Acting*, 1951.
              The Tragic Actor, 1959.
              Acting Shakespeare, 1960.
Nagler, A. M.: *Shakespeare's Stage*, Yale University Press, 1958.
Shakespeare Survey 12, Cambridge, 1959.
Watkins, R.: *On Producing Shakespeare*, 1950.

(6)   Shakespeare's Life.

Halliday, F. E.: *The Life of Shakespeare*, 1961.
Williams, C.: *A Short Life of Shakespeare*, 1933.
Alexander, P.: *Shakespeare*, Home University Library, 1964.

A map of the Mediterranean at the time of Antony and Cleopatra.

Pontus Euxinus

PAPHLAGONIA

PONTUS

ARME-
NIA

BITHYNIA

GALATIA

MYSIA

rgamum

PHRYGIA

CAPPADOCIA

COMMAGENE

MESOPOTAMIA

LYDIA

LYCA-
ONIA

R. Euphrates

Ephesus

Rodnus

CILICIA

PISIDIA

CARIA

Antioch

CILIC

Tarsus

LYCIA

SYRIA

CYPRUS

PHOENICIA

ETE

PALESTINE

n u m

Pelusium

Alexandria

IBYA

EGYPT

Antony and Cleopatra

MARK ANTONY
OCTAVIUS CAESAR   } *triumvirs*
LEPIDUS
SEXTUS POMPEIUS
DOMITIUS ENOBARBUS
EROS
SCARUS
DECRETAS
DEMETRIUS
PHILO
VENTIDIUS   } *Antony's followers*
CANIDIUS
SILIUS
LAMPRIUS
RANNIUS
LUCILLIUS

MAECENAS
AGRIPPA
DOLABELLA
PROCULEIUS   *Caesar's followers*
THIDIAS
GALLUS
TAURUS

MENAS
MENECRATES   *Pompey's followers*
VARRIUS

ALEXAS
MARDIAN   *Cleopatra's followers*
DIOMEDES
SELEUCUS

A SCHOOLMASTER, *ambassador from Antony to Caesar*
A SOOTHSAYER
A CLOWN

CLEOPATRA, *Queen of Egypt*
CHARMIAN } *Cleopatra's maids*
IRAS
OCTAVIA, *Caesar's sister*

OFFICERS, SOLDIERS, MESSENGERS *and* ATTENDANTS
*The scenes are laid in various parts of the Mediterranean world: in and around
Alexandria in Egypt, in Rome and Misenum in Italy, Messina in Sicily, Athens
and Actium in Greece, and in Syria.*

I.i.   The scene is set in Cleopatra's palace in the Egyptian city of Alexandria. Philo and Demetrius, two of Antony's Roman followers, are discussing Antony and Cleopatra, who enter talking of their love for each other. An attendant announces that messengers have arrived from Rome. Cleopatra cleverly taunts Antony so that he brushes aside the news from Rome unheard, and, as she has contrived he should do, turns his mind back to the pleasures of the moment. Alone again, Demetrius and Philo comment disapprovingly on this 'dotage' of their general.

Very briefly Shakespeare introduces us to his two main characters and reveals the essence of the relationship between them. He also establishes the central situation of the play, with Antony set in the middle between the two opposing forces of Rome and duty on the one hand, Egypt and pleasure on the other, and pulled now by one, now by the other. The tension between the two worlds is suggested by the support of Philo and Demetrius for the Roman values, and by the contempt which Cleopatra shows for them.

The circular structure of the scene, which begins and ends with the Roman viewpoint and encloses within this a glimpse of the Egyptian way of life, reflects the larger structure of the play as a whole. The love affair of Antony and Cleopatra is surrounded and finally dominated by the more powerful pressure of political events directed from Rome. The seeds of all the conflict that is to follow are present in this scene.

*   *Alexandria* is the famous Egyptian city founded by the Ptolemies, rulers of Egypt, and named after Alexander the Great who was buried there. It was the cultural centre of the Mediterranean world, celebrated for its magnificent library and museum, and also for its harbour and lighthouse, Pharos, one of the seven wonders of the ancient world. The name Alexandria was synonymous with magnificence and luxury.

1   *dotage:* infatuation.

2   *O'erflows the measure:* exceeds all limits. – This image, in which Antony's passion for Cleopatra is described as something spilling over the sides of a full measuring vessel, is the first of many images illustrating excess which run through the play. It suggests both the abundance and the lack of control in Antony's love.

3   *That o'er . . . plated Mars:* that have shone like the armoured Mars (the god of war) when he surveyed the lines (*files*) of his assembled troops (*musters*) during the war.

5   *The office . . . view:* the devoted service (*office*) of their gaze. – Antony's devotion to his army has been diverted to Cleopatra.

6   *tawny front:* dark-skinned face. – Shakespeare is probably playing on another meaning of *front*, i.e. the vanguard of an army, and in this way continuing the military images.

6   *His captain's heart* – i.e. Antony's heart, that of a commander.

8   *buckles* – i.e. those fastening his breastplate.

8   *reneges all temper:* casts off all self-control.

9   *the bellows* – The bellows could be used to cool, which is the sense intended here.

10   *gipsy's* – The word is derived from *Egyptian*, since Egypt was wrongly thought to be the original home of the gipsies. They were commonly supposed to be lustful and dishonest.

Flourish – i.e. a blast of trumpets like a bugle-call. This was the usual accompaniment to the entry or exit of royalty. The *Train* consists of Cleopatra's attendants.

10   *Look, where they come* – Philo is still speaking to Demetrius but his words draw the attention of the audience to one of the doors at the back of the stage (on each side of the inner stage) through which Antony and Cleopatra enter. See *Introduction*, p.lvii.

12   *The triple pillar* – After the defeat of Brutus and Cassius, the murderers of Caesar, at the Battle of Philippi in 42 B.C. the Roman empire was divided and ruled by three men (*triumvirs*). These were Antony, who ruled the eastern provinces, Octavius Caesar, ruler of the western provinces, and Lepidus, who ruled in Italy. Philo's description of Antony as an indispensable column supporting the huge structure of the Roman world, is a forewarning of the terrible destruction that will follow if Antony does not return to his duty. In the play Octavius is called Caesar throughout.

13   *a strumpet's fool:* (a) the lover, or (b) the entertainer, of a prostitute. – It was customary among the wealthy in Shakespeare's day to employ professional jesters to entertain them. In describing Antony as Cleopatra's *fool*, Philo suggests that he is no better than her hired servant, and also that he is duped by her.

15   *There's beggary . . . reckoned:* The kind of love that can be totalled up like a sum is a poor thing.

Antony and Cleopatra

ACT I scene i

Alexandria.* A room in CLEOPATRA'S *palace.*

Enter DEMETRIUS *and* PHILO.

PHILO   Nay, but this dotage* of our general's
O'erflows the measure:* those his goodly eyes
That o'er the files and musters of the war
Have glowed like plated Mars,* now bend, now turn
The office and devotion of their view*
Upon a tawny front.* His captain's heart,*
Which in the scuffles of great fights hath burst
The buckles* on his breast, reneges all temper,*
And is become the bellows* and the fan
To cool a gipsy's* lust.

Flourish.* Enter ANTONY, CLEOPATRA, *her Ladies, the Train,*
with Eunuchs fanning her.

                Look, where they come.*   10
Take but good note, and you shall see in him
The triple pillar* of the world transformed
Into a strumpet's fool.* Behold and see.

CLEOPATRA   If it be love indeed, tell me how much.

ANTONY   There's beggary in the love that can be reckoned.*   15

CLEOPATRA   I'll set a bourn how far to be beloved.*

ANTONY   Then must thou needs find out new heaven, new earth.

---

16   *a bourn . . . beloved:* a limit to how much you may love me. – Antony's reply that his love
is boundless, together with his first speech, coincides with what Philo has
said, and makes it clear that we can trust the factual basis of Philo's report of
the situation. Philo's opinion, however, reflects the restricted vision of a
Roman soldier; we are to be given a more complete picture on which to form
our judgement.

1

18	*Grates me. The sum:* (News from Rome) irritates me. Tell your news briefly. – The arrival of the messengers from Rome is the first of many intrusions which remind Antony of his political duty in the midst of his life of pleasure in Alexandria. Antony's irritated reaction is a sign of the conflict set up in his mind by this tension between duty and pleasure.
19	*them* – i.e. the news. *News* could be treated as either singular or plural in Shakespeare's time.
20	*Fulvia,* described by Plutarch as 'somewhat sour and crooked of condition' (i.e. perverse), is Antony's Roman wife. In this whole speech Cleopatra is mischievously taunting Antony by suggesting that he is at the beck and call of a woman or a boy. Her object is to strengthen his resistance to his Roman connections.
20	*perchance:* perhaps.
21	*the scarce-bearded Caesar* – Octavius Caesar is so young that his beard has hardly begun to grow. In fact, he was some twenty years younger than Antony, twenty-three at the time of the events chosen for the beginning of the play, thirty-two at its end.
23	*Take in:* capture.
23	*enfranchise:* set free.
24	*we damn thee:* I will condemn you. – Cleopatra suggests that Octavius gives orders to Antony like a ruler (using the royal 'we') commanding a subject.
24	*How:* Why do you say all this? – Antony's question suggests that he does not perceive her cunning intention, and so demonstrates one source of her power over him.
25	*Perchance* – Cleopatra repeats the word (see line 20), pretending not to hear Antony's question but to be seriously interested in what the message from Rome might be.
25	*like:* likely. – Many words used adjectively today were also used adverbially in Shakespeare's time, e.g. *like,* I.i.25; *sudden,* I.iii.5; *high,* I.v.49; *loud,* II.ii.21; *noble,* II.ii.102; *useful,* IV.xiv.80; *honourable,* V.i.58
26	*dismission:* dismissal, i.e. order to leave Egypt.
28	*process* – a legal term, meaning 'a summons to appear in a court of law'. By linking the names of Fulvia and Caesar, Cleopatra is hinting that any attempt by Fulvia to regain her husband is a political trick inspired by Caesar. This clever ruse is designed to stiffen Antony's resistance to any orders or appeals from Rome.
31	*homager:* dutiful servant. – Homage was the service owed by a man to his overlord in medieval times.
31	*else so:* or else. – Cleopatra suggests that Antony's blushes show his awe of Caesar or his shame at being scolded by Fulvia. Antony's blushes may have been caused by shame at his failure of duty to Rome and his wife, or by Cleopatra's taunts; whatever their cause, Cleopatra cleverly turns them to her own advantage.
33	*Let Rome . . . fall* – Cleopatra's cunning has succeeded. Antony says that he would let Rome dissolve into the River Tiber, and its widespread (*ranged*) empire (described as if it were a huge archway spanning the world) collapse in ruins, rather than leave her. The architectural image reminds us of Philo's description of Antony as a *triple pillar,* and all that it implied.
34	*Here is my space:* This small piece of earth here in Egypt is all I want.
35	*dungy earth . . . man:* dirty soil feeds animals just as much as men. – Ambition to conquer kingdoms, Antony implies, is mere folly.
36	*The nobleness . . . thus:* The noblest thing in life is to exchange love as we do. – It is unlikely that *do thus* means 'embrace', as some editors suggest. There is no stage direction to support this opinion, although the original Folio printing is rich in stage directions throughout. Since boys acted the women's parts Elizabethan dramatists tended to avoid this kind of physical intimacy. Rather, Shakespeare seems here to be putting into his own words a detail from Plutarch who twice refers to a way of life agreed upon between Antony and Cleopatra 'which they called *Amimetobion* (as much as to say, no life comparable and matchable with it)'.
37	*such a mutual . . . twain:* a pair who love each other equally, and of such outstanding greatness.
38	*in which . . . peerless:* I compel the whole world on penalty of punishment (if they refuse) to recognize (*weet*) that we stand without equal (*peerless*) as lovers of this kind.
40	*Excellent:* Exceptional.

Enter an ATTENDANT.

ATTENDANT News, my good lord, from Rome.
ANTONY   Grates me. The sum.*
CLEOPATRA Nay, hear them,* Antony.
    Fulvia* perchancc* is angry; or who knows   20
    If the scarce-bearded Caesar* have not sent
    His powerful mandate to you, 'Do this, or this;
    Take in* that kingdom, and enfranchise* that.
    Perform't or else we damn thee'.*
ANTONY   How,* my love?
CLEOPATRA Perchance?* Nay, and most like.*   25
    You must not stay here longer, your dismission*
    Is come from Caesar; therefore hear it, Antony.
    Where's Fulvia's process?* Caesar's I would say. Both?
    Call in the messengers. As I am Egypt's Queen,
    Thou blushest, Antony, and that blood of thine   30
    Is Caesar's homager:* else so* thy cheek pays shame
    When shrill-tongued Fulvia scolds. The messengers!
ANTONY Let Rome in Tiber melt, and the wide arch
    Of the ranged empire fall!* Here is my space.*
    Kingdoms are clay: our dungy earth alike   35
    Feeds beast as man.* The nobleness of life
    Is to do thus,* when such a mutual pair,
    And such a twain* can do't, in which I bind,
    On pain of punishment, the world to weet
    We stand up peerless.*
CLEOPATRA   Excellent* falsehood!   40
    Why did he marry Fulvia, and not love her?*

---

41   *Why did . . . her?* – This whole speech of Cleopatra is something of a riddle, and is possibly
        intended to be so. She could mean (a) 'Why did he marry Fulvia without loving
        her?' or (b) 'It is unthinkable that he married Fulvia without loving her'.

42   *I'll seem . . . not* – Either (a) 'I would be a fool if I believed him', or (b) 'I will pretend to
            believe him' (though that is the action of a fool and I am no fool).
42   *Antony . . . himself:* Antony will be true to his nature (which, Cleopatra pretends to
            believe, is false). – She also implies that while she will *seem* to be a fool, Antony
            will *be* one (i.e. if he expects her to believe what he has just said).
43   *But stirred:* Unless angered. – Antony takes up her words in another sense, pretending to
            believe that she meant 'Antony will be his noble self'. He replies, in effect,
            'Yes, I will, unless Cleopatra annoys me'.
44   *her soft hours:* the pleasant time spent in the service of Venus, goddess of love.
45   *confound:* waste.
45   *conference harsh:* quarrelling.
46   *should stretch:* (which) should pass.
48   *Hear the ambassadors* – Cleopatra is now so certain that she has won over Antony that
            she can remind him of the ambassadors from Rome knowing that he will refuse
            to hear them. In this way she can win the credit of appearing to be anxious that
            Antony should give his attention to state affairs.
48   *Fie, wrangling Queen:* Shame on you, you argumentative Queen.
49   *Whom everything . . . admired:* Everything you do, whether you are finding fault, laughing,
            or crying, is attractive (*becomes*); every passion in you does its best to appear
            beautiful and admirable.
52   *No messenger . . . thine:* I will listen to no messenger except yours.
54   *qualities* – either (a) characters or (b) occupations.
56   *with Antonius . . . slight:* so little valued by Antony. – Demetrius refers to Antony's
            refusal to receive Caesar's message.
57   *when he . . . with Antony:* when he is not his true self he shows himself lacking in that
            distinctive quality of greatness (*great property*) which should always (*still*) go
            with the name of Antony.
59   *full:* exceedingly.
60   *approves . . . liar:* proves that what the rumour-mongers say of him is true.
62   *Of:* for
62   *Rest you happy:* (May God) keep you happy.

I.ii.   As a soothsayer is telling the fortunes of Cleopatra's maids, Cleopatra enters worried by
         Antony's preoccupation with Roman affairs. She avoids him as he comes in with a
         messenger from Rome who reports that Fulvia, his wife, and Lucius, his brother, have
         made war on Caesar. Antony determines to break away from his entanglement with
         Cleopatra, and his resolution is strengthened when another messenger reports the death
         of Fulvia. He tells his decision to Enobarbus who prophesies some consummate acting
         from Cleopatra in her desire to retain Antony in Egypt. Apart from Fulvia's death the
         rising political power of Sextus Pompey, the son of Pompey the Great, demands Antony's
         presence in Rome. He gives Enobarbus orders for departure.
             The first part of the scene displays the habitual love of fun and the luxurious life of the
         Egyptian court, important elements in its attraction for Antony and a strong contrast with
         Roman life. The earthy humour of Cleopatra's maids in their ribald comments on the sooth-
         sayer's prophecies raises laughter, but the scene contains ominous and serious under-
         currents, such as the reference to Cleopatra's death. All the soothsayer's forecasts will
         prove to be true (a convention in Elizabethan drama) but in unexpected ways. They are
         thus a method of arousing interest and suspense in the audience. The second part of the
         scene prepares the way for the highly dramatic confrontation between Antony and
         Cleopatra in the next scene, in which Antony's resolution to leave Egypt is severely
         tested.

*   *a Soothsayer* – i.e. a fortune-teller. Shakespeare's stage direction names the three characters,
            Lamprius, Rannius and Lucillius, who do not speak and who do not appear in
            any other scene. It seems, by their names, that Shakespeare intended them to
            be Romans, who with Enobarbus form a group which comes in ahead of the
            Egyptian group made up of Charmian, Iras, Mardian and Alexas. It is possible
            that Lamprius, named after Plutarch's grandfather, who told him stories of
            Antony's life in Alexandria, is intended to be the name of the Soothsayer.
2   *absolute:* perfect.
3   *O that . . . which:* I wish I knew who this husband was, who . . .

I'll seem the fool I am not;* Antony
Will be himself.*
ANTONY   But stirred* by Cleopatra.
Now for the love of Love, and her soft hours,*
Let's not confound* the time with conference harsh.*   45
There's not a minute of our lives should stretch*
Without some pleasure now. What sport tonight?
CLEOPATRA Hear the ambassadors.*
ANTONY   Fie, wrangling Queen!*
Whom everything becomes – to chide, to laugh,
To weep – whose every passion fully strives   50
To make itself, in thee, fair and admired.*
No messenger but thine,* and all alone,
Tonight we'll wander through the streets, and note
The qualities* of people. Come, my Queen;
Last night you did desire it. [To the ATTENDANT] Speak not
to us.   55
                    [Exeunt all except DEMETRIUS and PHILO
DEMETRIUS Is Caesar with Antonius prized so slight?*
PHILO Sir, sometimes, when he is not Antony,
He comes too short of that great property
Which still should go with Antony.*
DEMETRIUS   I am full* sorry
That he approves the common liar,* who   60
Thus speaks of him at Rome; but I will hope
Of* better deeds tomorrow. Rest you happy.*
                                    [Exeunt

scene ii

Another room in the palace.

Enter ENOBARBUS, LAMPRIUS, *a* SOOTHSAYER,* RANNIUS,
LUCILLIUS, CHARMIAN, IRAS, MARDIAN *the Eunuch*
and ALEXAS.

CHARMIAN Lord Alexas, sweet Alexas, most any thing Alexas, almost
most absolute* Alexas, where's the soothsayer that you
praised so to the Queen? O that I knew this husband, which,*

4   *charge his horns with garlands* – Charmian is here quoting Alexas, who has been talking, off-stage, about a possible husband for Charmian and saying that as soon as he puts on the bridegroom's garland of flowers at his wedding he will have the cuckold's horns, i.e. Charmian will immediately be unfaithful to him. Possibly Alexas sees Charmian's prospective husband as a sacrificial victim, since horned beasts being led to sacrifice were garlanded.

7   *know things:* can see into the future.

8   *In Nature's . . . read:* I can discern some of Nature's innumerable secrets.

10   *banquet* – i.e. a light refreshment of fruit and wine.

10   *wine enough . . . drink:* (bring) enough wine to drink a toast to Cleopatra's health.

12   *give me good fortune:* provide a happy future for me.

13   *I make not, but foresee:* I cannot shape people's fortunes, only foresee them.

15   *far fairer* – The Soothsayer speaks in a riddling way. He means that Charmian will be a better person than she is (foreseeing her laying down her life for her mistress). Some of those present in this part of Scene ii would undoubtedly understand him to mean that Charmian will be more prosperous than she is. Charmian, flattering herself, takes him to mean that she will be more beautiful (*in flesh*).

17   *you shall paint* – Iras mockingly disagrees with Charmian's interpretation of the Soothsayer's words, saying that he simply means that Charmian will look *fairer* because she will use cosmetics to hide her age.

18   *Wrinkles forbid:* May I never have wrinkles (and so have no need of cosmetics to hide them).

19   *Vex not his prescience:* Do not annoy him in the middle of his fortune-telling.

21   *more beloving than beloved:* love others more than they love you.

22   *I had . . . drinking* – The liver was thought by the Elizabethans to be the seat of love. It was in the liver, too, they believed, that the intoxicating fumes of alcohol collected before passing to the head. Charmian would rather drink than love without being loved in return.

24   *Good now:* Now my good man.

26   *Herod* was traditionally the worst of tyrants. Charmian wishes for a son so powerfully tyrannical that Herod would bow to him. Charmian's wish for three kings as husbands recalls the three kings who came from the east to do homage to the Christ-child, and doubtless prompted the allusion to Herod who had dealings with them. Cf. III.iii.3.

27   *Find me . . . mistress:* Discover from the lines of my palm that I shall marry Octavius Caesar and so (as the wife of a triumvir) become the equal of Cleopatra.

31   *You have seen . . . approach:* You have already experienced a better fortune than that which lies ahead.

33   *belike . . . names:* it is likely that my children will be illegitimate.

33   *Prithee:* I pray you.

35   *If every . . . million:* If all your wishes had a womb and were fertile you would have a million children.

37   *Out . . . witch:* Away with you, you fool! I absolve you from the charge of being a magician. – Dealing in witchcraft and black magic was regarded as highly sinful and was heavily punished in Shakespeare's time. Charmian means that she thinks the Soothsayer has no real powers as a fortune-teller.

38   *none but . . . wishes:* nobody knows your secret thoughts but yourself.

43   *a palm presages chastity:* a hand which indicates that I shall always be chaste.

you say, must charge his horns with garlands!*
ALEXAS Soothsayer!   5
SOOTHSAYER Your will?
CHARMIAN Is this the man? Is't you, sir, that know things?*
SOOTHSAYER In Nature's infinite book of secrecy
A little I can read.*
ALEXAS   Show him your hand.
ENOBARBUS Bring in the banquet* quickly: wine enough   10
Cleopatra's health to drink.*
CHARMIAN Good sir, give me good fortune.*
SOOTHSAYER I make not, but foresee.*
CHARMIAN Pray then, foresee me one.
SOOTHSAYER You shall be yet far fairer* than you are.   15
CHARMIAN He means in flesh.
IRAS No, you shall paint* when you are old.
CHARMIAN Wrinkles forbid!*
ALEXAS Vex not his prescience;* be attentive.
CHARMIAN Hush!   20
SOOTHSAYER You shall be more beloving than beloved.*
CHARMIAN I had rather heat my liver with drinking.*
ALEXAS Nay, hear him.
CHARMIAN Good now,* some excellent fortune! Let me be married to
three kings in a forenoon, and widow them all. Let me have   25
a child at fifty, to whom Herod* of Jewry may do homage.
Find me to marry me with Octavius Caesar, and companion
me with my mistress.*
SOOTHSAYER You shall outlive the lady whom you serve.
CHARMIAN O excellent! I love long life better than figs.   30
SOOTHSAYER You have seen and proved a fairer former fortune
Than that which is to approach.*
CHARMIAN Then belike my children shall have no names.* Prithee*,
how many boys and wenches must I have?
SOOTHSAYER If every of your wishes had a womb,   35
And fertile every wish, a million.*
CHARMIAN Out, fool! I forgive thee for a witch.*
ALEXAS You think none but your sheets are privy to your wishes.*
CHARMIAN Nay, come, tell Iras hers.
ALEXAS We'll know all our fortunes.   40
ENOBARBUS Mine, and most of our fortunes tonight, shall be – drunk
to bed.
IRAS [Holding out her hand] There's a palm presages chastity,* if
nothing else.

45   *E'en as ... famine:* In the same way that the Nile when swollen with floodwater foretells
      famine, i.e. not at all. – The Nile brings down with it each year fertile alluvial
      silt. The higher the river rises, the more alluvium it deposits, and so the more
      abundant the crops. Charmian scornfully dismisses Iras's claim to chastity.
      Iras retorts by dismissing Charmian's claims as a soothsayer.

46   *wild:* (a) mad (b) wanton.

47   *an oily palm ... mine ear* – A moist hand was thought to reveal a lustful nature. In
      Charmian's opinion Iras's *oily palm* indicates that she will have many children
      (*a fruitful prognostication*). She is as sure of this as she is that she can scratch
      her ear.

48   *worky-day:* ordinary (like a working day).

51   *I have said:* I have said all I am going to say.

55   *husband's nose* – A large nose was thought to indicate a sensual nature.

56   *Our worser ... mend:* May heaven amend our baser thoughts. – Charmian pretends to be
      shocked at Iras's indelicacy.

56   *Alexas ... fortune:* Tell Alexas's fortune.

57   *cannot go:* Either (a) cannot bear children, or (b) cannot stand upright, or walk (i.e. an old
      crippled woman), or possibly both meanings.

58   *Isis* was the great Egyptian goddess of the earth, fertility and the moon.

60   *fiftyfold:* fifty times over.

60   *a cuckold* – i.e. a husband whose wife has been unfaithful to him.

61   *hear me ... weight:* answer this prayer even if you refuse more important requests of
      mine.

64   *loose-wived:* married to an unfaithful wife.

65   *a foul knave uncuckolded:* an ugly man whose wife has not been unfaithful.

66   *keep decorum ... accordingly:* act justly (as a goddess should) and give him the fortune he
      deserves – i.e. let him, because he is ugly, be cuckolded.

69   *if it lay ... do it:* if they were married to me and so had the power to make me a cuckold
      they would go as far as to become whores in order to do so.

75   *A Roman thought* – Either (a) a thought about Rome, or (b) a serious thought.

CHARMIAN E'en as the o'erflowing Nilus presageth famine.*   45
IRAS Go, you wild* bedfellow, you cannot soothsay.
CHARMIAN Nay, if an oily palm be not a fruitful prognostication, I cannot
         scratch mine ear.* Prithee, tell her but a worky-day* fortune.
SOOTHSAYER Your fortunes are alike.
IRAS But how, but how? Give me particulars.   50
SOOTHSAYER I have said.*
IRAS Am I not an inch of fortune better than she?
CHARMIAN Well, if you were but an inch of fortune better than I, where
         would you choose it?
IRAS Not in my husband's nose.*   55
CHARMIAN Our worser thoughts heavens mend!* Alexas – come, his
         fortune, his fortune!* O let him marry a woman that cannot
         go,* sweet Isis,* I beseech thee, and let her die too, and give
         him a worse, and let worse follow worse, till the worst of all
         follow him laughing to his grave, fiftyfold* a cuckold.* Good   60
         Isis, hear me this prayer, though thou deny me a matter of
         more weight.* Good Isis, I beseech thee.
IRAS Amen. Dear goddess, hear that prayer of the people! For, as
         it is a heart-breaking to see a handsome man loose-wived,* so
         it is a deadly sorrow to behold a foul knave uncuckolded.*   65
         Therefore, dear Isis, keep decorum, and fortune him accord-
         ingly.*
CHARMIAN Amen.
ALEXAS Lo now, if it lay in their hands to make me a cuckold, they
         would make themselves whores but they'ld do it.*   70
ENOBARBUS Hush, here comes Antony.

         Enter CLEOPATRA.

CHARMIAN   Not he, the Queen.
CLEOPATRA Saw you my lord?
ENOBARBUS   No lady.
CLEOPATRA   Was he not here?
CHARMIAN No madam.
CLEOPATRA He was disposed to mirth, but on the sudden
         A Roman thought* hath struck him. Enobarbus!   75
ENOBARBUS Madam.
CLEOPATRA Seek him, and bring him hither. Where's Alexas?
ALEXAS Here at your service. My lord approaches.

         Enter ANTONY *with a* MESSENGER *and* ATTENDANTS.

CLEOPATRA We will not look upon him. Go with us.
                                                          [*Exeunt*

80	*came into the field:* began war.
82	*the times state . . . drave them:* the state of affairs at that time forced them to be friends, joining their forces against Caesar, whose greater success (*better issue*) in the war drove them out of Italy after the first battle.
85	*what worst?:* (you have kept back) the worst news – what is it?
86	*The nature . . . teller:* Bad news makes people think the man who brings it similarly bad. – The messenger fears Antony's displeasure at his bad news.
88	*Things that are past . . . with me:* As far as I am concerned things done are finished with. – Antony is reassuring the messenger that he will not punish him for news of past events, however unpleasant.
89	*Who tells . . . flattered:* if a man tells me the truth, even if his news is fatal to me, I treat him as if he were saying the most flattering things.
90	*Labienus* was a follower of Brutus and Cassius. After their defeat at Philippi he continued to fight on against the Triumvirate in the eastern provinces, allying himself with the Parthians.
91	*stiff:* unpleasant.
92	*Extended:* seized.
92	*Asia* has three syllables here.
96	*Speak to . . . tongue:* Speak bluntly, without softening what everyone (*the general tongue*) is saying about me.
97	*Name Cleopatra . . . Rome:* give Cleopatra the kind of name she is given in Rome.
98	*Rail thou . . . phrase:* reproach me in the kind of terms that Fulvia uses.
99	*With such . . . utter:* with as much freedom as truth and ill-will could possibly have to express themselves.
100	*O then . . . earing* – Shakespeare uses agricultural imagery here, comparing man to a field. Our faults, says Antony, multiply when the keen breath of criticism is absent, just as weeds multiply in a field when piercing winds no longer blow. If we are told our faults they will be uprooted, just as the weeds are by ploughing (*earing*). Some editors change the Folio reading *winds* to *minds;* the general sense of the lines remains the same, however, whichever reading is adopted.
102	*Fare . . . awhile:* Go away for the present.
104	*Sicyon* was an ancient Greek city in the north-east of Peloponnesus.
104	*how:* what is.
106	*stays upon your will:* waits to know what you want him to do.
108	*lose myself in dotage:* ruin myself by my infatuation (for Cleopatra).
108	*What:* Who.

MESSENGER	Fulvia thy wife first came into the field.*	80
ANTONY	Against my brother Lucius?	
MESSENGER	Ay. But soon that war had end, and the time's state	
	Made friends of them, joining their force 'gainst Caesar,	
	Whose better issue in the war from Italy	
	Upon the first encounter drave them.*	
ANTONY	Well, what worst?*	85
MESSENGER	The nature of bad news infects the teller.*	
ANTONY	When it concerns the fool or coward. On!	
	Things that are past are done, with me.* 'Tis thus,	
	Who tells me true, though in his tale lie death,	
	I hear him as he flattered.*	
MESSENGER	Labienus *	90
	This is stiff* news – hath with his Parthian force	
	Extended* Asia;* from Euphrates	
	His conquering banner shook, from Syria	
	To Lydia, and to Ionia,	
	Whilst –	
ANTONY	Antony, thou wouldst say –	
MESSENGER	O my lord!	95
ANTONY	Speak to me home, mince not the general tongue,*	
	Name Cleopatra as she is called in Rome;*	
	Rail thou in Fulvia's phrase,* and taunt my faults	
	With such full licence as both truth and malice	
	Have power to utter.* O then we bring forth weeds	100
	When our quick winds lie still, and our ills told us	
	Is as our earing.* Fare thee well awhile.*	
MESSENGER	At your noble pleasure.	
	[Exit	
ANTONY	From Sicyon* how* the news? Speak there!	
FIRST ATTENDANT	The man from Sicyon! Is there such an one?	105
SECOND ATTENDANT	He stays upon your will.*	
ANTONY	Let him appear.	
	These strong Egyptian fetters I must break,	
	Or lose myself in dotage.*	

Enter another MESSENGER, *with a letter.*

	What* are you?	
MESSENGER	Fulvia thy wife is dead.	
ANTONY	Where died she?	
MESSENGER	In Sicyon.	110

111   *what else . . . know:* what other important news concerns you.
112   *Forbear me:* Leave me alone.
114   *What our . . . again:* What we throw away in disdain we often wish we had back again.
115   *The present . . . her on:* What pleases us now later displeases us, after time has passed and brought its changes. Now that she is gone I remember her good qualities, and my hand which (in imagination) pushed her to her death would willingly pull her back if it could. – Shakespeare depicts time as a revolving wheel: what is now at the top will in time be cast down (*By revolution lowering*).
119   *enchanting:* spell-binding. – This is one of many suggestions that Cleopatra possessed magical powers.
120   *Ten thousand . . . hatch:* my inactivity breeds ten thousand evils apart from those I know about.
124   *Why then . . . women:* If we go all our women will die of grief.
125   *if they . . . word:* if they have to bear our going away, it's death for them.
128   *Under a compelling occasion:* When it is absolutely necessary.
129   *between them . . . nothing:* if one has to choose between women and a great undertaking, women should be considered worthless.
131   *catching but the least noise:* hearing even the slightest rumour.
132   *upon far poorer moment:* with much less cause.
133   *there is mettle . . . dying:* there must be an ardent spirit in death which performs some loving action for her, since she is so ready to die. – Cleopatra rushes to embrace death as if it were a lover.
135   *past man's thought:* beyond anything a man could imagine.
136   *Alack:* Alas.
139   *Almanacs* which appeared annually giving weather forecasts for the coming year were very popular in the largely agricultural community of Shakespeare's day. They frequently forecast tremendous storms. Enobarbus is saying that even the most terrible storms described in the almanacs cannot equal the wind of Cleopatra's sighs or the floods of her tears. Her grief is on the grand scale. His tone is one of mingled admiration and scepticism.
140   *Jove* was a sky-deity with power to produce thunder, lightning and rain.
142   *piece:* masterpiece. – *Piece* was used then, as now, to refer humorously or contemptuously to a woman. Enobarbus possibly intends both meanings here.
143   *which not . . . travel:* if you had not been fortunate enough (*blest withal*) to see Cleopatra your reputation as a traveller would have suffered.

Her length of sickness, with what else more serious
Importeth thee to know,* this bears.   [*Gives a letter*
ANTONY   Forbear me.*
                    [MESSENGER *and* ATTENDANTS *go out*
There's a great spirit gone. Thus did I desire it.
What our contempts doth often hurl from us,
We wish it ours again.* The present pleasure,   115
By revolution lowering, does become
The opposite of itself: she's good, being gone;
The hand could pluck her back that shoved her on.*
I must from this enchanting* Queen break off;
Ten thousand harms, more than the ills I know,   120
My idleness doth hatch.* Ho now, Enobarbus!

Enter ENOBARBUS.

ENOBARBUS What's your pleasure, sir?
ANTONY I must with haste from hence.
ENOBARBUS Why then we kill all our women.* We see how mortal an
  unkindness is to them; if they suffer our departure, death's   125
  the word.*
ANTONY I must be gone.
ENOBARBUS Under a compelling occasion* let women die. It were pity to
  cast them away for nothing, though between them and a
  great cause they should be esteemed nothing.* Cleopatra,   130
  catching but the least noise* of this, dies instantly, I have
  seen her die twenty times upon far poorer moment.* I do
  think there is mettle in death, which commits some loving
  act upon her, she hath such a celerity in dying.*
ANTONY She is cunning past man's thought.*   135
ENOBARBUS Alack,* sir, no; her passions are made of nothing but the
  finest part of pure love. We cannot call her winds and waters
  sighs and tears; they are greater storms and tempests than
  almanacs* can report. This cannot be cunning in her; if it be,
  she makes a shower of rain as well as Jove.*   140
ANTONY Would I had never seen her!
ENOBARBUS O sir, you had then left unseen a wonderful piece* of work,
  which not to have been blest withal would have discredited
  your travel.*
ANTONY Fulvia is dead.   145
ENOBARBUS Sir?
ANTONY Fulvia is dead.
ENOBARBUS Fulvia?

150   *Why, sir . . . sorrow* – Enobarbus, in his rough and cynical fashion, attempts to console Antony by suggesting that having lost his old wife he can find a new one. He has not heard (as we have) Antony's regret at Fulvia's death, and wrongly imagines that Antony will feel so little grief that if he sheds any tears they will have to be produced by an onion. He expresses his thought in appropriately homespun images of tailoring, comparing the gods to tailors who provide the materials (*members*) to make new wives (*petticoats*) to replace the old (*old robes, old smock*) when they are dead (*worn out*). There is play on *cut* meaning (a) loss and (b) a tailored garment, and on *case* meaning (a) situation and (b) garment. A *smock* was a woman's linen petticoat.
159   *The business . . . absence:* The disturbance (*business*) she has set in motion (*broachèd*) in Rome demands my presence there.
161   *business:* affairs.
163   *your abode:* your staying here.
164   *light:* frivolous.
165   *Have notice what we purpose:* be forewarned of my intention (to leave). – Here and elsewhere Antony uses the royal 'we'.
165   *break:* tell.
166   *expedience:* (a) haste (b) expedition.
167   *part:* depart.
168   *more urgent touches:* more pressing affairs that concern me closely.
169   *speak to us:* call for my action.
170   *our contriving friends:* friends planning action on my behalf.
171   *Petition us at home:* beg me to come home.
172   *given the dare:* challenged.
173   *slippery:* fickle.
174   *linked to . . . past:* attached firmly to a deserving man until he no longer needs it (or possibly, until he no longer deserves it).
175   *to throw . . . son:* to clothe Sextus Pompeius in all the dignities of his father, Pompey the Great.
178   *Higher than . . . life:* greater than his reputation (*name*) and power in his courage and energy (*blood and life*).
178   *stands up . . . soldier:* sets himself up as the world's greatest soldier.
180   *whose quality . . . danger:* if he continues in this manner he may threaten the whole world. – *Sides:* bounds, limits.
180   *Much is breeding . . . poison:* Many things are coming to life, which, like a horse-hair, have life but are not yet poisonous. – It was commonly believed that a horse's hair placed in water would turn into a serpent, and also that a serpent became venomous only after it was fully grown. Antony means that by taking early action against these new developments in Rome he could prevent them from becoming dangerous to him.
184   *Say our pleasure . . . hence:* Tell my intention to those of my subordinates who need to know, which is, my quick departure from Egypt.

ANTONY   Dead.

ENOBARBUS   Why, sir, give the gods a thankful sacrifice. When it pleaseth   150
their deities to take the wife of a man from him, it shows to
man the tailors of the earth; comforting therein, that when
old robes are worn out, there are members to make new. If
there were no more women but Fulvia, then had you indeed
a cut, and the case to be lamented. This grief is crowned with   155
consolation: your old smock brings forth a new petticoat, and
indeed the tears live in an onion that should water this
sorrow.*

ANTONY   The business she hath broachèd in the state
Cannot endure my absence.*   160

ENOBARBUS   And the business* you have broached here cannot be without
you; especially that of Cleopatra's, which wholly depends on
your abode.*

ANTONY   No more light* answers. Let our officers
Have notice what we purpose.* I shall break*   165
The cause of our expedience* to the Queen,
And get her leave to part.* For not alone
The death of Fulvia, with more urgent touches,*
Do strongly speak to us,* but the letters too
Of many of our contriving friends* in Rome   170
Petition us at home.* Sextus Pompeius
Hath given the dare to Caesar,* and commands
The empire of the sea. Our slippery* people,
Whose love is never linked to the deserver
Till his deserts are past,* begin to throw   175
Pompey the Great and all his dignities
Upon his son,* who high in name and power,
Higher than both in blood and life,* stands up
For the main soldier;* whose quality, going on,
The sides o' th' world may danger.* Much is breeding,   180
Which, like the courser's hair, hath yet but life,
And not a serpent's poison.* Say our pleasure,
To such whose places under us require,
Our quick remove from hence.*

ENOBARBUS   I shall do't.   185

[*Exeunt*

I.iii.   Cleopatra uses all her wiles to prevent Antony's departure – pretended indifference, mockery, anger, simulated illness. When she sees that none of this succeeds, she accepts defeat, begs forgiveness and wishes him success.

The scene, though having little physical action, is full of drama. We applaud the variety and subtlety of Cleopatra's campaign against Antony, which concludes with the audacious irony that it is Antony who is play-acting. The scene is important in building up sympathy and admiration for Antony in holding firm against Cleopatra's battery; his resolution is firm, yet his love for her is evident in his patient forbearance. Antony's strength is seen here, and it is important that this should be established, since it is only a strong man who could win Cleopatra's love and submission. We have a further irony in the fact that Cleopatra's actions, though pretended, are an expression of her totally sincere desire to keep Antony beside her in Egypt.

3   *I did not send you:* Do not let him know I sent you.
3   *sad:* serious.
5   *sudden sick:* suddenly taken ill. – See note to i.i.25.
7   *hold the method . . . him:* follow the best method of compelling him to love you.
8   *I do not:* (that) I do not do.
9   *give him away:* give way to him.
10   *the way:* (that is) the way.
11   *Tempt . . . forbear:* Do not provoke him too far in this way. I wish you would refrain from doing this.
13   *I am sick and sullen* – Cleopatra tells Charmian that she will pretend to be ill and miserable.
14   *give breathing to my purpose:* have to tell you my intention.
15   *fall:* faint.
16   *It cannot . . . sustain it:* This agony cannot last long; human nature could not stand it. – Cleopatra is threatening to *die instantly* once again.
18   *stand farther from me* – i.e. give me air.
19   *I know . . . good news* – Cleopatra perversely pretends that the look she sees in Antony's eye indicates that he has good news for her. She deliberately makes it much harder for him to break his bad news.
20   *the married woman* – i.e Fulvia. By her phrase *you may go* Cleopatra sarcastically implies that Antony is dependent on Fulvia's permission to travel.
26   *I saw the treasons planted:* I saw that you intended to act treacherously. – The image could be of treason as a seed planted and maturing in the course of time, or as an explosive mine set in the ground.

scene iii

The same.

Enter CLEOPATRA, CHARMIAN, IRAS *and* ALEXAS.

CLEOPATRA Where is he?
CHARMIAN   I did not see him since.
CLEOPATRA See where he is, who's with him, what he does.
I did not send you.* If you find him sad,*
Say I am dancing: if in mirth, report
That I am sudden sick.* Quick, and return.   5
                                              [*Exit* ALEXAS
CHARMIAN Madam, methinks if you did love him dearly,
You do not hold the method to enforce
The like from him.*
CLEOPATRA   What should I do, I do not?*
CHARMIAN In each thing give him way,* cross him in nothing.
CLEOPATRA Thou teachest like a fool: the way* to lose him.   10
CHARMIAN Tempt him not so too far. I wish, forbear.*
In time we hate that which we often fear.

Enter ANTONY.

But here comes Antony.
CLEOPATRA   I am sick and sullen.*
ANTONY I am sorry to give breathing to my purpose - *
CLEOPATRA Help me away, dear Charmian, I shall fall.*   15
It cannot be thus long, the sides of nature
Will not sustain it.*
ANTONY   Now, my dearest Queen -
CLEOPATRA Pray you stand farther from me.*
ANTONY   What's the matter?
CLEOPATRA I know by that same eye there's some good news.*
What, says the married woman* you may go?   20
Would she had never given you leave to come!
Let her not say 'tis I that keep you here.
I have no power upon you; hers you are.
ANTONY The gods best know -
CLEOPATRA   O, never was there queen
So mightily betrayed! Yet at the first   25
I saw the treasons planted.*
ANTONY   Cleopatra -

28 *in swearing . . . gods:* shake the gods on their heavenly thrones with the power of your oaths.

29 *Riotous madness . . . swearing:* It would be wild madness to be deceived into believing your oaths which are broken as soon as you utter them.

32 *colour:* empty excuse.

33 *when you . . . going then:* when you begged to be allowed to stay here, then you had plenty to say: there was no talk of your going then.

35 *Eternity was . . . heaven:* then you were saying that you found eternal life in my lips and eyes, heavenly joy (*bliss*) in the curve of my eyebrows (*brow's bent*), and nothing about me (none our parts) that was not of divine origin.

39 *How now:* What are you saying.

40 *I would . . . Egypt:* I wish I was your size; then you would witness my courage. – Cleopatra implies that she would force Antony to submit by fighting him.

42 *The strong . . . awhile:* The compelling needs of the moment demand my active attention for a time.

43 *my full heart . . . you:* my whole heart remains in trust with you. – Use can mean (a) the legal right to enjoy the use and advantages of another person's property entrusted to one, and (b) interest from investment. Antony suggests that his love, entrusted to Cleopatra, will increase in his absence.

45 *Shines o'er . . . swords:* is covered with the glittering swords of Romans at war with each other.

46 *port* – Probably Ostia, the harbour for Rome, since Pompey commands a fleet, although it could mean the gate of the city of Rome.

47 *Equality . . . faction:* when there are two internal (*domestic*) powers in the state equally divided, distrustful (*scrupulous*) party strife (*faction*) is generated (*breeds*).

48 *the hated . . . love:* men who were hated, having acquired strength, suddenly find themselves loved.

49 *cóndemned Pompey . . . threaten:* Pompey, formerly censured, now loaded with the honour that was his father's, quickly finds his way into the affections of those who have not prospered under the present régime, whose large number threatens Rome.

53 *quietness . . . change:* peace having grown sick of inactivity (as well as ill because of it) wants to cure itself by any violent means, even blood-letting. – The *purge*, or letting of blood, was a common treatment for sickness at this time.

54 *My more particular . . . going:* My more personal reason for going, and one which should assure you that it is safe for me to go.

57 *Though age . . . childishness:* Though my advanced age has not exempted me from foolish behaviour, it does prevent me from being so childish as to believe you. – Cleopatra believes Antony is lying in order to leave her.

60 *at thy sovereign leisure:* when your majesty has time.

61 *garboils she awaked:* commotions she stirred up.

61 *At the last, best:* The best news is at the end of the letter. – Antony refers to the details of Fulvia's death.

63 *sacred vials:* precious bottles (of tears). – In this speech Cleopatra pretends to believe that Antony will mark her own death with a similar absence of grief.

CLEOPATRA Why should I think you can be mine and true
(Though you in swearing shake the thronèd gods)*
Who have been false to Fulvia? Riotous madness,
To be entangled with those mouth-made vows,   30
Which break themselves in swearing.*

ANTONY   Most sweet Queen –

CLEOPATRA Nay, pray you seek no colour* for your going,
But bid farewell, and go: when you sued staying,
Then was the time for words: no going then;*
Eternity was in our lips and eyes,   35
Bliss in our brows' bent; none our parts so poor
But was a race of heaven.* They are so still,
Or thou, the greatest soldier of the world,
Art turned the greatest liar.

ANTONY   How now,* lady?

CLEOPATRA I would I had thy inches; thou shouldst know   40
There were a heart in Egypt.*

ANTONY   Hear me, Queen.
The strong necessity of time commands
Our services awhile;* but my full heart
Remains in use with you.* Our Italy
Shines o'er with civil swords;* Sextus Pompeius   45
Makes his approaches to the port* of Rome;
Equality of two domestic powers
Breeds scrupulous faction;* the hated, grown to strength,
Are newly grown to love;* the cóndemned Pompey,
Rich in his father's honour, creeps apace   50
Into the hearts of such as have not thrived
Upon the present state, whose numbers threaten;*
And quietness, grown sick of rest, would purge
By any desperate change.* My more particular,
And that which most with you should safe my going,*   55
Is Fulvia's death.

CLEOPATRA Though age from folly could not give me freedom,
It does from childishness.* Can Fulvia die?

ANTONY She's dead, my Queen.
[*He gives her the letter*] Look here, and at thy sovereign
leisure* read   60
The garboils she awaked.* At the last, best:*
See when and where she died.

CLEOPATRA   O most false love!
Where be the sacred vials* thou shouldst fill

67	*bear:* have in mind.
67	*which are . . . advice:* which I will carry out, or abandon, according to your advice.
68	*By the fire . . . slime:* I swear by the sun which generates life (*quickens*) from the mud of the Nile.
71	*As thou affects:* whichever you prefer.
71	*Cut my lace* – Elizabethan ladies of fashion laced themselves tightly in whalebone stays which restricted breathing. Again Cleopatra pretends she is about to faint.
72	*let it be:* do not bother (to cut my lace).
73	*So Antony loves:* This is how Antony loves, i.e. badly (*ill*) one minute, *well* the next.
74	*to his love . . . trial:* about his love, which will prove honourable when put to trial.
75	*So Fulvia told me* – i.e. so Fulvia's case has taught me. Cleopatra taunts him ironically.
78	*Belong to Egypt:* are shed for me.
78	*Good now:* My good fellow. – Cleopatra speaks as if addressing an inferior, in this case, an actor.
79	*excellent dissembling:* perfect imitation.
80	*heat my blood:* make me angry.
81	*You can do better yet:* You can perform better than this.
81	*meetly:* quite good.
82	*target:* shield. – Cleopatra's addition turns Antony's dignified oath into one common among bragging soldiers.
82	*mends:* is improving.
83	*the best* – i.e. the best he can do.
84	*How this . . . chafe:* how skilfully this Roman descendant of Hercules performs his part as the angry man. – Antony claimed descent from Hercules. He is reputed to have looked like him and to have imitated him in his dress. Cf. IV.iii.15 and note.
89	*Something it is I would:* What I want to say is something. – She leaves the sentence unfinished, having forgotten, or pretending to have forgotten, what she wanted to say.
90	*O my oblivion . . . Antony:* my forgetfulness is like Antony himself.
91	*I am all forgotten:* (a) I am totally forgotten (by Antony), (b) I have forgotten entirely what I was going to say.
91	*But that . . . itself:* If it were not for the fact that you are the queen of frivolity, I should take you for the personification of frivolity.
93	*'Tis sweating . . . this:* To carry this burden of what you call idleness, which afflicts my heart so much, is work that makes me sweat. – Cleopatra in using the imagery of childbirth (*labour, bear*) is asserting the tenderness of her love for Antony.
96	*my becomings:* the feelings and behaviour natural to me in these circumstances.
97	*Eye:* appear.
97	*calls you hence:* demands that you leave here.

With sorrowful water? Now I see, I see
In Fulvia's death, how mine received shall be.   65
ANTONY Quarrel no more, but be prepared to know
The purposes I bear;* which are, or cease,
As you shall give th'advice.* By the fire
That quickens Nilus' slime,* I go from hence
Thy soldier, servant, making peace or war,   70
As thou affects.*
CLEOPATRA   Cut my lace,* Charmian, come –
But let it be,* I am quickly ill, and well.
So Antony loves.*
ANTONY   My precious Queen, forbear,
And give true evidence to his love, which stands
An honourable trial.*
CLEOPATRA   So Fulvia told me.*   75
I prithee turn aside and weep for her,
Then bid adieu to me, and say the tears
Belong to Egypt.* Good now,* play one scene
Of excellent dissembling,* and let it look
Like perfect honour.
ANTONY   You'll heat my blood.* No more!   80
CLEOPATRA You can do better yet;* but this is meetly*.
ANTONY Now, by my sword –
CLEOPATRA   And target.* Still he mends;*
But this is not the best.* Look, prithee, Charmian,
How this Herculean Roman does become
The carriage of his chafe.*
ANTONY   I'll leave you, lady.   85
CLEOPATRA Courteous lord, one word.
Sir, you and I must part, but that's not it:
Sir, you and I have loved, but there's not it:
That you know well. Something it is I would – *
O, my oblivion is a very Antony,*   90
And I am all forgotten.*
ANTONY   But that your royalty
Holds idleness your subject, I should take you
For idleness itself.*
CLEOPATRA   'Tis sweating labour
To bear such idleness so near the heart
As Cleopatra this.* But sir, forgive me,   95
Since my becomings* kill me when they do not
Eye* well to you. Your honour calls you hence;*

98   *be deaf . . . folly:* do not listen to what I say since you have no pity for my foolishness.
99   *Upon your sword . . . feet:* May you win the victor's laurel garland in your battles, and may
            your path to success be made smooth with rushes strewn by your admirers.
102   *Our separation . . . thee:* our separation from each other is such that we both stay and go,
            so that although you remain here physically you go with me in spirit, and I,
            hastening away, remain with you in spirit.

I.iv.   In Rome, Octavius Caesar is reading a report of Antony's self-indulgent life in Alexandria,
        of which he strongly disapproves. News is brought of the growing power of his opponent,
        Sextus Pompey, especially at sea, and Octavius laments that Antony, whose former
        exploits won everyone's admiration, should have fallen so low as to be absent at this time
        of emergency. Octavius and Lepidus determine to take the field against Pompey.
            The scene strengthens our consciousness of the unbridgeable gap between the two
        ways of life, the Roman and Egyptian. In Rome Octavius is the dominant figure; his
        fellow-triumvir Lepidus, pacific and temporising by nature, is very much a junior
        partner. Octavius's supremacy as a politician is balanced by Antony's military prowess,
        praised here and elsewhere, and it will be these opposed qualities that will form the basis
        of the coming struggle between them.

1   *see* – i.e. from the letter he holds which gives news of Antony.
2   *It is not . . . competitor* – Caesar insists that his opposition to Antony springs not from a
            natural dislike of him, which would be a *vice* in him, but from Antony's self-
            indulgent actions. *Competitor:* partner, with a play on its other meaning,
            rival. Octavius pompously refers to himself in the 3rd person as Caesar.
5   *lamps of night:* the stars, i.e. Antony spends all night in revelry (*revel*).
6   *the queen of Ptolemy* – Julius Caesar had arranged the marriage of Cleopatra to her young
            brother, later Ptolemy XIII.
7   *hardly gave audience:* was reluctant to give interviews to anyone.
8   *Vouchsafed to think:* deigned to remember.
8   *there* – i.e. described in the letter.
9   *abstract:* essence.
11   *enow:* enough.
12   *seems as . . . blackness:* like the stars shine out more clearly when set against the darkness
            of the night. – Lepidus argues that Antony's faults look greater than they are
            because they are set against the background of his general goodness.
13   *hereditary . . . purchased:* inherited from his ancestors rather than acquired through his
            own fault.
18   *give a kingdom . . . mirth* – Either (a) give away a kingdom for the fun of it, or (b) give away
            a kingdom in exchange for entertainment.
19   *keep the turn of tippling:* drink round for round.
20   *reel:* stagger drunkenly along.
20   *stand the buffet / With knaves:* endure the blows of rascals.
21   *smells* – The singular form was often used instead of the plural in Shakespeare's time.
21   *becomes:* is fitting for.
22   *As his . . . blemish:* although a man must have a very unusual character (*composure*) if
            these things do not taint it.

Therefore be deaf to my unpitied folly,*
And all the gods go with you! Upon your sword   100
Sit laurel victory, and smooth success
Be strewed before your feet!*

ANTONY   Let us go. Come;
Our separation so abides and flies,
That thou, residing here, goes yet with me,
And I, hence fleeting, here remain with thee.*   105
Away!

                                        [*Exeunt*

scene iv

Rome. A room in OCTAVIUS CAESAR'S *house.*

Enter OCTAVIUS *reading a letter,* LEPIDUS *and their Train.*

CAESAR You may see,* Lepidus, and henceforth know,
        It is not Caesar's natural vice to hate
        Our great competitor.* From Alexandria
        This is the news: he fishes, drinks, and wastes
        The lamps of night* in revel; is not more manlike   5
        Than Cleopatra, nor the queen of Ptolemy*
        More womanly than he; hardly gave audience,* or
        Vouchsafed to think* he had partners. You shall find there*
        A man who is the abstract* of all faults
        That all men follow.

LEPIDUS   I must not think there are   10
        Evils enow* to darken all his goodness.
        His faults, in him, seem as the spots of heaven,
        More fiery by night's blackness;* hereditary
        Rather than purchased;* what he cannot change
        Than what he chooses.   15

CAESAR You are too indulgent. Let's grant it is not
        Amiss to tumble on the bed of Ptolemy,
        To give a kingdom for a mirth,* to sit
        And keep the turn of tippling* with a slave,
        To reel* the streets at noon, and stand the buffet   20
        With knaves* that smells* of sweat: say this becomes* him,
        (As his composure must be rare indeed
        Whom these things cannot blemish)* yet must Antony

24	*foils:* disgraceful actions.
24	*when we . . . lightness:* when his levity throws such a great burden on us.
25	*If he filled . . . for't:* If he simply filled up his leisure time (*vacancy*) with his voluptuous behaviour, the violent sickness produced by excess (*full surfeits*) and the aching (*dryness*) of his bones will make him pay adequately (*call on him*) for it.
28	*But to . . . judgement:* But when he wastes (*confounds*) time that calls on (*drums*) him to leave his amusements, time that he ought to use for the important affairs of his part of the empire (*state*) and ours, he must be reproved (*chid*) in the same way that we scold boys who, being old enough to know better, exchange this knowledge for the pleasures of the moment and so betray their judgement.
37	*beloved of . . . Caesar:* loved by those who have only remained loyal to Caesar through fear.
39	*discontents repair:* discontented men make their way.
40	*Give him:* say that he has been.
40	*I should . . . less:* I ought to have known as much.
41	*from the primal . . . lacked:* from the beginning of time that he who is in power (*is*) was supported (*wished*) until he came to power; and he whose fortunes are at their lowest (*the ebbed man*), unloved until he no longer deserved love, comes to be wanted in power (*comes deared*) just because he is not there (*by being lacked*).
44	*This common . . . motion:* The common people, like a reed (*flag*) in the stream moving aimlessly about (*vagabond*), go backwards and forwards, servilely following (*lackeying*) every change (*the varying tide*), wearing themselves out with this constant movement. – Caesar's contempt for the common people is strongly conveyed in his comparison of them to a servile creature bowing and scraping to everyone, and in his use of the word *rot*, which suggests a moral as well as a physical decay.
49	*Makes for Make.* – Cf. note to line 21 above.
49	*ear:* plough. – Cf. I.ii.102. The keels of the ships are seen as ploughshares which cut through (*wound*) the fields of the sea.
50	*hot inroads:* fierce raids.
51	*the borders . . . revolt:* those living on the sea-coast turn pale at the thought of it, and hot-blooded young men go over to Pompey's side (*revolt*).
53	*peep forth:* put its nose outside the harbour.
54	*Taken:* captured.
54	*strikes more . . . resisted:* damages us more than war against him (*his war*) could cause if we fought him (*resisted*).
56	*lascivious wassails:* indecent revelry.
58	*consuls* – Two consuls, the chief military and judicial Roman officials before the founding of the empire, were elected annually by the people of Rome.
59	*whom* – *Famine* is spoken of as if a personal enemy of Antony.

No way excuse his foils,* when we do bear
So great weight in his lightness.* If he filled
His vacancy with his voluptuousness,   25
Full surfeits and the dryness of his bones
Call on him for't.* But to confound such time
That drums him from his sport and speaks as loud
As his own state and ours – 'tis to be chid,
As we rate boys, who, being mature in knowledge,   30
Pawn their experience to their present pleasure,
And so rebel to judgement.*

Enter a MESSENGER.

LEPIDUS   Here's more news.
MESSENGER Thy biddings have been done, and every hour,
Most noble Caesar, shalt thou have report   35
How 'tis abroad. Pompey is strong at sea
And it appears he is beloved of those
That only have feared Caesar:* to the ports
The discontents repair,* and men's reports
Give him* much wronged.
CAESAR   I should have known no less.*   40
It hath been taught us from the primal state
That he which is was wished, until he were;
And the ebbed man, ne'er loved till ne'er worth love,
Comes deared by being lacked.* This common body,
Like to a vagabond flag upon the stream,   45
Goes to and back, lackeying the varying tide,
To rot itself with motion.*
MESSENGER   Caesar, I bring thee word
Menecrates and Menas, famous pirates,
Makes* the sea serve them, which they ear* and wound
With keels of every kind. Many hot inroads*   50
They make in Italy; the borders maritime
Lack blood to think on't, and flush youth revolt.*
No vessel can peep forth,* but 'tis as soon
Taken* as seen, for Pompey's name strikes more
Than could his war resisted.*
CAESAR   Antony,   55
Leave thy lascivious wassails.* When thou once
Was beaten from Modena, where thou slew'st
Hirtius and Pansa, consuls,* at thy heel
Did famine follow, whom* thou fought'st against

60	*daintily:* delicately.
61	*Than savages could suffer:* than that which men of the roughest breeding could endure.
62	*stale:* urine.
62	*gilded:* covered with yellow scum.
63	*cough at:* reject.
63	*did deign:* accepted as fit to eat.
64	*rudest:* coarsest.
65	*the pasture sheets:* covers the fields.
66	*The barks . . . browsed:* you fed on the barks of trees.
68	*to look on:* just by looking at.
71	*So much as lanked not:* did not even grow thin.
71	*'Tis pity of him:* His case is pitiful.
73	*we twain* – Octavius means himself and Lepidus.
75	*Assemble we:* let us order.
77	*furnished:* in a position.
78	*I can . . . time:* I shall be able to provide to face the present situation.
79	*Till which . . . too:* Until that meeting I shall be busy over the same problem.
81	*know:* learn.
82	*stirs:* events.
84	*I knew it for my bond:* I knew it was my duty to do so.

I.v.   In Alexandria, Cleopatra is restless at Antony's protracted absence. She sends messengers to him daily and all her thoughts centre on him. She imagines him thinking of her, indulges in self-pitying reflections on her age and wrinkles, and characteristically derives comfort from the thought of her former conquest of Julius Caesar and Gnaeus, the son of Pompey the Great. Alexas arrives with the gift of a pearl from Antony and the promise of all the kingdoms of the east.

The scene assures us that whatever is happening in Rome, Antony's affections are still firmly rooted in Egypt, and prepares us for his ultimate return. His promise of the eastern kingdoms points to future strife between him and Octavius, who could never sanction such a gift. Cleopatra's love for Antony is not in doubt, but it is expressed in her own inimitable fashion: a blend of selfishness as she glories in her power over men, and selflessness as she thinks of him. Her violence and inconsistency emerge in her threat to give Charmian bloody teeth, when Charmian has only been echoing Cleopatra's own praise of Julius Caesar.

| 3 | *mandragora:* the sleep-producing juice of the mandrake plant. |

(Though daintily* brought up) with patience more   60
Than savages could suffer.* Thou didst drink
The stale* of horses and the gilded* puddle
Which beasts would cough at.* Thy palate then did deign*
The roughest berry on the rudest* hedge.
Yea, like the stag, when snow the pasture sheets,*   65
The barks of trees thou browsed.* On the Alps
It is reported thou didst eat strange flesh,
Which some did die to look on.* And all this
(It wounds thine honour that I speak it now)
Was borne so like a soldier that thy cheek   70
So much as lanked not.*

LEPIDUS   'Tis pity of him.*
CAESAR   Let his shames quickly
Drive him to Rome. 'Tis time we twain*
Did show ourselves i' th'field, and to that end
Assemble we* immediate council. Pompey   75
Thrives in our idleness.

LEPIDUS   Tomorrow, Caesar,
I shall be furnished* to inform you rightly
Both what by sea and land I can be able
To front this present time.*

CAESAR   Till which encounter,
It is my business too.* Farewell.   80

LEPIDUS Farewell, my lord. What you shall know* meantime
Of stirs* abroad, I shall beseech you, sir,
To let me be partaker.

CAESAR   Doubt not, sir;
I knew it for my bond.*

                                              [Exeunt

scene v

Alexandria. CLEOPATRA'S *palace.*

Enter CLEOPATRA, CHARMIAN, IRAS *and* MARDIAN.

CLEOPATRA Charmian!
CHARMIAN Madam?
CLEOPATRA [*Yawning*] Ha, ha. Give me to drink mandragora.*

7   *'tis treason* – It is not clear whether Cleopatra means that Antony has betrayed her by his long absence, or that Charmian's suggestion that Cleopatra thinks of Antony too much is treason.

10   *'Tis well . . . Egypt:* You are lucky that, being sexless, your mind is not distracted by thoughts of a lover outside Egypt. – Cleopatra contrasts Mardian's state with her own. She pictures thoughts as seeds blown by the wind. Since Mardian is seedless (*unseminared*) his thoughts cannot fly outside Egypt.

12   *affections:* passions.

15   *in deed* – Mardian takes up Cleopatra's expression of surprise (*indeed*) in the sense of 'in action'.

16   *honest:* chaste.

18   *What Venus . . . Mars* – Venus, the goddess of love, and Mars, the god of war, were lovers.

19   *he* – i.e. Antony.

22   *Do bravely:* Bear yourself proudly.

22   *wot'st thou:* you know.

23   *demi-Atlas* – According to Greek mythology the heavens were supported on the head, hands and shoulders of the Titan, Atlas. Antony is a half-Atlas (*demi-Atlas*) because he bears up half the world in Cleopatra's view. Cleopatra ignores Lepidus, the third triumvir. This is one of the many images suggesting a superhuman power and quality in Antony.

23   *the arm . . . of men:* matchless in both attack and defence. – The *arm* is symbolic of offensive action; the *burgonet*, a light steel helmet of Burgundian origin, which left no chink between head and chest, of defence.

25   *serpent of old Nile* – The ancient Egyptians revered the serpent as both royal and sacred. The pharaohs wore headdresses decorated with the *uraeus* or sacred cobra. Ironically, Cleopatra takes Antony's phrase for her as wholly complimentary; for Shakespeare's audience, however, familiar with Satan's guise as serpent in the Garden of Eden, the epithet would carry suggestions of deception.

27   *delicious poison* – Thinking of Antony delights Cleopatra, but is also, paradoxically, a poison, since it makes her more conscious of his absence and so increases her suffering.

27   *Think* – She is addressing the absent Antony.

28   *with Phoebus . . . black:* burnt dark with the sun's rays. – As always, Cleopatra's choice of image reveals her nature. She pictures the sun-god as her lover, whose *amorous pinches* have bruised her skin black. The sun, a symbol of royalty, is linked with the serpent images, since it gives life to the serpent, and is thus one of an associated group of images underlining Cleopatra's royalty.

29   *Broad-fronted Caesar* – She refers to the broad forehead of Caesar, whose lover she had been in her youth.

30   *above the ground* – i.e. alive.

31   *a morsel:* a tempting delicacy. – Cf. III.xiii.116.

31   *Pompey* – i.e. Gnaeus, the son of Pompey the Great.

32   *make his eyes grow in my brow:* (a) fix his eyes on my face as if they grew there, (b) open his eyes wide in wonder at the sight of my face.

33   *anchor his aspéct:* fix his gaze.

34   *looking on his life:* looking at what gave him life.

36   *that great med'cine . . . thee:* Antony has imparted some of his vitality and colour to you. – Cleopatra describes Antony as the elixir of life (known as the *great medicine* or *tinct*) which the alchemists believed would give perpetual life and turn base metals to gold.

CHARMIAN	Why, madam?
CLEOPATRA	That I might sleep out this great gap of time 5
	My Antony is away.
CHARMIAN	You think of him too much.
CLEOPATRA	O, 'tis treason!*
CHARMIAN	Madam, I trust not so.
CLEOPATRA	Thou, eunuch Mardian!
MARDIAN	What's your highness' pleasure?
CLEOPATRA	Not now to hear thee sing. I take no pleasure
	In aught an eunuch has. 'Tis well for thee 10
	That, being unseminared, thy freer thoughts
	May not fly forth of Egypt.* Hast thou affections?*
MARDIAN	Yes, gracious madam.
CLEOPATRA	Indeed?
MARDIAN	Not in deed,* madam, for I can do nothing 15
	But what indeed is honest* to be done:
	Yet have I fierce affections, and think
	What Venus did with Mars.*
CLEOPATRA	O Charmian!
	Where think'st thou he* is now? Stands he, or sits he?
	Or does he walk? Or is he on his horse? 20
	O happy horse, to bear the weight of Antony!
	Do bravely,* horse, for wot'st thou* whom thou mov'st,
	The demi-Atlas* of this earth, the arm
	And burgonet of men.* He's speaking now,
	Or murmuring, 'Where's my serpent of old Nile?'* 25
	For so he calls me. Now I feed myself
	With most delicious poison.* Think* on me,
	That am with Phoebus' amorous pinches black,*
	And wrinkled deep in time. Broad-fronted Caesar*,
	When thou wast here above the ground,* I was 30
	A morsel* for a monarch: and great Pompey*
	Would stand and make his eyes grow in my brow;*
	There would he anchor his aspéct,* and die
	With looking on his life.*

Enter ALEXAS *from* ANTONY.

ALEXAS	Sovereign of Egypt, hail!
CLEOPATRA	How much unlike art thou Mark Antony! 35
	Yet coming from him, that great med'cine hath
	With his tinct gilded thee.*
	How goes it with my brave Mark Antony?

41   *orient:* (a) eastern (b) brightly-shining.
41   *sticks in my heart:* is riveted in my mind.
43   *firm:* constant.
44   *treasure of an oyster* – i.e. a pearl.
44   *at whose foot:* in addition to which.
45   *mend the petty present:* make this trivial present worth-while.
45   *piece:* (a) add to (b) mend. – Note the use of tailoring images, *mend, piece.*
46   *opulent* – An anticipatory use of the word. Cleopatra's kingdom will be *opulent* after Antony
          has added to it.
48   *soberly:* in a serious mood.
48   *arm-gaunt* – The meaning of this word, which occurs nowhere else, is uncertain. It has
          been variously conjectured to mean 'worn thin with hard service in armour',
          'hungry for battle', 'looking fierce in armour', 'ready for conflict'. Many
          scholars have considered the word textually corrupt and have proposed such
          emendations as 'arm-girt', 'arrogant,' 'termagant', 'war-gaunt'.
49   *high:* loudly. – See note to I.i.25.
50   *beastly dumbed by him:* silenced by this beast.
52   *nor . . . nor:* neither . . . nor.
53   *O well-divided disposition!:* What a well-balanced temperament!
54   *'tis the man:* that is Antony exactly.
54   *but:* only
55   *for he would . . . his:* because he wanted to appear cheerful to those who take their mood
          from his.
57   *remembrance:* thoughts.
58   *his joy:* the object of his joy, i.e. Cleopatra herself.
59   *mingle:* mixture.
60   *the violence . . . becomes:* the extreme of either (sadness or merriment) suits you.
61   *So does it:* as it does.
61   *posts:* messengers. – Post-horses were those kept constantly ready at various stages on
          the roads, and so were the fastest means of travel in Shakespeare's time.
62   *several:* separate.
63   *so thick:* so many in quick succession.
65   *Shall die a beggar:* will never prosper. – Cleopatra appears to think that Fate would punish
          such a person.
68   *Be choked . . . emphasis:* May you be choked if you sing Caesar's praises so openly again.
71   *paragon:* compare.
73   *I sing but after you:* I merely repeat what you have said.
73   *My salad days:* (Those were) my young days.

ALEXAS Last thing he did, dear Queen,
        He kissed – the last of many doubled kisses –   40
        This orient* pearl. His speech sticks in my heart.*
CLEOPATRA Mine ear must pluck it thence.
ALEXAS   'Good friend,' quoth he,
        'Say the firm* Roman to great Egypt sends
        This treasure of an oyster;* at whose foot*
        To mend the petty present,* I will piece*   45
        Her opulent* throne with kingdoms. All the east
        (Say thou) shall call her mistress.' So he nodded
        And soberly* did mount an arm-gaunt* steed,
        Who neighed so high* that what I would have spoke
        Was beastly dumbed by him.*
CLEOPATRA   What, was he sad or merry?   50
ALEXAS Like to the time o'th'year between the extremes
        Of hot and cold, he was nor sad nor merry.*
CLEOPATRA O well-divided disposition!* Note him,
        Note him, good Charmian, 'tis the man;* but* note him.
        He was not sad, for he would shine on those   55
        That make their looks by his;* he was not merry,
        Which seemed to tell them his remembrance* lay
        In Egypt with his joy;* but between both.
        O heavenly mingle*! Be'st thou sad or merry,
        The violence of either thee becomes,*   60
        So does it* no man else. – Met'st thou my posts?*
ALEXAS Ay, madam, twenty several* messengers.
        Why did you send so thick?*
CLEOPATRA   Who's born that day
        When I forget to send to Antony
        Shall die a beggar.* Ink and paper, Charmian.   65
        Welcome, my good Alexas. Did I, Charmian,
        Ever love Caesar so?
CHARMIAN   O that brave Caesar!
CLEOPATRA Be choked with such another emphasis!*
        Say 'the brave Antony'.
CHARMIAN   The valiant Caesar!
CLEOPATRA By Isis, I will give thee bloody teeth   70
        If thou with Caesar paragon* again
        My man of men.
CHARMIAN   By your most gracious pardon,
        I sing but after you.*
CLEOPATRA   My salad days,*

74   *green:* inexperienced.
78   *I'll unpeople Egypt* – i.e. by sending out messengers. The only reason for Cleopatra not
       sending daily messengers to Antony would be that she had run out of subjects.

When I was green* in judgement, cold in blood,
To say as I said then. But come, away,   75
Get me ink and paper.
He shall have every day a several greeting,
Or I'll unpeople Egypt.*

                                                          [*Exeunt*

II.i.   At Messina in Sicily, Pompey is in confident mood. His power is growing; he is supreme at sea; many Romans are flocking to join him, and he is aware of internal dissensions in the Triumvirate. His messengers tell him that Octavius and Lepidus have put a large army into the field against him and that Antony is expected at any moment in Rome. This latter news daunts him, since he is aware that Antony is a far better soldier than the others, but he feels flattered that he should have forced Antony to leave Egypt.

As often, Shakespeare is doing several things at once. He exposes Pompey's character to us, throws into relief the divisions between the triumvirs, and the hypocrisy of their mutual flattery, and so gives us an insight into the political realities and the unspoken motives that lie beneath the surface discussion of the following scene, thus enriching its dramatic quality.

1	*shall:* must.
3	*what they . . . deny:* what they delay to perform they are not refusing to perform.
4	*Whiles we . . . sue for:* While we pray to the gods the thing we are begging for is losing its value.
5	*of ourselves:* of what is best for us.
6	*our own harms:* what is harmful to us.
8	*I shall do well:* I am certain to prosper.
10	*crescent:* increasing.
10	*auguring hope . . . full:* prophetic hope tells me that it will soon be fulfilled. – In *crescent* and *come to the full,* Pompey describes his power and hopes for the future in terms of the waxing moon.
13	*without doors:* out-of-doors, i.e. outside Egypt, in contrast to the feasting indoors.
13	*Caesar gets . . . hearts:* Caesar loses the affection of those whom he taxes.
15	*Of:* by.
15	*he neither . . . him:* he loves neither (Caesar nor Antony) nor does either of them care for him.
17	*in the field:* ready for battle.
20	*Looking for:* waiting for.
20	*all the charms:* (may) all the magic spells.
21	*Salt:* lustful.
21	*soften thy waned lip:* give youthful fullness to your withered lips. – Pompey continues the moon metaphor. He wants Cleopatra to detain Antony in Egypt.
23	*libertine:* one given to immoral pleasures.
23	*a field of feasts* – where there is nothing but feasting (in contrast to the field of battle earlier mentioned).
24	*fuming:* fuddled with alcohol. – The Elizabethans believed that alcohol caused fumes to rise from the stomach to the brain, overthrowing the controlling reason.
24	*Epicurean cooks:* cooks skilled in catering to epicures, i.e. those who value highly the pleasures of eating and drinking. – The Greek philosopher Epicurus (341–270 B.C.) taught that the pleasures of the mind were the only good and that the highest pleasure was a perfect harmony of mind and body to be sought in plain living and virtue. His philosophy became debased with time; by the sixteenth century epicureanism had come to mean indiscriminate pleasure-seeking in sensual things.
25	*cloyless sauce:* sauce so piquant that it cannot satisfy (cloy) the appetite it sharpens.
26	*prorogue . . . dullness:* make him put off (*prorogue*) honourable action until he becomes oblivious to all sense of honour. – *Lethe,* a river in Hades whose waters induced forgetfulness when they were drunk.
27	*How now:* What is it?

ACT II scene i

Messina. POMPEY'S *house.*

Enter POMPEY, MENECRATES *and* MENAS, *in warlike manner.*

POMPEY If the great gods be just, they shall* assist
       The deeds of justest men.

MENECRATES   Know, worthy Pompey,
       That what they do delay, they not deny.*

POMPEY Whiles we are suitors to their throne, decays
       The thing we sue for.*

MENECRATES   We, ignorant of ourselves,*   5
       Beg often our own harms,* which the wise powers
       Deny us for our good; so find we profit
       By losing of our prayers.

POMPEY   I shall do well:*
       The people love me, and the sea is mine;
       My powers are crescent,* and my auguring hope   10
       Says it will come to th' full.* Mark Antony
       In Egypt sits at dinner, and will make
       No wars without doors.* Caesar gets money where
       He loses hearts.* Lepidus flatters both,
       Of* both is flattered, but he neither loves,   15
       Nor either cares for him.*

MENECRATES   Caesar and Lepidus
       Are in the field;* a mighty strength they carry.

POMPEY Where have you this? 'Tis false.

MENECRATES   From Silvius, sir.

POMPEY He dreams: I know they are in Rome together
       Looking for* Antony. But all the charms* of love,   20
       Salt* Cleopatra, soften thy waned lip!*
       Let witchcraft join with beauty, lust with both!
       Tie up the libertine* in a field of feasts,*
       Keep his brain fuming.* Epicurean cooks*
       Sharpen with cloyless sauce* his appetite,   25
       That sleep and feeding may prorogue his honour
       Even till a Lethe'd dullness – *

Enter VARRIUS.

                How now,* Varrius?

28	*deliver:* announce.
30	*'tis / A space . . . travel:* there has been time for him to have travelled farther than to Rome.
31	*I could . . . ear:* I would have been more willing to hear less important news.
33	*amorous surfeiter:* lover given to excesses.
33	*donned his helm:* put on his helmet.
34	*His soldiership . . . twain:* His skill as a soldier is twice as great as that of the other two (Octavius and Lepidus).
35	*rear . . . opinion:* think more highly of ourselves.
37	*Egypt's widow* – i.e. Cleopatra, formerly married to her brother. See note to I.iv.6.
38	*ne'er lust-wearied:* never exhausted by pleasure.
39	*well greet:* meet each other amicably.
40	*did trespasses:* opposed and attacked.
42	*moved:* incited.
43	*How lesser . . . greater:* how far the smaller reasons for enmity (between Caesar and Antony) may be forgotten in the presence of their greater enmity (towards me).
45	*pregnant:* obvious.
45	*square:* quarrel.
46	*entertainèd:* received (from each other).
48	*cément their divisions:* patch up their quarrel.
50	*It only . . . hands:* Our lives depend solely on the use of our utmost strength.

II.ii.	At the meeting of the triumvirs in Rome, Antony, in reply to the complaints of Caesar, assures him that he had nothing to do with the wars waged against him by his wife and brother, that he was not sober when he rejected Octavius's messenger in Alexandria, and that he had neglected, not refused, the arms and aid he had promised him. Lepidus and Maecenas urge their reconciliation and Arippa proposes that it be cemented by the marriage of Antony to Caesar's sister, Octavia. Antony agrees. When the triumvirs have left to see Octavia and plan their campaign against Pompey, Maecenas and Agrippa eagerly question Enobarbus about Cleopatra and about life in Alexandria. He describes the first meeting of Cleopatra and Antony on the river Cydnus, and assures them that Antony will never leave her for Octavia.
	The scene underlines the irreconcilable differences between Octavius and Antony. We get several pointers that the alliance is a patched-up affair, its motivation political not personal. Octavius remarks ominously that their 'conditions' are 'so differing', and Enobarbus's certainty that Octavia's beauty, wisdom and modesty will prove no match for Cleopatra, who 'pursed up' Antony's heart at their first meeting by her mysterious magnetism, persuades us of the precariousness of this political reconciliation which is made to rest on Antony's fidelity to Octavia.

2	*become you well:* be very fitting for you. – Lepidus flatters Enobarbus: the worthy deed requires a worthy person to perform it.

VARRIUS This is most certain that I shall deliver:*
         Mark Antony is every hour in Rome
         Expected. Since he went from Egypt 'tis   30
         A space for farther travel.*
POMPEY   I could have given less matter
         A better ear.* Menas, I did not think
         This amorous surfeiter* would have donned his helm*
         For such a petty war. His soldiership
         Is twice the other twain;* but let us rear   35
         The higher our opinion,* that our stirring
         Can from the lap of Egypt's widow* pluck
         The ne'er lust-wearied Antony.*
MENAS   I cannot hope
         Caesar and Antony shall well greet* together:
         His wife that's dead did trespasses* to Caesar;   40
         His brother warred upon him, although I think
         Not moved* by Antony.
POMPEY   I know not, Menas,
         How lesser enmities may give way to greater.*
         Were't not that we stand up against them all,
         'Twere pregnant* they should square* between themselves, 45
         For they have entertainèd* cause enough
         To draw their swords; but how the fear of us
         May cément their divisions* and bind up
         The petty difference, we yet not know.
         Be't as our gods will have't! It only stands   50
         Our lives upon to use our strongest hands.*
         Come, Menas.
                                                    [*Exeunt*

scene ii

Rome. The house of LEPIDUS.

Enter ENOBARBUS *and* LEPIDUS.

LEPIDUS Good Enobarbus, 'tis a worthy deed,
         And shall become you well,* to entreat your captain
         To soft and gentle speech.

4	*like himself:* in a manner worthy of him.
4	*move:* anger.
5	*Let Antony . . . head:* I hope Antony will treat Caesar with contempt.
6	*as loud as Mars* – Enobarbus apparently thinks of Mars, the god of war, as having a voice as loud as the noise of battle.
8	*I would not shave't:* (a) I would not bother to show Caesar the courtesy of meeting him freshly shaved, or (b) I would not remove the temptation for Caesar to pluck it if he dare. – In Shakespeare's time to pluck another's beard was tantamount to challenging him to a fight. Enobarbus is so bluntly unwilling that Antony should make any concessions to Caesar that he possibly intends both meanings.
9	*private stomaching:* personal resentment.
9	*Every time . . . in't:* Matters can be pursued whenever they arise. – Enobarbus rejects all appeals that he should persuade Antony to be tactful in his meeting with Caesar.
12	*Not if . . . first* – Enobarbus counters the argument of Lepidus that trifling matters must give way to important ones, by pointing out that if the *small matters* occur before the great ones they take precedence and cannot be said to *give way.*
12	*passion:* emotional (as opposed to rational).
13	*stir no embers up:* do not rake up old quarrels.
15	*compose well:* reach a satisfactory agreement.
15	*to Parthia:* we will set out for Parthia. – Antony and Caesar studiously avoid talking to each other, leaving Lepidus to try to reconcile them.
18	*That which combined us:* the reason which led to our alliance in the Triumvirate.
19	*A leaner action:* a matter of much less importance.
19	*rend:* divide.
19	*What's amiss . . . heard:* Whatever is wrong, let it be stated politely.
21	*loud:* loudly. – See note to I.i.25.
21	*we do . . . wounds:* we are like a clumsy surgeon who kills his patient in healing his wounds.
23	*The rather . . . beseech:* all the more readily because it is I who request it.
24	*Touch you . . . terms:* discuss the most controversial points with the utmost politeness.
25	*Nor curstness . . . matter:* do not allow ill-temper to increase our differences.
26	*and to fight:* and about to fight.
27	*I should do thus* – At this point Antony perhaps shakes Caesar's hand or embraces him, though possibly he simply means that he would speak temperately, as Lepidus has suggested, whatever the situation.

ENOBARBUS   I shall entreat him
To answer like himself:* if Caesar move* him,
Let Antony look over Caesar's head*   5
And speak as loud as Mars.* By Jupiter,
Were I the wearer of Antonio's beard,
I would not shave't* today.
LEPIDUS   'Tis not a time
For private stomaching.*
ENOBARBUS   Every time
Serves for the matter that is then born in't.*   10
LEPIDUS But small to greater matters must give way.
ENOBARBUS Not if the small come first.*
LEPIDUS   Your speech is passion;*
But pray you, stir no embers up.* Here comes
The noble Antony.

Enter ANTONY *and* VENTIDIUS *talking together.*

ENOBARBUS   And yonder, Caesar.

Enter CAESAR, MAECENAS *and* AGRIPPA *from the other side.*

ANTONY If we compose well* here, to Parthia.*   15
Hark, Ventidius.
CAESAR   I do not know,
Maecenas; ask Agrippa.
LEPIDUS   Noble friends,
That which combined us* was most great, and let not
A leaner action* rend* us. What's amiss,
May it be gently heard.* When we debate   20
Our trivial difference loud,* we do commit
Murder in healing wounds.* Then, noble partners,
The rather for I earnestly beseech,*
Touch you the sourest points with sweetest terms,*
Nor curstness grow to th' matter.*
ANTONY   'Tis spoken well.   25
Were we before our armies, and to fight,*
I should do thus.*
                                        [*Flourish*
CAESAR Welcome to Rome.
ANTONY Thank you.
CAESAR Sit.   30
ANTONY Sit, sir.

32	*Nay then:* Well, if you insist. – He sits down.
34	*Or being:* or, if they are offensive (*ill*).
34	*must be:* would deserve to be.
35	*or . . . or:* either . . . or.
36	*say myself . . . world:* say that I have been offended – and offended by you in particular.
37	*more laughed at, that:* (deserve to be) laughed at all the more, if . . .
38	*derogately:* disparagingly.
38	*when to sound . . . me:* when talking about you was none of my business.
40	*what was't to you:* concern of yours was it.
43	*Did practise . . . state:* plotted against my authority.
44	*my question:* a matter for me to investigate.
44	*How . . . 'practised':* What do you mean by that word 'practised'?
45	*You may . . . me:* You may if you wish understand my meaning from what happened to me here in Rome.
47	*contestation:* conflict.
48	*Was theme for you:* had you as its subject.
48	*you were . . . war:* the war was about you.
49	*mistake your business:* your anxiety (*business*) is mistaken.
50	*urge me in his act:* make use of my name in his wars.
50	*did inquire it:* made inquiries about it.
51	*learning:* information.
52	*That drew their swords with you:* from men who fought on your side.
53	*Discredit . . . yours:* bring my authority into discredit along with yours. – Antony argues that his brother, in defying the authority of one triumvir, defied them all.
54	*stomach:* desire.
55	*Having alike your cause:* since I have the same interests as you.
56	*If you'll . . . this:* If you insist on creating a quarrel out of odds and ends of material (*patch*) even when (*As*) you have a whole piece of cloth (*matter whole*) to make it from, you must not do it with this scrap, i.e. this feeble argument about my brother's behaviour.
59	*laying:* imputing.
60	*patched up your excuses:* worked up some unconvincing excuses.
61	*lack:* fail (to understand).
62	*Very necessity . . . thought:* the thought was inescapable.
64	*with graceful . . . attend:* look favourably on.
65	*fronted:* opposed.
66	*you had . . . another:* you had a wife with such a formidable spirit as hers.
67	*a snaffle . . . easy:* you may easily keep under control with a light bridle. – A *snaffle* is a horse's bridle-bit a curb, used with tractable animals.

CAESAR   Nay, then.* [*He sits, followed by* ANTONY]
ANTONY   I learn you take things ill which are not so,
          Or being,* concern you not.
CAESAR   I must be* laughed at
          If, or for nothing, or a little,* I   35
          Should say myself offended, and with you
          Chiefly i' th' world;* more laughed at, that* I should
          Once name you derogately,* when to sound your name
          It not concerned me.*
ANTONY   My being in Egypt,
          Caesar, what was't to you?*   40
CAESAR   No more than my residing here at Rome
          Might be to you in Egypt: yet if you there
          Did practise on my state,* your being in Egypt
          Might be my question.*
ANTONY   How intend you, 'practised'?*
CAESAR   You may be pleased to catch at mine intent   45
          By what did here befall me.* Your wife and brother
          Made wars upon me, and their contestation*
          Was theme for you;* you were the word of war.*
ANTONY   You do mistake your business;* my brother never
          Did urge me in his act.* I did inquire it,*   50
          And have my learning* from some true reports
          That drew their swords with you.* Did he not rather
          Discredit my authority with yours,*
          And make the wars alike against my stomach,*
          Having alike your cause?* Of this, my letters   55
          Before did satisfy you. If you'll patch a quarrel,
          As matter whole you have to make it with,
          It must not be with this.*
CAESAR   You praise yourself
          By laying* defects of judgement to me, but
          You patched up your excuses.*
ANTONY   Not so, not so: 60
          I know you could not lack,* I am certain on't,
          Very necessity of this thought,* that I
          Your partner in the cause 'gainst which he fought,
          Could not with graceful eyes attend* those wars
          Which fronted* mine own peace. As for my wife,   65
          I would you had her spirit in such another:*
          The third o' th' world is yours, which with a snaffle
          You may pace easy,* but not such a wife.

71   *much uncurbable:* uncontrollable.
72   *not wanted . . . policy:* was not lacking in political astuteness.
73   *grieving grant . . . disquiet:* regretfully admit caused you too much trouble.
75   *But:* only.
77   *pocket up:* put, unread, in your pocket.
77   *with taunts . . . audience:* drove my messenger (*missive*) out of your presence (*audience*)
         with contemptuous remarks.
79   *fell . . . admitted:* burst in on me suddenly before obtaining permission to enter.
80   *did want/Of what I was:* was not as sober as I had been.
82   *told him of myself:* explained my condition to him.
84   *nothing of:* no part of.
85   *question:* conversation.
86   *article:* exact terms.
87   *Have tongue . . . with:* be able to say about me.
87   *Soft:* Go carefully. – Lepidus is afraid that Caesar's words will provoke Antony to anger
         and prevent the reconciliation he hopes for.
89   *The honour . . . it:* the honour he is now speaking about, which he supposes that I lack,
         is a sacred matter.
90   *on, Caesar:* go on, Caesar, with what you were saying about . . .
93   *The which . . . denied:* both of which you refused.
94   *poisoned hours . . . knowledge:* harmful pleasures had overcome me so that I forgot myself.
95   *As nearly as I may:* As far as I can (without dishonour).
96   *play the penitent:* confess my faults.
96   *mine honesty . . . it:* my frankness (in admitting my faults) will not diminish my great-
         ness, nor will I use my power dishonourably (*without it,* i.e. honesty).
99   *To have:* in order to get.
100 *ignorant motive:* unconscious cause.
102 *noble* for *nobly.* – See note to I.i.25.
103 *enforce:* emphasize.
104 *griefs:* grievances.

ENOBARBUS Would we had all such wives, that the men might go to
    wars with the women!   70
ANTONY So much uncurbable,* her garboils, Caesar,
    Made out of her impatience (which not wanted
    Shrewdness of policy* too), I grieving grant
    Did you too much disquiet:* for that you must
    But* say, I could not help it.
CAESAR   I wrote to you: 75
    When rioting in Alexandria you
    Did pocket up* my letters, and with taunts
    Did gibe my missive out of audience.*
ANTONY   Sir,
    He fell upon me, ere admitted,* then.
    Three kings I had newly feasted, and did want 80
    Of what I was* i' th' morning; but next day
    I told him of myself,* which was as much
    As to have asked him pardon. Let this fellow
    Be nothing of* our strife: if we contend,
    Out of our question* wipe him.
CAESAR   You have broken 85
    The article* of your oath, which you shall never
    Have tongue to charge me with.*
LEPIDUS   Soft,* Caesar!
ANTONY No, Lepidus, let him speak;
    The honour is sacred which he talks on now,
    Supposing that I lacked it.* But on, Caesar,* 90
    The article of my oath.
CAESAR To lend me arms and aid when I required them,
    The which you both denied.*
ANTONY   Neglected, rather.
    And then when poisoned hours had bound me up
    From mine own knowledge.* As nearly as I may,* 95
    I'll play the penitent* to you; but mine honesty
    Shall not make poor my greatness, nor my power
    Work without it.* Truth is, that Fulvia,
    To have* me out of Egypt, made wars here,
    For which myself, the ignorant motive,* do 100
    So far ask pardon as befits mine honour
    To stoop in such a case.
LEPIDUS   'Tis noble* spoken.
MAECENAS If it might please you, to enforce* no further
    The griefs* between ye, to forget them quite,

105	*Were to remember:* would show that you are aware.
106	*speaks to atone you:* demands that you should be reconciled.
107	Enobarbus's speech expresses his scepticism about the reconciliation of Antony and Caesar. The *love*, he cynically implies, will be replaced by the old wrangling as soon as Pompey is disposed of.
111	*a soldier only,* and therefore, Antony implies, ignorant of politics.
113	*presence:* distinguished company.
114	*Go to . . . stone:* Very well, then; I will be as silent as a stone, though that will not stop me thinking. – *Considerate:* reflective.
116	*his,* i.e. Enobarbus's. Caesar disapproves of the bluntness and lack of respect of Enobarbus's manner of speech, but agrees with the substance of what he says.
117	*our conditions . . . acts:* since our dispositions lead us to act so differently.
119	*hoop . . . staunch:* bond would hold us firmly together. – The image is taken from the cooper's practice of strengthening barrels by the use of iron hoops. Caesar implies that firm friendship between them will bring security to the whole world.
119	*edge to edge:* end to end. – Many Elizabethans thought that the world was a flat plane, thus having edges.
120	*leave:* permission to speak. – There is a strong contrast between Agrippa's *manner* and that of Enobarbus.
122	*the mother's side* – Plutarch mistakenly thought that Octavia had a different mother from Octavius and so was his half-sister. In fact they had the same mother, Atia. Shakespeare repeats Plutarch's error.
125	*your reproof . . . rashness:* you would fully deserve censure for your rashness.
131	*take Antony:* let Antony take.
132	*claims / No worse:* demands no less.
134	*general graces . . . utter:* general excellent qualities are such as no one else can boast.
136	*jealousies:* suspicions.
137	*import their dangers:* carry with them their own dangers.
138	*truths would . . . truths:* disturbing facts would be disbelieved, whereas at the moment half-truths are believed.
140	*Would each . . . her:* would compel Antony and Caesar to love each other, and everyone else to love them both.
142	*a studied . . . ruminated:* an idea I have long thought about (*studied*) which has been turning over in my mind (*ruminated*) prompted by my duty to you, not one which has just occurred to me (*present*).

Were to remember* that the present need   105
Speaks to atone you.*

LEPIDUS   Worthily spoken, Maecenas.

ENOBARBUS Or if you borrow one another's love for the instant, you may,
when you hear no more words of Pompey, return it again:
you shall have time to wrangle in when you have nothing
else to do.*   110

ANTONY Thou art a soldier only;* speak no more.

ENOBARBUS That truth should be silent I had almost forgot.

ANTONY You wrong this presence;* therefore speak no more.

ENOBARBUS Go to, then; your considerate stone.*

CAESAR I do not much dislike the matter, but   115
The manner of his* speech; for't cannot be
We shall remain in friendship, our conditions
So differing in their acts.* Yet if I knew
What hoop should hold us staunch* from edge to edge*
O' th' world, I would pursue it.

AGRIPPA   Give me leave,* Caesar.   120

CAESAR Speak, Agrippa.

AGRIPPA Thou hast a sister by the mother's side,*
Admired Octavia. Great Mark Antony
Is now a widower.

CAESAR   Say not so, Agrippa:
If Cleopatra heard you, your reproof   125
Were well deserved of rashness.*

ANTONY I am not married, Caesar: let me hear
Agrippa further speak.

AGRIPPA To hold you in perpetual amity,
To make you brothers, and to knit your hearts   130
With an unslipping knot, take Antony*
Octavia to his wife; whose beauty claims
No worse* a husband than the best of men;
Whose virtue and whose general graces speak
That which none else can utter.* By this marriage   135
All little jealousies* which now seem great,
And all great fears which now import their dangers,*
Would then be nothing: truths would be tales,
Where now half tales be truths:* her love to both
Would each to other and all loves to both   140
Draw after her.* Pardon what I have spoke,
For 'tis a studied, not a present thought,
By duty ruminated.*

144   *how Antony . . . / With:* what Antony thinks of.
147   *make this good:* bring this about.
148   *unto:* with regard to.
149   *so fairly shows:* looks so promising.
150   *Dream of impediment:* dream of raising any objection.
150   *thy* – Antony changes from the formal pronoun *you* to the more friendly and familiar *thy*.
            Caesar continues to use *you*.
151   *Further this act of grace:* to support this gracious act, i.e. the giving of Octavia in marriage.
152   *The heart . . . designs:* may brotherly love rule our hearts and direct our great plans.
156   *never / Fly off . . . again:* may our love for each other never desert us.
157   *Happily:* This has ended happily.
158   *laid strange courtesies:* done unusual favours.
161   *Lest . . . report:* if my reputation for remembering favours done to me is not to be attacked.
162   *At heel . . . him:* immediately after that has been done, I must challenge him to battle.
162   *upon's:* upon us.
163   *Of:* By.
163   *presently:* at once.
164   *seeks:* will seek.
165   *About:* Near. – *Mesena,* correctly spelt *Misenum,* was an Italian port near Naples.
168   *So is the fame:* So the rumour goes.
169   *spoke together:* joined battle.
169   *for it:* to prepare for it.
170   *despatch we:* let us conclude.
171   *The business* – i.e. the marriage with Octavia. The term reflects the nature of the marriage.
171   *most:* the utmost.
172   *my sister's view:* see my sister.
175   *not sickness should:* not even sickness would.

ANTONY   Will Caesar speak?
CAESAR Not till he hears how Antony is touched
        With* what is spoke already.
ANTONY   What power is in Agrippa,   145
        If I would say, 'Agrippa be it so,'
        To make this good?*
CAESAR   The power of Caesar, and
        His power unto* Octavia.
ANTONY   May I never
        To this good purpose, that so fairly shows,*
        Dream of impediment!* Let me have thy* hand   150
        Further this act of grace;* and from this hour,
        The heart of brothers govern in our loves
        And sway our great designs!*
CAESAR   There's my hand.
        A sister I bequeath you, whom no brother
        Did ever love so dearly. Let her live   155
        To join our kingdoms and our hearts, and never
        Fly off our loves again!*
LEPIDUS   Happily,* amen.
ANTONY I did not think to draw my sword 'gainst Pompey,
        For he hath laid strange courtesies* and great
        Of late upon me. I must thank him only,   160
        Lest my remembrance suffer ill report:*
        At heel of that, defy him.*
LEPIDUS   Time calls upon's.*
        Of* us must Pompey presently* be sought,
        Or else he seeks* out us.
ANTONY Where lies he?
CAESAR   About* the Mount Mesena.   165
ANTONY What is his strength by land?
CAESAR   Great and increasing;
        But by sea he is an absolute master.
ANTONY So is the fame.*
        Would we had spoke together!* Haste we for it:*
        Yet ere we put ourselves in arms, despatch we*   170
        The business* we have talked of.
CAESAR   With most* gladness,
        And do invite you to my sister's view,*
        Whither straight I'll lead you.
ANTONY Let us, Lepidus, not lack your company.
LEPIDUS Noble Antony, not sickness should detain me.*   175

177   *Half the heart* – i.e. Close friend.
180   *disgested:* settled. – This is an old form of *digest*.
181   *stayed well by't:* had a good time of it.
182   *we did . . . countenance:* we disconcerted the day (by treating it as night and sleeping
            through it).
183   *light:* (a) bright (b) merry.
186   *by:* compared with.
187   *monstrous . . . feast:* astounding kinds of feast.
188   *triumphant:* magnificent.
188   *square:* faithful.
189   *pursed up:* put in her purse, i.e. took total possession of.
190   *Cydnus* was a river in Cilicia in Asia Minor.
191   *appeared indeed:* appeared in all her glory.
191   *devised well:* invented freely.
194   *burnished:* polished.
195   *the poop . . . gold:* the stern was covered in sheets of hammered gold.
197   *The winds . . . them:* the winds were so enamoured of the sails that they pursued them,
            filling them out.
199   *to follow faster* – The water, in rushing to fill the vacuum made by the oars in the water,
            seemed to be in love with them.
200   *As amorous:* as if in love with.
200   *For:* As for.
201   *beggared all description:* made any description of her (no matter how spendid) seem
            beggarly in comparison with the reality.
202   *pavilion,* a large tent or awning.
202   *cloth of gold, of tissue* was a rich fabric having twisted silk threads running one way (the
            warp), and gold threads (the woof) running the other.
203   *O'er-picturing . . . nature:* looking more beautiful (*o'er-picturing*) than the painting of
            Venus in which the imagination of the artist (*fancy*) has created a beauty
            greater than that found in nature.
205   *smiling cupids* – Cupid, the Roman god of love, was from Roman times represented in
            art as a naked baby boy with dimpled cheeks.
206   *did seem . . . did:* seemed to make the delicate cheeks they cooled burn instead, thus
            reversing their cooling effect. – The paradox in which fanning caused heat
            (*did*) is only an apparent one, as the verb *seem* indicates. Cleopatra's glowing
            cheeks were not caused by the fans, but by her own excitement at the prospect
            of her confrontation with Antony.
208   *O, rare for Antony:* What a splendid experience for Antony! – Enobarbus's description
            has stressed the uniqueness of Cleopatra and her barge with its golden poop,
            purple sails, silver oars and silken tackle.
209   *Nereides* – i.e. the fifty daughters of Nereus the sea-god, sea nymphs having human shape.
210   *So many mermaids:* like mermaids.
210   *tended her . . . adornings:* waited upon her in her sight, and their graceful movements
            (*bends*) made an ornamental frame around her (*adornings*).
212   *A seeming mermaid:* a gentlewoman disguised as a mermaid.
213   *Swell . . . hands:* swell with pride at the touch of hands as delicately soft as the bloom of
            flower-petals. – *Swell* is plural since *tackle,* including sails, ropes and rigging,
            is treated as a collective plural.

Flourish. Exeunt all escept ENOBARBUS, AGRIPPA *and*
MAECENAS.

MAECENAS Welcome from Egypt, sir.

ENOBARBUS Half the heart* of Caesar, worthy Maecenas! My honourable
friend Agrippa!

AGRIPPA Good Enobarbus!

MAECENAS We have cause to be glad that matters are so well disgested.*   180
You stayed well by't* in Egypt.

ENOBARBUS Ay, sir, we did sleep day out of countenance,* and made the
night light* with drinking.

MAECENAS Eight wild boars roasted whole at a breakfast, and but
twelve persons there. Is this true?   185

ENOBARBUS This was but as a fly by* an eagle: we had much more
monstrous matter of feast,* which worthily deserved noting.

MAECENAS She's a most triumphant* lady, if report be square* to her.

ENOBARBUS When she first met Mark Antony, she pursed up* his heart
upon the river of Cydnus.*   190

AGRIPPA There she appeared indeed,* or my reporter devised well*
for her.

ENOBARBUS I will tell you.
The barge she sat in, like a burnished* throne
Burned on the water: the poop was beaten gold;*   195
Purple the sails, and so perfumèd that
The winds were love-sick with them;* the oars were silver,
Which to the tune of flutes kept stroke, and made
The water which they beat to follow faster,*
As amorous of their strokes.* For* her own person,   200
It beggared all description:* she did lie
In her pavilion,* cloth of gold, of tissue,*
O'er-picturing that Venus where we see
The fancy outwork nature.* On each side her
Stood pretty dimpled boys, like smiling Cupids,*   205
With divers-coloured fans, whose wind did seem
To glow the delicate cheeks which they did cool,
And what they undid did.*

AGRIPPA   O, rare for Antony!*

ENOBARBUS Her gentlewomen, like the Nereides,*
So many mermaids,* tended her i' th' eyes,   210
And made their bends adornings.* At the helm
A seeming mermaid* steers: the silken tackle
Swell with the touches of those flower-soft hands*

214   *yarely frame the office:* promptly perform the task.
216   *the adjacent wharfs* – i.e. the people on the nearby river banks.
217   *upon her:* to see her.
219   *but for . . . gone:* if it had not been for the fact that it would have caused a vacuum, would
                  have gone.
226   *Whom ne'er . . . speak:* whom no woman ever heard say 'No'.
227   *Being barbered:* having had his beard trimmed.
228   *for his ordinary:* as the price of his supper. – In Shakespeare's time the *ordinary* was a
                  public dinner at a tavern or eating-house in which each man paid for himself.
                  It was cheaper than a private meal. Antony, however, instead of saving, paid
                  his heart and could eat nothing. All he could do was consume Cleopatra with
                  his eyes.
                       The terms in which Enobarbus describes Antony – whistling to keep up
                  his courage, being repeatedly barbered, and going to the *ordinary* – serve to
                  accentuate his nervousness and helplessness in the face of Cleopatra's magnifi-
                  cence and magnetism. Her careful stage-management of the scene has the
                  effect she intends.
230   *Caesar . . . bed:* Julius Caesar put away his sword.
231   *cropped:* had a child,. i.e. Caesarion.
234   *That she . . . forth:* in such a way that she made her panting, a defect, seem a perfection,
                  and though breathless she breathed charm. – *Perfection* has four syllables
                  here.
238   *custom stale . . . variety* – Cleopatra's behaviour is so endlessly varied that she never loses
                  her fascination through repetition.
239   *cloy:* satiate to the point of disgust.
242   *Become themselves:* are attractive.
242   *that:* so that.
243   *riggish:* wanton.
246   *blessed lottery:* adorable prize.
248   *abide here:* stay in Rome.

That yarely frame the office.* From the barge
A strange invisible perfume hits the sense   215
Of the adjacent wharfs.* The city cast
Her people out upon her, and Antony,
Enthroned i' th' market-place, did sit alone,
Whistling to th' air, which, but for vacancy,
Had gone* to gaze on Cleopatra too,   220
And made a gap in nature.

AGRIPPA   Rare Egyptian!

ENOBARBUS Upon her landing, Antony sent to her,
Invited her to supper. She replied,
It should be better he became her guest,
Which she entreated. Our courteous Antony,   225
Whom ne'er the word of 'No' woman heard speak,*
Being barbered* ten times o'er, goes to the feast,
And, for his ordinary,* pays his heart
For what his eyes eat only.

AGRIPPA   Royal wench!
She made great Caesar lay his sword to bed:*   230
He ploughed her, and she cropped.*

ENOBARBUS   I saw her once
Hop forty paces through the public street,
And having lost her breath, she spoke, and panted,
That she did make defect perfection,
And, breathless, power breathe forth.*   235

MAECENAS Now Antony must leave her utterly.

ENOBARBUS Never; he will not.
Age cannot wither her, nor custom stale
Her infinite variety:* other women cloy*
The appetites they feed, but she makes hungry   240
Where most she satisfies; for vilest things
Become themselves* in her, that* the holy priests
Bless her when she is riggish.*

MAECENAS If beauty, wisdom, modesty, can settle
The heart of Antony, Octavia is   245
A blessed lottery* to him.

AGRIPPA   Let us go.
Good Enobarbus, make yourself my guest
Whilst you abide here*.

ENOBARBUS   Humbly, sir, I thank you.

                                              [Exeunt

II.iii.   The scene opens with the conclusion of Antony's introduction by Caesar to Octavia. Antony admits his former backsliding but promises to reform. The Soothsayer, alone with Antony, prophesies that Caesar's fortunes will outshine Antony's, and warns him to get away from Caesar, so that his guardian spirit, overshadowed in Caesar's presence, can regain its nobility. This is why Antony loses all sporting contests against Caesar, he says. When the Soothsayer has gone Antony concedes the truth of what he has said. He reveals that his intention in marrying Octavia was to secure peace, but that he intends to return to Cleopatra. He arranges to give Ventidius his orders for the military campaign against the Parthians.

The scene shows Antony's fatally divided mind. A few moments after promising reform, possibly sincerely intended when he spoke it, we find him resolving to return to Cleopatra. Shakespeare carefully mitigates the loss of audience sympathy for Antony in two ways: firstly, by the evidence of Antony's diminution in Caesar's presence, which he can do nothing to avoid, so that we accept his decision to leave Rome, and secondly, by the fact that he does not immediately leave Octavia for Cleopatra. Antony's revelation, however, amounts to a declaration of war with Caesar.

*   The entry of Octavia between Caesar and Antony is a forceful visual symbol of her role in keeping them together, and later in keeping them apart. Cf. the report of the messenger to Cleopatra, III.iii.9-10.

1   *The world . . . office:* State affairs and my heavy duties as triumvir.
2   *Divide:* separate.
2   *All which time:* Whenever that happens.
5   *Read not . . . report:* do not believe what the general rumours say about my faults.
6   *not kept my square:* wandered off the right path. – The carpenter's *square,* a set square for measuring right angles, is used here to mean a guide to right action.
6   *that to come . . . rule* – i.e. I will go straight in future. The *rule* is another of the carpenter's tools.
10   *sirrah* was a term used in addressing social inferiors.
11   *Would I . . . thither:* I wish I had never left there, and that you had never gone there.
12   *your reason:* (give me) your reason.
13   *I see . . . tongue:* I feel it intuitively but cannot explain. – *Motion,* a movement of the brain, i.e. intuition.
13   *hie you:* go quickly.
19   *Thy demon . . . thee:* Your guardian angel, that spirit of yours which safeguards (*keeps*) you.
21   *Where Caesar's is not:* where Caesar's *demon* is not present.
23   *Make space enough:* put as much distance as you can.
24   *no more but when to thee:* never except when I speak to you.
26   *of:* because of.
27   *'gainst the odds:* even when the chances (*odds*) are in your favour.
27   *Thy lustre thickens:* Your brilliance is dimmed.
28   *by:* near by.
30   *he away:* when he is not there.

scene iii

Rome. CAESAR'S *house.*

Enter ANTONY *and* CAESAR *with* OCTAVIA *between them.**

ANTONY   The world and my great office* will sometimes
                Divide* me from your bosom.

OCTAVIA   All which time*
                Before the gods my knee shall bow my prayers
                To them for you.

ANTONY   Good night, sir. My Octavia,
                Read not my blemishes in the world's report:*   5
                I have not kept my square,* but that to come
                Shall all be done by th' rule.* Good night, dear lady.

OCTAVIA   Good night, sir.

CAESAR   Good night.
                                [*Exeunt* CAESAR *and* OCTAVIA

Enter SOOTHSAYER.

ANTONY   Now, sirrah;* you do wish yourself in Egypt?   10

SOOTHSAYER Would I had never come from thence, nor you thither.*

ANTONY   If you can, your reason?*

SOOTHSAYER I see it in my motion, have it not in my tongue;* but yet hie
            you* to Egypt again.

ANTONY   Say to me, whose fortunes shall rise higher,   15
            Caesar's or mine?

SOOTHSAYER Caesar's.
            Therefore, O Antony, stay not by his side.
            Thy demon, that thy spirit which keeps thee,* is
            Noble, courageous, high, unmatchable,   20
            Where Caesar's is not.* But near him, thy angel
            Becomes afeard, as being o'erpowered; therefore
            Make space enough* between you.

ANTONY   Speak this no more.

SOOTHSAYER To none but thee; no more but when to thee.*
            If thou dost play with him at any game,   25
            Thou art sure to lose; and of* that natural luck
            He beats thee 'gainst the odds.* Thy lustre thickens*
            When he shines by.* I say again, thy spirit
            Is all afraid to govern thee near him,
            But he away,* 'tis noble.

ANTONY   Get thee gone.   30

32   *He* – i.e. Ventidius.
32   *art or hap:* magical skill or chance. – Antony refers to the Latin *ars magica* or magic art.
33   *He* – i.e. the Soothsayer.
33   *obey him:* turn up the score he (Caesar) wants.
34   *better cunning . . . chance:* greater skill is overcome by his luck.
35   *speeds:* is successful.
36   *cocks* – i.e. fighting cocks.
36   *still of mine:* always over mine.
37   *it is all to nought:* the odds are overwhelmingly in my favour.
37   *quails* are small birds like partridges.
38   *inhooped:* enclosed in a hoop (and so forced to fight each other). Combats with quails
                  were common in Roman times.
38   *at odds:* against the odds.
39   *for my peace:* to ensure peace (with Caesar).
41   *commission* – i.e. papers authorising the expedition.

II.iv.   This ten-line scene showing preparations in Rome for the military expedition against
          Sextus Pompey is transitional in function, leading economically into the meeting at
          Misenum in II.vi between the Triumvirate and Pompey. It also effects that sense of speed
          and efficiency which is the keynote of all Caesar's military and political activity.

2   *Your generals after:* after your generals.
3   *e'en but kiss Octavia:* just kiss Octavia farewell.
5   *become:* suit.
6   *conceive:* plan.
6   *th'Mount* – i.e. Mount Mesena, mentioned earlier at II.ii.165.
8   *draw me much about:* force me to take a roundabout route.
9   *win two days upon me:* be there two days before me.

Say to Ventidius I would speak with him.

[*Exit* SOOTHSAYER

He* shall to Parthia. Be it art or hap,*
He* hath spoken true. The very dice obey him,*
And in our sports my better cunning faints
Under his chance.* If we draw lots, he speeds;*   35
His cocks* do win the battle still of mine*
When it is all to nought,* and his quails* ever
Beat mine, inhooped,* at odds.* I will to Egypt;
And though I make this marriage for my peace,*
I' th' East my pleasure lies.

Enter VENTIDIUS.

                      O, come, Ventidius,   40
You must to Parthia. Your commission's* ready:
Follow me, and receiv't.

                          [*Exeunt*

scene iv

Rome. A street.

Enter LEPIDUS, MAECENAS *and* AGRIPPA.

LEPIDUS Trouble yourselves no further: pray you, hasten
Your generals after.*

AGRIPPA   Sir, Mark Antony
Will e'en but kiss Octavia,* and we'll follow.

LEPIDUS Till I shall see you in your soldier's dress,
Which will become* you both, farewell.

MAECENAS   We shall,   5
As I conceive* the journey, be at th' Mount*
Before you, Lepidus.

LEPIDUS   Your way is shorter;
My purposes do draw me much about.*
You'll win two days upon me.*

MAECENAS *and*   Sir, good success.
AGRIPPA

LEPIDUS Farewell.   10

                        [*Exeunt*

II.v.   In Alexandria, Cleopatra, chafing without Antony, reminisces about their former escapades. A messenger arrives reporting Antony's marriage to Octavia. Cleopatra loses self-control, assaulting him and drawing a dagger to stab him, so that he flees in terror. She regains control of herself and the terrified messenger is induced to return and confirm his news. She instructs that he be sent to Rome to obtain details of Octavia's appearance and disposition.

The scene deepens our knowledge of Cleopatra. Her violence towards the messenger while expressing her anger and jealousy is also a manifestation of the strength of her feeling for Antony. Our realization of this, together with her regret at her loss of nobility, in striking an inferior, tend to excuse her savagery to some extent. The scene is further evidence of her vitality and passion, two qualities which so powerfully attract Antony, and for which the mild manners of Octavia will be no match.

1   *moody:* melancholy. – There is probably a pun on *mood* meaning the key in which music is composed.

2   *trade in:* engage in the business of.

3   *billiards* – There is no evidence that the game was known to the Romans, but anachronisms of this kind did not worry Shakespeare or his contemporaries.

4   *best:* you had better.

5   *As well . . . played:* A woman might as well play with a eunuch.

8   *when good . . . pardon:* when someone has shown goodwill he can be forgiven if his performance is poor. – Cleopatra will not blame Mardian if he plays badly since he was willing to do his best.

9   *I'll none now:* I do not want to play now.

10   *angle:* angling rod.

11   *betray:* deceive.

15   *y'are:* you are.

16   *wagered on your angling:* laid bets on who would catch the most fish.

17   *salt-fish:* dried fish.

18   *with fervency:* eagerly.

19   *laughed him out of patience:* laughed at him until he lost his temper.

21   *the ninth hour* – i.e. 9 a.m.

21   *drunk him to his bed:* drank with him until he had to take to his bed.

22   *tires and mantles:* head-dresses and cloaks.

23   *Philippan,* the sword that Antony used in his victory over Brutus and Cassius at Philippi. Shakespeare invented this detail, basing it on a hint in Plutarch's *Comparison of Demetrius with Antonius* which refers to Omphale who 'secretly stealeth away Hercules' club and took his lion skin from him; even so Cleopatra oftentimes unarmed Antonius'. The Omphale/Hercules story was well known in Shakespeare's day, and frequently cited as an example of the hero unmanned and made effeminate, so that the parallel with Antony and Cleopatra would be evident to many in the audience.

24   *fruitful tidings:* good news.

25   *barren* – i.e. without any good news.

27   *mistress* has three syllables here.

27   *well and free . . . him:* if you report that he is well and free.

scene v

Alexandria. CLEOPATRA'S *palace.*

Enter CLEOPATRA, CHARMIAN, IRAS *and* ALEXAS.

CLEOPATRA   Give me some music; music, moody* food
Of us that trade in* love.

ALL   The music, ho!

Enter MARDIAN *the Eunuch.*

CLEOPATRA   Let it alone, let's to billiards:* come, Charmian.
CHARMIAN   My arm is sore; best* play with Mardian.
CLEOPATRA   As well a woman with an eunuch played*   5
As with a woman. Come. You'll play with me, sir?
MARDIAN   As well as I can, madam.
CLEOPATRA   And when good will is showed, though't come too short,
The actor may plead pardon.* I'll none now.*
Give me mine angle;* we'll to th'river there,   10
My music playing far off. I will betray*
Tawny-finned fishes: my bended hook shall pierce
Their slimy jaws, and as I draw them up,
I'll think them every one an Antony,
And say, 'Ah ha! y'are* caught.'

CHARMIAN   'Twas merry when   15
You wagered on your angling;* when your diver
Did hang a salt-fish* on his hook, which he
With fervency* drew up.

CLEOPATRA   That time – O times! –
I laughed him out of patience;* and that night
I laughed him into patience; and next morn,   20
Ere the ninth hour,* I drunk him to his bed,*
Then put my tires and mantles* on him, whilst
I wore his sword Philippan.*

Enter a MESSENGER.

                                    O, from Italy!
Ram thou thy fruitful tidings* in mine ears,
That long time have been barren.*

MESSENGER   Madam, madam –   25
CLEOPATRA   Antonio's dead! If thou say so, villain,
Thou kill'st thy mistress:* but well and free,

29	*bluest veins* – An allusion to the belief that royal blood was blue.
30	*lipped, and trembled kissing:* touched with their lips and trembled as they kissed.
32	*use:* are accustomed.
33	*well* – i.e. in the sense that they have gone to heaven.
33	*bring it to that:* if that is what you have to report.
37	*But there's . . . healthful* – Cleopatra cannot reconcile the messenger's assurance that Antony is well with his expression, which suggests that he has bad news to tell.
38	*tart a favour:* sour an expression.
39	*trumpet:* announce.
39	*not well:* (Antony is) not well.
40	*a Fury* – The Furies (also called the Erinyes or Eumenides) were the ancient Greek goddesses sent from the underworld to punish crime. They are represented as winged women having black bodies, with snakes entwined in their hair and eyes dripping blood, and so were regarded as types of the horrifying. Cleopatra feels that if the news of Antony is bad, only the ugliest messenger would be appropriate to deliver it.
41	*a formal man:* an ordinary man in appearance.
45	*set thee . . . gold:* shower gold upon you.
49	*Make thee . . . me:* Ask me for anything you want.
50	*does allay . . . precedence:* takes away from the previous good news.
51	*Fie upon* – An exclamation of disgust.
52	*as a gaoler to:* like a gaoler who will.
54	*pack of matter:* all you have to say. – She wants him, like a pedlar, to reveal all the contents of his pack at once.
58	*bound:* joined (in marriage).
58	*good turn:* favour. – Cleopatra takes him to mean that Antony is indebted to Octavia for some favour she has done him.
59	*For the . . . bed* – i.e. Antony is bound to Octavia by the ties of the marriage bed.
59	*I am pale* – Cleopatra's physical response is real this time.

If thou so yield him,* there is gold, and here
My bluest veins* to kiss, a hand that kings
Have lipped, and trembled kissing.*   30
MESSENGER First, madam, he is well.
CLEOPATRA   Why, there's more gold.
But, sirrah, mark, we use*
To say the dead are well:* bring it to that,*
The gold I give thee will I melt and pour
Down thy ill-uttering throat.   35
MESSENGER Good madam, hear me.
CLEOPATRA   Well, go to, I will;
But there's no goodness in thy face, if Antony
Be free and healthful.* So tart a favour*
To trumpet* such good tidings! If not well,*
Thou shouldst come like a Fury* crowned with snakes,   40
Not like a formal man.*
MESSENGER   Will't please you hear me?
CLEOPATRA I have a mind to strike thee ere thou speak'st:
Yet if thou say Antony lives, is well,
Or friends with Caesar, or not captive to him,
I'll set thee in a shower of gold,* and hail   45
Rich pearls upon thee.
MESSENGER   Madam, he's well.
CLEOPATRA   Well said.
MESSENGER And friends with Caesar.
CLEOPATRA   Th'art an honest man.
MESSENGER Caesar and he are greater friends than ever.
CLEOPATRA Make thee a fortune from me.*
MESSENGER   But yet, madam –
CLEOPATRA I do not like 'But yet'; it does allay   50
The good precedence.* Fie upon* 'But yet'!
'But yet' is as a gaoler to* bring forth
Some monstrous malefactor. Prithee, friend,
Pour out the pack of matter* to mine ear,
The good and bad together. He's friends with Caesar,   55
In state of health, thou say'st, and thou say'st, free.
MESSENGER Free, madam, no; I made no such report.
He's bound* unto Octavia.
CLEOPATRA   For what good turn?*
MESSENGER For the best turn i' th' bed.*
CLEOPATRA   I am pale,* Charmian.
MESSENGER Madam, he's married to Octavia.   60

61   *pestilence:* plague.
63   *spurn:* kick.
65   *stewed in brine:* pickled in salt.
66   *smarting in lingering pickle:* kept stinging for a long time (*lingering*) in the pickling solution.
69   *proud:* magnificent.
70   *make thy peace:* atone.
71   *boot thee:* reward you in addition.
72   *Thy modesty can beg:* you can, in moderation, ask for.
74   *made no fault:* done no wrong.
75   *within yourself:* under control.
78   *kindly:* of gentle nature.
84   *Have given myself the cause* – i.e. by loving Antony so much.
86   *give to . . . tongues:* deliver a pleasing message at great length.
88   *when they be felt:* when they are experienced.

CLEOPATRA   The most infectious pestilence* upon thee!

                                              [*She strikes him down*

MESSENGER   Good madam, patience.

CLEOPATRA   What say you?

                                              [*She strikes him again*

                                                   Hence,
            Horrible villain, or I'll spurn* thine eyes
            Like balls before me; I'll unhair thy head

                                              [*She drags him up and down*

            Thou shalt be whipped with wire, and stewed in brine,*   65
            Smarting in lingering pickle.*

MESSENGER   Gracious madam,
            I that do bring the news made not the match.

CLEOPATRA   Say 'tis not so, a province I will give thee,
            And make thy fortunes proud.* The blow thou hadst
            Shall make thy peace* for moving me to rage,   70
            And I will boot* thee with what gift beside
            Thy modesty can beg.*

MESSENGER   He's married, madam.

CLEOPATRA   Rogue, thou hast lived too long.

                                              [*She draws a knife*

MESSENGER   Nay, then I'll run.
            What mean you, madam? I have made no fault.*

                                              [*Exit*

CHARMIAN   Good madam, keep yourself within yourself:*   75
           The man is innocent.

CLEOPATRA   Some innocents scape not the thunderbolt.
            Melt Egypt into Nile, and kindly* creatures
            Turn all to serpents! Call the slave again:
            Though I am mad, I will not bite him. Call!   80

CHARMIAN   He is afeard to come.

CLEOPATRA   I will not hurt him.
            These hands do lack nobility, that they strike
            A meaner than myself, since I myself
            Have given myself the cause.* Come hither, sir.

           Enter the MESSENGER *again.*

            Though it be honest, it is never good   85
            To bring bad news: give to a gracious message
            An host of tongues,* but let ill tidings tell
            Themselves, when they be felt.*

MESSENGER   I have done my duty.

90   *worser* – The double comparative was common in Shakespeare's day.
92   *confound:* destroy.
92   *hold there still:* still stick to that story.
94   *So:* even if.
95   *cistern:* pond.
96   *Hadst thou . . . face:* even if your face were as beautiful as that of Narcissus. – In Greek mythology Narcissus fell in love with the beauty of his own reflection in a fountain, and died of despair at being unable to reach it. He became a type of the beautiful.
99   *Take no . . . you:* Do not be offended because I hesitate to give you an answer that would offend you. – He has just tried to evade her question.
101   *much unequal:* very unjust.
102   *O that . . . thee:* To think that Antony's fault should make you a subject for punishment.
103   *That art not what th'art sure of:* who are not guilty of the fault which you are so sure about. – Cleopatra recognizes the injustice of punishing the messenger as if he were guilty of Antony's fault.
104   *merchandise:* goods. – The word is treated here as a collective plural and so followed by a plural verb. Cf. *tackle,* II.ii.212.
105   *dear:* (a) grievous (b) expensive. – In both senses the news is too much for her.
105   *Lie they . . . 'em:* May they remain unsold on your hands and ruin you. – Cleopatra carries through the commercial image began with *merchandise* (line 104).
108   *paid:* punished.
112   *feature:* appearance (not just the face).
113   *inclination:* disposition.
115   *Let him for ever go:* Let him (i.e. Antony) never return.
116   *one way . . . Mars:* to look like a Gorgon from one angle, from the other he looks like Mars. – The Gorgon is Medusa who was so frighteningly ugly that whoever looked at her turned to stone. The allusion is to the perspective paintings, very popular with the Elizabethans, which showed contrasting faces when viewed from opposite sides.
117   *way's:* It is not certain whether this means (a) way is, or (b) way he is. The sense, however, is clear.

CLEOPATRA Is he married?
  I cannot hate thee worser* than I do,   90
  If thou again say 'Yes'.
MESSENGER   He's married, madam.
CLEOPATRA The gods confound* thee! Dost thou hold there still?*
MESSENGER Should I lie, madam?
CLEOPATRA   O, I would thou didst,
  So* half my Egypt were submerged and made
  A cistern* for scaled snakes! Go get thee hence: 95
  Hadst thou Narcissus in thy face,* to me
  Thou wouldst appear most ugly. He is married?
MESSENGER I crave your Highness' pardon.
CLEOPATRA   He is married?
MESSENGER Take no offence that I would not offend you:*
  To punish me for what you make me do   100
  Seems much unequal.* He's married to Octavia.
CLEOPATRA O that his fault should make a knave of thee,*
  That art not what th'art sure of!* Get thee hence:
  The merchandise* which thou hast brought from Rome
  Are all too dear* for me. Lie they upon thy hand,   105
  And be undone by 'em!*
                                        [Exit MESSENGER
CHARMIAN   Good your Highness, patience.
CLEOPATRA In praising Antony, I have dispraised Caesar.
CHARMIAN Many times, madam.
CLEOPATRA   I am paid* for't now.
  Lead me from hence.
  I faint. O Iras, Charmian! 'Tis no matter.   110
  Go to the fellow, good Alexas; bid him
  Report the feature* of Octavia, her years,
  Her inclination;* let him not leave out
  The colour of her hair. Bring me word quickly.
                                        [Exit ALEXAS
  Let him for ever go!* Let him not, Charmian!   115
  Though he be painted one way like a Gorgon,
  The other way's* a Mars.* [To MARDIAN] Bid you Alexas
  Bring me word how tall she is. Pity me, Charmian,
  But do not speak to me. Lead me to my chamber.
                                        [Exeunt

II.vi.   In Misenum, Pompey tells the Triumvirate that he has opposed them because of their support of the tyrannical Caesar, but despite this he accepts their offer of Sicily and Sardinia on condition that he clears the Mediterranean of pirates. They arrange for a treaty to this effect to be drawn up and plan to feast each other in turn. They go out, leaving Menas, Pompey's lieutenant, and Enobarbus commenting on the meeting. Menas disapproves of the reconciliation. Enobarbus dismisses Menas's belief that Antony's marriage will promote amity with Caesar, prophesying that Antony will return to Cleopatra, so that the marriage bond will be the cause of greater dissension than ever before.

The scene fascinatingly reveals the political realities and illuminates the character of the participants. Pompey emerges as a slight and uncertain figure, talkative and tactless, and politically out of his depth. Caesar's handling of him, a blend of threat, bribery and promise, is masterly. He allows Pompey to talk out his grievances – 'Take your time' – making no attempt to contradict or to discuss Pompey's arguments, but gradually bringing him to the desired end. His succinct domination of the scene illustrates visually and dramatically the superiority of his genius over Antony's when they are together, observed earlier by the Soothsayer. Antony appears inept and clumsy by contrast. His illegal possession of the house of Pompey's father, Pompey the Great, and his failure to thank Sextus for giving his mother hospitality, come near to wrecking the negotiation. The scene confirms that Lepidus is a political nonentity.

Menas and Enobarbus perform a function like that of the Chorus in Greek tragedy which comments upon and interprets the action of the play for the benefit of the audience, guiding their response. Their realistic comments make explicit the implications of the meeting. They make it clear to us that Pompey has been outwitted, and that the marriage of Antony and Octavia was a political device which will end in failure. The firm conviction with which Enobarbus prophesies future events accentuates that he has a keener understanding of his master and of political realities than Antony himself – another of Shakespeare's methods of stressing Antony's lack of self-awareness and helplessness.

2   *meet:* fitting.
3   *come to words* – i.e. before we come to blows.
4   *Our written . . . sent:* previously sent you our proposals in writing.
6   *tie up:* cause you to sheathe.
7   *tall:* brave.
9   *senators alone:* sole rulers.
10   *factors:* agents.
11   *Wherefore . . . friends:* why my father should lack avengers (*revengers want*), seeing that he has a son and friends. – See page ix for an outline of the events referred to here.
13   *ghosted:* haunted in the form of a spirit. – This incident is represented in Shakespeare's *Julius Caesar*, IV.iii.
14   *labouring for him:* striving to avenge him.
17   *the armed rest:* the rest of those who armed themselves for the same cause.
17   *courtiers of beauteous freedom:* noble men who tried to win the beauty of freedom. – *Courtiers* combines the two senses (a) men of distinction, and (b) men paying court, or wooing.
18   *To drench* – i.e. in Caesar's blood.
18   *the Capitol* was the summit of the Capitoline hill in Rome on which the great temple of Jupiter stood. It was here that Julius Caesar was murdered.
18   *would . . . but a man:* were determined that a single man (Julius Caesar as a citizen of the republic) should be no more than (*but*) a man – i.e. and not a king or demi-god.
19   *that is it:* it is the same motive that.
20   *rig:* fit out for sea.
20   *at whose . . . foams* – Pompey personifies the sea as a man foaming at the mouth with anger at having a heavy burden imposed on him.
22   *despiteful:* malicious. – Pompey is making two points in this speech: firstly, that in taking up arms to avenge his father, he is doing no more than they, the triumvirs, did for Julius Caesar; and secondly, that his motivation was the same as that of Brutus and the other conspirators against Caesar, namely the assertion of freedom against tyranny.
23   *Take your time:* Speak freely.

scene vi

Near Misenum.

Flourish. Enter POMPEY *and* MENAS *at one door, with drummers and trumpeters; at another* CAESAR, LEPIDUS, ANTONY, ENOBARBUS, MAECENAS, AGRIPPA, *with soldiers marching.*

POMPEY Your hostages I have, so have you mine;
And we shall talk before we fight.

CAESAR   Most meet*
That first we come to words,* and therefore have we
Our written purposes before us sent,*
Which, if thou hast considered, let us know   5
If 'twill tie up* thy discontented sword,
And carry back to Sicily much tall* youth
That else must perish here.

POMPEY   To you all three,
The senators* alone of this great world,
Chief factors* for the gods: I do not know   10
Wherefore my father should revengers want,
Having a son and friends,* since Julius Caesar,
Who at Philippi the good Brutus ghosted,*
There saw you labouring for him.* What was't
That moved pale Cassius to conspire? And what   15
Made the all-honoured, honest Roman, Brutus,
With the armed rest,* courtiers of beauteous freedom,*
To drench* the Capitol,* but that they would
Have one man but a man?* And that is it*
Hath made me rig* my navy, at whose burden   20
The angered ocean foams,* with which I meant
To scourge th' ingratitude that despiteful* Rome
Cast on my noble father.

CAESAR   Take your time.*

24	*fear:* frighten.
24	*thy sails:* the strength of your navy.

24   *fear:* frighten.
24   *thy sails:* the strength of your navy.
25   *speak with thee:* meet you (in battle).
26   *o'ercount:* outnumber.
27   *o'ercount me:* cheat me out of. – Antony had acquired Pompey the Great's house at a public auction but later refused to pay for it.
28   *since the cuckoo . . . mayst:* since the cuckoo does not build its own nest (but steals that of other birds) stay in it while you can.
30   *this is from the present:* this matter (of Pompey's house) has nothing to do with our present negotiations. – Lepidus, as usual, tries to keep the peace.
32   *Which do . . . embraced:* Do not accept them just because we ask you to, but consider how advantageous they are to you if you accept them.   . .
34   *To try a larger fortune:* (a) if you attempt to win more (by fighting us) (b) if you join us and aim at greater things. – Caesar is deliberately ambiguous: his sentence is at once both a threat and a promise.
36   *to send:* I must send.
37   *this 'greed . . . undinted:* if I agree to this we must return home with undamaged swords (*unhacked edges*) and undented shields (*targes undinted*) – i.e. without fighting.
42   *Put me to some impatience:* annoyed me a good deal.
42   *lose . . . by telling:* forfeit any praise due to me (i.e. for protecting Antony's mother) because I am telling you about it myself.
43   *you must know:* I must tell you (Antony).
47   *am well . . . thanks:* am well prepared, having thought about it so much, to give you the hearty thanks. – Pompey's friendliness towards Antony's mother was one of the *strange courtesies* which Antony has earlier spoken of. See II.ii.159 and note.
51   *called me . . . hither:* made me come here sooner than I had intended.

ANTONY Thou canst not fear* us, Pompey, with thy sails.*
        We'll speak with thee* at sea. At land thou know'st   25
        How much we do o'ercount* thee.

POMPEY   At land indeed
        Thou dost o'ercount me* of my father's house;
        But since the cuckoo builds not for himself,
        Remain in't as thou mayst.*

LEPIDUS   Be pleased to tell us –
        For this is from the present* – how you take   30
        The offers we have sent you.

CAESAR   There's the point.

ANTONY Which do not be entreated to, but weigh
        What it is worth embraced.*

CAESAR   And what may follow,
        To try a larger fortune.*

POMPEY   You have made me offer
        Of Sicily, Sardinia; and I must   35
        Rid all the sea of pirates. Then, to send*
        Measures of wheat to Rome; this 'greed upon,
        To part with unhacked edges and bear back
        Our targes undinted.*

CAESAR, ANTONY   That's our offer.
and LEPIDUS

POMPEY   Know then
        I came before you here a man prepared   40
        To take this offer, but Mark Antony
        Put me to some impatience.* Though I lose
        The praise of it by telling,* you must know,*
        When Caesar and your brother were at blows,
        Your mother came to Sicily and did find   45
        Her welcome friendly.

ANTONY   I have heard it, Pompey,
        And am well studied for a liberal thanks*
        Which I do owe you.

POMPEY   Let me have your hand.
        I did not think, sir, to have met you here.

ANTONY The beds i' th' East are soft, and thanks to you,   50
        That called me timelier than my purpose hither,*
        For I have gained by't

CAESAR   Since I saw you last
        There's a change upon you.

POMPEY   Well, I know not

54   *counts:* total (of lines and wrinkles).
54   *casts:* (a) throws (b) adds up. – The metaphor is from book-keeping. Pompey describes
         hostile fortune as an accountant writing cruel entries in her account book,
         Pompey's face.
56   *vassal:* servant. – His misfortunes, Pompey says, will never subjugate his spirit.
56   *Well met:* Welcome.
58   *composition:* agreement.
59   *sealed between us:* be ratified by our seals.
59   *next to do:* next thing to be done.
61   *That will I:* I will begin.
62   *take the lot:* take part in the drawing of lots.
62   *first or last:* whether you give the first or the last feast.
64   *fame:* highest praise.
66   *I have fair meanings:* My intentions were good. – Pompey sees that Antony did not like
         the reference to Julius Caesar (Cleopatra's former lover) and hastens to assure
         him that he meant nothing by it.
69   *No more of that.* Pompey is about to tell the story of how Apollodorus wrapped Cleopatra
         in a mattress and carried her secretly to Caesar. Enobarbus, observing his
         tactlessness, cuts him short.
71   *know:* recognize.
72   *well am like to do:* am likely to go on doing well.
73   *toward:* imminent.
78   *Enjoy thy plainness:* Continue your plain speaking.
79   *It nothing ill becomes thee:* it suits you very well.
81   *Show's:* Show us.

What counts* harsh fortune casts* upon my face,
But in my bosom shall she never come,   55
To make my heart her vassal.*

LEPIDUS   Well met* here.
POMPEY I hope so, Lepidus. Thus we are agreed.
I crave our composition* may be written
And sealed between us.*
CAESAR   That's the next to do.*
POMPEY We'll feast each other ere we part, and let's   60
Draw lots who shall begin.
ANTONY   That will I,* Pompey.
POMPEY No, Antony, take the lot;* but, first or last,*
Your fine Egyptian cookery shall have
The fame.* I have heard that Julius Caesar
Grew fat with feasting there.
ANTONY   You have heard much.   65
POMPEY I have fair meanings, sir.*
ANTONY   And fair words to them.
POMPEY Then so much have I heard.
And I have heard, Apollodorus carried –
ENOBARBUS No more of that:* he did so.
POMPEY   What, I pray you?
ENOBARBUS A certain queen to Caesar in a mattress.   70
POMPEY I know* thee now: how far'st thou, soldier?
ENOBARBUS   Well,
And well am like to do,* for I perceive
Four feasts are toward.*
POMPEY   Let me shake thy hand.
I never hated thee. I have seen thee fight
When I have envied thy behaviour.
ENOBARBUS   Sir,   75
I never loved you much, but I ha' praised you
When you have well deserved ten times as much
As I have said you did.
POMPEY   Enjoy thy plainness;*
It nothing ill becomes thee.*
Aboard my galley I invite you all.   80
Will you lead, lords?
CAESAR, ANTONY
and LEPIDUS   Show's* the way, sir.
POMPEY   Come.

[*Exeunt all except* ENOBARBUS *and* MENAS

84	*known:* met before.
95	*There . . . land service:* In that matter of theft (*There*) I deny that I have done that kind of military service. – Enobarbus does not deny the charge of theft, but denies (quite safely) that it was any part of his military duties.
96	*authority:* the power of officers of the law.
97	*take two thieves kissing:* (a) arrest two thieves fraternizing (b) see our two hands (*thieves*) clasping.
98	*true:* (a) honest, (b) a true reflection of their character (c) natural, not altered with cosmetics.
98	*whatsome'er:* whatever.
100	*No slander:* That is no slander.
103	*laugh away his fortune:* throw away the good fortune that was in store for him (by allying himself with the triumvirs).
104	*weep't back again:* get it back again by shedding tears over it.
105	*looked not for:* did not expect.
110	*Pray ye, sir?* What did you say? – Menas is incredulous.
113	*bound:* obliged.
114	*divine:* predict the future.
115	*policy . . . made more:* political motives behind that resolution (*purpose*) counted for more.
118	*of:* between.
119	*of a holy . . . conversation:* religious, unemotional and quiet in behaviour.
122	*dish:* appetizing food. – He refers to Cleopatra.
122	*sighs:* Enobarbus foresees Antony's desertion of Octavia, whose sighs of grief will be like a wind fanning the flames of Caesar's anger.

MENAS   [*Aside*] Thy father, Pompey, would ne'er have made this
             treaty.
             [*To* ENOBARBUS] You and I have known,* sir.

ENOBARBUS At sea, I think.   85

MENAS   We have, sir.

ENOBARBUS You have done well by water.

MENAS   And you by land.

ENOBARBUS I will praise any man that will praise me, though it cannot be
             denied what I have done by land.   90

MENAS   Nor what I have done by water.

ENOBARBUS Yes, something you can deny for your own safety: you have
             been a great thief by sea.

MENAS   And you by land.

ENOBARBUS There I deny my land service.* But give me your hand,   95
             Menas: if our eyes had authority,* here they might take two
             thieves kissing.*

MENAS   All men's faces are true,* whatsome'er* their hands are.

ENOBARBUS But there is never a fair woman has a true* face.

MENAS   No slander;* they steal hearts.   100

ENOBARBUS We came hither to fight with you.

MENAS   For my part, I am sorry it is turned to a drinking. Pompey
             doth this day laugh away his fortune.*

ENOBARBUS If he do, sure he cannot weep't back again.*

MENAS   Y'have said, sir. We looked not for* Mark Antony here. Pray   105
             you, is he married to Cleopatra?

ENOBARBUS Caesar's sister is called Octavia.

MENAS   True, sir; she was the wife of Caius Marcellus.

ENOBARBUS But she is now the wife of Marcus Antonius.

MENAS   Pray ye, sir?*   110

ENOBARBUS 'Tis true.

MENAS   Then is Caesar and he for ever knit together.

ENOBARBUS If I were bound* to divine* of this unity, I would not prophesy
             so.

MENAS   I think the policy of that purpose made more* in the marriage 115
             than the love of the parties.

ENOBARBUS I think so too. But you shall find the band that seems to tie
             their friendship together will be the very strangler of* their
             amity: Octavia is of a holy, cold, and still conversation.*

MENAS   Who would not have his wife so?   120

ENOBARBUS Not he that himself is not so, which is Mark Antony. He will
             to his Egyptian dish* again: then shall the sighs* of Octavia
             blow the fire up in Caesar, and, as I said before, that which is

124   *author of their variance:* cause of their dissension.
125   *use his affection:* gratify his passion.
125   *where it is* – i.e. in Egypt.
126   *but his occasion:* only out of political expedience.
127   *a health for you:* a toast I wish to drink with you.
129   *take:* accept.
129   *used our throats:* had plenty of drinking practice.

II.vii.   Pompey is feasting the triumvirs aboard his galley. While Antony is making fun of the
tipsy Lepidus, Menas draws Pompey aside and proposes to make him ruler of the world
by cutting the throats of the triumvirs. Pompey replies that if Menas had done it without
discussion he would have approved, but that his honour forbids him to do it. Menas, in an
aside, decides to desert Pompey's service. Lepidus is carried off in a drunken stupor.
After some singing and dancing, Caesar takes his leave, while Pompey and Antony plan
to continue their drinking ashore.
    This scene, though richly comic, has serious dramatic functions. It is an ironic commen-
tary on Menas's assertion in the previous scene that 'All men's faces are true'. In fact, no
one here can trust anyone else, nothing is as it appears. Beneath the surface joviality and
camaraderie lurks the imminent reality of assassination; while Lepidus drinks himself
senseless, Antony and Caesar 'pinch one another by the disposition'. Their host, Pompey,
would have applauded their murder had it been presented as a *fait accompli*. His 'honour'
prevents his involvement in the action itself. He exclaims to Antony as they leave,

> O Antony
> You have my father's house. But what, we are friends.

and we are invited to evaluate this honour and friendship at their true worth. By
establishing the treachery and instability of the political world, the scene casts the love
affair of Antony and Cleopatra, the other way of life explored by the play, in a much more
favourable light. We should note, too, that in contrast to the previous scene, Antony is here
the dominant figure. At a feast he is in his element, Caesar very much out of it; as he
expands, Caesar contracts. The two men differ so fundamentally in their personality and
outlook on life – a difference stressed by the opposition between Antony's philosophy,
'Be a child o'th'time', and Caesar's, 'Possess it' – that we realize that lasting peace and
friendship between them are impossible. This incompatibility is seen more and more clearly
as the play proceeds.

          *   A *banquet* was a dessert of fruit, sweets and wine which followed the main meal.
1   *Here they'll be:* This is where they will come.
1   *plants* – There is a play on the word meaning (a) feet (from the Latin *planta*, the sole of the
                foot). The servant is saying that some are so drunk and insecure on their feet
                (*ill-rooted*), that a very little more drink will knock them over; and (b) the
                things that the triumvirs have 'planted', e.g. their insecure friendship.
3   *high-coloured:* flushed with drink.
4   *alms-drink* – i.e. the remains of drink left in the glass or cup. These were sometimes thrown
                together and given away as alms to the poor.
5   *pinch . . . disposition:* find fault with one another as a result of their differing characters.
6   *reconciles . . . drink:* persuades them to accept his plea (to stop quarrelling) and re-unites
                himself with his drink.
8   *But it . . . discretion* – The servant observes the irony of the fact that while Lepidus effects
                peace by reconciling his companions, he produces internal war by 'reconciling'
                himself to his drink, since it separates him from his powers of reason and
                judgement (*discretion*).
9   *this it . . . fellowship:* this is what comes of wanting to be called the friend of great men.
9   *I had . . . heave:* I would as soon (*lief*) have a reed which would be useless as a weapon,
                as a spear (*partisan*) I could not throw. – The servants are critical of Lepidus
                whom they see as one out of his depth, a small man trying to be great.
12   *To be called . . . cheeks:* To be called upon to fill a high office, and then to do nothing in it, is
                like having eyeless sockets which greatly disfigure the face. – The metaphor is
                made up of terms from Ptolemaic astronomy, which held that seven crystalline
                concentric *spheres*, each containing a planet including the sun, moved around
                the earth once a day. Eyes were often compared to stars, and a *disaster* was the
                unfavourable aspect of a star.

the strength of their amity shall prove the immediate author
of their variance.* Antony will use his affection* where it is.*   125
He married but his occasion* here.

MENAS And thus it may be. Come, sir, will you aboard? I have a
health for you.*

ENOBARBUS I shall take* it, sir: we have used our throats* in Egypt.

MENAS Come, let's away.   130

[*Exeunt*

scene vii

On board POMPEY'S *galley, off Misenum.*

Music plays. Enter two or three SERVANTS *with a banquet.**

FIRST SERVANT Here they'll be,* man. Some o' their plants* are ill-rooted
already; the least wind i' the world will blow them down.

SECOND
SERVANT Lepidus is high-coloured.*

FIRST SERVANT They have made him drink alms-drink.*

SECOND As they pinch one another by the disposition,* he cries out   5
SERVANT 'No more', reconciles them to his entreaty and himself to the
drink.*

FIRST SERVANT But it raises the greater war between him and his discretion.*

SECOND Why, this it is to have a name in great men's fellowship.* I
SERVANT had as lief have a reed that will do me no service, as a partisan   10
I could not heave.*

FIRST SERVANT To be called into a huge sphere, and not to be seen to move
in't, are the holes where eyes should be, which pitifully
disaster the cheeks.*

*A Sennet** is sounded. Enter* CAESAR, ANTONY, POMPEY, LEPIDUS,
AGRIPPA, MAECENAS, ENOBARBUS, MENAS, *with other captains.*

---

*   A *Sennet* was a piece of formal music usually played by cornets to mark the processional
entry or exit of people of high rank.

15   *take the flow:* measure the depth.
16   *scales:* graduated marks.
17   *the mean* – i.e. a midway reading between high and low.
17   *dearth / Or foison:* famine or plenty.
24   *Your serpent* – The undefined use of the pronoun to mean vaguely 'that you know of',
        was a common colloquialism among the lower classes of Elizabethan society.
        It was often intended to suggest the speaker's familiarity with his subject.
        Lepidus uses it four times in this short speech, which underlines that he is
        trying to show off his knowledge, and that the tone of his speech has dropped
        from the level befitting a triumvir – further evidence of his unfitness to rule
        with great men. The phrase, of course, recalls Cleopatra to mind, since she is
        Antony's 'serpent of old Nile'.
24   The theory that life could be generated by the action of the sun upon inanimate matter was
        widely believed in Shakespeare's day.
28   *I am not so well* – Lepidus's befuddled mind hears the word 'health' and takes it in its
        usual sense.
28   *I'll ne'er out:* I will not fall out, i.e. by refusing to drink in answer to the toast to his
        health.
29   *in:* (a) in drink, i.e. drunk, (b) in the game, i.e. the opposite of Lepidus's *out* in line 28.
30   *pyramises* is apparently Lepidus's tipsy attempt to say 'pyramids'.
31   *very goodly things* – The feeble vagueness of Lepidus's comment on the pyramids contrasts
        strongly with Antony's precise and knowledgeable description, another
        means used by Shakespeare to reveal character.
32   *Say in mine ear:* Whisper to me.
33   *Forsake thy seat:* Menas wants Pompey to leave his companions so that he can talk to him
        in private.
35   *Forbear me till anon:* Leave me alone for a while.
38   *it:* its. – The uninflected genitive form was common at this time.
39   *the elements:* its life-principle. In Shakespeare's time it was thought that the world and
        all its creatures were made up of a mixture of the four elements of earth, water,
        air and fire. See also IV.x.3.
40   *transmigrates:* passes into another body.
44   *tears* – It was a popular belief that the crocodile, having killed a man, shed tears.
46   *With . . . epicure:* (It will satisfy him) as well as the health that Pompey makes him drink;
        if it does not he is a perfect epicurean. – Antony means that after this last
        drink Lepidus will not be able to take any more, and also that he is so drunk
        that this absurd description of the crocodile will satisfy him. See note on
        Epicurus at II.i.24.
48   *Tell me of that?:* What nonsense are you talking?
50   *for the sake of merit:* as a reward for my services to you.

ANTONY   [*To* CAESAR] Thus do they, sir: they take the flow* o' th' Nile   15
By certain scales* i' th' pyramid. They know
By th' height, the lowness, or the mean,* if dearth
Or foison* follow. The higher Nilus swells,
The more it promises; as it ebbs, the seedsman
Upon the slime and ooze scatters his grain,   20
And shortly comes to harvest.

LEPIDUS   Y'have strange serpents there?

ANTONY   Ay, Lepidus.

LEPIDUS   Your serpent* of Egypt is bred now of your mud by the
operation of your sun: so is your crocodile.*   25

ANTONY   They are so.

POMPEY   Sit, – and some wine! A health to Lepidus!

LEPIDUS   I am not so well* as I should be, but I'll ne'er out.*

ENOBARBUS   Not till you have slept; I fear me you'll be in* till then.

LEPIDUS   Nay, certainly, I have heard the Ptolemies' pyramises* are   30
very goodly things;* without contradiction I have heard that.

MENAS   [*Aside to* POMPEY] Pompey, a word.

POMPEY   [*Aside to* MENAS] Say in mine ear,* what is't?

MENAS   [*Aside to* POMPEY] Forsake thy seat,* I do beseech thee,
captain,
And hear me speak a word.

POMPEY   [*Aside to* MENAS] Forbear me till anon* –
                        [MENAS *whispers to* POMPEY
This wine for Lepidus!   35

LEPIDUS   What manner o' thing is your crocodile?

ANTONY   It is shaped, sir, like itself, and it is as broad as it hath breadth.
It is just so high as it is, and moves with it* own organs. It
lives by that which nourisheth it, and the elements* once out
of it, it transmigrates.*   40

LEPIDUS   What colour is it of?

ANTONY   Of it own colour too.

LEPIDUS   'Tis a strange serpent.

ANTONY   'Tis so, and the tears* or it are wet.

CAESAR   Will this description satisfy him?   45

ANTONY   With the health that Pompey gives him, else he is a very
epicure.*

POMPEY   [*Aside to* MENAS] Go hang, sir, hang! Tell me of that?* Away!
Do as I bid you. – Where's this cup I called for?

MENAS   [*Aside to* POMPEY] If for the sake of merit* thou wilt hear me,   50
Rise from thy stool.

POMPEY   [*Aside to* MENAS] I think th'art mad. The matter?

53	*held my cap off:* faithfully served. – Servants went bareheaded in the presence of their masters.
55	*Be jolly:* Carry on enjoying yourselves.
55	*These quicksands* – Lepidus is either staggering about or has collapsed. He is unconscious when Pompey toasts him at line 79.
59	*should that be:* could that possibly come about.
59	*But entertain it:* Only accept the idea.
61	*Hast thou drunk well?* – Pompey thinks Menas must be drunk to suggest it.
63	*earthly Jove:* sole ruler of the earth (as Jóve is of heaven).
64	*pales:* encloses (as with *pales*, i.e. stakes).
64	*inclips:* embraces.
65	*ha't:* have it.
66	*competitors:* partners and rivals.
68	*put off:* out to sea.
68	*fall to:* cut.
69	*All there is, thine:* The whole world is then yours.
70	*In me:* For me to do it.
71	*'t had:* it would have.
73	*'Tis not . . . it* – i.e. my guiding motive for action is not profit, but honour.
74	*betrayed thine act:* revealed your intended action before it was performed.
74	*Being done unknown:* If it had been done without my knowledge.
76	*Desist:* Give up this idea.
77	*palled:* decayed.
78	*Who:* Whoever.
80	*pledge* – i.e. drink in response to the toast.
82	*hid* – i.e. filled to the brim.

[He gets up and they go to one side

MENAS   I have ever held my cap off* to thy fortunes.

POMPEY   Thou hast served me with much faith. What's else to say? –
[To the others] Be jolly,* lords.

ANTONY   These quicksands,* Lepidus,   55
Keep off them, for you sink.

MENAS   *[Aside to POMPEY]* Wilt thou be lord of all the world?

POMPEY   What say'st thou?

MENAS   Wilt thou be lord of the whole world? That's twice.

POMPEY   How should that be?*

MENAS   But entertain it,*
And though thou think me poor, I am the man   60
Will give thee all the world.

POMPEY   Hast thou drunk well?*

MENAS   No, Pompey, I have kept me from the cup.
Thou art, if thou dar'st be, the earthly Jove:*
Whate'er the ocean pales,* or sky inclips,*
Is thine, if thou wilt ha't.*

POMPEY   Show me which way.   65

MENAS   These three world-sharers, these competitors,*
Are in thy vessel. Let me cut the cable,
And when we are put off,* fall to* their throats.
All there is, thine.*

POMPEY   Ah, this thou shouldst have done,
And not have spoke on't! In me* 'tis villainy;   70
In thee 't had* been good service. Thou must know,
'Tis not my profit that does lead mine honour;
Mine honour, it.* Repent that e'er thy tongue
Hath so betrayed thine act.* Being done unknown,*
I should have found it afterwards well done,   75
But must condemn it now. Desist,* and drink.

[POMPEY returns to his guests

MENAS   *[Aside]* For this I'll never follow thy palled* fortunes more.
Who* seeks and will not take, when once 'tis offered,
Shall never find it more.

POMPEY   This health to Lepidus!

ANTONY   Bear him ashore. I'll pledge* it for him, Pompey.   80

ENOBARBUS   Here's to thee, Menas!

MENAS   Enobarbus, welcome!

POMPEY   Fill till the cup be hid.*

ENOBARBUS   There's a strong fellow, Menas.

[Pointing to the Attendant carrying off LEPIDUS

83	*'A*: He.
86	*go on wheels:* run quickly and easily. – The phrase was proverbial.
87	*reels:* (a) revelry (b) drunken staggering.
89	*an Alexandrian feast:* equal to the famous feasts of Alexandria.
90	*ripens towards it:* grows very like it.
90	*Strike the vessels* – The meaning is uncertain. Some think it means 'clink glasses'; others suggest 'open the casks'. The latter seems unlikely, since Pompey, not Antony, is the host who would give such an order.
91	*well forbear't:* happily leave it alone. – Caesar is no drinker.
92	*monstrous . . . fouler:* unnatural work when washing my brain (with drink) makes it muddier. *And* (sometimes *An*): if.
93	*Be a child o' th' time,* i.e. submit to the demands of the occasion (by drinking like everyone else).
94	*Possess it . . . answer:* Control it (i.e. the time) is my answer to that.
95	*fast from all:* refrain from drinking at all.
97	*Egyptian bacchanals:* rites in honour of Bacchus (the Greek god of wine) as they are performed in Egypt.
98	*celebrate:* consecrate, make sacred. – Their drinking, Enobarbus is saying, will be made holy by having the religious motive of honouring the god Bacchus.
100	*steeped our sense:* bathed our senses.
101	*Lethe* – i.e. forgetfulness. See note to II.i.27.
102	*make battery to:* bombard.
103	*The while . . . you:* meanwhile I will put you in position.
103	*the boy* would be one of the boy actors of the company. They were usually accomplished singers.
104	*holding:* chorus.
104	*bear . . . volley:* sing as loudly as the strength of his lungs will bear.
107	*Plumpy:* plump.
107	*pink eyne:* (a) small, half-closed eyes, (b) eyes made red with drinking. – *Eyne* is the old plural of eye.
108	*fats:* vats. – *Fats* is the northern dialect form, *vats* the southern form.
110	*Cup us . . . round:* Keep our cups filled with drink until the world reels.
112	*What would you more:* What more do you want? i.e. We have done everything. – Caesar puts an end to the feasting.
113	*request you off:* beg you to leave the ship with me.
113	*our graver . . . levity:* our weightier business disapproves of this light behaviour.

MENAS   Why?
ENOBARBUS   'A* bears
The third part of the world, man; see'st not?
MENAS The third part then is drunk. Would it were all,   85
That it might go on wheels!*
ENOBARBUS Drink thou; increase the reels.*
MENAS Come.
POMPEY This is not yet an Alexandrian feast.*
ANTONY It ripens towards it.* Strike the vessels,* ho!   90
Here's to Caesar!
CAESAR   I could well forbear't.*
It's monstrous labour when I wash my brain
And it grow fouler.*
ANTONY   Be a child o' th' time.*
CAESAR Possess it, I'll make answer.*
But I had rather fast from all,* four days,   95
Than drink so much in one.
ENOBARBUS   [To ANTONY] Ha, my brave Emperor,
Shall we dance now the Egyptian bacchanals,*
And celebrate* our drink?
POMPEY   Let's ha't good soldier.
ANTONY Come, let's all take hands,
Till that the conquering wine hath steeped our sense*   100
In soft and delicate Lethe.*
ENOBARBUS   All take hands.
Make battery to* our ears with the loud music:
The while, I'll place you;* then the boy* shall sing.
The holding* every man shall bear as loud
As his strong sides can volley.*   105
        [Music plays. ENOBARBUS places them hand in hand.

                    The Song
        Come, thou monarch of the vine,
        Plumpy* Bacchus with pink eyne!*
        In thy fats* our cares be drowned,
        With thy grapes our hairs be crowned.
            Cup us till the world go round,*   110
            Cup us till the world go round!

CAESAR What would you more?* Pompey, good night. Good brother,
Let me request you off:* our graver business
Frowns at this levity.* Gentle lords, let's part;
You see we have burnt our cheeks. Strong Enobarb   115

117   *splits what it speaks:* speaks indistinctly. – Cf. Lepidus's struggles with the word *pyramids*
             at line 30.
117   *disguise . . . us all:* drunken revelry has almost made fools of us all.
118   *What needs . . . words* – i.e. There is no need to say more.
119   *try you . . . shore:* test your drinking powers when we get ashore.
120   *But what:* What does it matter.
123   *I'll not:* I will not go.
125   *Neptune:* the sea god, and the appropriate deity since they are on board ship.
127   *Hoo, says 'a:* Hooray, he says. – Enobarbus joins in the farewell to the 'great fellows'
             by cheering and throwing his cap in the air.

Is weaker than the wine, and mine own tongue
Splits what it speaks:* the wild disguise hath almost
Anticked us all.* What needs more words?* Good night.
Good Antony, your hand.

POMPEY   I'll try you on the shore.*

ANTONY And shall, sir. Give's your hand.

POMPEY   O Antony,   120
You have my father's house. But what,* we are friends!
Come down into the boat.

ENOBARBUS   Take heed you fall not.

                 [*Exeunt all except* ENOBARBUS *and* MENAS
Menas, I'll not* on shore.

MENAS   No, to my cabin.
These drums, these trumpets, flutes! What!
Let Neptune* hear we bid a loud farewell   125
To these great fellows. Sound and be hanged, sound out!

                 [*Flourish and drums sound*

ENOBARBUS Hoo, says 'a.* There's my cap.

MENAS Hoa! Noble captain, come.

                          [*Exeunt*

III.i.   In Syria, Ventidius, Antony's lieutenant, has avenged the humiliating defeat of the Roman Marcus Crassus by defeating the Parthians. He rejects the advice of Silius to press home his victory by pursuing the fleeing Parthians because too much success would arouse Antony's envy. As it is, he must give all credit for the victory to Antony.

This scene follows up the previous one, in its exposure of the pretence and meanness underlying Roman politics. Both Caesar and Antony, we are told, have always won 'more in their officer than person' while taking the credit themselves. Their followers are inhibited from doing their best for Rome by the jealousy of their masters. There are numerous defections and disloyalties among the followers of both sides and an atmosphere of distrust. The scene also shows how the activities (and inactivities) of the political leaders have world-wide repercussions.

Pacorus was the son of Orodes, the Parthian King who had inflicted a humiliating defeat on the Romans under Marcus Crassus in 53 B.C. In 60 B.C. Crassus, Julius Caesar and Pompey formed a coalition known as the First Triumvirate. Crassus was treacherously put to death by Orodes while negotiating a truce. The Romans see the death of Orodes' son Pacorus in battle as a fitting revenge for Crassus.

1   *darting Parthia* – The Parthian cavalry avoided fighting at close quarters by hurling their spears from a distance and then retreating, shooting arrows as they went. Nevertheless they have now, in their turn, been struck, says Ventidius.

5   *this* – i.e. his life.

7   *The fugitive Parthians follow:* pursue the fleeing Parthians.

8   *the shelters . . . fly:* the hiding places to which the fugitives fly.

11   *garlands* – i.e. the laurel crown of the victor.

12   *A lower . . . act:* One in a subordinate position, you should observe, may perform a feat which is too great (for his own safety).

15   *him we serve's away:* he whom we serve is absent (and so unable to claim the credit).

16   *ever won . . . person:* always won more through the actions of their officers than by their own efforts.

18   *my place:* the same rank as myself.

18   *his* – i.e. Antony's.

19   *For quick . . . renown:* because he won fame quickly.

20   *by th' minute:* all the time, continually.

23   *rather makes . . . him:* prefers to lose rather than win something that puts him into eclipse.

26   *in his offence . . . perish:* because of the offence he would take my service would be forgotten and go unrewarded.

27   *that . . . distinction:* that quality (i.e. discretion) without which there would hardly be any difference between a soldier and his sword.

30   Ventidius says ironically that he will report that all this has been achieved through the terror which Antony's name inspired among the Parthians.

ACT III scene i

A plain in Syria.

Enter VENTIDIUS *in triumph, with* SILIUS *and other Romans.*
The body of PACORUS* *is carried in front of him.*

VENTIDIUS Now, darting Parthia,* art thou struck, and now
             Pleased Fortune does of Marcus Crassus' death
             Make me revenger. Bear the king's son's body
             Before our army. Thy Pacorus, Orodes,
             Pays this* for Marcus Crassus.
SILIUS   Noble Ventidius,   5
             Whilst yet with Parthian blood thy sword is warm,
             The fugitive Parthians follow.* Spur though Media,
             Mesopotamia, and the shelters whither
             The routed fly*. So thy grand captain, Antony,
             Shall set thee on triumphant chariots, and   10
             Put garlands* on thy head.
VENTIDIUS   O Silius, Silius,
             I have done enough. A lower place, note well,
             May make too great an act.* For learn this, Silius:
             Better to leave undone, than by our deed
             Acquire too high a fame when him we serve's away.*   15
             Caesar and Antony have ever won
             More in their officer than person.* Sossius,
             One of my place* in Syria, his* lieutenant,
             For quick accumulation of renown,*
             Which he achieved by th' minute,* lost his favour.   20
             Who does i' th' wars more than his captain can,
             Becomes his captain's captain; and ambition,
             The soldier's virtue, rather makes choice of loss,
             Than gain which darkens him.*
             I could do more to do Antonius good,   25
             But 'twould offend him, and in his offence
             Should my performance perish.*
SILIUS   Thou hast, Ventidius, that
             Without the which a soldier and his sword
             Grants scarce distinction.* Thou wilt write to Antony?
VENTIDIUS I'll humbly signify what in his name,   30

31   *word of war* – Antony's name frightens his enemies like magic, because of his prowess as
        a soldier.
34   *jaded:* driven like worn-out horses.
35   *purposeth:* intends to go.
36   *weight . . . with's:* heavy baggage we must carry with us.

III.ii.   In Rome, Enobarbus and Agrippa remark on the general air of melancholy as Antony and
        Octavia are about to set out for Athens: Octavia weeps, Caesar is sad, and Lepidus, whom
        they mock for his fulsome flattery of his fellow-triumvirs, is sick. Caesar exhorts Antony
        not to disturb their new-found amity by failing to cherish Octavia. Antony professes his
        love for Caesar and assures him that there is not the least cause for his fears.
            The scene generates a sense of foreboding through the general gloom and through
        Caesar's evident distrust of Antony and his scarcely-veiled threats in the event of any
        maltreatment of Octavia, and a sense of mounting crisis as we learn that the whole future
        has narrowed down to a dependence on Antony's treatment of Octavia. After Antony's
        earlier resolution to return to Egypt and Enobarbus's conviction that he will, we can have
        little faith in Antony's promises here, although it is probable that in his unawareness of
        himself, he really believes what he is saying.

1   *are . . . parted:* have Antony and Caesar (brothers-in-law) gone?
2   *dispatched:* settled matters. – Enobarbus possibly intends to suggest also that they have
        finished Pompey off as a political force.
3   *the other three* – (i.e. of the four) the triumvirs.
3   *sealing:* fixing their seals to the agreement.
6   *green-sickness,* a form of anaemia thought to be common among love-sick girls. Lepidus is
        green-sick after his drinking bout (i.e. bilious), but also because of his love for
        Antony and Caesar. Enobarbus and Agrippa go on to echo and to mock
        ironically Lepidus's extravagant flattery of their masters. In their hymn of
        praise Agrippa directs his mockery at Antony, Enobarbus at Caesar. In their
        single-line exchanges (lines 6–14) they employ the device known as *sticho-
        mythia* found in ancient Greek and Roman plays, but also found in hymns of
        praise used in Christian services since the Middle Ages.
11   *How!:* What!
11   *nonpareil:* one without an equal.
12   *Arabian bird* – i.e. the phoenix. It was unique among birds in that only one existed; when
        it died it rose again from its own ashes.
13   *say 'Caesar'* – According to Lepidus the word 'Caesar' is the supremest possible praise.
16   *figures* – i.e. figures of rhetoric.
17   *cast:* sum up. – Each noun in line 16 has its appropriate verb in line 17. This was a favourite
        device among the sonneteers of the time, whom Enobarbus is here parodying.
17   *number:* write verse. – 'Numbers' is an old name for verse.
20   *They are . . . so:* They are the wings (*shards*) that make this beetle fly in this way (*so*). –
        Enobarbus refers to Lepidus's flights of fancy.
21   *to horse:* a signal to mount and be off.

That magical word of war,* we have effected;
How with his banners and his well-paid ranks,
The ne'er-yet-beaten horse of Parthia
We have jaded* out o' th' field.*

SILIUS   Where is he now?
VENTIDIUS He purposeth* to Athens, whither, with what haste   35
The weight we must convey with's* will permit,
We shall appear before him. – On there; pass along!

                                                          [Exeunt

scene ii

Rome. CAESAR'S *house.*

Enter AGRIPPA *at one door,* ENOBARBUS *at another.*

AGRIPPA What, are the brothers parted?*
ENOBARBUS They have dispatched* with Pompey; he is gone;
The other three* are sealing.* Octavia weeps
To part from Rome; Caesar is sad, and Lepidus,
Since Pompey's feast, as Menas says, is troubled   5
With the green-sickness.*
AGRIPPA   'Tis a noble Lepidus.
ENOBARBUS A very fine one. O, how he loves Caesar!
AGRIPPA Nay, but how dearly he adores Mark Antony!
ENOBARBUS Caesar? Why, he's the Jupiter of men.
AGRIPPA What's Antony? The god of Jupiter.   10
ENOBARBUS Spake you of Caesar? How!* The nonpareil!*
AGRIPPA O Antony! O thou Arabian bird!*
ENOBARBUS Would you praise Caesar, say 'Caesar':* go no further.
AGRIPPA Indeed he plied them both with excellent praises.
ENOBARBUS But he loves Caesar best; yet he loves Antony.   15
Hoo! Hearts, tongues, figures,* scribes, bards, poets, cannot
Think, speak, cast,* write, sing, number* – hoo! –
His love to Antony. But as for Caesar,
Kneel down, kneel down, and wonder.
AGRIPPA   Both he loves.
ENOBARBUS They are his shards, and he their beetle, so.*   20

                                              [*Trumpet sounds*
This is to horse.* Adieu, noble Agrippa.

23	*No further:* Do not trouble to come any further with me.
24	*a great . . . myself* – Caesar refers to Octavia. She is as dear to him as himself, and in giving her to Antony he is giving a part of himself.
25	*Use me well in't* – i.e. treat Octavia well. Caesar implies a warning that he will take any affront to Octavia as an affront to himself.
26	*As my . . . approof:* as I think you will be, and as I would stake (*pass*) everything (*my farthest band*) you will prove to be (*pass on thy approof*). – *Band* is a variant form of *bond*.
28	*piece:* masterpiece.
30	*builded:* intact.
30	*the ram* – A battering ram was a large, heavy log, often tipped with an iron head used in war to knock down the walls and gates of fortresses.
31	*better might . . . cherished:* it might have been better for us to have been reconciled without this intermediary (Octavia), if she is not equally loved by both of us. – Caesar gives Antony another veiled warning.
33	*Make me . . . distrust:* Do not offend me by your distrust.
34	*I have said:* (a) I have finished speaking (b) I mean what I have said. – Another of Caesar's characteristically ambiguous utterances.
35	*curious:* minutely particular.
40	*elements* – Caesar could mean (a) air and water, i.e. wishing for good weather on Octavia's journey, or (b) the world, or life in general.
40	*make . . . comfort:* keep you in good spirits.
43	*The April's . . . eyes:* She is about to shed showers of tears. – April is traditionally the month of soft spring showers.
43	*love's spring:* (a) the springtime of love (b) a stream (i.e. the flow of Octavia's tears at parting) springing from love.
44	*bring it on:* (a) advance the springtime (b) show her love.
46	*I'll tell you in your ear:* Octavia engages in whispered conversation with her brother, with Antony watching them. This enables Shakespeare to interject the secret asides of Enobarbus and Agrippa with their comments on Caesar and Antony, lines 50–59.
47	*Her tongue . . . tongue:* Her tongue cannot utter what she feels, and her heart is too full to convey her feelings to her tongue.
48	*the swan's-down . . . inclines:* like a floating feather of swan's-down which, just at the turning of the tide, moves neither one way nor the other. – Octavia is torn between love and sorrow, silence and speech, her love for Caesar and for Antony.
51	*a cloud:* a sorrowful look, threatening tears (as a cloud threatens rain).
52	*He were . . . horse:* He would be less highly regarded for having a dark face if he were a horse. – The absence of a white mark on a horse's forehead was thought to indicate bad temper.
53	*So is . . .* Enobarbus thinks Caesar's emotion unmanly.

AGRIPPA Good fortune, worthy soldier, and farewell.

Enter CAESAR, ANTONY, LEPIDUS *and* OCTAVIA.

ANTONY No further,* sir.
CAESAR You take from me a great part of myself:*
    Use me well in't.* Sister, prove such a wife   25
    As my thoughts make thee, and as my farthest band
    Shall pass on thy approof.* Most noble Antony,
    Let not the piece* of virtue which is set
    Betwixt us as the cément of our love
    To keep it builded,* be the ram* to batter   30
    The fortress of it; for better might we
    Have loved without this mean, if on both parts
    This be not cherished.*
ANTONY   Make me not offended
    In your distrust.*
CAESAR   I have said.*
ANTONY   You shall not find,
    Though you be therein curious,* the least cause   35
    For what you seem to fear. So, the gods keep you,
    And make the hearts of Romans serve your ends!
    We will here part.
CAESAR Farewell, my dearest sister, fare thee well.
    The elements* be kind to thee, and make   40
    Thy spirits all of comfort.* Fare thee well.
OCTAVIA My noble brother!
ANTONY The April's in her eyes:* it is love's spring,*
    And these the showers to bring it on.* Be cheerful.
OCTAVIA Sir, look well to my husband's house, and –
CAESAR   What,   45
    Octavia?
OCTAVIA   I'll tell you in your ear.*
ANTONY Her tongue will not obey her heart, nor can
    Her heart inform her tongue* – the swan's-down feather
    That stands upon the swell at the full of tide,
    And neither way inclines.*
ENOBARBUS   [*Aside to* AGRIPPA] Will Caesar weep?   50
AGRIPPA [*Aside to* ENOBARBUS] He has a cloud* in's face.
ENOBARBUS [*Aside to* AGRIPPA] He were the worse for that were he a
    horse;*
    So is he being a man.*

54   Agrippa refers to Antony's tears over the murdered body of Julius Caesar in front of the Capitol in Rome, 44 B.C., and over the body of his opponent Brutus at the Battle of Philippi in Macedonia in 42 B.C.

57   *a rheum:* a watering of the eyes. – Enobarbus is cynically suggesting that on the two occasions mentioned by Agrippa, Antony's tears were insincere.

58   *What willingly . . . wailed:* He wept for the loss of what he wished to destroy (*confound*).

60   *still:* continually.

60   *the time . . . you* – i.e. I shall be thinking of you all the time. *Outgo:* go faster than.

62   *wrestle . . . love:* compete with you in the strength of my love.

66   *fair way* – Octavia's way will be made *fair* by her beauty and by the light of the stars.

III.iii.   In Alexandria, Cleopatra's messenger has just returned with his report on Octavia. With the memory of Cleopatra's former anger fresh in his mind, he gives a false account of Octavia's appearance and attributes, telling Cleopatra everything he knows she wants to hear, and Charmian assists him in this indirect flattery of Cleopatra.

With this pattern of alternated Roman and Egyptian scenes, Shakespeare keeps Cleopatra firmly in our minds and prepares for Antony's ultimate return to her. Cleopatra's jealousy, deplorable from one point of view, is at the same time a means of winning our sympathy, since it reveals her vulnerability and the desperation of her need for Antony.

1   *afeard:* afraid.

2   *Go to:* Nonsense.

*   *as before.* i.e. the same messenger as in II.v.

3   *Herod,* i.e. even the fiercest of men. See note to I.ii.26.

4   *But:* except.

AGRIPPA   [*Aside to* ENOBARBUS] Why, Enobarbus,
          When Antony found Julius Caesar dead,
          He cried almost to roaring; and he wept   55
          When at Philippi he found Brutus slain.*
ENOBARBUS [*Aside to* AGRIPPA] That year, indeed, he was troubled with
          a rheum.*
          What willingly he did confound he wailed,*
          Believe't, till I wept too.
CAESAR   No, sweet Octavia,
          You shall hear from me still;* the time shall not   60
          Outgo my thinking on you.*
ANTONY   Come, sir, come;
          I'll wrestle with you in my strength of love.*
          Look, here I have you; thus I let you go,
          And give you to the gods.
CAESAR   Adieu; be happy!
LEPIDUS   Let all the number of the stars give light
          To thy fair way!*   65
CAESAR   Farewell, farewell!
                                        [*Kisses* OCTAVIA
ANTONY   Farewell!
                                        [*Trumpets sound. Exeunt*

scene iii

Alexandria. CLEOPATRA'S *palace.*

Enter CLEOPATRA, CHARMIAN, IRAS *and* ALEXAS.

CLEOPATRA Where is the fellow?
ALEXAS   Half afeard* to come.
CLEOPATRA Go to, go to.* Come hither, sir.

Enter the MESSENGER *as before.*

ALEXAS   Good Majesty,
          Herod* of Jewry dare not look upon you
          But* when you are well pleased.
CLEOPATRA   That Herod's head
          I'll have: but how, when Antony is gone,   5
          Through whom I might command it? Come thou near.

12   *Is she . . . low:* Is her voice loud and piercing or quiet?
14   *That's not so good* – It is not certain whether Cleopatra means (a) that is not such good news (as the fact that Octavia is not tall), or (b) a low voice is not so good as a shrill one. In favour of (a) is the fact that Cleopatra calls Fulvia *shrill-tongued* (I.i.32) intending it as a criticism of her. King Lear (v.iii.273) speaks of a low voice as 'an excellent thing in woman'. In favour of (b) is Cleopatra's following description of Octavia as *dull of tongue* and her opinion that Antony *cannot like her long,* and that *there's nothing in her yet,* though these statements could be interpreted as Cleopatra's efforts to look on the bright side or to distort the facts in her own favour.
17   *gait:* manner of walking.
18   *creeps:* moves in an abject way.
19   *Her motion . . . one:* her movement and the way she stands still are the same, i.e. she is lacking in liveliness, stiff in movement.
20   *shows:* seems to be.
21   *a breather:* someone endowed with life.
22   *Or I have no observance:* If not then I have no powers of observation.
22   *Three in Egypt . . . note:* There are not three in Egypt with better observation.
23   *knowing:* intelligent.
24   *There's nothing . . . yet:* So far there is nothing remarkable about her.
27   *Charmian, hark:* Do you hear that, Charmian? – Cleopatra takes Octavia's widowhood as a fact favourable to herself.
28   *thirty* – Cleopatra, being thirty-eight, can take no comfort from Octavia's age, and so makes no comment.
32   *her forehead . . . it* – A low forehead was considered ugly, denoting stupidity. If Octavia's forehead were any lower, the messenger implies, she would be positively ugly.

MESSENGER   Most gracious Majesty.
CLEOPATRA   Didst thou behold
             Octavia?
MESSENGER   Ay, dread queen.
CLEOPATRA   Where?
MESSENGER   Madam, in Rome.
             I looked her in the face, and saw her led
             Between her brother and Mark Antony.   10
CLEOPATRA   Is she as tall as me?
MESSENGER   She is not, madam.
CLEOPATRA   Didst hear her speak? It she shrill-tongued or low?*
MESSENGER   Madam, I heard her speak; she is low-voiced.
CLEOPATRA   That's not so good.* He cannot like her long.
CHARMIAN   Like her? O Isis! 'Tis impossible.   15
CLEOPATRA   I think so, Charmian. Dull of tongue and dwarfish.
             What majesty is in her gait?* Remember,
             If e'er thou look'dst on majesty.
MESSENGER   She creeps:*
             Her motion and her station are as one.*
             She shows* a body rather than a life,   20
             A statue than a breather.*
CLEOPATRA   Is this certain?
MESSENGER   Or I have no observance.*
CHARMIAN   Three in Egypt
             Cannot make better note.*
CLEOPATRA   He's very knowing;*
             I do perceiv't. There's nothing in her yet.*
             The fellow has good judgement.
CHARMIAN   Excellent.   25
CLEOPATRA   Guess at her years, I prithee.
MESSENGER   Madam,
             She was a widow –
CLEOPATRA   Widow? Charmian, hark.*
MESSENGER   And I do think she's thirty.*
CLEOPATRA   Bear'st thou her face in mind? Is't long or round?
MESSENGER   Round, even to faultiness.   30
CLEOPATRA   For the most part, too, they are foolish that are so.
             Her hair, what colour?
MESSENGER   Brown, madam; and her forehead
             As low as she would wish it.*
CLEOPATRA   There's gold for thee.
             Thou must not take my former sharpness ill;

35   *back again* – i.e. to take letters back to Antony.
37   *proper:* honest.
38   *I repent . . . him:* I am very sorry I treated him so harshly.
39   *by him . . . thing:* according to his report Octavia (*this creature*) is nothing to talk of.
41   *should:* ought to.
42   *Isis else defend:* Isis forbid that it should be otherwise – i.e. it could not be otherwise
              (since he has served you).
47   *warrant you:* assure you it will.

III.iv.   In Athens Antony complains that Caesar has offended his honour in various ways – by
          fighting Pompey, by publishing his will and by denigrating him. Octavia is torn between
          love for her husband and love for her brother, and Antony agrees that she shall travel to
          Rome to act as mediator between them, although meanwhile he proposes to raise an
          army against Caesar.
              The scene confirms our apprehensions of trouble, as the cracks in the amity between
          Caesar and Antony show through, despite the 'cement' of Octavia's love.

2   *were:* would be.
2   *thousands . . . import:* countless other faults of similar gravity.
4   *New wars* – i.e. contrary to their agreement.
5   *To public ear* – Antony complains that Caesar has curried popular favour by making known
              that he has left money in his will to the people of Rome. This detail is
              Shakespeare's invention.
6   *scantly:* grudgingly.
6   *when perforce . . , them:* when circumstances compelled him to speak of me in honourable
              terms he uttered them (*vented*) in a half-hearted and feeble way (*cold and
              sickly*).
8   *most . . . me:* gave very little credit.
9   *best hint:* most favourable opportunity (to praise me).
9   *not took't:* did not take it.
10   *from his teeth* – i.e. insincerely, not from the heart.
12   *stomach:* resent.
13   *division chance:* split occurs.
14   *parts:* parties.

I will employ thee back again:* I find thee   35
Most fit for business. Go, make thee ready;
Our letters are prepared.

[*Exit* MESSENGER

CHARMIAN   A proper* man.
CLEOPATRA Indeed he is so. I repent me much
That I so harried him.* Why, methinks, by him,
This creature's no such thing.*
CHARMIAN   Nothing, madam.   40
CLEOPATRA The man hath seen some majesty, and should* know.
CHARMIAN Hath he seen majesty! Isis else defend,*
And serving you so long!
CLEOPATRA I have one thing more to ask him yet, good Charmian;
But 'tis no matter, thou shalt bring him to me   45
Where I will write. All may be well enough.
CHARMIAN I warrant you,* madam.

[*Exeunt*

scene iv

Athens. ANTONY'S *house.*

Enter ANTONY *and* OCTAVIA.

ANTONY Nay, nay, Octavia, not only that –
That were* excusable, that and thousands more
Of semblable import* – but he hath waged
New wars* 'gainst Pompey; made his will, and read it
To public ear;*   5
Spoke scantly* of me; when perforce he could not
But pay me terms of honour, cold and sickly
He vented them;* most narrow measure lent me;*
When the best hint* was given him, he not took't,*
Or did it from his teeth.*
OCTAVIA   O my good lord,   10
Believe not all, or if you must believe,
Stomach* not all. A more unhappy lady,
If this division chance,* ne'er stood between,
Praying for both parts.*

15   *presently:* at once.
17   *Undo* – i.e. and then undo.
18   *Husband win . . . prayer* – A prayer which asks that both her husband and her brother
        may win, inevitably cancels itself out.
19   *no:* (there is) no.
21   *Let your . . . preserve it:* let your strongest love support that side which does most to
        protect it.
23   *better I . . . branchless:* it would be better for me not to be your husband than to be your
        husband without my honour (*branchless*).
25   *go between's:* act as mediator between us.
26   *raise . . . your brother:* make preparations for war which will eclipse (*stain*) any that your
        brother may make.
28   *So your desires are yours:* in this way you have what you want, i.e. permission to act as
        peacemaker.
30   *Wars twixt . . . the rift:* War between you two (*twixt you twain*) would be like the splitting
        in two of the world, which only the bodies of those killed in the war could
        cement (*solder*) together again.
33   *where this begins:* which of us caused this dissension.
34   *our faults . . . them:* one of us must be more at fault than the other, so that you cannot
        love both sides equally.
36   *Provide your going:* Make arrangements for your departure.
37   *command with cost:* give orders for whatever expenses.

III.v.   We learn from the conversation between Eros and Enobarbus that Caesar and Lepidus
          have made war on Pompey, who has later been killed by one of Antony's officers, and
          that Caesar has subsequently arrested and imprisoned Lepidus. Enobarbus sees these
          events as the prelude to the final confrontation of Caesar and Antony for world supremacy.
          Antony's navy is fitted out, ready to sail against Caesar.
              This scene is by no means the clumsy repetition of the previous scene that it has some-
          times been held to be. It is dramatically important at this point in the action, when Antony
          is about to desert Octavia and so earn our censure, that sufficient sympathy be retained
          for him. Shakespeare effects this by establishing, through the independent and impartial
          remarks of Enobarbus and Eros, a high degree of culpability in Caesar for the destruction
          of friendship between him and Antony. Our disapproval of Antony's desertion of Octavia
          is less extreme since we see that it is not the cause of the war which follows, but is a
          fortuitous pretext for a course of political action which Caesar has already decided to
          follow. He has been systematically removing the obstacles to sole rulership of the Roman
          world.

5   *success:* result.

The good gods will mock me presently*   15
When I shall pray, 'O, bless my lord and husband!'
Undo* that prayer, by crying out as loud,
'O, bless my brother!' Husband win, win brother,
Prays and destroys the prayer;* no* midway
'Twixt these extremes at all.

ANTONY   Gentle Octavia,   20
Let your best love draw to that point which seeks
Best to preserve it.* If I lose mine honour,
I lose myself: better I were not yours
Than yours so branchless.* But, as you requested,
Yourself shall go between's;* the meantime, lady,   25
I'll raise the preparation of a war
Shall stain your brother.* Make your soonest haste;
So your desires are yours.*

OCTAVIA   Thanks to my lord.
The Jove of power make me, most weak, most weak,
Your reconciler! Wars 'twixt you twain would be   30
As if the world should cleave, and that slain men
Should solder up the rift.*

ANTONY   When it appears to you where this begins,*
Turn your displeasure that way, for our faults
Can never be so equal that your love   35
Can equally move with them.* Provide your going,*
Choose your own company, and command what cost*
Your heart has mind to.

                                        [Exeunt

scene v

Athens. Another room in ANTONY'S *house.*

Enter ENOBARBUS *and* EROS.

ENOBARBUS How now, friend Eros?
     EROS There's strange news come, sir.
ENOBARBUS What, man?
     EROS Caesar and Lepidus have made wars upon Pompey.
ENOBARBUS This is old. What is the success?*   5

6	*him* – i.e. Lepidus.
7	*rivality:* equal partnership.
9	*upon his own appeal:* on the strength of his (Caesar's) own accusation.
10	*the poor third is up:* Lepidus is imprisoned (*up*).
10	*enlarge his confine:* free him from prison.
12	*Then, world . . . other* – The removal of Lepidus leaves Caesar and Antony to fight it out like two dogs for control of the world. Although each has more than enough already, conflict is inevitable. *Chaps:* jaws.
15	*thus* – Here Eros imitates Antony's manner of walking.
15	*spurns / The rush:* kicks aside any straw.
17	*threats . . . officer:* threatens to cut the throat of that officer of his.
20	*presently:* immediately.
20	*My news . . .hereafter:* I ought to have told you this first and kept the news till later.
21	*'Twill be . . . be* – Either (a) It will be nothing important that Antony wants me for, but no matter, or (b) It will be something disastrous (*naught*), but never mind.

III.vi.   In Rome Caesar informs his followers that Antony has returned to Egypt and has given several Roman provinces to Cleopatra and to his sons. He says he will concede half his spoils as Antony demands, provided Antony will do the same for him. Octavia arrives unheralded in Rome to mediate between her brother and her husband only to learn that Antony has returned to Cleopatra. Caesar counsels her to patience, arguing that destiny and necessity have determined this state of affairs.

Shakespeare carefully orders events so that Antony's return to Egypt is seen as partly provoked by Caesar's anterior actions in breaking the treaties with Pompey and Lepidus without any consultation with Antony, and this is important in lightening the burden of Antony's guilt in his desertion of Octavia, an action which makes conflict inevitable.

1	*Contemning:* Despising.
3	*tribunal silvered:* raised platform plated with silver.
6	*my father's* – i.e. Julius Caesar's. Octavius was his adopted son.
7	*unlawful issue:* illegitimate children.
9	*stablishment:* possession.
11	*This . . . eye?:* Did he do this in front of the public?
12	*common show-place . . . exercise:* public arena where the athletes exercise.

EROS Caesar, having made use of him* in the wars 'gainst Pompey,
presently denied him rivality,* would not let him partake in
the glory of the action; and not resting here, accuses him of
letters he had formerly wrote to Pompey; upon his own
appeal,* seizes him. So the poor third is up,* till death enlarge   10
his confine.*

ENOBARBUS Then, world, thou hast a pair of chaps, no more;
And throw between them all the food thou hast,
They'll grind the one the other.* Where's Antony?

EROS He's walking in the garden – thus* – and spurns   15
The rush* that lies before him; cries 'Fool Lepidus!'
And threats the throat of that his officer*
That murdered Pompey.

ENOBARBUS   Our great navy's rigged.

EROS For Italy and Caesar. More, Domitius,
My lord desires you presently.* My news   20
I might have told hereafter.*

ENOBARBUS   'Twill be naught,
But let it be.* Bring me to Antony.

EROS Come, sir.

                                     [Exeunt

scene vi

Rome. CAESAR'S *house.*

Enter CAESAR, AGRIPPA *and* MAECENAS.

CAESAR Contemning* Rome, he has done all this and more
In Alexandria. Here's the manner of't:
I' th' market-place, on a tribunal silvered,*
Cleopatra and himself in chairs of gold
Were publicly enthroned. At the feet sat   5
Caesarion, whom they call my father's* son,
And all the unlawful issue* that their lust
Since then hath made between them. Unto her
He gave the stablishment* of Egypt, made her
Of lower Syria, Cyprus, Lydia,   10
Absolute queen.

MAECENAS   This in the public eye?*

17	*habiliments:* dress.
19	*so* – i.e. dressed as Isis.
20	*Who* – i.e. the inhabitants of Rome.
20	*queasy with:* sickened by.
21	*their good . . . him:* withdraw their good opinion of him.
22	*received:* heard.
25	*spoiled:* plundered.
25	*rated him:* allotted him his share.
27	*unrestored:* which was not given back.
28	*of:* from.
29	*being* – i.e. being deposed.
34	*change* – i.e. from triumvir to prisoner.
34	*For:* As for.
37	*the like:* an equivalent share.
40	*That ever . . . castaway:* I never expected to have to call you discarded.
42	*stolen upon us thus:* come to us in this stealthy way.
44	*for an usher:* to announce her coming.
46	*by th' way:* along your route.
47	*borne:* been full of.
47	*expectation . . . had not:* those waiting to see her should have grown faint, waiting longingly for the sight of her.

CAESAR I' th' common show-place, where they exercise.*
His sons he there proclaimed the kings of kings:
Great Media, Parthia, and Armenia,
He gave to Alexander; to Ptolemy he assigned   15
Syria, Cilicia, and Phoenicia. She
In th'habiliments* of the goddess Isis
That day appeared, and oft before gave audience,
As 'tis reported, so.*
MAECENAS   Let Rome be thus informed.
AGRIPPA Who,* queasy* with his insolence already,   20
Will their good thoughts call from him.*
CAESAR The people knows it, and have now received*
His accusations.
AGRIPPA   Who does he accuse?
CAESAR Caesar: and that having in Sicily
Sextus Pompeius spoiled,* we had not rated him*   25
His part o' th' isle. Then does he say, he lent me
Some shipping unrestored.* Lastly, he frets
That Lepidus of* the triumvirate
Should be deposed; and, being,* that we detain
All his revénue.
AGRIPPA   Sir, this should be answered.   30
CAESAR 'Tis done already, and the messenger gone.
I have told him Lepidus was grown too cruel,
That he his high authority abused
And did deserve his change.* For* what I have conquered
I grant him part; but then in his Armenia,   35
And other of his conquered kingdoms, I
Demand the like.*
MAECENAS   He'll never yield to that.
CAESAR Nor must not then be yielded to in this.

Enter OCTAVIA *with her train.*

OCTAVIA Hail, Caesar, and my lords! Hail, most dear Caesar!
CAESAR That ever I should call thee castaway!*   40
OCTAVIA You have not called me so, nor have you cause.
CAESAR Why have you stolen upon us thus?* You come not
Like Caesar's sister. The wife of Antony
Should have an army for an usher,* and
The neighs of horse to tell of her approach   45
Long ere she did appear. The trees by th' way*
Should have borne* men, and expectation fainted,

50   *populous:* numerous.
51   *A market-maid:* like a girl on her way to market.
52   *ostentation:* public display.
52   *left unshown . . . unloved* – Another example of Caesar's habitual ambiguity. It could mean that when love is not openly demonstrated it (a) is often thought not to exist, (b) is unrequired (c) ceases to be felt.
53   *should:* ought to have.
54   *supplying . . . greeting:* at every stage of your journey giving you a greater welcome.
58   *acquainted . . . withal:* told me and grieved me with the news.
60   *pardon:* permission.
61   *abstract* – A puzzling word. Possibly Caesar means that Octavia's return (a) draws out of the way an obstacle between Antony and his love for Cleopatra, or (b) is a short cut to his love.
63   *on the wind:* speedily.
66   *nodded:* beckoned with a nod. – In this metaphor Caesar conveys his contempt for Antony whom he represents as unable to resist the slightest gesture of command from Cleopatra.
67   *who:* and they.
67   *levying:* enrolling.
76   *a more larger . . . sceptres:* a much longer list of kings.
78   *parted:* divided.
79   *does* for *do.* Cf. I.iv.21.
80   *did withhold . . . danger:* prevented me from showing my anger (*breaking forth*) until I saw that you were being misled and that I was in danger through not acting (*negligent danger*).
83   *the time:* the present state of affairs.

Longing for what it had not.* Nay, the dust
Should have ascended to the roof of heaven,
Raised by your populous* troops. But you are come   50
A market-maid* to Rome, and have prevented
The ostentation* of our love, which, left unshown,
Is often left unloved.* We should* have met you
By sea and land, supplying every stage
With an augmented greeting.*

OCTAVIA   Good my lord,   55
To come thus was I not constrained, but did it
On my free will. My lord, Mark Antony,
Hearing that you prepared for war, acquainted
My grievèd ear withal;* whereon I begged
His pardon* for return.

CAESAR   Which soon he granted,   60
Being an abstract* 'tween his lust and him.

OCTAVIA Do not say so, my lord.

CAESAR   I have eyes upon him,
And his affairs come to me on the wind.*
Where is he now?

OCTAVIA   My lord, in Athens.

CAESAR No, my most wronged sister, Cleopatra   65
Hath nodded* him to her. He hath given his empire
Up to a whore, who* now are levying*
The kings o' th' earth for war. He hath assembled
Bocchus, the King of Libya, Archelaus
Of Cappadocia, Philadelphos, King   70
Of Paphlagonia, the Thracian King Adallas,
King Manchus of Arabia, King of Pont,
Herod of Jewry, Mithridates, King
Of Comagene, Polemon and Amyntas,
The Kings of Mede and Lycaonia,   75
With a more larger list of sceptres.*

OCTAVIA Ay me, most wretched,
That have my heart parted* betwixt two friends
That does* afflict each other.

CAESAR   Welcome hither.
Your letters did withhold our breaking forth   80
Till we perceived both how you were wrong led,
And we in negligent danger.* Cheer your heart:
Be you not troubled with the time,* which drives
O'er your content these strong necessities,

83   *drives . . . their way:* forces these strong measures to trample on your happiness, but let predestined events (*determined things*) continue on their appointed way (*to destiny*) without lamenting. – Caesar hopes that Octavia will accept calmly the cruel developments which, he tells her, have been decided by fate.

87   *abused . . . thought:* wronged beyond all conceivable limits. – The *mark* was the target or butt in archery.

89   *makes his ministers . . . love you:* make me and those who love you their agents of justice.

90   *Best of comfort* – Either (a) May the best of comfort be yours, or (b) You are my greatest comfort.

94   *large / In his abominations:* unrestrained in his hateful actions.

96   *potent regiment . . . us:* powerful authority to a prostitute who raises a tumult against me.

99   *Be ever known to patience:* let patience be your constant companion.

III.vii.   The action moves to Actium where the two armies face each other. Cleopatra is angry at Enobarbus's hostility to her presence on the battlefield which he fears will be a disastrous distraction to Antony. Cleopatra supports Antony's decision to fight at sea, against advice from his general Canidius, from Enobarbus, and from a veteran soldier.

An ominous atmosphere is created through the numerous divisions within Antony's camp. Firstly, Cleopatra quarrels with Enobarbus – and so many of his opinions have proved correct that our sympathies continue to be on his side in the matter. Secondly, Cleopatra rebukes Antony for his 'negligence' which contrasts unfavourably with Caesar's speed. Thirdly, there is a fatal division over the strategy of the war between Antony and his followers who suspect that it is Cleopatra's idea to fight at sea. Set menacingly against this discord is the uncanny speed and cleverness with which Caesar has fooled all Antony's spies about his troop movements, crossed the Ionian Sea and captured Toryne. All the signs point to Antony's defeat.

3   *forspoke:* spoken against.

5   *If not . . . not we:* Even if the war had not been declared (*denounced*) against me, why should I not. – Cleopatra claims that she has a right to be present in any case, and particularly in view of the fact that Caesar declared war on her alone, not on Antony.

8   *were merely:* would be completely – Enobarbus answers in an aside which he does not intend Cleopatra to hear, that women on the battlefield are a distraction to men.

10   *needs must puzzle:* would inevitably confuse.

But let determined things to destiny   85
Hold unbewailed their way.* Welcome to Rome;
Nothing more dear to me. You are abused
Beyond the mark of thought,* and the high gods,
To do you justice, makes his ministers
Of us and those that love you.* Best of comfort,*   90
And ever welcome to us.

AGRIPPA   Welcome, lady.
MAECENAS Welcome, dear madam,
Each heart in Rome does love and pity you.
Only th' adulterous Antony, most large
In his abominations,* turns you off,   95
And gives his potent regiment to a trull,
That noises it against us.*

OCTAVIA   Is it so, sir?
CAESAR Most certain. Sister, welcome. Pray you,
Be ever known to patience.* My dear'st sister!

                                                         [*Exeunt*

scene vii

Actium. ANTONY'S *camp.*

Enter CLEOPATRA *and* ENOBARBUS.

CLEOPATRA I will be even with thee, doubt it not.
ENOBARBUS But why, why, why?
CLEOPATRA Thou hast forspoke* my being in these wars,
And say'st it is not fit.
ENOBARBUS   Well, is it, is it?
CLEOPATRA If not denounced against us, why should not we*   5
Be there in person?
ENOBARBUS   [*Aside*] Well, I could reply,
'If we should serve with horse and mares together,
The horse were merely* lost; the mares would bear
A soldier and his horse.'
CLEOPATRA   What is't you say?
ENOBARBUS Your presence needs must puzzle* Antony,   10
Take from his heart, take from his brain, from's time,

13	*Traduced for levity:* censured for frivolity.
14	*an eunuch* – i.e. Mardian.
16	*A charge we bear:* I bear part of the expenses.
17	*president:* sovereign ruler.
18	*for a man:* as if I were a man.
19	*Nay, I have done:* Well, I will say no more (about your presence with the army).
22	*cut:* cross (by cutting a path through with his ships).
23	*take in:* capture.
23	*on't:* about it.
24	*Celerity . . . negligent:* Nobody admires swift action more than those who are slow to act.
26	*becomed:* suited.
27	*taunt at slackness:* reproach slackness with.
29	*For that:* Because.
30	Enobarbus is making the point that the fact that Caesar has issued a challenge is no reason why Antony should accept it, especially since Caesar has not accepted Antony's challenge.
33	*serve not for his vantage:* are not to his advantage.
33	*shakes off:* rejects.
35	*muleters:* mule-drivers.
36	*Ingrossed by swift impress:* hastily assembled by forced conscription.
37	*Are those . . . fought* – Enobarbus makes the point that Caesar's sailors are experienced while Antony's are not.
38	*yare:* nimble.
38	*No disgrace . . . you:* You will suffer no loss of reputation.
40	*Being prepared for land:* since you are prepared for a land battle.
42	*absolute soldiership:* complete supremacy in military experience.

What should not then be spared. He is already
Traduced for levity,* and 'tis said in Rome
That Photinus, an eunuch,* and your maids
Manage this war.

CLEOPATRA   Sink Rome, and their tongues rot   15
That speak against us! A charge we bear* i' th' war,
And as the president* of my kingdom will
Appear there for a man.* Speak not against it;
I will not stay behind.

Enter ANTONY *and* CANIDIUS.

ENOBARBUS   Nay, I have done.*
Here comes the Emperor.

ANTONY   Is it not strange, Canidius,   20
That from Tarentum and Brundisium
He could so quickly cut* the Ionian Sea
And take in* Toryne? – You have heard on't* sweet?

CLEOPATRA Celerity is never more admired
Than by the negligent.*

ANTONY   A good rebuke,   25
Which might have well becomed* the best of men,
To taunt at slackness.* Canidius, we
Will fight with him by sea.

CLEOPATRA   By sea? What else?
CANIDIUS Why will my lord do so?
ANTONY   For that* he dares us to't.
ENOBARBUS So hath my lord dared him to single fight.*   30
CANIDIUS Ay, and to wage this battle at Pharsalia,
Where Caesar fought with Pompey. But these offers,
Which serve not for his vantage,* he shakes off,*
And so should you.

ENOBARBUS   Your ships are not well manned;
Your mariners are muleters,* reapers, people   35
Ingrossed by swift impress.* In Caesar's fleet
Are those that often have 'gainst Pompey fought;*
Their ships are yare,* yours heavy. No disgrace
Shall fall you* for refusing him at sea,
Being prepared for land.*

ANTONY   By sea, by sea.   40
ENOBARBUS Most worthy sir, you therein throw away
The absolute soldiership* you have by land,

43   *Distract:* (a) divide (b) confuse.
43   *most consist . . . footmen:* consists for the most part of veteran infantrymen. – *war-marked:* battle-scarred.
44   *leave unexecuted . . . knowledge:* fail to use the military knowledge for which you are famous.
46   *assurance:* certain success.
47   *merely:* wholly.
48   *From firm security:* from a position of certain safety.
49   *sails:* ships.
50   *overplus of shipping* – Antony had more warships than he needed. By burning this excess (*overplus*) he would be able to man fully with crews and fighting men those ships (the best that he had) that remained.
51   *from the head . . . Beat:* beat away from the headland of Actium.
54   *is descried:* has been sighted.
57   *power:* army.
58   *hold:* command.
60   *Thetis,* a sea-nymph, one of the fifty daughters of Nereus, and mother of Achilles. See note to II.ii.209. Cleopatra, powerful at sea, is identified with the sea-goddess by Antony.
62   *misdoubt:* distrust.
64   *go a-ducking:* (a) take to the water (like ducks), (b) be ducked in the sea.
65   *Have used:* are accustomed.
66   *foot to foot:* in close combat.
68   *whole action . . . on't:* plan of action is being formed without regard to where his real strength lies.
70   *womens men:* the servants of women.
71   *The legions . . . whole:* the infantry and cavalry together.
73   *for sea:* to fight by sea.

Distract* your army, which doth most consist
Of war-marked footmen,* leave unexecuted
Your own renownèd knowledge,* quite forgo   45
The way which promises assurance,* and
Give up yourself merely* to chance and hazard
From firm security.*

ANTONY   I'll fight at sea.
CLEOPATRA I have sixty sails,* Caesar none better.
ANTONY Our overplus of shipping* will we burn,   50
And with the rest full-manned, from th' head of Actium
Beat* th' approaching Caesar. But if we fail
We then can do't at land.

Enter a MESSENGER.

                                 Thy business?
MESSENGER The news is true, my lord; he is descried.*
Caesar has taken Toryne.   55
ANTONY Can he be there in person? 'Tis impossible;
Strange that his power* should be. Canidius,
Our nineteen legions thou shalt hold* by land,
And our twelve thousand horse. We'll to our ship.
Away, my Thetis!*

Enter a SOLDIER.

                                 How now, worthy soldier?   60
SOLDIER O noble Emperor, do not fight by sea;
Trust not to rotten planks. Do you misdoubt*
This sword, and these my wounds? Let th' Egyptians
And the Phoenicians go a-ducking:* we
Have used* to conquer standing on the earth   65
And fighting foot to foot.*
ANTONY   Well, well, away!
                    [*Exeunt* ANTONY, CLEOPATRA *and* ENOBARBUS
SOLDIER By Hercules, I think I am i' th' right.
CANIDIUS Soldier, thou art. But his whole action grows
Not in the power on't:* so our leader's led,
And we are women's men.*
SOLDIER   You keep by land   70
The legions and the horse whole,* do you not?
CANIDIUS Marcus Octavius, Marcus Justeius,
Publicola and Caelius, are for sea,*

75	*Carries:* propels him forward. – The term is taken from the flight of the arrow in archery.
76	*His power . . . spies:* his army (*power*) marched off in so many divided units (*distractions*) that all Antony's spies were deceived.
80	*With news . . . some* – i.e. there is fresh news every minute. The image is one of pregnancy and birth, with a possible play on *throws,* which has the same sound as *throes,* meaning birth-pains, creating an atmosphere of anxious expectancy.

| III.viii. | Caesar and then Antony are briefly glimpsed giving their orders for battle. |
| – ix. | The structure of several short, rapid and contrasting scenes at this point in the play admirably establishes the required sense of urgency and excitement. |

3	*keep whole:* keep your forces together.
5	*The prescript of this scroll:* the instructions in this paper.
5	*lies / Upon this jump:* depends on the outcome of this venture.

| 1 | *squadrons:* bodies of troops. |
| 2 | *In eye . . . battle:* within sight of Caesar's line of battle. |

But we keep whole by land. This speed of Caesar's
Carries* beyond belief.

SOLDIER   While he was yet in Rome,   75
His power went out in such distractions as
Beguiled all spies.*

CANIDIUS   Who's his lieutenant, hear you?

SOLDIER   They say, one Taurus.

CANIDIUS   Well I know the man.

Enter a MESSENGER.

MESSENGER   The Emperor calls Canidius.

CANIDIUS   With news the time's with labour, and throws forth   80
Each minute some.*

                                                    [*Exeunt*

scene viii

Near Actium.

Enter CAESAR *marching with his army.*

CAESAR   Taurus!

TAURUS   My lord?

CAESAR   Strike not by land, keep whole,* provoke not battle
Till we have done at sea. Do not exceed
The prescript of this scroll.* Our fortune lies   5
Upon this jump.*

                                                    [*Exeunt*

scene ix

Actium.

Enter ANTONY *and* ENOBARBUS.

ANTONY   Set we our squadrons* on yond side o' th'hill
In eye of Caesar's battle;* from which place
We may the number of the ships behold,
And so proceed accordingly.

                                                    [*Exeunt*

III.x.   A distraught Enobarbus enters, describing the flight of Cleopatra's fleet. Next comes
Scarus, infuriated by Cleopatra's defection, who reports that Antony has shamefully
followed her. They are joined by Canidius, who tells them that six kings have followed
Antony's example and capitulated and that he too proposes to surrender his forces
Enobarbus sees that all is lost, but determines, against his reason, to remain loyal to
Antony.

   Shakespeare, unable to represent the sea-battle on stage, is forced to report it. His
technique of constructing the scene around a series of individual entries, each character
rushing in in a state of excitement and anger, achieves the necessary pace and movement
and a cumulative sense of disintegration and despair.

*   *Alarum*. A call to arms, or warning that action is imminent.
1   *Naught*: Reduced to nothing, ruined.
2   *Th'Antoniad* – Cleopatra's flagship (*admiral*) is named in honour of Antony, a detail
              invented by Shakespeare.
3   *their sixty* – i.e. the Egyptian fleet.
4   *blasted*: destroyed (as if by a withering blight).
5   *synod*: assembly. – Ancient mythology represents the gods and goddesses as meeting
              together from time to time to decide quarrels and issues of various kinds.
5   *thy passion*: the emotion that disturbs you.
6   *cantle*: segment (of a sphere).
7   *very ignorance*: sheer stupidity.
7   *kissed away* – i.e. lost through Antony's infatuation.
9   *the tokened pestilence*: the spots denoting the plague. – These were invariably fatal, and a
              familiar phenomenon in Elizabethan England. Some twenty-five thousand
              Londoners had died of plague a few years before in 1603.
10   *ribaudred nag*: wanton creature. – A *nag* is literally a small horse.
11   *Whom leprosy o'ertake*: may she be stricken with leprosy.
12   *When vantage . . . appeared*: when the fight was so even that neither side appeared to
              have the advantage.
13   *ours the elder* – i.e. we were slightly ahead.
14   *The breeze upon her* – There is play on the two meanings of *breeze*, 'wind', and 'horsefly':
              (a) as if she had been stung by a horsefly, (b) the wind blowing her.
17   *being loofed*: (a) having luffed, i.e. turned her ship's head close to the wind in order to
              sail off, (b) having made herself scarce (playing on *aloof* meaning 'at a distance').
18   *The noble . . . magic*: the once-noble man ruined by her witchcraft.
19   *Claps on his sea-wing*: sets sail for flight.
19   *doting mallard*: wild drake flying after the duck. – To *dote* is to love foolishly or
              excessively.
20   *in heighth*: at its height.
22   *ne'er before . . . itself*: never before disgraced themselves in this way.

scene x

Near Actium.

CANIDIUS *marches with his army one way across the stage, and*
TAURUS, *with* CAESAR'S *army, the other way. The noise of a sea-*
*fight is heard. Alarum.**

Enter ENOBARBUS.

ENOBARBUS Naught, naught, all naught!* I can behold no longer.
Th' Antoniad,* the Egyptian admiral,
With all their sixty,* fly and turn the rudder.
To see't, mine eyes are blasted.*

Enter SCARUS.

SCARUS   Gods and goddesses,
All the whole synod* of them!
ENOBARBUS   What's thy passion?*   5
SCARUS The greater cantle* of the world is lost
With very ignorance.* We have kissed away*
Kingdoms and provinces.
ENOBARBUS   How appears the fight?
SCARUS On our side like the tokened pestilence,*
Where death is sure. Yon ribaudred nag* of Egypt –   10
Whom leprosy o'ertake!* – i'th'midst o' th'fight,
When vantage like a pair of twins appeared,*
Both as the same, or rather ours the elder,*
The breeze upon her,* like a cow in June,
Hoists sails and flies.
ENOBARBUS   That I beheld: 15
Mine eyes did sicken at the sight, and could not
Endure a further view.
SCARUS   She once being loofed,*
The noble ruin of her magic,* Antony,
Claps on his sea-wing,* and, like a doting mallard,*
Leaving the fight in heighth,* flies after her.   20
I never saw an action of such shame;
Experience, manhood, honour, ne'er before
Did violate so itself.*
ENOBARBUS   Alack, alack!

24	*out of breath:* exhausted.
26	*Been what he knew himself:* acted like the leader he knows he is.
26	*had:* would have.
27	*he has given . . . own:* his shameful running away has set the example for us to do the same (*grossly:* with unpleasant clarity).
28	*are you thereabouts:* is that what you are thinking of?
29	*Why then . . . indeed:* If that is so then it is certainly the end.
31	*to't* – i.e. to get to Peloponnesus.
31	*attend:* wait and see.
32	*render:* surrender.
34	*Show . . . yielding:* set me an example by their surrender.
35	*wounded chance:* damaged fortunes.
36	*Sits in the wind:* blows. – Enobarbus believes that his decision is irrational.

III.xi.   Having reached Alexandria. Antony is in a mood of profound self-disgust. He tells his followers to divide his treasure and submit to Caesar and promises letters to his friends on their behalf. He hints that he has determined to commit suicide. Cleopatra, genuinely frightened, begs forgiveness for her flight. Antony is tortured by the thought of defeat at the hands of one he knows to be his inferior as a soldier, and also by the memory of his former power and glory, now lost. He reproaches Cleopatra, but then forgives her, calling for food and drink and professing his scorn of Fortune.

Antony's defeat marks an important turning point in the play. Good fortune hitherto has demonstrated Antony's less admirable qualities. With his fortunes at their lowest he shows at his best. His concern for the welfare of his faithful followers despite his own suffering, his magnanimity in forgiving Cleopatra, and the nobility of his total devotion to her, however misplaced, win powerful support for him.

1   *Hark . . . bear me* – Shakespeare probably intended the actor taking Antony's part to indicate his deep dejection by walking so heavily across the boards of the stage that they re-echoed his tread. As he says (at line 73), he is *full of lead.* In *Troilus and Cressida* (I.iii.153–6) Shakespeare censures

> a strutting player whose conceit
> Lies in his hamstring, and doth think it rich
> To hear the wooden dialogue and sound
> 'Twixt his stretched footing and the scaffoldage.

Antony here interprets 'the wooden dialogue' as the earth's expression of its disapproval of him.

3	*lated:* belated, like a traveller overtaken on his journey by darkness.
7	*instructed* – i.e. taught them by his example, not verbally.
8	*show their shoulders:* turn their backs in flight.
9	*a course* – Antony means suicide.
12	*that:* what.
13	*mutiny:* quarrel.
14	*they them* – i.e. the brown hairs reprove the white. Antony is saying that the mature part of his make-up (the white hair) blames his immaturity (the brown hair) in rashly accepting Caesar's challenge to fight at sea and the brown blames the white for fear and infatuated love in following Cleopatra in her flight.

Enter CANIDIUS.

CANIDIUS Our fortune on the sea is out of breath,*
          And sinks most lamentably. Had our general   25
          Been what he knew himself,* it had* gone well.
          O, he has given example for our flight
          Most grossly by his own!*
ENOBARBUS   Ay, are you thereabouts?*
          Why then, good night indeed.*
CANIDIUS Toward Peloponnesus are they fled.   30
SCARUS   'Tis easy to't,* and there I will attend*
          What further comes.
CANIDIUS   To Caesar will I render*
          My legions and my horse; six kings already
          Show me the way of yielding.*
ENOBARBUS   I'll yet follow
          The wounded chance* of Antony, though my reason   35
          Sits in the wind* against me.

                                                    [*Exeunt*

scene xi

Alexandria. CLEOPATRA'S *palace.*

Enter ANTONY *with* ATTENDANTS.

ANTONY Hark, the land bids me tread no more upon't;
        It is ashamed to bear me.* Friends, come hither.
        I am so lated* in the world that I
        Have lost my way for ever. I have a ship
        Laden with gold: take that, divide it; fly,   5
        And make your peace with Caesar.
ALL   Fly? Not we.
ANTONY I have fled myself, and have instructed* cowards
        To run and show their shoulders.* Friends, be gone.
        I have myself resolved upon a course*
        Which has no need of you. Be gone.   10
        My treasure's in the harbour. Take it. O,
        I followed that* I blush to look upon.
        My very hairs do mutiny,* for the white
        Reprove the brown for rashness, and they them*

17	*Sweep your way:* smooth things out.
18	*loathness:* unwillingness.
18	*the hint* – i.e. his hint at suicide.
19	*Let that . . . itself:* Leave him who is about to leave himself, i.e. die – Antony is telling them that since he is resolved on suicide their loyalty to him is against their interests.
21	*possess you:* put you in possession of.
23	*I have lost command:* (a) I have no right to order you; and possibly (b) my emotions overcome me. – Antony's short disjointed phrases at the end of this speech support the second interpretation.
28	*O Juno!* – Juno, the chief Roman goddess, and protectress of women, was among other things a moon goddess, which would make this invocation by Cleopatra, the earthly Isis, appropriate here.
29	*No . . . no!* – Antony is lost in bitter reflections as he relives the battle. At line 35 he does not recognize Eros and addresses him as *my lord.*
30	*See you here:* Do you see Cleopatra here beside you?
35	*He* – i.e. Octavius.
35	*kept . . . dancer:* did not draw his sword, but wore it as an ornament like a dancer.
38	*the mad Brutus ended:* defeated the mad Brutus. – Brutus committed suicide. Antony means that by being instrumental in his defeat, he brought about his destruction.
38	*He alone . . . lieutenantry:* Only Octavius relied on his subordinate officers to do the fighting.
40	*squares* – i.e. troops drawn up in square formations.
41	*stand by:* stand near me. – Cleopatra addresses her maids as she pretends to be about to faint.
44	*is unqualitied:* has lost all self-possession.
45	*Well then, sustain me:* If I do go to him you must hold me up. – Cleopatra is so apprehensive at this moment that she may really need their help.
47	*declined:* bowed down.
47	*but:* unless.
49	*offended reputation:* injured my good name.
50	*unnoble swerving:* dishonourable transgression.
52	*convey . . . dishonour:* remove my shame from your sight by turning back and reflecting on my dishonourable actions. – Antony is turned away from her physically and mentally, so that she will not see the shame written on his face or hidden in his thoughts. *'Stroyed:* destroyed.

For fear and doting. Friends, be gone. You shall   15
Have letters from me to some friends that will
Sweep your way* for you. Pray you, look not sad,
Nor make replies of loathness;* take the hint*
Which my despair proclaims. Let that be left
Which leaves itself.* To the sea-side straightway.   20
I will possess you* of that ship and treasure.
Leave me, I pray, a little: pray you now,
Nay, do so; for indeed I have lost command,*
Therefore I pray you. I'll see you by and by.

                    [*He sits down. Exeunt Attendants*

    Enter CLEOPATRA *led by* CHARMIAN, IRAS *and* EROS.

EROS   Nay, gentle madam, to him, comfort him.   25
IRAS   Do, most dear Queen.
CHARMIAN   Do? Why, what else?
CLEOPATRA   Let me sit down. O Juno!*
ANTONY   No, no, no, no, no!*
EROS   See you here,* sir?   30
ANTONY   O fie, fie, fie!
CHARMIAN   Madam!
IRAS   Madam, O, good empress!
EROS   Sir, sir!
ANTONY   Yes, my lord, yes. He* at Philippi kept   35
His sword e'en like a dancer,* while I struck
The lean and wrinkled Cassius, and 'twas I
That the mad Brutus ended.* He alone
Dealt on lieutenantry,* and no practice had
In the brave squares* of war, yet now – no matter.   40
CLEOPATRA   Ah, stand by.*
EROS   The Queen, my lord, the Queen.
IRAS   Go to him, madam, speak to him;
He is unqualitied* with very shame.
CLEOPATRA   Well then, sustain me.* O!   45
EROS   Most noble sir, arise, the Queen approaches:
Her head's declined,* and death will seize her, but*
Your comfort makes the rescue.
ANTONY   I have offended reputation;*
A most unnoble swerving.*
EROS   Sir, the Queen.   50
ANTONY   O, whither hast thou led me, Egypt? See
How I convey my shame out of thine eyes

55   *my fearful sails:* my sailing away in such fear.
57   *th'strings* – i.e. the heart strings, the most intense affections or emotions.
60   *Thy beck . . . me:* your slightest gesture (*beck*) would force me to obey, even against the
         command (*from the bidding*) of the gods.
61   *my pardon:* pardon me.
62   *treaties:* peace proposals.
62   *dodge . . . lowness:* be shifty (*dodge*) and equivocate (*palter*) using the tricks (*shifts*) of
         one whose fortunes are low.
64   *bulk:* mass.
68   *on all cause:* whatever the reason.
69   *Fall:* Let fall.
69   *rates:* is worth.
72   *our schoolmaster* – i.e. Euphronius, the tutor of his children by Cleopatra.
73   *full of lead:* depressed in spirit.
74   *viands:* food.

III.xii. Caesar rejects Antony's requests to be allowed to live in Egypt, or as a private citizen in
          Athens, which are brought by his ambassador, an Egyptian schoolmaster. He will concede
          Cleopatra's request that her children should rule Egypt provided that she expels or kills
          Antony. Caesar sends Thidias to promise anything in his name that will win Cleopatra
          away from Antony and to observe how Antony takes his defeat.
              Caesar's strategy of driving a wedge between Antony and Cleopatra through bribery,
          based on his cynical conviction that all women have their price, and his cruel interest in
          Antony's suffering, swing audience sympathy away from him towards Antony.

3   *An argument . . . wing:* a proof that he is stripped of his power when he sends here such a
         humble follower.

By looking back what I have left behind
'Stroyed in dishonour.*

CLEOPATRA   O my lord, my lord,
Forgive my fearful sails!* I little thought   55
You would have followed.

ANTONY   Egypt, thou knew'st too well
My heart was to thy rudder tied by th'strings,*
And thou shouldst tow me after. O'er my spirit
Thy full supremacy thou knew'st, and that
Thy beck might from the bidding of the gods   60
Command me.*

CLEOPATRA   O, my pardon!*

ANTONY   Now I must
To the young man send humble treaties*, dodge
And palter in the shifts of lowness,* who
With half the bulk* o' th'world played as I pleased,
Making and marring fortunes. You did know   65
How much you were my conqueror, and that
My sword, made weak by my affection, would
Obey it on all cause.*

CLEOPATRA   Pardon, pardon!

ANTONY Fall* not a tear, I say; one of them rates*
All that is won and lost. Give me a kiss.   70
Even this repays me.
We sent our schoolmaster;* is 'a come back?
Love, I am full of lead.* Some wine
Within there, and our viands!* Fortune knows
We scorn her most when most she offers blows.   75

[*Exeunt*

scene xii

Egypt. CAESAR's *camp.*

Enter CAESAR, AGRIPPA, DOLABELLA *and* THIDIAS, *with others.*

CAESAR Let him appear that's come from Antony.
Know you him?

DOLABELLA   Caesar, 'tis his schoolmaster –
An argument that he is plucked, when hither
He sends so poor a pinion of his wing,*

5	*Which:* who.
8	*of late . . . ends:* until recently as insignificant in his plans.
10	*To his grand sea:* to the great sea that is Antony.
12	*Requires:* requests.
12	*which not granted:* and if this request is not granted.
13	*lessons:* teaches a lesson, disciplines – with a play on *lessens*. Some editors emend *lessons* to *lessens*, but this robs the pedantic schoolmaster of a pun appropriate to his nature and occupation.
15	*This for him:* This is the message I have to deliver for him.
18	*circle:* crown.
19	*hazarded to thy grace:* dependent on your favour.
21	*Of audience . . . fail:* shall not fail to get either a hearing or her wish.
21	*so:* provided that.
22	*friend:* lover.
24	*unheard:* in vain.
24	*So –* i.e. Deliver this answer.
25	*Bring . . . bands:* Conduct him safely past our troops.
26	*To try . . . Dispatch:* It is now time for you to see what your eloquence can do. Hurry away from here.
27	*From Antony win Cleopatra:* Persuade Cleopatra to turn against Antony.
28	*in our name:* on my authority.
28	*add . . . offers:* make her further offers as you think fit.
29	*Women are . . . vestal:* Women are not steadfast (*strong*) even when their fortunes are at their highest, but urgent need (*want*) will make the most virtuous (*ne'er touched*) break her vows (*perjure*). – The *vestals* were the Roman virgin priestesses of the goddess Vesta, symbols of innocence and virtue.
31	*cunning:* skill. – The word was rarely used in the sixteenth century with the modern connotation of 'crafty'.
32	*Make thine . . . law:* decree your own reward for your efforts, which I will give you as if bound by law.
34	*becomes his flaw:* adapts himself to his broken fortunes.
35	*And what . . . moves:* and what you think his behaviour in everything he does tells about his state of mind.

Which* had superfluous kings for messengers   5
Not many moons gone by.

Enter AMBASSADOR *from* ANTONY.

CAESAR   Approach, and speak.
AMBASSADOR Such as I am, I come from Antony.
I was of late as petty to his ends*
As is the morn-dew on the myrtle leaf
To his grand sea.*
CAESAR   Be't so. Declare thine office.   10
AMBASSADOR Lord of his fortunes he salutes thee, and
Requires* to live in Egypt, which not granted,*
He lessons* his requests, and to thee sues
To let him breathe between the heavens and earth,
A private man in Athens. This for him.*   15
Next, Cleopatra does confess thy greatness,
Submits her to thy might, and of thee craves
The circle* of the Ptolemies for her heirs,
Now hazarded to thy grace.*
CAESAR   For Antony,
I have no ears to his request. The Queen   20
Of audience nor desire shall fail,* so* she
From Egypt drive her all-disgracèd friend,*
Or take his life there. This if she perform,
She shall not sue unheard.* So* to them both.
AMBASSADOR Fortune pursue thee!
CAESAR   Bring him through the bands.*   25

                                     [*Exit* AMBASSADOR
[*To* THIDIAS] To try thy eloquence now 'tis time. Dispatch.*
From Antony win Cleopatra:* promise,
And in our name,* what she requires; add more,
From thine invention, offers.* Women are not
In their best fortunes strong, but want will perjure   30
The ne'er-touched vestal.* Try thy cunning,* Thidias;
Make thine own edict for thy pains, which we
Will answer as a law.*
THIDIAS   Caesar, I go.
CAESAR Observe how Antony becomes his flaw,*
And what thou think'st his very action speaks   35
In every power that moves.*
THIDIAS   Caesar, I shall.

                                     [*Exeunt*

III.xiii. When Antony has heard Caesar's reply from the schoolmaster he goes off to write a letter challenging Caesar to single combat, and Enobarbus tells himself that it is folly to be loyal to someone behaving so foolishly. Thidias arrives from Caesar saying that his master knows that Cleopatra's relationship with Antony was forced upon her. When Enobarbus hears Cleopatra apparently agreeing with this he hurries off to fetch Antony, who enters to find Thidias kissing Cleopatra's hand. He has him whipped and returned to Caesar, and turns savagely on Cleopatra. She protests her love for him and they are again reconciled. In a final speech of mingled rant and hopefulness, Antony decides to fight on against Caesar after 'one other gaudy night'. Enobarbus resolves to leave him.

Antony's savagery towards Thidias is very like that of Cleopatra to the messenger in II.v. The two scenes are close parallels in structure and substance, with a quiet beginning, a swift rise to impassioned climax, and a calmer ending with a note of suspense about the outcome of events. Just as Cleopatra's jealousy was provoked by her passion for Antony whom, she feared had deserted her, so now Antony's anger stems from his passion for Cleopatra whom he suspects of betraying his love, and in both cases while we deplore the outburst of violence against an innocent man we pity the protagonist because we understand that it is prompted by love and suffering. The deliberate parallelism of structure and situation powerfully suggests the closeness of the lovers through identity of temperament and passion. Suspense is aroused through our speculation about Cleopatra's motives in showing favours to Thidias – a question that Shakespeare carefully avoids answering in the play.

1	*Think and die* – Enobarbus believes that if they meditate on their present situation they will be so profoundly depressed that death will inevitably follow.
2	*or we:* or are we.
3	*would make . . . reason:* insisted on subjecting his reason to his desire (*will*).
4	*What though:* What did it matter that.
5	*ranges:* lines of warships.
7	*itch of his affection:* craving of his passion.
8	*nicked* – Either (a) got the better of, or (b) maimed (from *nick*, to cut a piece out of).
8	*captainship:* leadership.
9	*When half . . . question:* when one half of the world was fighting the other, and he was the whole (*mered*) cause of the dispute (*question*).
11	*course:* chase.
12	*gazing:* looking on in astonishment.
15	*courtesy, so:* kind treatment, if.
19	*principalities* – i.e. regions for Cleopatra to rule over as prince.
20	*rose* – i.e. rosy bloom.
21	*from which . . . particular:* on account of which (his *youth*) the world ought to see him perform some outstanding feat (*something particular*).
23	*ministers:* agents.
23	*prevail:* be victorious.
26	*comparisons* – i.e. the ships, legions and other things which made him Antony's superior by comparison.
27	*answer me:* accept my invitation to fight. – The verb is used in the same sense in line 36 also.
27	*declined* – i.e. in both age and fortunes.

scene xiii

Alexandria. CLEOPATRA'S *palace.*

Enter CLEOPATRA, ENOBARBUS, CHARMIAN *and* IRAS.

CLEOPATRA	What shall we do, Enobarbus?
ENOBARBUS	Think, and die.*
CLEOPATRA	Is Antony, or we,* in fault for this?
ENOBARBUS	Antony only, that would make his will

     Lord of his reason.* What though* you fled
     From that great face of war, whose several ranges*   5
     Frighted each other? Why should he follow?
     The itch of his affection* should not then
     Have nicked* his captainship* at such a point,
     When half to half the world opposed, he being
     The merèd question.* 'Twas a shame no less   10
     Than was his loss, to course* your flying flags
     And leave his navy gazing.*

CLEOPATRA   Prithee, peace.

Enter ANTONY *with the* AMBASSADOR.

ANTONY	Is that his answer?
AMBASSADOR	Ay, my lord.
ANTONY	The Queen shall then have courtesy,* so she 15

     Will yield us up.

AMBASSADOR   He says so.

ANTONY   Let her know't.
     To the boy Caesar send this grizzled head,
     And he will fill thy wishes to the brim
     With principalities.*

CLEOPATRA   That head, my lord?

ANTONY   To him again. Tell him he wears the rose*   20
     Of youth upon him, from which the world should note
     Something particular.* His coin, ships, legions,
     May be a coward's, whose ministers* would prevail*
     Under the service of a child as soon
     As i' th'command of Caesar. I dare him therefore   25
     To lay his gay comparisons* apart
     And answer me* declined,* sword against sword,
     Ourselves alone. I'll write it. Follow me.

         [*Exeunt* ANTONY *and the* AMBASSADOR

29   *like enough . . . sworder:* it is highly likely that Caesar who commands great armies (*high-battled*) will abdicate (*unstate*) his present good fortune, and come on-stage to make an exhibition (*show*) of himself against a professional swordsman (*sworder*). – Public sword-fights for money were popular in Elizabethan London. Enobarbus is contemptuous at the stupidity of Antony's suggestion.

32   *A parcel of:* of the same nature as. – Cf. the modern phrase 'part and parcel of'.

32   *things outward . . . alike:* external misfortunes (*things outward*) compel the inner character to follow them, so that both deteriorate together.

35   *Knowing all measures:* having experience of every degree (*all measures*) of fortune. – The image is that of filling and emptying vessels, as in line 18 above.

38   *no more ceremony* – Cleopatra is indignant at the servant's unceremonious announcement.

39   *Against . . . buds* – i.e. those who showed us respect when we had power, openly reject us now that we have lost it. *Blown:* dying, having bloomed.

41   *honesty . . . square:* honour and self-interest begin to oppose each other.

42   *loyalty . . . folly:* firm (*well held*) loyalty to fools makes our fidelity altogether foolish.

45   *Does conquer . . . conquer:* shows his superiority over the one who conquered his master.

46   *earns a place i' th'story:* deserves renown. – Enobarbus is torn between loyalty and self-interest.

47   *None but friends:* Everyone here is a friend.

48   *haply:* perhaps.

49   *He needs . . . not us* – Enobarbus means that if Caesar's terms are favourable then Antony needs all the friends he can get; if unfavourable, then he needs no friends since his situation is hopeless.

51   *For us . . . Caesar's:* As for us, you know that whoever Antony belongs to, so do we, and he belongs to Caesar.

52   *So:* Very well.

53   *Caesar . . . Caesar:* Caesar begs you not to worry about your position, except to remember that he is Caesar (and therefore magnanimous).

55   *right royal:* a truly royal message.

57   *As:* because.

59   *constrainèd blemishes:* faults forced on you.

ENOBARBUS [*Aside*] Yes, like enough, high-battled Caesar will
          Unstate his happiness, and be staged to th' show   30
          Against a sworder!* I see men's judgements are
          A parcel* of their fortunes, and things outward
          Do draw the inward quality after them,
          To suffer all alike.* That he should dream,
          Knowing all measures,* the full Caesar will   35
          Answer his emptiness! Caesar, thou hast subdued
          His judgement too.

          Enter a SERVANT.

SERVANT   A messenger from Caesar.
CLEOPATRA What, no more ceremony?* See, my women,
          Against the blown rose may they stop their nose
          That kneeled unto the buds.* Admit him, sir.   40

                                                    [*Exit* SERVANT

ENOBARBUS [*Aside*] Mine honesty and I begin to square.*
          The loyalty well held to fools does make
          Our faith mere folly:* yet he that can endure
          To follow with allegiance a fall'n lord
          Does conquer him that did his master conquer,*   45
          And earns a place i' th'story.*

          Enter THIDIAS.

CLEOPATRA   Caesar's will?
THIDIAS   Hear it apart.
CLEOPATRA   None but friends.* Say boldly.
THIDIAS   So, haply,* are they friends to Antony.
ENOBARBUS He needs as many, sir, as Caesar has,
          Or needs not us.* If Caesar please, our master   50
          Will leap to be his friend. For us, you know,
          Whose he is, we are, and that is Caesar's.*
THIDIAS   So.*
          Thus then, thou most renowned, Caesar entreats
          Not to consider in what case thou stand'st
          Further than he is Caesar.*
CLEOPATRA   Go on: right royal.*   55
THIDIAS   He knows that you embraced not Antony
          As* you did love, but as you feared him.
CLEOPATRA   O!
THIDIAS   The scars upon your honour, therefore, he
          Does pity as constrainèd* blemishes,

61   *right:* true.
62   *merely:* completely.
63   *leaky . . . sinking* – The image suggests rats leaving a sinking ship, and so is a powerful, though unconscious, piece of self-criticism by Enobarbus, and a means of evoking sympathy for Antony.
66   *require:* request. – Cf. III.xii.12, 28.
66   *partly . . . desired:* almost begs to be asked.
71   *shroud* – i.e. protection.
72   *universal landlord:* lord of the whole world.
74   *in deputation:* as my representative.
75   *prompt:* ready.
77   *all-obeying breath:* words which all obey.
77   *I hear . . . Egypt:* I accept the judgement on myself.
79   *Wisdom . . . shake it:* When there is a contest (*combating together*) between prudence (*wisdom*) and taking a chance (*fortune*), if prudence is allowed to make the decision, chance cannot bring misfortune.
81   *grace:* permission.
81   *lay . . . hand:* pay my respects by kissing your hand.
82   *Caesar's father* – Cleopatra refers to Julius Caesar, who was, in fact, the brother of Octavius's grandmother.
83   *hath mused of taking kingdoms in:* was thinking about capturing kingdoms.
85   *As:* as if.
85   *Favours?* – Antony refers to Cleopatra's allowing Thidias to kiss her hand.
85   *Jove that thunders* – Jove was, among other things, the god of thunder.
87   *fullest:* most complete in character and fortunes.

Not as deserved.

CLEOPATRA   He is a god, and knows   60
What is most right.* Mine honour was not yielded,
But conquered merely.*

ENOBARBUS   [*Aside*] To be sure of that,
I will ask Antony. Sir, sir, thou art so leaky
That we must leave thee to thy sinking,* for
Thy dearest quit thee.

                                        [*Exit* ENOBARBUS

THIDIAS   Shall I say to Caesar   65
What you require* of him? For he partly begs
To be desired* to give. It much would please him
That of his fortunes you should make a staff
To lean upon. But it would warm his spirits
To hear from me you had left Antony,   70
And put yourself under his shroud,*
The universal landlord.*

CLEOPATRA   What's your name?

THIDIAS My name is Thidias.

CLEOPATRA   Most kind messenger,
Say to great Caesar this in deputation*:
I kiss his conqu'ring hand. Tell him I am prompt*   75
To lay my crown at's feet, and there to kneel.
Tell him, from his all-obeying breath* I hear
The doom of Egypt.*

THIDIAS   'Tis your noblest course.
Wisdom and fortune combating together,
If that the former dare but what it can,   80
No chance may shake it.* Give me grace* to lay
My duty on your hand.*

CLEOPATRA   Your Caesar's father* oft,
When he hath mused of taking kingdoms in,*
Bestowed his lips on that unworthy place,
As* it rained kisses.

Enter ANTONY *and* ENOBARBUS.

ANTONY   Favours?* By Jove that thunders!*   85
What art thou fellow?

THIDIAS   One that but performs
The bidding of the fullest* man, and worthiest
To have command obeyed.

ENOBARBUS   [*Aside*] You will be whipped.

89   *kite:* bird of prey. – It is not certain whether Antony is addressing Cleopatra or Thidias, though the latter seems most likely since the image of the bird of prey is singularly appropriate as Antony catches sight of Thidias bending over Cleopatra's hand, and the word *feeders* (line 109) applied to him tends to confirm this interpretation.

89   *Now, gods and devils* – Antony is incensed because the servants are so slow to obey.

90   *Of late:* Until recently.

91   *unto a muss:* to a scrambling game. – *Muss* was a game in which small objects were thrown down to be scrambled for by those taking part.

91   *start forth:* jump forward.

93   *Jack:* rascal.

94   *better* – i.e. safer.

94   *lion's whelp* – Enobarbus possibly alludes to Octavius.

96   *tributaries* – i.e. rulers paying tribute.

98   *saucy:* insolent.

98   *she* – The pronoun is used as a noun.

98   *what's . . . Cleopatra* – Antony will not call her Cleopatra because she is not behaving as he, in his present mood, thinks she ought to, namely, like a great queen.

100   *cringe:* distort.

102   *Being:* When he has been.

104   *Bear us an errand:* carry a message for me.

105   *blasted:* withered.

106   *my pillow left unpressed* – i.e. deserted my home.

107   *Forborne . . . race:* refrained from begetting legitimate offspring.

108   *a gem* – i.e. Octavia.

108   *abused:* wronged.

109   *feeders:* servants (i.e. those whom one feeds).

110   *boggler:* fickle waverer.

111   *in our viciousness grow hard:* become hardened in our vices.

112   *seel:* stitch up. – In falconry the hawk eyelids were temporarily stitched up or *seeled* to train it to become accustomed to the use of the hood, the leather cap that covered the eyes when the hawk was not in action – a hawk blindfolded in either of these ways would sit quietly on the owner's hand.

113   *In our . . . judgements:* make our evil inclinations swamp our right judgements.

114   *at's while . . . our confusion:* at us while we swagger to our destruction.

117   *trencher:* wooden plate.

118   *hotter:* more sensual.

119   *Unregistered in vulgar fame:* not recorded in the rumours of the common people.

120   *Luxuriously picked out:* lecherously selected.

121   *temperance should be:* chastity ought to be.

122   *Wherefore is this?:* Why are you saying all this?

ANTONY   [*Calling for* SERVANTS] Approach there! – Ah, you kite!* –
Now, gods and devils!*
Authority melts from me. Of late,* when I cried 'Ho!'   90
Like boys unto a muss,* kings would start forth*
And cry 'Your will?' Have you no ears?
I am Antony yet.
Enter SERVANTS.
                        Take hence this Jack,* and whip him.

ENOBARBUS [*Aside*] 'Tis better* playing with a lion's whelp,*
Than with an old one dying.

ANTONY   Moon and stars!   95
Whip him! Were't twenty of the greatest tributaries*
That do acknowledge Caesar, should I find them
So saucy* with the hand of she* here – what's her name
Since she was Cleopatra?* Whip him, fellows,
Till like a boy you see him cringe* his face   100
And whine aloud for mercy. Take him hence.

THIDIAS   Mark Antony!

ANTONY   Tug him away! Being* whipped,
Bring him again. This Jack of Caesar's shall
Bear us an errand* to him.   [*Exeunt* SERVANTS *with* THIDIAS
You were half blasted* ere I knew you. Ha?   105
Have I my pillow left unpressed* in Rome,
Forborne the getting of a lawful race,*
And by a gem of women,* to be abused*
By one that looks on feeders?*

CLEOPATRA   Good my lord, –

ANTONY   You have been a boggler* ever,   110
But when we in our viciousness grow hard – *
O misery on't! – the wise gods seel* our eyes,
In our own filth drop our clear judgements,* make us
Adore our errors, laugh at's while we strut
To our confusion.*

CLEOPATRA   O, is't come to this?   115

ANTONY   I found you as a morsel, cold upon
Dead Caesar's trencher;* nay, you were a fragment
Of Gnaeus Pompey's, besides what hotter hours,*
Unregistered in vulgar fame,* you have
Luxuriously picked out.* For I am sure,   120
Though you can guess what temperance should be,*
You know not what it is.

CLEOPATRA   Wherefore is this?*

124   *God quit you:* God reward you. – The phrase was common among beggars.
125   *kingly seal . . . hearts!* – Cleopatra's hand is described as the royal seal ratifying the agreement of these two monarchs (*high hearts*) to love each other.
127   *the hill of Basan,* mentioned in Psalms 22 and 68.
128   *The hornèd herd:* (a) the fat bulls which grazed on Basan (b) the men whom Cleopatra has cuckolded, among whom Antony includes himself.
128   *savage:* bitter.
129   *to proclaim . . . about him:* to talk about it politely would be like a prisoner with the rope round his neck thanking the hangman for hanging him quickly.
132   *'a:* he.
134   *let him . . . daughter* – i.e. so that he would have escaped this whipping.
138   *fever thee:* make you shiver with fear.
140   *thy entertainment:* how you have been received.
140   *Look:* Be sure.
146   *orbs:* spheres. Ptolemaic astronomy held that every star was fixed inside an invisible hollow sphere (*orb*).
147   *abysm:* abyss.
147   *mislike:* dislike.
149   *enfranchèd bondman:* freed slave.
151   *quit:* repay.
151   *Urge it thou:* You can insist on it.
152   *Stripes:* marks made by the whip.
153   *terrene moon:* earthly moon – i.e. Cleopatra is the earthly Isis, goddess of the moon.
154   *portends alone:* foretells only. – Elizabethans regarded an eclipse as an evil omen. In Antony's view, Cleopatra's light has been extinguished by her behaviour.
155   *stay his time:* wait till he recovers.
156   *mingle eyes:* exchange loving looks.
157   *ties his points:* laces up his (i.e. Caesar's) clothes. – *Points* were laces with tags for fastening various parts of Elizabethan clothes where we would use buttons. Antony refers to Thidias as if he were a mere valet or manservant of Caesar's
157   *Not know me yet?* i.e. Do you still know so little of me as to believe this?

ANTONY   To let a fellow that will take rewards
    And say, 'God quit you!'* be familiar with
    My playfellow, your hand, this kingly seal   125
    And plighter of high hearts!* O that I were
    Upon the hill of Basan,* to outroar
    The hornèd herd,* for I have savage* cause
    And to proclaim it civilly were like
    A haltered neck, which does the hangman thank   130
    For being yare about him.*

    Enter a SERVANT *with* THIDIAS.

                         Is he whipped?
SERVANT   Soundly, my lord.
ANTONY   Cried he? And begged 'a* pardon?
SERVANT   He did ask favour.
ANTONY   If that thy father live, let him repent
    Thou wast not made his daughter;* and be thou sorry   135
    To follow Caesar in his triumph, since
    Thou hast been whipped for following him. Henceforth
    The white hand of a lady fever thee;*
    Shake thou to look on't. Get thee back to Caesar;
    Tell him thy entertainment.* Look* thou say   140
    He makes me angry with him, for he seems
    Proud and disdainful, harping on what I am,
    Not what he knew I was. He makes me angry,
    And at this time most easy 'tis to do't,
    When my good stars that were my former guides   145
    Have empty left their orbs* and shot their fires
    Into th' abysm* of hell. If he mislike*
    My speech, and what is done, tell him he has
    Hipparchus, my enfranchèd bondman,* whom
    He may at pleasure whip, or hang, or torture,   150
    As he shall like, to quit* me. Urge it thou.*
    Hence with thy stripes,* be gone!   [*Exit* THIDIAS
CLEOPATRA   Have you done yet?
ANTONY   Alack, our terrene moon*
    Is now eclipsed, and it portends alone*
    The fall of Antony.
CLEOPATRA   I must stay his time.*   155
ANTONY   To flatter Caesar, would you mingle eyes*
    With one that ties his points?*
CLEOPATRA   Not know me yet?*

159   *engender:* produce.
160   *in:* on.
161   *determines:* comes to an end (by melting).
162   *The next Caesarion smite:* May the next stone strike down Caesarion (i.e. her eldest
                child by Julius Caesar).
163   *by degrees . . . womb:* one by one all my children. – *Memory:* memorials.
165   *discandying of this pelleted storm:* melting of this storm of pellets, i.e. hailstones
166   *graveless:* unburied.
167   *buried them:* consumed them.
169   *sits down in:* will besiege.
169   *his fate:* what he is destined to achieve.
170   *held:* kept intact.
171   *knit:* joined together.
171   *fleet:* float.
171   *most sea-like:* in a most seaworthy way.
172   *heart:* Most editors take this to mean 'courage', i.e. Antony talking to himself and not
                addressing Cleopatra here.
174   *in blood:* (a) covered with blood (b) with my fighting spirit roused.
175   *earn our chronicle:* win their place in history.
176   *in't:* in this situation.
177   *treble-sinewed, hearted, breathed:* be like three men in strength, courage and endurance.
178   *maliciously:* fiercely.
179   *nice:* luxurious.
179   *did ransom . . . jests:* won their freedom as a result of telling me jokes.
180   *set my teeth* – i.e. grit them against any kind of clemency.
182   *gaudy:* festive.
184   *mock* – i.e. by ignoring.
185   *I had . . . poor:* I had expected to celebrate it in a miserable way.
190   *peep:* to show itself.
191   *sap:* life.
192   *contend . . . scythe:* strive to kill as many as he does in times of plague. – Death is pictured
                as an old man carrying a scythe with which he cuts down his victims.

ANTONY   Cold-hearted toward me?

CLEOPATRA   Ah, dear, if I be so,
From my cold heart let heaven engender* hail
And poison it in* the source, and the first stone   160
Drop in my neck. As it determines,* so
Dissolve my life! The next Caesarion smite,*
Till by degrees the memory of my womb,*
Together with my brave Egyptians all,
By the discandying of this pelleted storm,*   165
Lie graveless,* till the flies and gnats of Nile
Have buried them* for prey.

ANTONY   I am satisfied.
Caesar sits down in* Alexandria, where
I will oppose his fate.* Our force by land
Hath nobly held;* our severed navy too   170
Have knit* again, and fleet,* threat'ning most sea-like.*
Where hast thou been, my heart?* Dost thou hear, lady?
If from the field I shall return once more
To kiss these lips, I will appear in blood;*
I and my sword will earn our chronicle.*   175
There's hope in't* yet.

CLEOPATRA   That's my brave lord!

ANTONY   I will be treble-sinewed, hearted, breathed,*
And fight maliciously;* for when mine hours
Were nice* and lucky, men did ransom lives
Of me for jests;* but now I'll set my teeth,*   180
And send to darkness all that stop me. Come,
Let's have one other gaudy* night. Call to me
All my sad captains; fill our bowls once more;
Let's mock* the midnight bell.

CLEOPATRA   It is my birthday.
I had thought t'have held it poor.* But since my lord   185
Is Antony again, I will be Cleopatra.

ANTONY   We will yet do well.

CLEOPATRA   Call all his noble captains to my lord.

ANTONY   Do so, we'll speak to them; and tonight I'll force
The wine peep* through their scars. Come on, my Queen,   190
There's sap* in't yet! The next time I do fight
I'll make Death love me, for I will contend
Even with his pestilent scythe.*

                              [*Exeunt all except* ENOBARBUS

194   *he'll outstare the lightning* – i.e. he thinks he can achieve the impossible.
194   *To be . . . of fear:* To be mad with fury is to lose fear.
196   *peck the estridge:* attack the goshawk (a fierce member of the falcon family).
197   *A diminution . . . heart:* As Antony's reason diminishes his courage revives.
199   *It eats . . . with:* destroys its best weapon. – Enobarbus's desertion is prompted by what
         seems to him the wild irrationality of Antony's behaviour.

ENOBARBUS Now he'll outstare the lightning.* To be furious
Is to be frighted out of fear,* and in that mood   195
The dove will peck the estridge;* and I see still
A diminution in our captain's brain
Restores his heart.* When valour preys on reason,
It eats the sword it fights with.* I will seek
Some way to leave him.   200
                                                                        [*Exit*

IV.i. Caesar reports to his followers Antony's reception of Thidias. He laughs contemptuously at Antony's challenge and declares that they will fight their last battle on the following day.

Caesar's cool control suggests his assured mastery of events, and is in striking contrast to Antony's fury. He describes Antony as 'the old ruffian', a phrase which earns more sympathy for Antony than for the speaker. Again, in contrast to Antony's liberality and warm relationship with his followers, we have Caesar's description of the feast he orders for his soldiers as 'the waste', one which he knows he can well afford since he has abundant stores.

1	*calls me 'boy'* – a gross insult in Shakespeare's day.
1	*chides as:* finds fault as if.
3	*He hath . . . rods:* he has had whipped with canes.
4	*Caesar to Antony:* This is Caesar's answer to Antony.
8	*falling:* the point of death.
8	*breath:* breathing space. – Antony is depicted as a hunted animal at bay.
9	*Make boot of his distraction:* take advantage of his mad rage.
9	*Never anger . . . itself:* An angry man never defended himself wisely. – Maecenas echoes what Enobarbus has just been saying.
10	*best heads:* ablest officers.
12	*files:* ranks.
13	*but late:* only recently.
14	*fetch him in:* capture him.
15	*store:* plentiful supplies.
16	*waste:* unnecessary expense.

IV.ii. Caesar's rejection of the challenge has reached Antony who now bids farewell to his servants, telling them that this will be their last night of service. When Enobarbus points out that his speech is making his followers weep, Antony attempts to assure them that he is hopeful of victory the next day. Antony and Cleopatra go off to supper.

In this moving scene, the effect of Antony's speech on the servants and on the hard-bitten Enobarbus indicates the audience response which Shakespeare aimed at. The devotion of his followers and his real concern for them enhance the pathos of his situation.

ACT IV scene i

Near Alexandria. CAESAR'S *camp.*

Enter CAESAR, AGRIPPA *and* MAECENAS, *with his army;*
CAESAR *reading a letter.*

CAESAR He calls me 'boy',* and chides as* he had power
To beat me out of Egypt. My messenger
He hath whipped with rods,* dares me to personal combat.
Caesar to Antony:* let the old ruffian know
I have many other ways to die; meantime   5
Laugh at his challenge.
MAECENAS   Caesar must think,
When one so great begins to rage, he's hunted
Even to falling.* Give him no breath,* but now
Make boot of his distraction.* Never anger
Made good guard for itself.*
CAESAR   Let our best heads*   10
Know that tomorrow the last of many battles
We mean to fight. Within our files* there are,
Of those that served Mark Antony but late,*
Enough to fetch him in.* See it done,
And feast the army; we have store* to do't,   15
And they have earned the waste.* Poor Antony!

                                             [*Exeunt*

scene ii

Alexandria. CLEOPATRA'S *palace.*

Enter ANTONY, CLEOPATRA, ENOBARBUS, CHARMIAN, IRAS,
ALEXAS *with others.*

ANTONY He will not fight with me, Domitius?
ENOBARBUS   No.
ANTONY Why should he not?
ENOBARBUS He thinks, being twenty times of better fortune,
He is twenty men to one.

135

5	*or:* either.
6	*Or bathe . . . live again:* or, if I die, I will cleanse my honour in my enemies' blood so that it will be restored.
7	*Woo't:* Will you . . .
8	*I'll strike . . . all':* (a) I'll surrender to the enemy and say 'Take everything', (b) I'll fight and let the winner take all, i.e. fight to the death. – Enobarbus equivocates, playing on the two meanings of *strike,* 'surrender' and 'fight', but Antony notices only the second meaning.
11	*rightly:* truly.
13	*your fellows* – i.e. my servants, like you.
14	*tricks:* unexpected actions.
16	*made so many men:* made into as many men as you all.
17	*clapped up together in:* made together into. – The literal meaning of 'clap up' is 'imprison'.
21	*Scant not my cups:* do not restrict the supply of wine.
23	*suffered:* obeyed.
24	*Tend:* Attend.
25	*period:* end.
26	*Haply:* perhaps.
26	*or if . . . shadow:* or if you do, it will be as a mutilated corpse.
30	*like a master . . . death:* Antony, echoing the Christian marriage service, insists that he will be parted from his servants only by death (as one partner in marriage is wedded to the other until death), and begs them, on their side, to be faithful till then.
33	*yield:* reward.

ANTONY   Tomorrow, soldier,
          By sea and land I'll fight; or* I will live,   5
          Or bathe my dying honour in the blood
          Shall make it live again.* Woo't thou fight well?*
ENOBARBUS I'll strike, and cry 'Take all'.*
ANTONY   Well said, come on.
          Call forth my household servants; let's tonight
          Be bounteous at our meal.

          Enter three or four SERVANTS.

                                Give me thy hand;   10
                         [*He shakes each one by the hand*
          Thou hast been rightly* honest – so hast thou –
          Thou – and thou – and thou. You have served me well,
          And kings have been your fellows.*
CLEOPATRA   [*Aside to* ENOBARBUS] What means this?
ENOBARBUS [*Aside to* CLEOPATRA] 'Tis one of those odd tricks* which
          sorrow shoots
          Out of the mind.
ANTONY   And thou art honest too.   15
          I wish I could be made so many men,*
          And all of you clapped up together in*
          An Antony, that I might do you service
          So good as you have done.
ALL   The gods forbid!   20
ANTONY Well, my good fellows, wait on me tonight:
          Scant not my cups,* and make as much of me
          As when mine empire was your fellow too,
          And suffered* my command.
CLEOPATRA   [*Aside to* ENOBARBUS] What does he mean?
ENOBARBUS [*Aside to* CLEOPATRA] To make his followers weep.
ANTONY   Tend* me tonight.
          May be it is the period* of your duty;   25
          Haply* you shall not see me more, or if,
          A mangled shadow.* Perchance tomorrow
          You'll serve another master. I look on you
          As one that takes his leave. Mine honest friends,
          I turn you not away, but like a master   30
          Married to your good service, stay till death.*
          Tend me tonight two hours – I ask no more –
          And the gods yield* you for't!

35   *am onion-eyed* – i.e. have tears in my eyes. – Cf. I.ii.157–8. Enobarbus's tears, however,
          are real.
36   *Ho, ho, ho* – Antony tries to laugh off pathos in his words and manner.
37   *the witch take me:* may I be bewitched.
38   *Grace grow:* (a) May God's favour increase (b) May the herb of grace (i.e. rue, esteemed for
          its medicinal properties) grow.
39   *take me . . . sense:* interpret my words in too mournful a sense.
40   *for your comfort:* to console you.
41   *burn this night with torches* – i.e. pass the night in revelry.
45   *consideration:* serious thought.

IV.iii.   Antony's sentries on night guard in Alexandria hear mysterious music in the air and
          from under the earth which they interpret as a sign that Antony's great forbear and
          examplar, Hercules, is now leaving him.
              An atmosphere of nervous uncertainty is established, with the soldiers trying to keep
          their spirits up at the prospect of the coming battle and discussing the lastest rumours in
          worried exchanges. The eerie music unnerves them, and their interpretation of it points
          strongly to Antony's defeat.

1   *the day* – i.e. the decisive day.
2   *determine one way:* decide things one way or the other.
2   *Fare you well:* May things go well with you.
5   *Belike:* Probably.
8   *Here we:* Here is our post.
9   *absolute:* certain.
10   *stand up:* stand firm.
11   *purpose:* resolution.
*   *hautboys,* wood-wind instruments. In Shakespeare's time the hautboy was a louder and
          more strident instrument than its descendant, the modern oboe.

ENOBARBUS   What mean you, sir,
To give them this discomfort? Look, they weep,
And I, an ass, am onion-eyed.* For shame;   35
Transform us not to women.
ANTONY   Ho, ho, ho!*
Now the witch take me* if I meant it thus!
Grace grow* where those drops fall, my hearty friends!
You take me in too dolorous a sense,*
For I spake to you for your comfort;* did desire you   40
To burn this night with torches.* Know, my hearts,
I hope well of tomorrow, and will lead you
Where rather I'll expect victorious life
Than death and honour. Let's to supper, come,
And drown consideration.*   45

                                        [*Exeunt*

scene iii

Alexandria. Near CLEOPATRA'S *palace.*

Enter a Company of Soldiers.

FIRST SOLDIER Brother, good night. Tomorrow is the day.*
SECOND SOLDIER It will determine one way.* Fare you well.*
Heard you of nothing strange about the streets?
FIRST SOLDIER Nothing. What news?
SECOND SOLDIER Belike* 'tis but a rumour. Good night to you.   5
FIRST SOLDIER Well, sir, good night.

                              [*They meet other soldiers*
THIRD SOLDIER   Soldiers, have careful watch.
FIRST SOLDIER And you. Good night, good night.

                  [*They place themselves in every corner of the stage*
SECOND SOLDIER Here we;* and if tomorrow
Our navy thrive, I have an absolute* hope
Our landsmen will stand up.*
FIRST SOLDIER   'Tis a brave army,   10
And full of purpose.*

                  [*The music of hautboys* is heard under the stage*

11   *List:* Listen.
13   *signs well:* signifies something good.
14   *should:* can.
15   *Hercules* – Shakespeare alters Plutarch's Bacchus to Hercules here and so enhances the
      sense of tragic inevitability. Antony is being deserted by his tutelary god and
      ancestor, Hercules. Cf. I.iii.84 and note.
16   *watchmen:* sentries.
17   *How now, masters:* What is it friends?
20   *so far . . . quarter:* as far as the area of our watch extends.
21   *give off:* end.
21   *Content:* I agree.

IV.iv. Antony, in a mood of elation at the thought of the coming battle, boasts of the deeds he
        will perform, as Cleopatra and Eros help to put on his armour. He takes a brief soldierly
        farewell, and when he has gone Cleopatra reveals her fear that he will be defeated.
            The scene gives an important glimpse of Antony's inspiring qualities as a leader; his
        gaiety and confidence infect his men, and we understand and accept his reputation as the
        foremost soldier of the world, which we have heard repeatedly asserted, but not yet seen
        demonstrated. His brevity in bidding farewell to Cleopatra and her self-control at this
        moment which may be their last sight of each other win our admiration. Cleopatra's
        courage is reflected in her assumed gaiety as she buckles on Antony's armour, contrasted
        with Eros's fumbling, and in her concealment of her fears of Antony's defeat.

2   *chuck:* chick, a term of endearment.
3   *thine iron:* that armour of mine you have there.
5   *brave:* defy.
6   *this* – Cleopatra picks up a piece of Antony's armour.

SECOND SOLDIER	Peace! What noise?
FIRST SOLDIER	List, list!*
SECOND SOLDIER	Hark!
FIRST SOLDIER	Music i' th'air.
THIRD SOLDIER	Under the earth.
FOURTH SOLDIER	It signs well,* does it not?
THIRD SOLDIER	No.
FIRST SOLDIER	Peace, I say!

What should* this mean?

SECOND SOLDIER   'Tis the god Hercules,* whom Antony loved,   15
Now leaves him.

FIRST SOLDIER   Walk; let's see if other watchmen*
Do hear what we do.

SECOND SOLDIER   How now, masters?

ALL   [*Speaking together*] How now?*
How now? Do you hear this?

FIRST SOLDIER   Ay, is't not strange?

THIRD SOLDIER   Do you hear, masters? Do you hear?

FIRST SOLDIER   Follow the noise so far as we have quarter.*   20
Let's see how it will give off.*

ALL   Content.* 'Tis strange.

              [*Exeunt*

scene iv

Alexandria. CLEOPATRA'S *palace.*

Enter ANTONY, CLEOPATRA, CHARMIAN *and* ATTENDANTS.

ANTONY	Eros! Mine armour, Eros!
CLEOPATRA	Sleep a little.
ANTONY	No, my chuck.* Eros! Come, mine armour, Eros!

Enter EROS *with armour.*

Come, good fellow, put thine iron* on.
If fortune be not ours today, it is
Because we brave* her. Come.

CLEOPATRA   Nay, I'll help too.   5
What's this* for?

6	*let be:* leave it.
7	*the armourer of my heart:* the one who steels my heart with courage.
7	*False, false; this, this* – Cleopatra picks up the wrong piece; Antony shows her the right one.
8	*Sooth:* Indeed.
8	*la,* an exclamation without meaning in itself, used to add emphasis.
8	*Thus it must be:* This is the way it must go.
9	*thrive:* be successful.
9	*Seest thou* – i.e. Do you see how well she is doing it?
10	*thy defences:* your own armour.
10	*Briefly:* Soon.
11	*Rarely:* Splendidly.
13	*dafft:* take it off.
13	*hear a storm* – i.e. have a rough passage.
14	*a squire* was a body-servant or valet, one of whose duties was to arm his master for war.
15	*tight:* skilful.
16	*my wars* – i.e. the way I shall make war.
17	*The royal occupation:* the profession that belongs to kings. – One of the chief attributes of the ideal king was prowess in war.
18	*workman:* true craftsman.
19	*him that . . . charge:* one who has a warlike message to deliver.
20	*betime:* early.
22	*riveted trim* – Either (a) armour, properly adjusted, or (b) riveted finery, i.e. armour.
23	*port:* city gate.
23	*expect:* wait for.
25	*'Tis well blown:* It is not clear whether this refers to the trumpet call (S.D line 23), or to the morning which is now blossoming, i.e. well-advanced.
27	*be of note:* do outstanding deeds.
28	*So, so* – Antony is still putting on his armour.
28	*that* – i.e. that piece of armour.
28	*Well said:* Well done.
30	*rebukable . . . mechanic compliment:* I would deserve rebuke and censure if I spent a long time kissing goodbye as the vulgar do. – *mechanic:* belonging or pertaining to a working-man. Antony makes a distinction between the businesslike behaviour of the professional soldier and other mortals when going off to war. Antony's crisp, decisive speech here reflects the military leader.

ANTONY   Ah, let be, let be!* Thou art
          The armourer of my heart.* False, false; this, this.*
CLEOPATRA Sooth,* la,* I'll help. Thus it must be.*
ANTONY   Well, well,
          We shall thrive* now. Seest thou,* my good fellow?
          Go, put on thy defences.*
EROS   Briefly,* sir.   10
CLEOPATRA Is not this buckled well?
ANTONY   Rarely,* rarely.
          He that unbuckles this, till we do please
          To daff't* for our repose, shall hear a storm.*
          Thou fumblest, Eros, and my Queen's a squire*
          More tight* at this than thou. Dispatch. O love,   15
          That thou couldst see my wars* today, and knew'st
          The royal occupation!* Thou shouldst see
          A workman* in't.

          Enter an armed SOLDIER.

                           Good morrow to thee; welcome.
          Thou look'st like him that knows a warlike charge.*
          To business that we love we rise betime,*   20
          And go to't with delight.
SOLDIER   A thousand, sir,
          Early though't be, have on their riveted trim,*
          And at the port* expect* you.
                                    [*Shouting. Trumpets sound*

          Enter CAPTAINS *and* SOLDIERS.

CAPTAIN The morn is fair. Good morrow, general.
    ALL Good morrow, general.
ANTONY   'Tis well blown,* lads.   25
          This morning, like the spirit of a youth
          That means to be of note,* begins betimes.
          So, so.* Come, give me that.* This way. Well said.*
          Fare thee well, dame, whate'er becomes of me.
          This is a soldier's kiss: rebukable   30
          And worthy shameful check it were, to stand
          On more mechanic compliment.* I'll leave thee,
          Now like a man of steel. You that will fight,
          Follow me close; I'll bring you to't. Adieu.
                      [*Exeunt all except* CLEOPATRA *and* CHARMIAN

35   *Please you:* Do you wish to.
36   *That:* I wish that.
38   *Then Antony – but now* – Cleopatra feels certain that Antony would beat Caesar in single combat, but she has strong doubts about his chances in the general battle that is about to take place.

IV.v.   Antony meets the soldier who had advised him against a sea-battle at Actium and admits his error. The soldier tells him that Enobarbus has deserted to Caesar. Antony instructs Eros to send 'gentle adieus and greetings' to Enobarbus with all the treasure that he has left behind.
     Sympathy grows for Antony at this desertion of his friend, which follows so closely upon the symbolic desertion of Hercules. Antony gains in stature through the humility of his admission of error to the soldier, and through the magnanimity of his reaction to the news of Enobarbus's defection. He offers no reproach but censures himself for corrupting honest men. The jubilant mood of the previous scene is destroyed by this event.

1   *happy:* fortunate.
2   *Would thou . . . land* – Antony admits his error to the soldier who had wanted him to fight on land at Actium (III.vii.61–6)
4   *revolted:* deserted. – Cf. IV.vi.9,12 and IV.ix.8.
8   *or from . . . thine:* or, if he does hear you, his answer, 'I am not one of your followers', will come from Caesar's camp. – In Plutarch, Enobarbus deserts before the battle of Actium. Shakespeare changes the timing for the reason suggested in the Introduction (p.lii).
13   *jot:* small part.
14   *subscribe:* sign it.
17   *Dispatch:* Hurry.

CHARMIAN Please you* retire to your chamber?
CLEOPATRA   Lead me.   35
          He goes forth gallantly. That* he and Caesar might
          Determine this great war in single fight!
          Then Antony – but now* – Well, on.

                                            [Exeunt

scene v

Alexandria. ANTONY'S *camp.*

Trumpets sound. Enter ANTONY *and* EROS *who meet a* SOLDIER.

SOLDIER The gods make this a happy* day to Antony!
ANTONY   Would thou and those thy scars had once prevailed
         To make me fight at land!*
SOLDIER   Hadst thou done so,
         The kings that have revolted,* and the soldier
         That has this morning left thee, would have still   5
         Followed thy heels.
ANTONY   Who's gone this morning?
SOLDIER   Who?
         One ever near thee. Call for Enobarbus,
         He shall not hear thee, or from Caesar's camp
         Say 'I am none of thine'.*
ANTONY   What sayest thou?
SOLDIER   Sir,
         He is with Caesar.
EROS   Sir, his chests and treasure   10
         He has not with him.
ANTONY   Is he gone?
SOLDIER   Most certain.
ANTONY   Go, Eros, send his treasure after; do it,
         Detain no jot,* I charge thee. Write to him –
         I will subscribe* – gentle adieus and greetings;
         Say that I wish he never find more cause   15
         To change a master. O, my fortunes have
         Corrupted honest men! Dispatch.* Enobarbus!

                                            [Exeunt

IV.vi. Caesar orders that Antony is to be taken alive. Enobarbus, alone on-stage after Caesar's departure, expresses remorse at his disloyalty, a feeling which is made more painful by the arrival of his treasure from Antony. If his broken heart does not kill him, he determines on suicide, and seeks out a ditch to die in.

Our regard for Antony is further built up by Enobarbus's heartbreak. He describes Antony as a 'mine of bounty', and Caesar's soldier sees Antony as 'a Jove'.

6   *Prove this:* If this proves.
6   *three-nooked:* three-cornered. – This term is possibly used because of the division of the world into three by the triumvirs, possibly because in Roman times the world was thought to consist of the three continents, Europe, Asia and Africa.
7   *bear the olive freely:* bring forth the olive (the symbol of peace) in abundance.
9   *Plant those . . . vant:* to place the deserters from Antony's army in the front (of our army). – Caesar plans to force Antony to waste his strength (*spend his fury*) fighting his own deserters (*himself*) while Caesar's own legions are kept in reserve.
12   *Jewry:* Judaea.
13   *dissuade:* persuade. – Enobarbus is grimly ironic about Caesar's cruelty in killing Alexas who was trying to please Caesar by deserting Antony and persuading Herod to support Caesar. Enobarbus too has had a cold reception from Caesar.
15   *pains:* trouble that he took.
17   *That fell . . . trust:* who deserted have been employed by Caesar but not given positions of trust.
18   *done ill:* acted wickedly.
19   *sorely:* severely.
20   *joy:* be happy.
22   *His bounty overplus:* gifts from himself in addition.
23   *on my guard:* while I was on guard.

scene vi

Alexandria. CAESAR'S *camp.*

Flourish. Enter CAESAR, AGRIPPA *and* DOLABELLA, *with*
ENOBARBUS.

CAESAR   Go forth, Agrippa, and begin the fight.
Our will is Antony be took alive;
Make it so known.
AGRIPPA   Caesar, I shall.

[*Exit* AGRIPPA

CAESAR   The time of universal peace is near.   5
Prove this* a prosperous day, the three-nooked* world
Shall bear the olive freely.*

Enter a MESSENGER.

MESSENGER   Antony
Is come into the field.
CAESAR   Go charge Agrippa
Plant those* that have revolted in the vant,*
That Antony may seem to spend his fury   10
Upon himself.

[*Exeunt all except* ENOBARBUS

ENOBARBUS   Alexas did revolt, and went to Jewry* on
Affairs of Antony; there did dissuade*
Great Herod to incline himself to Caesar,
And leave his master Antony. For this pains*   15
Caesar hath hanged him. Canidius and the rest
That fell away have entertainment, but
No honourable trust.* I have done ill,*
Of which I do accuse myself so sorely*
That I will joy* no more.

Enter a SOLDIER *of* CAESAR'S *army.*

SOLDIER   Enobarbus, Antony   20
Hath after thee sent all thy treasure, with
His bounty overplus.* The messenger
Came on my guard,* and at thy tent is now
Unloading of his mules.
ENOBARBUS   I give it you.

26   *Best you . . . host:* You had better see that the man who has brought it gets safe conduct
          through the army (i.e. on his return through Caesar's army to Antony).
27   *attend my office:* get back to my work.
28   *a Jove* – i.e. to behave like a god.
29   *alone the villain:* the only villain.
30   *And feel I am so most:* and no one feels it more than I do.
32   *turpitude:* baseness.
33   *crown:* reward.
33   *blows:* swells to breaking point.
34   *If swift . . . outstrike thought:* if remorse is not quick enough in breaking it, I shall use a
          means that will do so more quickly than remorse.
37   *the foul'st . . . of life:* the most loathsome is most suited to the latter part of my life.

IV.vii. Antony's army gets the better of Caesar's and returns to the city.
          This reversal of all expectations reinforces Antony's military reputation and creates
      suspense by holding out a hope of victory against Caesar.

1   *engaged ourselves too far:* involved ourselves with the enemy too far forward.
2   *has work:* is having trouble.
2   *our oppression:* the pressure on us.
4   *fought indeed:* real fighting.
5   *done so* – i.e. fought like this.
5   *had droven:* would have driven. – *Droven* is an old form of the past participle.
6   *clouts:* (a) blows (b) bandages.
7   *like a T* – i.e. shaped like the letter T.
8   *made an H* – i.e. by the addition of another cut at right angles to the upright of the T. There
          is also play on *ache*, pronounced *aitch* in Shakespeare's time.
9   *bench holes* – i.e. holes in a privy, or latrine.
10   *scotches:* gashes.

SOLDIER Mock not, Enobarbus; I tell you true.   25
         Best you safed the bringer out of the host:*
         I must attend mine office,* or would have done't myself.
         Your Emperor continues still a Jove.*

                                              [*Exit* SOLDIER

ENOBARBUS I am alone the villain* of the earth,
           And feel I am so most.* O Antony,   30
           Thou mine of bounty, how wouldst thou have paid
           My better service, when my turpitude*
           Thou dost so crown* with gold! This blows* my heart;
           If swift thought break it not, a swifter mean
           Shall outstrike thought;* but thought will do't, I feel.   35
           I fight against thee? No, I will go seek
           Some ditch wherein to die: the foul'st best fits
           My latter part of life.*

                                                        [*Exit*

scene vii

The battlefield between the camps.

Alarum. Drums and trumpets sound. Enter AGRIPPA *and*
SOLDIERS.

AGRIPPA Retire; we have engaged ourselves too far.*
         Caesar himself has work,* and our oppression*
         Exceeds what we expected.

                                                        [*Exeunt*

Alarums. Enter ANTONY, *and* SCARUS *wounded.*

SCARUS O my brave Emperor, this is fought indeed!*
        Had we done so* at first, we had droven* them home   5
        With clouts* about their heads.
ANTONY   Thou bleed'st apace.
SCARUS I had a wound here that was like a T,*
        But now 'tis made an H.*

                                     [*Trumpet sounds the retreat*
ANTONY   They do retire.
SCARUS We'll beat 'em into bench-holes.* I have yet
        Room for six scotches* more.   10

11	*serves/For:* is sufficient to give us.
12	*score:* cut notches in.
13	*take:* catch.
14	*sport to maul a runner:* fun to beat someone running away.
15	*spritely:* high-spirited.
16	*halt after:* limp behind you.

IV.viii. A jubilant Antony praises his troops for their brave devotion and leads them into Alexandria where they are greeted by Cleopatra, overjoyed at the victory sounded by Antony's trumpets and drums.

1	*Run one before:* Someone run ahead.
2	*gests:* deeds.
5	*doughty-handed* – i.e. brave men of action.
6	*Not as . . . mine:* not as if you were hired servants, but as if the cause were as much yours as mine.
7	*shown all Hectors:* all appeared like Hectors. – Hector, the son of King Priam of Troy in Greek mythology, was the type of the perfect warrior.
8	*clip:* embrace.
10	*congealment* – i.e. congealed blood.
10	*kiss . . . gashes whole:* heal your honourable wounds by kissing them.
12	*fairy:* enchantress.
13	*day* – i.e. light.
14	*Chain* – i.e. by putting your arms about me.
14	*attire and all:* dressed as you are.
15	*proof of harness* – i.e. armour tested and proved impenetrable.
16	*Ride . . . triumphing* – Antony's panting breast is spoken of as the triumphal chariot on which Cleopatra will ride.

Enter EROS.

EROS They are beaten, sir, and our advantage serves
For* a fair victory.

SCARUS   Let us score* their backs
And snatch 'em up, as we take* hares, behind.
'Tis sport to maul a runner.*

ANTONY   I will reward thee,
Once for thy spritely* comfort and tenfold   15
For thy good valour. Come thee on.

SCARUS   I'll halt after.*

                                        [*Exeunt*

scene viii

Near Alexandria.

Alarum. Enter ANTONY *marching with* SCARUS *and his army.*

ANTONY We have beat him to his camp. Run one before,*
And let the Queen know of our gests.* Tomorrow,
Before the sun shall see's, we'll spill the blood
That has today escaped. I thank you all,
For doughty-handed* are you, and have fought   5
Not as you served the cause, but as't had been
Each man's like mine:* you have shown all Hectors.*
Enter the city, clip* your wives, your friends;
Tell them your feats, whilst they with joyful tears
Wash the congealment* from your wounds, and kiss   10
The honoured gashes whole.*

Enter CLEOPATRA.

                    [*To* SCARUS] Give me thy hand;
To this great fairy* I'll commend thy acts,
Make her thanks bless thee. [*To* CLEOPATRA] O thou day* o'
th'world,
Chain* mine armed neck; leap thou, attire and all,*
Through proof of harness* to my heart, and there   15
Ride on the pants triumphing!*

17	*virtue:* manly power.
18	*world's great snare* – i.e. war.
18	*nightingale* – A compliment to the enchantment of Cleopatra's voice.
19	*beat them to their beds:* hurled them back to their camp.
19	*grey . . . mingle:* grey hairs are mixed to some extent – We are reminded of Antony's earlier reference to his hair at III.xi.13 and his very different mood on that occasion.
20	*ha':* have.
21	*A brain . . . of youth:* a mind that sustains my muscles, and can achieve as much as young men can. – The guile that comes from experience, Antony is saying, makes up for his loss of youthful agility. It is this mood in Antony that Enobarbus considered a *diminution in our captain's brain.* Cf. III.xiii.197.
23	*Commend . . . hand:* let him kiss (*commend:* give kindly) your gracious hand.
26	*Destroyed in such a shape:* killed in his (*Scarus's*) shape.
28	*carbuncled:* jewelled.
29	*Phoebus' car:* Phoebus's chariot. – Ovid, in his *Metamorphoses*, a work which greatly influenced the writers of the sixteenth century, describes the chariot of the sun-god Phoebus as set with chrysolites and gems.
31	*Bear . . . owe them:* hold up our battered shields (*targets*) with pride like that of the men who own (*owe*) them. – The men, too, are *hacked* but hold themselves proudly.
33	*camp:* accommodate.
34	*carouses:* deep draughts.
35	*royal peril:* supreme danger.
36	*brazen* – i.e. produced by brass trumpets, with possibly also the sense of 'bold', 'fearless'.
37	*Make mingle:* let the noise mix.
37	*tabourines:* long, narrow drums.
38	*That heaven . . . together:* so that the earthly sounds will be echoed at the same time in the heavens.

| IV.ix. | In Caesar's camp three sentries listen while Enobarbus, unaware of their presence, reproaches himself for his disloyalty. He collapses and dies broken-hearted. The sentries carry him off to the guard-room. |
| | Enobarbus's death is one of the emotional climaxes of the play. The death of this hard-bitten soldier of a broken heart affirms the superiority of the emotional values of loyalty and friendship over the more rational value of prudence in whose name Enobarbus has acted in leaving Antony. Shakespeare has brought his point out by altering the historical source in which Enobarbus dies from disease. |

1	*relieved* – i.e. by the oncoming guard.
2	*must:* shall have to.
2	*court of guard:* guardroom.
3	*shiny:* moonlit.
3	*embattle:* draw up in line of battle.

CLEOPATRA   Lord of lords!
          O infinite virtue,* com'st thou smiling from
          The world's great snare* uncaught?
ANTONY   My nightingale,*
          We have beat them to their beds.* What, girl! Though grey
          Do something mingle* with our younger brown, yet ha'* we   20
          A brain that nourishes our nerves, and can
          Get goal for goal of youth.* Behold this man:
          Commend unto his lips thy favouring hand.* –
          Kiss it my warrior. – He hath fought today
          As if a god in hate of mankind had   25
          Destroyed in such a shape.*
CLEOPATRA   I'll give thee, friend,
          An armour all of gold. It was a king's.
ANTONY   He has deserved it, were it carbuncled*
          Like holy Phoebus' car.* Give me thy hand.
          Through Alexandria make a jolly march;   30
          Bear our hacked targets like the men that owe them.*
          Had our great palace the capacity
          To camp* this host, we all would sup together
          And drink carouses* to the next day's fate,
          Which promises royal peril.* Trumpeters,   35
          With brazen* din blast you the city's ear;
          Make mingle* with our rattling tabourines,*
          That heaven and earth may strike their sounds together,*
          Applauding our approach.
                                                        [*Exeunt*

scene ix

CAESAR'S *camp.*

Enter a SENTRY *and his Company.* ENOBARBUS *follows.*

SENTRY   If we be not relieved* within this hour,
          We must* return to th'court of guard.* The night
          Is shiny,* and they say we shall embattle*
          By th'second hour i' th'morn.

5   *A shrewd one to's:* a harmful one for us. – He alludes to Antony's victory over them.
6   *Stand close:* Keep hidden.
8   *When men . . . memory:* when deserters are remembered with hatred in history (*upon record*).
12   *sovereign . . . melancholy:* supreme ruler over the deepest melancholy. – The moon was thought to cause and control mental disease.
13   *poisonous damp* – The Elizabethans believed that the dew fell from the sky and that the damp airs of the night spread disease and were generally unhealthy.
13   *dispone:* drop (as from a sponge).
14   *That life . . . will:* so that life, which continues against my will.
17   *Which* – i.e. his heart. – Sorrow, it was thought, dried up the blood, leaving the heart brittle and so easily broken.
19   *revolt:* desertion.
20   *in thine own particular:* as far as you yourself are concerned. – He does not ask pardon for his offence, so much as for Antony's personal forgiveness.
21   *rank me in register:* list me in the history book.
22   *A master-leaver . . . fugitive:* a runaway servant and a deserter.
26   *so bad . . . for sleep:* a bad prayer like this has never yet been a request for sleep. – The sentry cannot believe that this 'bad' prayer which he has overheard could ever have been answered by sleep. Enobarbus, he believes, must have fainted.
29   *raught:* seized.
*   The quiet sound of the drums which awaken the sleeping soldiers also serves as a funeral roll to mark the death of Enobarbus. This cross pattern of death and awakening is one example of a wider pattern of contrasts in the play as a whole, such as the pervasive references to waxing and waning, filling and emptying, flowers blooming and dying, which stress the rise of Caesar and the fall of Antony.

FIRST   This last day was
WATCHMAN A shrewd one to's.*

ENOBARBUS   O bear me witness, night –   5

SECOND   What man is this?
WATCHMAN

FIRST   Stand close,* and list him.
WATCHMAN

ENOBARBUS Be witness to me, O thou blessed moon,
          When men revolted shall upon recórd
          Bear hateful memory,* poor Enobarbus did
          Before thy face repent.

SENTRY   Enobarbus?

SECOND   Peace!   10
WATCHMAN Hark further.

ENOBARBUS O sovereign mistress of true melancholy,*
          The poisonous damp* of night disponge* upon me,
          That life, a very rebel to my will,*
          May hang no longer on me. Throw my heart   15
          Against the flint and hardness of my fault,
          Which,* being dried with grief, will break to powder,
          And finish all foul thoughts. O Antony,
          Nobler than my revolt* is infamous,
          Forgive me in thine own particular,*   20
          But let the world rank me in register*
          A master-leaver and a fugitive.*
          O Antony! O Antony!   [He dies

FIRST   Let's speak to him.
WATCHMAN

SENTRY   Let's hear him, for the things he speaks
          May concern Caesar.

SECOND   Let's do so. But he sleeps.   25
WATCHMAN

SENTRY   Swoons rather, for so bad a prayer as his
          Was never yet for sleep.*

FIRST   Go we to him.
WATCHMAN

SECOND   Awake, sir, awake; speak to us.
WATCHMAN

FIRST   Hear you, sir?
WATCHMAN

SENTRY   The hand of death hath raught* him.
                        [Drums are heard in the distance*

30   *demurely* – i.e. with subdued sounds.
31   *of note:* an important man.
32   *Our hour is fully out:* Our hour of guard duty has ended.

IV.x.   Antony and Scarus go to take up position in the hills to watch the sea battle that is about
         to take place. Antony is confident that he can beat Caesar in any element.

3   *I would . . . th'air:* I wish they would fight in the elements of fire or air (i.e. as well as, or
                 instead of, the other two elements earth and water). – Antony is so elated by
                 his success the day before that he is confident he can beat Caesar in any element
                 he chooses.
4   *foot:* infantry.
6   *Order for sea is given:* I have given orders for a naval battle.
7   *put forth the haven:* left harbour.
8   *Where:* by which action.
8   *appointment:* appearance, equipment.
8   *their endeavour:* their efforts in battle.

IV.xi.   Caesar gives his orders that a land fight is to be avoided unless Antony attacks.

1   *But being . . . we shall:* Unless (*But*) we are attacked, we will remain inactive (*still*) by land,
                 which I imagine we shall be left to do.
4   *hold our best advantage:* take up the best possible position.

Hark! The drums demurely* wake the sleepers. 30
Let's bear him to th' court of guard: he is of note.*
Our hour is fully out.*

SECOND Come on, then. He may recover yet.
WATCHMAN

[*Exeunt*

scene x

Between the two camps.

Enter ANTONY *and* SCARUS *with their army.*

ANTONY Their preparation is today by sea;
We please them not by land.
SCARUS   For both, my lord.
ANTONY I would they'ld fight i' th'fire or i' th'air:*
We'ld fight there too. But this it is. Our foot*
Upon the hills adjoining to the city   5
Shall stay with us. Order for sea is given;*
They have put forth the haven,*
Where* their appointment* we may best discover,
And look on their endeavour.*

[*Exeunt*

scene xi

Between the two camps.

Enter CAESAR *and his army.*

CAESAR But being charged, we will be still by land,
Which, as I take't we shall,* for his best force
Is forth to man his galleys. To the vales,
And hold our best advantage.*

[*Exeunt*

IV.xii.   Antony and Scarus are now in the hills. While Antony goes off to get a better view of the battle, Scarus speaks of omens unfavourable to Antony, and of Antony's fluctuating moods of hope and fear. An infuriated Antony returns having witnessed the surrender of the Egyptian fleet to Caesar. He is certain that Cleopatra has betrayed him and threatens revenge. Cleopatra appears but when she sees how angry he is she runs off. Alone again, Antony vows to kill her.

Antony's momentary success makes the totality of his defeat now more bitter. It is cruelly ironic that his conviction of Cleopatra's treachery should be totally unfounded, and the titanic anger it gives rise to should lead to her flight and a course of events which leads directly to their destruction.

1	*yet*: still.
1	*joined* – i.e. in battle.
1	*yond pine* – Antony probably points to a property tree, which he ascends. See Introduction, p. lviii.
3	*Straight . . . go*: directly how the battle is likely to go.
4	*The augurers . . . know not*: The official interpreters of the omen say they do not know what it means. – Augurs were Roman religious officials who claimed to foretell future events by observing the actions of birds or examining their entrails. Antony had his own augurs in Alexandria.
7	*starts*: outbursts in quick succession.
8	*fretted*: (a) decayed (b) chequered, i.e. up and down, contrasting like the squares in a check pattern.
8	*hope . . . has not*: hope of winning what he has not, and fear of losing what he has.
12	*cast their caps up* – throw up their hats, i.e. in their delight at avoiding battle.
13	*Triple-turned* – Cleopatra has turned from Julius Caesar to Gnaeus Pompey, from Pompey to Antony, and now, Antony believes, from himself to Octavius.
14	*novice*: inexperienced youth.
15	*Makes only wars on thee*: makes war on you alone. – His only enemy now, he says, is Cleopatra.
16	*my charm*: the thing that has bewitched me.
19	*part*: separate from one another, disengage.
20	*shake hands* – i.e. in parting.
20	*All come to this*: Has everything ended like this?
21	*spanielled*: followed me as devotedly as a spaniel.
22	*discandy*: melt away.
23	*barked*: stripped of its bark. – This *pine* is Antony himself, in contrast to the pine he has just climbed to view the battle. Having lost his power, his followers, and, as he thinks, Cleopatra, he sees himself reduced to his essential self, like the naked trunk of the stripped tree.
25	*grave charm*: deadly enchantress.
26	*Whose eye . . . home*: whose glance was enough to send me off to war for her, or recall me home from war.
27	*Whose bosom . . . end*: whose love was the crown and object of all I did.
28	*right*: true.
28	*fast and loose* – a game of deception formerly played at fairs by gipsies. Having tied a knot in a belt or string, the gipsy would get people to bet that it was real (*fast*), and would then pull the two ends, removing the knot and showing that it was only an apparent one (*loose*).

scene xii

Near Alexandria.

Enter ANTONY *and* SCARUS.

ANTONY Yet* they are not joined.* Where yond pine* does stand
    I shall discover all. I'll bring thee word
    Straight how 'tis like to go.*

                                 [Exit
           [The noise of a distant naval battle is heard
SCARCUS   Swallows have built
    In Cleopatra's sails their nests. The augurers
    Say they know not,* they cannot tell, look grimly,   5
    And dare not speak their knowledge. Antony
    Is valiant, and dejected, and by starts*
    His fretted* fortunes give him hope and fear
    Of what he has, and has not.*

    Enter ANTONY.

ANTONY   All is lost!
    This foul Egyptian hath betrayèd me.   10
    My fleet hath yielded to the foe, and yonder
    They cast their caps up* and carouse together
    Like friends long lost. Triple-turned* whore! 'Tis thou
    Hast sold me to this novice,* and my heart
    Makes only wars on thee.* Bid them all fly;   15
    For when I am revenged upon my charm*
    I have done all. Bid them all fly, be gone.

                           [Exit SCARUS
    O sun, thy uprise shall I see no more.
    Fortune and Antony part* here; even here
    Do we shake hands.* All come to this?* The hearts   20
    That spanielled* me at heels, to whom I gave
    Their wishes, do discandy,* melt their sweets
    On blossoming Caesar; and this pine is barked,*
    That overtopped them all. Betrayed I am.
    O this false soul of Egypt! This grave charm,*   25
    Whose eye becked forth my wars, and called them home,*
    Whose bosom was my crownet, my chief end,*
    Like a right* gipsy hath at fast and loose*

29	*the very heart of loss:* total ruin.
30	*spell* – Antony's disgust is such that he addresses Cleopatra as something abstract rather than human. Cf. *charm*, lines 16, 25.
30	*Avaunt:* Get away! – This was a term used to dismiss witches and evil spirits.
32	*thy deserving:* what you deserve, i.e. death.
33	*blemish Caesar's triumph:* spoil Caesar's triumphal march through Rome (by making it impossible for him to display Cleopatra as his prisoner).
34	*hoist thee up* – i.e. as a spectacle.
34	*plébeians:* common people.
35	*spot:* blemish.
36	*monster-like be shown:* be exhibited like a freak. – Deformed people and animals were often exhibited at fairs and other popular entertainments in Shakespeare's time.
37	*For poor'st . . . dolts:* for the enjoyment of the poorest and meanest citizens (*diminutives*), for fools.
38	*Patient:* long-suffering. – Antony acknowledges the suffering he has caused Octavia, but in this forecast of her reactions shows that he totally misunderstands her nature.
38	*visage:* face.
39	*preparèd* – i.e. either by being allowed to grow long, or by being sharpened for the purpose. There is a powerful irony in the fact that Antony's fury at this point, caused by his mistaken belief in Cleopatra's treachery, forces her to fly to the refuge of her monument and feign death, and is thus a direct cause of his own death.
39	*Tis well . . . well to live:* It is a good thing for you that you have gone, if you want to go on living. – Playing on the word *well*, Antony implies that if she had stayed he would have killed her.
41	*fell'st into my fury:* had been killed by my fury.
42	*prevented many* – i.e. prevented the many moments of terror she will suffer, which will be as bad as death.
43	*shirt of Nessus* – In Greek mythology Deianira sent Lichas with a shirt for her husband Hercules, unaware that it had been poisoned by being dipped in the blood of Nessus the Centaur, whom Hercules had killed with a poisoned arrow. Hercules suffered such torment when he put it on that he hurled Lichas high into the air with such force that he turned into a pebble and fell into the sea. Hercules then had himself burned to death on Mount Oeta.
44	*Alcides* – i.e. Hercules, son of Alceus.
45	*lodge:* impale.
47	*Subdue:* destroy.
47	*worthiest:* most heroic (i.e. sharing the heroic nature of his ancestor Hercules).
48	*fall / Under:* fall a victim to.

IV.xiii. Terrified by Antony's fury, Cleopatra rushes off to lock herself in her funeral monument, and sends Mardian to tell Antony she is dead and bring word how he receives the news.
    Pathetically and fatally, Cleopatra behaves characteristically even in this moment of panic, hoping to win Antony over by a piece of play-acting.

2	*Telamon* – i.e. Ajax, son of Telamon. When Ulysses beat him in the contest to discover the bravest of the Greeks and so was awarded the shield and armour of Achilles, Ajax went mad and killed himself.
2	*the boar of Thessaly* – When Oeneus, King of Calydon, omitted the sacrifices to Artemis, she sent a great boar to ravage his country.
3	*embossed:* foaming at the mouth.
4	*the monument* – This was the tomb which Cleopatra, following the custom of her time, had built for herself.

Beguiled me, to the very heart of loss.*
What, Eros, Eros!

Enter CLEOPATRA.

                Ah, thou spell!* Avaunt!*   30

CLEOPATRA Why is my lord enraged against his love?
ANTONY Vanish, or I shall give thee thy deserving*
And blemish Caesar's triumph.* Let him take thee
And hoist thee up* to the shouting plébeians;*
Follow his chariot, like the greatest spot*   35
Of all thy sex; most monster-like be shown*
For poor'st diminutives, for dolts,* and let
Patient* Octavia plough thy visage* up
With her preparèd* nails.

                              [*Exit* CLEOPATRA
                  'Tis well th'art gone,
If it be well to live;* but better 'twere   40
Thou fell'st into my fury,* for one death
Might have prevented many.* Eros, ho!
The shirt of Nessus* is upon me: teach me
Alcides,* thou mine ancestor, thy rage.
Let me lodge* Lichas on the horns o' th'moon,   45
And with those hands that grasped the heaviest club
Subdue* my worthiest* self. The witch shall die.
To the young Roman boy she hath sold me, and I fall
Under this plot.* She dies for't. Eros, ho!

                                    [*Exit*

scene xiii

Alexandria. CLEOPATRA'S *palace.*

Enter CLEOPATRA, CHARMIAN, IRAS, MARDIAN.

CLEOPATRA Help me, my women! O, he's more mad
Than Telamon* for his shield; the boar of Thessaly*
Was never so embossed.*
CHARMIAN   To the monument:*
There lock yourself, and send him word you are dead.

5   *rive . . . going off:* are not more painfully torn apart when they separate, than a man whose
        greatness leaves him.
10   *bring me how:* bring me news of how.

IV.xiv. Antony, convinced that Cleopatra is in league with Caesar, decides to take his own life.
        When Mardian arrives with the false report of Cleopatra's suicide, Antony unarms,
        preparing to join her in death and ask pardon. He orders Eros to kill him, but as he turns
        his face away, Eros stabs himself. Antony then falls on his own sword, but fails to kill
        himself. Hearing the noise, Decretas and the guard enter, but refuse to kill him. Decretas
        purloins Antony's sword to win favour by taking it to Caesar. As he leaves, Diomedes
        comes in to tell Antony that Cleopatra has only pretended death out of fear. Antony
        commands that he be taken to her.
            The tone of this scene is in marked contrast to Antony's last appearance. His rage has
        given way to a calm resignation which draws tears from Eros. At the thought of Cleopatra's
        supposed treachery Antony's world collapses, so that he even feels a loss of personal
        identity. Eros's self-sacrifice is eloquent and moving testimony of the lovableness of
        Antony, and his love is in contrast to the selfish prudence of Decretas. This love, together
        with the totality of Antony's love for Cleopatra, his courage and characteristic magnani-
        mity in not uttering a word of reproach at Cleopatra's fatal deception, raises Antony to
        the proportions of a tragic hero.

1   *thou yet behold'st me?:* can you still see me? – Antony, in profound dejection, feels that he
        has lost his identity with the departure of his greatness.
2   *dragonish:* shaped like a dragon.
3   *vapour:* mist, or cloud.
4   *pendant:* overhanging.
5   *forkèd:* having two or more peaks.
6   *nod* – i.e. bow in the wind.
7   *mock our eyes with air:* deceive us into taking airy illusion for reality.
8   *black vesper's pageants:* deceptive shows that approaching night puts on. – A *pageant,*
        originally the cart on which plays were acted in the middle ages, later becomes
        the name for the dramatic performance itself. The pageant, like the clouds,
        represents an appearance, not a reality.
9   *even with . . . dislimns:* as swift as thought the drifting cloud (*rack*) robs of its shape
        (*dislimns*).
12   *knave:* servant.
15   *Egypt* – i.e. Cleopatra.
17   *Which . . . million moe:* (my heart) which before I lost it to Cleopatra, had a million more
        hearts attached to it.
19   *Packed cards . . . triumph:* cheated in dealing the cards, and played so dishonestly that
        she has caused me to lose my glory to Caesar's trump card. – Antony believes
        that Cleopatra has conspired with Caesar against him. There is play on *triumph*
        meaning (a) Roman triumph (b) trump card.

The soul and body rive not more in parting   5
Than greatness going off.*
CLEOPATRA   To the monument!
Mardian, go tell him I have slain myself:
Say that the last I spoke was 'Antony',
And word it, prithee, piteously. Hence, Mardian,
And bring me how* he takes my death to th'monument.   10

                                                    [*Exeunt*

scene xiv

Alexandria. CLEOPATRA'S *palace*.

Enter ANTONY *and* EROS.

ANTONY Eros, thou yet behold'st me?*
EROS   Ay, noble lord.
ANTONY Sometime we see a cloud that's dragonish,*
A vapour* sometime like a bear or lion,
A towered citadel, a pendant* rock,
A forkèd* mountain, or blue promontory   5
With trees upon't that nod* unto the world
And mock our eyes with air.* Thou hast seen these signs:
They are black vesper's pageants.*
EROS   Ay, my lord.
ANTONY That which is now a horse, even with a thought
The rack dislimns,* and makes it indistinct   10
As water is in water.
EROS   It does, my lord.
ANTONY My good knave* Eros, now thy captain is
Even such a body. Here I am, Antony,
Yet cannot hold this visible shape, my knave.
I made these wars for Egypt,* and the Queen –   15
Whose heart I thought I had, for she had mine,
Which, whilst it was mine, had annexed unto't
A million moe,* now lost – she, Eros, has
Packed cards with Caesar, and false-played my glory
Unto an enemy's triumph.*   20

21	*there is . . . ourselves:* I am still free to take my life.
23	*my sword* – i.e. the symbol of his manly power.
24	*mingled . . . entirely:* were completely interwoven with yours.
29	*unto thy hand:* for you already.
31	*a tearing . . . lips:* a groan which tore her life apart left the word 'Antony' only half-uttered; her lips spoke the first half of it, the other was buried in her heart.
33	*rendered life:* surrendered to death.
36	*That thou . . . richly:* That I allow you to leave here safely is a rich reward for the message you have brought. – Antony implies that Mardian deserves death for bringing such a message as Cleopatra's death.
38	*The sevenfold shield of Ajax* – Ajax's shield was made of brass and lined with seven layers of oxhide.
38	*keep . . . my heart:* prevent this news from battering my heart.
39	*O cleave . . . case* – The Elizabethans believed that on death the heart broke. Antony begs that his heart should remain whole, for once proving stronger than its containing (*continent*) body (*frail case*) which he wishes to split (*cleave*) instead.
42	*No more:* I am no longer. – He looks at the dented armour. (*Bruisèd pieces*) which has been stripped from him.
43	*From me awhile:* Leave me alone for a while.
45	*Weep for my pardon:* beg forgiveness with tears (for misjudging her).
46	*length* – i.e. continuance of life.
46	*the torch* – i.e. the light of his life, Cleopatra.
47	*all labour . . . does:* all activity is a waste of time.
48	*very force . . . strength:* strength itself only gets more firmly tied up when it exerts itself. – The image is apparently that of an animal struggling in the nets which have trapped it.
49	*Seal:* Let me finish life. – The image is that of affixing the wax seal which completes a written agreement.
50	*Stay:* Wait. – Antony is addressing Cleopatra.

Nay, weep not, gentle Eros, there is left us
Ourselves to end ourselves.*

Enter MARDIAN.

                        O, thy vile lady!
She has robbed me of my sword.*
MARDIAN   No, Antony,
My mistress loved thee, and her fortunes mingled
With thine entirely.*
ANTONY   Hence, saucy eunuch, peace!   25
She hath betrayed me, and shall die the death.
MARDIAN Death of one person can be paid but once,
And that she has discharged. What thou wouldst do
Is done unto thy hand.* The last she spake
Was 'Antony! most noble Antony!'   30
Then in the midst a tearing groan did break
The name of Antony; it was divided
Between her heart and lips.* She rendered life*
Thy name so buried in her.
ANTONY   Dead, then?
MARDIAN   Dead.
ANTONY Unarm, Eros; the long day's task is done,   35
And we must sleep. [*To* MARDIAN] That thou depart'st hence
safe
Does pay thy labour richly.* Go.
                           [*Exit* MARDIAN
                    Off, pluck off.
               [EROS *unbuckles* ANTONY'S *breastplate*
The sevenfold shield of Ajax* cannot keep
The battery from my heart.* O, cleave, my sides!
Heart, once be stronger than thy continent,   40
Crack thy frail case!* Apace, Eros, apace!
No more* a soldier. Bruisèd pieces, go;
You have been nobly borne. – From me awhile.*
                           [*Exit* EROS
I will o'ertake thee, Cleopatra, and
Weep for my pardon.* So it must be, for now   45
All length* is torture. Since the torch* is out,
Lie down and stray no farther. Now all labour
Mars what it does:* yea, very force entangles
Itself with strength.* Seal* then, and all is done.
Eros! – I come my Queen – Eros! – Stay* for me;   50

51   *couch on flowers:* lie on banks of flowers. – Antony refers to the Elysian fields where, according to Greek mythology, those whom the gods favoured lived after death in perpetual bliss.

52   *sprightly port:* (a) high-spirited behaviour (b) bearing as spirits.

53   *Dido and her Aeneas* – i.e. Dido, Queen of Carthage, and Aeneas, her lover. When Aeneas deserted her to go to Italy, she killed herself. In Virgil's *Aeneid* she scornfully repels Aeneas when he visits her in Hades, the Roman Elysium.

53   *want troops:* lack followers (because Antony and Cleopatra will attract them all away).

54   *all the haunt be ours:* (a) the whole company will follow us (b) the resort of ghosts will be entirely ours.

58   *Quartered:* divided up.

59   *With ships made cities* – Antony's ships were so numerous that they looked like cities at sea.

59   *to lack:* for lacking.

60   *less noble mind* – Possibly *mind* is in apposition to *I* (line 57). If not, then we have to supply a verb: (I have a) less noble mind.

61   *Caesar tells:* tells Caesar.

63   *exigent:* moment of urgent need.

65   *inevitable prosecution:* unavoidable pursuit.

68   *Thou strik'st . . . defeat'st:* You will not be doing me any harm; your blow will be directed at Caesar. – Antony is trying to get Eros to accept the idea that in killing him he is not acting against him, but doing him a favour by spoiling Caesar's triumph.

70   *Parthian darts* – See note to III.i.1.

71   *lost aim* – i.e. in trying to do.

72   *windowed:* placed in a window.

73   *pleached:* folded. – Standing with folded arms was one of the symptoms of the Elizabethan melancholy man.

73   *bending down . . . ensued:* bowing his head and submitting to correction (*corrigible*), his face dejected by profound (*penetrative*) shame, while the chariot (*wheeled seat*) of the fortunate Caesar, drawn in front of him, made the humiliation (*baseness*) of him who followed more conspicuous (*branded*). – In former times the brand was the identifying mark burned into the skin of criminals and animals.

77   *would not:* do not want to.

80   *useful* for *usefully*. Cf note to I.i.25.

80   *pardon me:* excuse me from performing this act.

83   *thy precédent . . . unpurposed:* I will consider all your former services as unintentional actions, i.e. not as inspired by affectionate loyalty.

Where souls do couch on flowers,* we'll hand in hand,
And with our sprightly port* make the ghosts gaze.
Dido and her Aeneas* shall want troops,*
And all the haunt be ours.* – Come, Eros, Eros!

Enter EROS.

EROS   What would my lord?

ANTONY   Since Cleopatra died,   55
I have lived in such dishonour that the gods
Detest my baseness. I, that with my sword
Quartered* the world, and o'er green Neptune's back
With ships made cities,* condemn myself to lack*
The courage of a woman; less noble mind*   60
Than she which by her death our Caesar tells*
'I am conqueror of myself'. Thou art sworn, Eros,
That when the exigent* should come, which now
Is come indeed, when I should see behind me
Th' inevitable prosecution* of   65
Disgrace and horror, that, on my command
Thou then wouldst kill me. Do't, the time is come.
Thou strik'st not me, 'tis Caesar thou defeat'st.*
Put colour in thy cheek.

EROS   The gods withhold me.
Shall I do that which all the Parthian darts,*   70
Though enemy, lost aim* and could not?

ANTONY   Eros,
Wouldst thou be windowed* in great Rome, and see
Thy master thus with pleached* arms, bending down
His corrigible neck, his face subdued
To penetrative shame, whilst the wheeled seat   75
Of fortunate Caesar, drawn before him, branded
His baseness that ensued?*

EROS   I would not* see't.

ANTONY   Come then: for with a wound I must be cured.
Draw that thy honest sword, which thou hast worn
Most useful* for thy country.

EROS   O, sir, pardon me!*   80

ANTONY   When I did make thee free, swor'st thou not then
To do this when I bade thee? Do it at once,
Or thy precédent services are all
But accidents unpurposed.* Draw, and come.

86   *Wherein . . . lies:* which contains all that commands the world's devotion.
87   *Lo, thee:* Here you are.
89   *why:* for which.
98   *got upon . . . record:* taken precedence over me in the chronicle of noble actions.
102   *dies thy scholar:* is your pupil in dying, i.e. taught by Eros's example.
104   *dispatch me:* kill me quickly.
105   *ill:* badly.
106   *The star:* The day star, i.e. the sun.
107   *his period:* its end.
111   *but:* only.
112   *enter me:* get me a favourable reception.

EROS   Turn from me then that noble countenance   85
        Wherein the worship of the whole world lies.*
ANTONY [*Turning away from him*] Lo, thee!*
EROS   My sword is drawn.
ANTONY   Then let it do at once
        The thing why* thou hast drawn it.
EROS   My dear master,
        My captain, and my Emperor, let me say,   90
        Before I strike this bloody stroke, farewell.
ANTONY 'Tis said, man, and farewell.
EROS   Farewell, great chief. Shall I strike now?
ANTONY   Now, Eros.
EROS   [*Stabbing himself*] Why, there then! Thus do I escape the
        sorrow
        Of Antony's death.
ANTONY   Thrice-nobler than myself,   95
        Thou teachest me, O valiant Eros, what
        I should, and thou couldst not. My Queen and Eros
        Have by their brave instruction got upon me
        A nobleness in record.* But I will be
        A bridegroom in my death, and run into't   100
        As to a lover's bed. [*Drawing his sword*] Come, then; and, Eros,
        Thy master dies thy scholar.* To do thus
                            [*Falling on his sword*
        I learnt of thee. How! Not dead? Not dead?
        The guard, ho! O, dispatch me!*

        Enter GUARDS *followed by* DECRETAS.

FIRST GUARD   What's the noise?
ANTONY I have done my work ill,* friends. O, make an end   105
        Of what I have begun.
SECOND GUARD   The star* is fall'n.
FIRST GUARD And time is at his period.*
ALL   Alas, and woe!
ANTONY Let him that loves me, strike me dead.
FIRST GUARD   Not I.
SECOND GUARD Nor I.
THIRD GUARD   Nor anyone.
                                    [*Exeunt* GUARDS
DECRETAS Thy death and fortunes bid thy followers fly.   110
        This sword but* shown to Caesar, with this tidings,
        Shall enter me* with him.

116   *Sufficing strokes for death:* blows sufficient to cause death.
119   *a prophesying fear:* a presentiment.
121   *found:* proved true.
122   *disposed:* made an agreement.
123   *purged:* expelled.
124   *how it might work:* what effect it might produce.
132   *live . . . followers out:* outlive all your faithful servants (i.e. by wearing them out in your service).
134   *To grace it with your sorrows:* by doing it the favour of sorrowing.
135   *Bid . . . punish it:* If we welcome what comes to punish us, we punish it (by robbing it of all satisfaction).

Enter DIOMEDES.

DIOMEDES   Where's Antony?

DECRETAS There, Diomed, there.

DIOMEDES   Lives he? Wilt thou
          Not answer, man?

                                        [*Exit* DECRETAS

ANTONY   Art thou there, Diomed?
          Draw thy sword, and give me   115
          Sufficing strokes for death.*

DIOMEDES   Most absolute lord,
          My mistress Cleopatra sent me to thee.

ANTONY When did she send thee?

DIOMEDES   Now, my lord.

ANTONY   Where is she?

DIOMEDES Locked in her monument. She had a prophesying fear*
          Of what hath come to pass; for when she saw –   120
          Which never shall be found* – you did suspect
          She had disposed* with Caesar, and that your rage
          Would not be purged,* she sent you word she was dead;
          But fearing since how it might work,* hath sent
          Me to proclaim the truth, and I am come,   125
          I dread, too late.

ANTONY Too late, good Diomed. Call my guard, I prithee.

DIOMEDES What ho! The Emperor's guard! The guard, what ho!
          Come, your lord calls.

          Enter four of five of ANTONY'S GUARD.

ANTONY Bear me, good friends, where Cleopatra bides;   130
          'Tis the last service that I shall command you.

FIRST GUARD Woe, woe are we, sir, you may not live to wear
          All your true followers out.*

ALL   Most heavy day!

ANTONY Nay, good my fellows, do not please sharp fate
          To grace it with your sorrows.* Bid that welcome   135
          Which comes to punish us, and we punish it,*
          Seeming to bear it lightly. Take me up.
          I have led you oft: carry me now, good friends,
          And have my thanks for all.

                          [*Exeunt carrying* ANTONY *and* EROS

IV.xv. Cleopatra declares that she will never leave the monument. Antony is brought dying to to the foot of it and is hauled up by Cleopatra and her maids. He advises her to seek safety with Caesar, but to trust only Proculeius. Antony dies, fortified by the thought that he has not surrendered, but has in true Roman fashion conquered himself. Cleopatra in her turn feels the emptiness of life without her lover; she will bury Antony and follow his example by taking her own life.

With the successive deaths of Enobarbus, Eros and Antony there is a tragic darkening of the universe, emphasised by the imagery employed. Antony has given expression to this is his phrase, 'The long day's task is done' and now Cleopatra remarks 'Our lamp is spent' since the gods have 'stolen our jewels'. Defeat, death and desertion have eaten away her power so that she is now isolated with her maids, her kingdom reduced to the monument, defying Caesar and the world which he owns. As Shakespeare focuses audience attention upon her he raises her to unprecedented heights by her spirit in defeat, and by her exquisite epitaph over the dead body of Antony.

4   *we* – i.e. I.
4   *Our size . . . makes it:* My sorrow must be as great as what causes it. – The cause of her grief is Antony's angry rejection of her and his possible death.
10   *sphere:* – See note to II.vii.12–14. If Cleopatra's plea were answered, the sun would drop from its sphere into space and eternal darkness would follow on the earth.
10   *Darkling stand . . . world:* May the constantly changing (*varying*) shores of the earth remain in darkness. – Cleopatra wants the universe to go into mourning for Antony.
19   *importune death awhile:* beg death to wait for a while.
21   *I dare not* – i.e. dare not receive his kiss by coming down to him or by unlocking the gates of the monument to let him enter.
23   *Not th'imperious . . . with me:* The victorious Caesar's imperial march of triumph (through Rome) shall never have me as its chief ornament (*brooch*).

scene xv

Alexandria. CLEOPATRA'S *monument.*

Enter CLEOPATRA *and her* MAIDS, CHARMIAN *and* IRAS *on the upper stage.*

CLEOPATRA O Charmian, I will never go from hence.
CHARMIAN Be comforted, dear madam.
CLEOPATRA   No, I will not.
    All strange and terrible events are welcome,
    But comforts we* despise. Our size of sorrow,
    Proportioned to our cause, must be as great   5
    As that which makes it.*

Enter DIOMEDES *below.*

                How now? Is he dead?
DIOMEDES His death's upon him, but not dead.
    Look out o' th'other side your monument:
    His guard have brought him thither.

Enter the GUARD *below, carrying* ANTONY.

CLEOPATRA   O sun,
    Burn the great sphere* thou mov'st in! Darkling stand   10
    The varying shore o' th'world!* O Antony,
    Antony, Antony! Help, Charmian, help, Iras, help:
    Help, friends below; let's draw him hither.
ANTONY   Peace!
    Not Caesar's valour hath o'erthrown Antony,
    But Antony's hath triumphed on itself.   15
CLEOPATRA So it should be, that none but Antony
    Should conquer Antony, but woe 'tis so.
ANTONY I am dying, Egypt, dying; only
    I here importune death awhile,* until
    Of many thousand kisses, the poor last   20
    I lay upon thy lips.
CLEOPATRA   I dare not,* dear.
    Dear my lord, pardon: I dare not,
    Lest I be taken. Not th'imperious show
    Of the full-fortuned Caesar ever shall
    Be brooched with me,* if knife, drugs, serpents, have   25

26	*operation:* power to work (referring to *drugs*).
28	*still conclusion:* silent judgement of me. – Cleopatra imagines Octavia silently weighing her up and forming an unfavourable opinion of her.
29	*Demuring upon:* looking demurely at.
32	*sport* – The word pathetically underlines the contrast between the present occasion and the diversions of former times, as described earlier at II.v.15-8.
33	*heaviness:* (a) sorrow (b) weight. – Their grief enfeebles them and makes it harder to lift Antony.
35	*Mercury* – (or Hermes) was the messenger of the gods generally, and of Jove particularly.
37	*Wishers were ever fools* – i.e. wishing without acting is foolish. Cleopatra exhorts herself to further efforts to lift Antony.
38	*Die when thou hast lived* – i.e. Live once more before you die.
39	*Quicken:* come to life.
39	*that power* – i.e. power to give life by kissing.
43	*rail so high . . . offence:* complain so strongly that the treacherous hussy Fortune, angered by my attack, will break her wheel. – The allusion is to the Roman goddess Fortuna, who whimsically turned her wheel so that those at the height of their fortune one moment (i.e. at the top of her wheel in its turning) would be hurled down to misfortune the next, as Antony has been. Cleopatra hopes that Fortune will break her wheel and consequently have no power to bring misfortunes into the lives of mortals. *Huswife* was pronounced *hussif* and stressed on the first syllable.
46	*Of:* From.
47	*They do not go together* – i.e. they are incompatible. If she seeks safety she loses her honour.
49	*My resolution . . . trust:* I will trust only my determination and my hands (i.e. to take her own life).
52	*The miserable . . . sorrow at:* Do not grieve over (*lament*) or be saddened by the misfortune that the end of my life has brought.
55	*do:* I do.
56	*Not cowardly . . . helmet:* do not yield in a cowardly fashion.
59	*woo't:* will you.
60	*Hast thou no care of me?* Do you not care for me?

Edge, sting, or operation.* I am safe.
Your wife Octavia, with her modest eyes
And still conclusion,* shall acquire no honour
Demuring upon* me. But come, come, Antony, –
Help me, my women – we must draw thee up.   30
Assist, good friends.

ANTONY   O quick, or I am gone.

CLEOPATRA Here's sport,* indeed! How heavy weighs my lord!
Our strength is all gone into heaviness;*
That makes the weight. Had I great Juno's power,
The strong-winged Mercury* should fetch thee up   35
And set thee by Jove's side. Yet come a little –
Wishers were ever fools* – O come, come, come!

                    [*They heave* ANTONY *up to* CLEOPATRA

And welcome, welcome! Die when thou hast lived,*
Quicken* with kissing. Had my lips that power,*
Thus would I wear them out.

ALL   A heavy sight!   40

ANTONY I am dying, Egypt, dying.
Give me some wine, and let me speak a little.

CLEOPATRA No, let me speak, and let me rail so high
That the false huswife Fortune break her wheel,
Provoked by my offence.*

ANTONY   One word, sweet Queen.   45
Of* Caesar seek your honour, with your safety. O!

CLEOPATRA They do not go together.*

ANTONY   Gentle, hear me:
None about Caesar trust but Proculeius.

CLEOPATRA My resolution and my hands I'll trust;*
None about Caesar.   50

ANTONY The miserable change now at my end
Lament nor sorrow at,* but please your thoughts
In feeding them with those my former fortunes
Wherein I lived: the greatest prince o' th' world,
The noblest; and do* now not basely die,   55
Not cowardly put off my helmet* to
My countryman; a Roman, by a Roman
Valiantly vanquished. Now my spirit is going,
I can no more.

CLEOPATRA   Noblest of men, woo't* die?
Hast thou no care of me?* Shall I abide   60
In this dull world, which in thy absence is

64   *garland:* (a) crown (b) flower. – The word seems to have suggested *pole* (line 65), the may-
     pole, decorated with garlands of flowers, around which people danced at
     summer festivities, and also *young boys and girls* (line 65).
65   *pole:* (a) maypole (b) pole-star (c) standard (around which troops rallied).
66   *Are level now* – Now that Antony, who towered above everyone else, has gone, the rest
     of mankind are indistinguishable.
66   *The odds is gone:* The distinction between great and small no longer exists.
67   *remarkable:* to be wondered at. – The word had stronger connotations of amazement in
     Shakespeare's time than it has now.
68   *the visiting moon* – The moon in its waxing and waning is described as a visitor to earth,
     coming and going.
73   *No more but e'en:* Nothing more than.
73   *commanded . . . passion:* ruled by the same common emotions.
75   *chares:* chores, menial tasks.
75   *It were for me:* It would be fitting for me.
78   *our jewel* – i.e. Antony.
79   *sottish:* stupid.
79   *does / Become:* is characteristic of.
83   *good cheer:* be cheerful.
85   *lamp is spent* – i.e. Antony is dead. Cf. Antony's words of Cleopatra at IV.xiv.46.
85   *sirs* – The word was commonly applied to women at this time.
87   *after the high Roman fashion:* in the exalted Roman manner. – Cleopatra refers to suicide,
     an action considered brave and noble by the Romans.
89   *This case* – i.e. the body of Antony. Cf. IV.xiv.41.

No better than a sty? O, see, my women,
The crown o' th'earth doth melt. My lord!

                                        [ANTONY *dies*

O, withered is the garland* of the war,
The soldier's pole* is fall'n: young boys and girls   65
Are level now* with men. The odds is gone,*
And there is nothing left remarkable*
Beneath the visiting moon.*

CHARMIAN   O quietness, lady.

                                        [CLEOPATRA *faints*

IRAS   She's dead too, our sovereign!
CHARMIAN   Lady!
IRAS   Madam!
CHARMIAN   O madam, madam, madam!
IRAS   Royal Egypt!   70
    Empress!
CHARMIAN   Peace, peace, Iras!
CLEOPATRA   No more but e'en* a woman, and commanded
    By such poor passion* as the maid that milks
    And does the meanest chares.* It were for me*   75
    To throw my sceptre at the injurious gods,
    To tell them that this world did equal theirs
    Till they had stol'n our jewel.* All's but naught:
    Patience is sottish,* and impatience does
    Become* a dog that's mad. Then is it sin   80
    To rush into the secret house of death
    Ere death dare come to us? How do you, women?
    What, what, good cheer!* Why, how now, Charmian?
    My noble girls! Ah, women, women! Look,
    Our lamp is spent,* it's out. Good sirs,* take heart;   85
    We'll bury him; and then what's brave, what's noble,
    Let's do it after the high Roman fashion,*
    And make death proud to take us. Come, away.
    This case* of that huge spirit now is cold.
    Ah, women, women! Come, we have no friend   90
    But resolution, and the briefest end.

                            [*Exeunt carrying* ANTONY'S *body*

v.i.   After Caesar has sent Dolabella to order Antony to surrender, Decretas arrives bearing
          Antony's sword and announcing his death, news which causes Caesar to weep. He assures
          Cleopatra's messenger that his intentions towards her are honourable and kindly. The
          messenger leaves and Caesar sends Proculeius to allay her fears lest she kill herself and
          prevent him displaying her in his triumph through Rome. He sends Gallus after him.
              The generous praise of Antony by Caesar and his followers sustains the exalted note
          of Antony's end. The tone here is quiet and businesslike after the lyrical heroism of the
          previous scene. Shakespeare eases the tension before the build-up to the final climax of
          the meeting of Cleopatra and Caesar.

2   *Being so . . . makes:* since he is so soundly beaten, tell him his delays in surrendering are
                     ridiculous. - There is dramatic irony in that Caesar's anxieties are mocked by
                     the fact that Antony is dead. Dramatic irony is the device in which characters
                     speak and act in ignorance of the true significance of what they or other
                     characters are saying, or in which actions produce results opposite to what they
                     expect. Sometimes, as in this case, the audience perceives the irony at once,
                     since it knows facts unknown to the speaker(s).
4   *Wherefore is that:* What is that for? - Caesar has caught sight of Antony's sword which
                     Decretas is carrying.
5   *thus* - i.e. unannounced and holding a naked sword.
8   *I wore . . . haters:* I spent my life in opposing his enemies. - The opportunism of Decretas
                     is in strong contrast with the true loyalty of Antony's servants (IV.ii) and is well
                     brought out in his clothing image. His service is like a garment which can be
                     cast off and changed at will.
14   *breaking:* (a) destruction (b) report.
15   *crack:* (a) break (b) explosion.
16   *shook . . . their dens:* shaken lions out of their dens into the streets of the city, and thrown
                     citizens into the lions' dens. - Caesar expected startling signs to mark Antony's
                     death as they had done when Julius Caesar died. In Shakespeare's *Julius
                     Caesar* much is made of these signs and portents, and lions on the streets of
                     Rome are twice mentioned.
18   *doom:* death.
19   *moiety:* half.
21   *self:* same.

ACT V scene i

Alexandria. CAESAR'S *camp.*

Enter CAESAR, AGRIPPA, DOLABELLA, MAECENAS, GALLUS *and*
PROCULEIUS.

CAESAR Go to him, Dolabella, bid him yield:
Being so frustrate, tell him, he mocks
The pauses that he makes.*

DOLABELLA   Caesar, I shall.   [*Exit*

Enter DECRETAS *with* ANTONY'S *sword.*

CAESAR Wherefore is that?* And what art thou that dar'st
Appear thus* to us?

DECRETAS   I am called Decretas.   5
Mark Antony I served, who best was worthy
Best to be served. Whilst he stood up and spoke,
He was my master, and I wore my life
To spend upon his haters.* If thou please
To take me to thee, as I was to him   10
I'll be to Caesar; if thou pleasest not,
I yield thee up my life.

CAESAR   What is't thou say'st?

DECRETAS I say, O Caesar, Antony is dead.

CAESAR The breaking* of so great a thing should make
A greater crack.* The round world   15
. Should have shook lions into civil streets,
And citizens to their dens.* The death of Antony
Is not a single doom;* in the name lay
A moiety* of the world.

DECRETAS   He is dead, Caesar,
Not by a public minister of justice,   20
Nor by a hired knife; but that self* hand
Which writ his honour in the acts it did,
Hath, with the courage which the heart did lend it,
Splitted the heart. This is his sword;
I robbed his wound of it. Behold it stained   25
With his most noble blood.

179

27   *rebuke me* – i.e. because he is shedding tears.
28   *wash the eyes of kings:* make kings weep.
29   *nature . . . persisted deeds:* natural feelings force us to lament those deeds (like the destruction of Antony) which we have most persistently tried to perform.
31   *Waged equal with:* were equally matched in.
32   *Did steer humanity:* guided men through life.
32   *will give:* persist in giving.
34   *When such . . . himself* – Antony's career is like a mirror (*spacious* because of the greatness of Antony's achievements) in which Caesar can see reflected what his own fate might have been, or might be.
36   *followed:* pursued.
36   *launch:* lance.
37   *I must perforce . . . thine:* I was forced either to suffer such a fall as yours and to display it to you, or to witness yours. – Caesar reveals through the image he uses that he regards Antony's career as a disease threatening to infect his own political well-being.
39   *stall:* live. – The metaphor is that of two animals living peaceably side by side in the same stall.
40   *In the whole world:* anywhere in the world.
41   *sovereign:* (a) potent (b) royal.
42   *competitor . . . design:* partner (and rival) in the loftiest enterprises.
46   *Where mine . . . kindle:* where my deepest thoughts were inspired. – *his:* its.
47   *Unreconciliable:* unable to be brought into harmony.
47   *divide / Our equalness to this:* divide our equality in this unequal way.
49   *meeter season:* more appropriate time. – The arrival of the Egyptian interrupts him; unlike Antony, Caesar is not the man to let less important matters hold up the more important business of the state.
50   *business . . . of him:* the urgency of this man's business can be seen in his face.
53   *Confined . . . monument:* locked in her only possession, her monument.
54   *intents:* intentions.
55   *preparedly may frame herself:* by preparation may adapt herself.
56   *have good heart:* keep her spirits up.
57   *of us, by some of ours:* from me, by some messengers.
58   *honourable* for *honourably*. Cf. note to I.i.25.
59   *live / To be ungentle:* be harsh, however long he lives.

CAESAR   Look you sad, friends?
                  The gods rebuke me,* but it is tidings
                  To wash the eyes of kings.*
AGRIPPA   And strange it is
                  That nature must compel us to lament
                  Our most persisted deeds.*
MAECENAS   His taints and honours   30
                  Waged equal with* him.
AGRIPPA   A rarer spirit never
                  Did steer humanity:* but you gods will give* us
                  Some faults to make us men. Caesar is touched.
MAECENAS When such a spacious mirror's set before him,
                  He needs must see himself.*
CAESAR   O Antony,   35
                  I have followed* thee to this. But we do launch*
                  Diseases in our bodies. I must perforce
                  Have shown to thee such a declining day,
                  Or look on thine:* we could not stall* together
                  In the whole world.* But yet let me lament   40
                  With tears as sovereign* as the blood of hearts,
                  That thou, my brother, my competitor
                  In top of all design,* my mate in empire,
                  Friend and companion in the front of war,
                  The arm of mine own body, and the heart   45
                  Where mine his thoughts did kindle,* that our stars,
                  Unreconciliable,* should divide
                  Our equalness to this.* Hear me, good friends –

Enter an EGYPTIAN.

                  But I will tell you at some meeter season:*   50
                  The business of this man looks out of him.*
                  We'll hear him what he says. Whence are you?
EGYPTIAN A poor Egyptian, yet the Queen my mistress,
                  Confined in all she has, her monument,*
                  Of thy intents* desires instruction,
                  That she preparedly may frame herself*   55
                  To th'way she's forced to.
CAESAR   Bid her have good heart.*
                  She soon shall know of us, by some of ours,*
                  How honourable* and how kindly we
                  Determine for her; for Caesar cannot live
                  To be ungentle.*

63	*quality:* nature.
64	*greatness* – i.e. of spirit. Caesar fears she will commit suicide.
65	*her life . . . triumph:* to have her alive in my triumph in Rome would make it everlasting.
67	*with your speediest:* as fast as you can.
68	*how you find of her:* what state of mind you find her in.
69	*along* – i.e. with Proculeius.
74	*hardly:* reluctantly.
75	*still:* always.
77	*What I can show in this:* what proofs of this I can show you.

v.ii.   In the monument Cleopatra expresses scorn for Caesar and Fortune. Proculeius arrives outside the monument and while Cleopatra is talking to him, Gallus and his men break in and she is thwarted in her attempt to stab herself. Dolabella, who arrives to take command, confirms her fear that Caesar intends to show her in his triumph. At this point Caesar enters and warns her that he will kill her children if she takes her own life. She gives him an inventory of her treasure and calls on her Treasurer, Seleucus, to verify it. She furiously assaults him when he reveals that she has kept back at least half her treasure. Caesar professes friendship and allows her to keep the treasure. After he has gone, aware that she cannot trust him, she orders her maids to dress her in the regalia in which she first met Antony. An Egyptian rustic delivers a basket of figs in which asps are concealed. When he has left, her maids dress her. Iras dies, having apparently taken an asp from the basket. Cleopatra applies an asp to her breast and dies rejoicing at having foiled Caesar's plans. A guard rushes in just before Charmian dies, shortly followed by Caesar who feared some such attempt by Cleopatra to outwit him. He orders that she should be buried beside Antony.

A number of separate incidents are skilfully woven into a single, swiftly moving scene, which maintains suspense up to the last minute and provides plenty of visual excitement. At the beginning of the scene Cleopatra tries to nerve herself to take her life, and we are in some doubt about her resolution as she parleys with Proculeius. When the Romans break into the monument she impulsively tries to stab herself but is prevented. Her anxiety to discover Caesar's intentions, and her deception over the treasure, suggest her irresolution and the strong appeal that life still has for her. After her humiliation by Seleucus and her certainty that Caesar intends to display her in his triumph she decides calmly and irrevocably on death. Dressed for a second Cydnus she sheds her womanly fear and is 'marble constant' for the first time. The accompanying deaths of Charmian and Iras serve, as that of Eros did for Antony, to lend a tragic exaltation to her end.

1	*My desolation . . . life:* My desolate state is a beginning, leading to a better life. – When Cleopatra's fortunes were at their height she did not value them at their true worth. Now that they have fallen, she is able to evaluate them objectively and despise them. Death, she goes on to argue, gives command over Fortune.
3	*knave:* servant.
4	*minister:* agent.
5	*do that thing* – i.e. commit suicide.
6	*shackles . . . change:* prevents chance happenings and change from harming us. – Accidents and change are personified as prisoners chained and locked up by Death.
7	*palates . . . Caesar's:* tastes again base earthly food, which nourishes beggar and emperor alike. – *Dung* here stands for food grown with the aid of manure. Cleopatra echoes Antony's words at I.i.35.
10	*study on:* consider carefully.

EGYPTIAN   So the gods preserve thee!   [*Exit*   60
CAESAR   Come hither, Proculeius. Go and say
         We purpose her no shame. Give her what comforts
         The quality* of her passion shall require,
         Lest in her greatness* by some mortal stroke
         She do defeat us: for her life in Rome   65
         Would be eternal in our triumph.* Go,
         And with your speediest* bring us what she says
         And how you find of her.*
PROCULEIUS   Caesar, I shall.   [*Exit*
CAESAR   Gallus, go you along.* [*Exit* GALLUS] Where's Dolabella,
         To second Proculeius?
ALL   Dolabella!   70
CAESAR   Let him alone, for I remember now
         How he's employed. He shall in time be ready.
         Go with me to my tent, where you shall see
         How hardly* I was drawn into this war,
         How calm and gentle I proceeded still*   75
         In all my writings. Go with me, and see
         What I can show in this.*
                                                          [*Exeunt*

scene ii

Alexandria. The monument.

Enter CLEOPATRA, CHARMIAN *and* IRAS.

CLEOPATRA   My desolation does begin to make
            A better life.* 'Tis paltry to be Caesar:
            Not being Fortune, he's but Fortune's knave,*
            A minister* of her will. And it is great
            To do that thing* that ends all other deeds,   5
            Which shackles accidents and bolts up change;*
            Which sleeps, and never palates more the dung,
            The beggar's nurse, and Caesar's.*

Enter PROCULEIUS.

PROCULEIUS   Caesar sends greeting to the Queen of Egypt,
             And bids thee study on* what fair demands   10
             Thou mean'st to have him grant thee.
CLEOPATRA   What's thy name?

14   *to be deceived . . . trusting:* whether I am deceived or not, since I have no need for trust.
16   *keep decorum . . . beg than:* act in the manner fitting to it, has to ask for nothing less than.
20   *as:* that.
23   *Make your full reference freely:* Submit your whole case frankly.
24   *grace:* goodwill.
26   *sweet dependency:* willing submission to his authority.
27   *pray in aid for kindness:* beg your help to instruct him how he can show kindness to you. -
            Pray in aid is a legal term used in a petition to call in another's help in a court
            case.
28   *Where . . . kneeled to:* when people beg for his favour.
29   *I am his fortune's vassal:* I pay homage to his good fortune (like a servant or vassal,
            acknowledging the supremacy of his overlord).
29   *I send . . . has got:* I acknowledge his greatness.
31   *doctrine:* lesson.
34   *Of:* by.
39   *Hold:* Stop!
40   *who are . . . betrayed:* since by this action (i.e. Gallus's capture of her) you are rescued not
            betrayed.
41   *of death . . . languish:* (rescued) from death too, which puts an end to (even) the lingering
            diseases of dogs.

PROCULEIUS My name is Proculeius

CLEOPATRA   Antony
Did tell me of you, bade me trust you, but
I do not greatly care to be deceived
That have no use for trusting.* If your master   15
Would have a queen his beggar, you must tell him
That majesty, to keep decorum, must
No less beg than* a kingdom. If he please
To give me conquered Egypt for my son,
He gives me so much of mine own as* I   20
Will kneel to him with thanks.

PROCULEIUS   Be of good cheer:
Y'are fall'n into a princely hand; fear nothing.
Make your full reference freely* to my lord,
Who is so full of grace* that it flows over
On all that need. Let me report to him   25
Your sweet dependency,* and you shall find
A conqueror that will pray in aid for kindness,*
Where he for grace is kneeled to.*

CLEOPATRA   Pray you, tell him
I am his fortune's vassal,* and I send him
The greatness he has got.* I hourly learn   30
A doctrine* of obedience, and would gladly
Look him i' th'face.

PROCULEIUS   This I'll report, dear lady.
Have comfort, for I know your plight is pitied
Of* him that caused it.

Enter GALLUS *with* ROMAN SOLDIERS.

GALLUS You see how easily she may be surprised.   35
[*To* PROCULEIUS *and the soldiers*] Guard her till Caesar come.

IRAS Royal Queen!

CHARMIAN O Cleopatra, thou art taken, Queen!

CLEOPATRA [*Drawing a dagger*] Quick, quick, good hands!

PROCULEIUS   Hold,* worthy lady, hold!
                                   [*He disarms her*
Do not yourself such wrong, who are in this   40
Relieved, but not betrayed.*

CLEOPATRA   What, of death too,
That rids our dogs of languish?*

PROCULEIUS   Cleopatra,

44	*undoing:* destruction.
45	*nobleness well acted:* nobility admirably shown in action.
46	*let come forth:* allow to appear.
48	*babes and beggars* – i.e. those most susceptible to death. – The death rate among babies was very high in Elizabethan times.
48	*temperance:* moderation.
50	*If idle . . . necessary:* if for once I must indulge in empty talk. – The line is parenthetic. The horrifying thought of the humiliation of being Caesar's prisoner, enduring Octavia's censure, and being made a spectacle to please the Roman mob, gives rise to this impassioned speech by Cleopatra, and explains her attempt at line 39 to take her life rather than endure such a fate.
51	*This mortal house* – i.e. her body.
52	*Do Caesar what he can:* whatever Caesar can do to prevent it.
53	*pinioned* – i.e. with wings clipped, and so a virtual prisoner.
54	*sober:* modest.
56	*varletry:* rabble.
60	*Blow me into abhorring:* lay their eggs on me and make my body loathsome with the maggots that grow from them.
61	*pyrámides:* pyramides is a four-syllabled word, stressed on the second.
66	*For:* As for.
67	*to my guard:* into my charge.
68	*It shall content me best:* nothing would please me more.
70	*If you'll . . . him:* if you wish me to represent anything to him on your behalf.
70	*would:* wish to.
71	*Empress* – Dolabella flatters her by acknowledging her as Antony's wife and co-ruler.

Do not abuse my master's bounty by
Th'undoing* of yourself. Let the world see
His nobleness well acted,* which your death   45
Will never let come forth.*

CLEOPATRA   Where art thou, death?
Come hither, come! Come, come, and take a queen
Worth many babes and beggars!*

PROCULEIUS   O, temperance,* lady!

CLEOPATRA Sir, I will eat no meat; I'll not drink, sir, –
If idle talk will once be necessary –*   50
I'll not sleep neither. This mortal house* I'll ruin,
Do Caesar what he can.* Know, sir, that I
Will not wait pinioned* at your master's court,
Nor once be chástised with the sober* eye
Of dull Octavia. Shall they hoist me up   55
And show me to the shouting varletry*
Of censuring Rome? Rather a ditch in Egypt
Be gentle grave unto me! Rather on Nilus' mud
Lay me stark-naked and let the waterflies
Blow me into abhorring!* Rather make   60
My country's high pyrámides* my gibbet
And hang me up in chains!

PROCULEIUS   You do extend
These thoughts of horror further than you shall
Find cause in Caesar.

        Enter DOLABELLA.

DOLABELLA   Proculeius,
What thou hast done thy master Caesar knows,   65
And he hath sent for thee. For the Queen,
I'll take her to my guard.*

PROCULEIUS   So, Dolabella,
It shall content me best.* Be gentle to her.
[*To* CLEOPATRA] To Caesar I will speak what you shall please,
If you'll employ me to him.*

CLEOPATRA   Say, I would* die.   70
                                    [*Exit* PROCULEIUS

DOLABELLA Most noble Empress,* you have heard of me?
CLEOPATRA I cannot tell.
DOLABELLA   Assuredly you know me.
CLEOPATRA No matter, sir, what I have heard or known.
You laugh when boys or women tell their dreams;

75   *trick:* habit.
77   *such* – i.e. for such.
80   *A sun and moon* – i.e. Antony's eyes.
81   *The little O, the earth* – Shakespeare frequently uses the letter O to describe circular
                    objects. Cleopatra sees the earth as tiny, partly because of her new mood in
                    which material things appear insignificant, partly because it is minute when
                    measured against Antony's transcendent qualities.
82   *bestrid:* straddled. – Cleopatra pictures Antony as a super Colossus, whose statue,
                    standing astride the entrance to the harbour of Rhodes, was one of the seven
                    wonders of the world.
82   *his reared . . . world:* his raised arm dominated the world.
83   *propertied . . . spheres:* endowed with the heavenly music of the spheres. – This is an
                    allusion to the Pythagorean theory that the spheres in their movement produced
                    music of transcendent beauty.
84   *that to friends:* that music was heard when he was among his friends. – The music of the
 ·   spheres was said to be heard only by a few mortals favoured by the gods.   ·
85   *quail and shake the orb:* make the world cower and tremble with fear.
86   *For his bounty:* As for his generosity.
87   *winter:* cold meanness.
87   *an autumn . . . reaping:* it was a harvest that grew more abundant the more it was reaped.
88   *His delights . . . lived in* – Just as the dolphin's back rises above its element, the sea, so
                    Antony's greatness stood out, even when he was immersed in pleasures.
90   *In his . . . crownets:* Kings and princes wore his colours (*livery*) – i.e. were his servants.
92   *plates:* silver coins.
97   *It's past the size of dreaming:* no dream could equal the reality.
97   *nature . . . with fancy:* nature lacks materials to compete with imagination in creating
                    strange forms.
99   *were nature's . . . quite:* would be a masterpiece of conception by nature, wholly dis-
                    crediting fancy's shadowy creations.
101   *you bear . . . weight* – Cleopatra shows her magnanimity in the way she bears her loss, her
                    greatness corresponding to (*answering to*) the grievousness of her loss.
102   *Would I . . . do feel:* May I never attain any success I seek if I do not (*but I do*) feel.
104   *of yours* – i.e. of your grief. Cleopatra's grief stands out starkly against the background of
                    Roman success, discussed here. The dramatic effect of Dolabella's sympathy at
                    Cleopatra's suffering is to deepen ours.
107   *would you knew:* want you to know.

Is't not your trick?*
DOLABELLA   I understand not, madam.   75
CLEOPATRA I dreamt there was an Emperor Antony.
O such* another sleep, that I might see
But such another man!
DOLABELLA   If it might please ye –
CLEOPATRA His face was as the heavens, and therein stuck
A sun and moon,* which kept their course, and lighted   80
The little O, the earth.*
DOLABELLA   Most sovereign creature –
CLEOPATRA His legs bestrid* the ocean, his reared arm
Crested the world;* his voice was propertied
As all the tunèd spheres,* and that to friends.*
But when he meant to quail and shake the orb,*   85
He was as rattling thunder. For his bounty,*
There was no winter* in't; an autumn 'twas
That grew the more by reaping.* His delights
Were dolphin-like, they showed his back above
The element they lived in.* In his livery   90
Walked crowns and crownets;* realms and islands were
As plates* dropped from his pocket.
DOLABELLA   Cleopatra!
CLEOPATRA Think you there was, or might be, such a man
As this I dreamt of?
DOLABELLA   Gentle madam, no.
CLEOPATRA You lie up to the hearing of the gods.   95
But if there be, or ever were one such,
It's past the size of dreaming:* nature wants stuff
To vie strange forms with fancy,* yet t'imagine
An Antony were nature's piece 'gainst fancy,
Condemning shadows quite.*
DOLABELLA   Hear me, good madam.   100
Your loss is as yourself, great; and you bear it
As answering to the weight.* Would I might never
O'ertake pursued success, but I do feel,*
By the rebound of yours,* a grief that smites
My very heart at root.
CLEOPATRA   I thank you, sir.   105
Know you what Caesar means to do with me?
DOLABELLA I am loath to tell you what I would you knew.*
CLEOPATRA Nay, pray you, sir, –
DOLABELLA   Though he be honourable, –

117	*Take to you no hard thoughts* – i.e. Do not be afraid of my intentions towards you.
119	*written in our flesh* – i.e. shown in our war wounds.
120	*sir:* lord.
121	*project . . . cause:* put forward my own case (i.e. her own *record of . . . injuries* against Caesar).
122	*clear:* blameless.
123	*like frailties:* frailties like those.
125	*extenuate rather than enforce:* excuse rather than stress (your faults).
126	*apply yourself to our intents:* accede to my plans.
128	*change* – i.e. of fortunes.
129	*lay on me a cruelty:* have the charge of cruelty brought against me.
130	*Antony's course* – i.e. suicide.
130	*bereave . . . good purposes:* deprive yourself of the good things I intend for you.
133	*thereon* – i.e. on his *good purposes.*
134	*And may through all the world:* And you are free to come and go as you like anywhere in the world. – The world, that is, belongs to Caesar.
135	*scutcheons* – shields depicting the coat-of-arms of the owners. In Shakespeare's time a victor displayed those of his captured enemies. Cleopatra's use of the word *scutcheons* here is anachronistic, since they did not come into use until the Middle Ages.
137	*in all for Cleopatra* – i.e. in everything that concerns you.
138	*brief:* summary list.
140	*Not petty things admitted:* with trifles omitted.

CLEOPATRA   He'll lead me then, in triumph?
DOLABELLA   Madam, he will. I know't.   110

       Flourish. Enter PROCULEIUS, CAESAR, GALLUS, MAECENAS *and
       others of his train.*

     ALL   Make way there! Caesar!
  CAESAR   Which is the Queen of Egypt?
DOLABELLA   It is the Emperor, madam.

                                        [CLEOPATRA *kneels*
  CAESAR   Arise, you shall not kneel:
       I pray you rise, rise, Egypt.
CLEOPATRA   Sir, the gods   115
       Will have it thus. My master and my lord
       I must obey.
  CAESAR   Take to you no hard thoughts.*
       The record of what injuries you did us,
       Though written in our flesh,* we shall remember
       As things but done by chance.
CLEOPATRA   Sole sir* o' th'world,   120
       I cannot project mine own cause* so well
       To make it clear,* but do confess I have
       Been laden with like frailties* which before
       Have often shamed our sex.
  CAESAR   Cleopatra, know,
       We will extenuate rather than enforce.*   125
       If you apply yourself to our intents,*
       Which towards you are most gentle, you shall find
       A benefit in this change*; but if you seek
       To lay on me a cruelty* by taking
       Antony's course,* you shall bereave yourself   130
       Of my good purposes,* and put your children
       To that destruction which I'll guard them from
       If thereon* you rely. I'll take my leave.
CLEOPATRA   And may through all the world:* 'tis yours, and we
       Your scutcheons* and your signs of conquest, shall   135
       Hang in what place you please. [*Handing him a paper*]
       Here, my good lord.
  CAESAR   You shall advise me in all for Cleopatra.*
CLEOPATRA   This is the brief* of money, plate, and jewels
       I am possessed of. 'Tis exactly valued,
       Not pretty things admitted.* Where's Seleucus?   140

143   *Upon his peril:* at the risk of punishment if he lies.
146   *seel:* sew up. – Cf. note to III.xiii.112.
151   *How pomp is followed:* how men pursue those in power. – Cleopatra refers to Seleucus's betrayal of his loyalty to her in order to placate Caesar because his fortunes are now in the ascendant, and hers in decline.
151   *Mine* – i.e. my servants.
152   *shift estates:* exchange situations.
155   *goest thou back:* are you backing away? – The words indicate how this is to be acted, with Seleucus retreating as Cleopatra moves menacingly towards him.
156   *catch* – presumably with her nails.
158   *rarely:* exceptionally.
159   *O Caesar . . . envy* – The clause beginning *That thou vouchsafing* is not completed. Cleopatra switches in mid-sentence to a new construction, beginning *that mine own servant.* Possibly Shakespeare intended by this incoherence to stress the strength of her anger at Seleucus.
159   *wounding shame:* deep humiliation.
160   *vouchsafing:* condescending.
161   *Doing . . . so meek:* honouring by your exalted presence one so lowly.
163   *Parcel . . . his envy:* make up the sum total of my shames by adding the item of his malice to it.
164   *Say:* Suppose.
165   *lady:* feminine, such as would appeal to a woman.
166   *Immoment toys:* unimportant odds and ends.
166   *dignity:* value.
167   *modern:* ordinary.
167   *withal:* with.
168   *token:* sign (of my respect).
169   *Livia,* Caesar's wife.
169   *induce / Their mediation:* encourage them to intercede for me.
170   *unfolded / With:* exposed by.
171   *one that I have bred* – i.e. Seleucus, the Treasurer, her servant and *bred* by her in that sense.
172   *smites me . . . have* – i.e. makes my fall even greater.
173   *cinders . . . my chance:* the living fire of my spirit which is hidden beneath the ashes of my fortunes (*chance*).
174   *a man* – Seleucus is a eunuch.
175   *Thou wouldst have mercy on me:* you would pity me (and not have betrayed me as you have done).
175   *Forbear:* Withdraw.

Enter SELEUCUS.

SELEUCUS Here, madam.

CLEOPATRA This is my treasurer; let him speak, my lord,
Upon his peril,* that I have reserved
To myself nothing. Speak the truth, Seleucus.

SELEUCUS Madam,   145
I had rather seel* my lips than to my peril
Speak that which is not.

CLEOPATRA   What have I kept back?

SELEUCUS Enough to purchase what you have made known.

CAESAR Nay, blush not, Cleopatra; I approve
Your wisdom in the deed.

CLEOPATRA   See, Caesar! O, behold   150
How pomp is followed!* Mine* will now be yours,
And should we shift estates,* yours would be mine.
The ingratitude of this Seleucus does
Even make me wild. O slave, of no more trust
Than love that's hired! What, goest thou back?* Thou shalt   155
Go back, I warrant thee; but I'll catch* thine eyes
Though they had wings. Slave, soulless villain, dog!
O rarely* base!

CAESAR   Good Queen, let us entreat you.

CLEOPATRA O Caesar,* what a wounding shame* is this,
That thou vouchsafing* here to visit me,   160
Doing the honour of thy lordliness
To one so meek,* that mine own servant should
Parcel the sum of my disgraces by
Addition of his envy.* Say,* good Caesar,
That I some lady* trifles have reserved,   165
Immoment toys,* things of such dignity*
As we greet modern* friends withal;* and say
Some nobler token* I have kept apart
For Livia* and Octavia, to induce
Their mediation;* must I be unfolded   170
With* one that I have bred?* The gods! It smites me
Beneath the fall I have.* [*To* SELEUCUS] Prithee go hence,
Or I shall show the cinders of my spirits
Through th'ashes of my chance.* Wert thou a man,*
Thou wouldst have mercy on me.*

CAESAR   Forbear,* Seleucus.   175

[*Exit* SELEUCUS

| 176 | *misthought:* misjudged. |

176 *misthought:* misjudged.
178 *We answer . . . name:* we are held personally responsible for the misdeeds of others. – *merits:* deserts, whether reward or punishment.
180 *reserved, nor what acknowledged:* kept back, or admitted to possessing.
181 *Put we i'th'roll of conquest:* do I list as mine by right of conquest.
183 *make prize with you/Of:* haggle with you over.
185 *Make not . . . prisons:* do not think you are a prisoner.
186 *dispose you:* make arrangements concerning you.
191 *he words . . . myself:* tries to win me over by words to prevent my doing the noble thing to myself (i.e. committing suicide).
194 *for the dark:* bound for death.
194 *Hie:* Hurry.
195 *I have . . . provided:* I have already given orders and it is all arranged. – By *it* (line 195) Cleopatra refers to the provision of the asps; Shakespeare maintains suspense, however, by not revealing the fact at this point.
196 *put it to the haste:* do it quickly.
199 *my love . . . obey:* my love for you makes it a sacred duty to obey.
202 *before:* ahead of him.
203 *Make your best use of this:* Use this information as best you can.
203 *performed/Your pleasure:* done what you asked me to do.

CLEOPATRA Be it known that we, the greatest, are misthought*
              For things that others do, and when we fall,
              We answer others' merits in our name,*
              Are therefore to be pitied.

CAESAR   Cleopatra,
              Not what you have reserved, nor what acknowledged,*   180
              Put we i'th'roll of conquest;* still be't yours,
              Bestow, it at your pleasure, and believe,
              Caesar's no merchant, to make prize with you
              Of* things that merchants sold. Therefore be cheered;
              Make not your thoughts your prisons.* No, dear Queen,   185
              For we intend so to dispose you* as
              Yourself shall give us counsel. Feed, and sleep:
              Our care and pity is so much upon you
              That we remain your friend. And so adieu.

CLEOPATRA My master and my lord!

CAESAR   Not so. Adieu.   190
                         [*Flourish. Exeunt* CAESAR *and his Train*

CLEOPATRA He words me, girls, he words me, that I should not
              Be noble to myself.* But hark thee, Charmian.
                         [*She whispers to* CHARMIAN

IRAS Finish, good lady, the bright day is done,
              And we are for the dark.*

CLEOPATRA   Hie* thee again:
              I have spoke already, and it is provided.*   195
              Go put it to the haste.*

CHARMIAN   Madam, I will.

Enter DOLABELLA.

DOLABELLA Where's the Queen?

CHARMIAN   Behold, sir.   [*Exit*

CLEOPATRA   Dolabella?

DOLABELLA Madam, as thereto sworn, by your command
              (Which my love makes religion to obey*)
              I tell you this: Caesar through Syria   200
              Intends his journey, and within three days
              You with your children will he send before.*
              Make your best use of this.* I have performed
              Your pleasure,* and my promise.

CLEOPATRA   Dolabella,
              I shall remain your debtor.

DOLABELLA   I your servant.   205

208	*puppet:* (a) actor in a play or show (b) doll (c) woman (used in a contemptuous way). – Shakespeare possibly intended something of all three meanings here. Cleopatra thinks of Iras as a puppet manipulated by Caesar, and as a performer in his triumphal march through Rome, representing the conquest of Egypt. Puppet shows, depicting contemporary events and people, were popular in London at this time.
209	*Mechanic* – i.e. engaged in manual work. Cf. IV.iv.32 and note.
210	*rules:* carpenters' rulers.
211	*thick:* foul.
212	*Rank of gross diet* ×offensive because of their coarse diet.
212	*enclouded:* enveloped.
213	*drink their vapour* – i.e. inhale what they breathe out.
214	*Saucy:* (a) Insolent (b) Lascivious.
214	*lictors* – Roman officials who kept the streets clear and carried out the punishments imposed by the magistrates.
215	*catch at us like strumpets:* apprehend us as if we were prostitutes. – Shakespeare apparently thought of the lictors as the equivalent of the Elizabethan beadles, one of whose functions was to deal with prostitutes.
215	*scald rhymers . . . tune:* contemptible poets will compose tuneless ballads about us. – Like the puppet shows, ballads were often a commentary on contemporary people and affairs. Despite their generally low literary quality, these precursors of the modern newspaper were highly popular.
216	*quick comedians:* lively writers (or actors) of comedy.
217	*Extemporally . . . present:* without any preparation will put us on the stage and represent.
220	*squeaking . . . whore:* shrill-voiced boy reducing my greatness by representing me as a whore. – It is a measure of the skill of the boy actors that Shakespeare could give this line to one of them, confident that he would not 'squeak' or imitate Cleopatra's greatness unconvincingly.
223	*my nails . . . mine eyes* – Iras will tear out her eyes rather than witness it.
228	*again for Cydnus . . . Antony* – Cleopatra alludes to her first meeting with Antony, described by Enobarbus at II.ii.189f.
229	*Sirrah* – Like *sir* (IV.xv.85) the word was often used to address women.
230	*dispatch:* (a) hurry (b) finish off.
231	*chare:* chore – Cf. IV.xv.75 and note.
232	*play till doomsday,* i.e. to do no more work during your lifetime.
234	*will not be:* refuses to be.

Adieu, good Queen! I must attend on Caesar.

CLEOPATRA Farewell, and thanks.   [*Exit* DOLABELLA

                     Now, Iras, what think'st thou?
Thou, an Egyptian puppet,* shalt be shown
In Rome as well as I. Mechanic* slaves
With greasy aprons, rules* and hammers, shall   210
Uplift us to the view. In their thick* breaths,
Rank of gross diet,* shall we be enclouded,*
And forced to drink their vapour.*

IRAS   The gods forbid!

CLEOPATRA Nay, 'tis most certain, Iras. Saucy* lictors*
Will catch at us like strumpets,* and scald rhymers   215
Ballad us out o' tune.* The quick comedians*
Extemporally will stage us, and present*
Our Alexandrian revels: Antony
Shall be brought drunken forth, and I shall see
Some squeaking Cleopatra boy my greatness   220
I' th'posture of a whore.*

IRAS   O the good gods!

CLEOPATRA Nay, that's certain.

IRAS I'll never see't, for I am sure my nails
Are stronger than mine eyes!*

CLEOPATRA   Why, that's the way
To fool their preparation, and to conquer   225
Their most absurd intents.

Enter CHARMIAN.

                     Now, Charmian!
Show me, my women, like a Queen. Go fetch
My best attires. I am again for Cydnus,
To meet Mark Antony.* Sirrah* Iras, go –
Now, noble Charmian, we'll dispatch* indeed –   230
And when thou hast done this chare,* I'll give thee leave
To play till doomsday.* Bring our crown and all.
        [*Exeunt* CHARMIAN *and* IRAS. *A noise is heard within*
Wherefore's this noise?

Enter a GUARDSMAN.

GUARDSMAN   Here is a rural fellow
That will not be* denied your Highness' presence.
He brings you figs.   235

CLEOPATRA Let him come in.   [*Exit* GUARDSMAN

235   *What:* How.
238   *placed:* immovably fixed.
238   *nothing/Of woman:* no womanly weaknesses.
239   *marble-constant:* as unchanging as marble.
239   *now the fleeting . . . mine:* the inconstant moon is no longer the planet guiding me (inconstant because it waxes and wanes).
      Clown was the name given to the actor who took the part of the rustic fool, as here. The Clown is a stock figure found in many of Shakespeare's plays. He is a man of low social status and, accordingly, speaks prose (see Introduction, p. lxvi). Despite his simple-mindedness he possesses a sound folk wisdom which enables him to hold his own with his social and intellectual superiors. His wisdom is often expressed in comic fashion, in a muddled or paradoxical way, and sometimes his speech is wiser than he knows.
242   *Avoid:* Go away.
243   *worm of Nilus:* snake of the Nile, i.e. the asp, a small venomous snake found in Egypt and Libya.
246   *immortal* – The Clown means *mortal* (i.e. deadly), but as often in Shakespeare, the malapropism makes a sense of its own. The biting is immortal in the sense that it sends those bitten into eternity.
249   *heard of:* heard from.
250   *something:* somewhat.
251   *lie:* (a) tell lies (b) lie down.
252   *honesty:* (a) truthfulness (b) chastity.
253   *makes . . . report:* reports well of.
253   *but he . . . they do* – This is the Clown's muddled way of saying that one cannot believe all one hears, since people say much more than they perform.
255   *falliable* – He means *infallible,* 'undeniable'.
260   *do his kind:* act according to its nature, i.e. bite.
265   *Take thou no care:* Don't worry.
265   *it shall be heeded:* care will be taken with it.
269   *simple but:* foolish that I do not.
270   *dish:* appetizing food. – Cf. II.vi.122.
271   *dress:* prepare.
272   *whoreson* – a term of abuse or contempt (literally, 'son of a whore'), often used as here, in a generalized and humorous way.
272   *in their women:* with regard to their (i.e. the gods') women.

>   What* poor an instrument
> May do a noble deed! He brings me liberty.
> My resolution's placed,* and I have nothing
> Of woman* in me: now from head to foot
> I am marble-constant;* now the fleeting moon   240
> No planet is of mine.*

Enter GUARDSMAN *with* CLOWN* *who carries a basket.*

GUARDSMAN   This is the man.
CLEOPATRA Avoid,* and leave him.   [*Exit* GUARDSMAN
Hast thou the pretty worm of Nilus* there,
That kills and pains not?
CLOWN Truly I have him, but I would not be the party that should   245
desire you to touch him, for his biting is immortal:* those that
do die of it do seldom or never recover.
CLEOPATRA Remember'st thou any that have died on't?
CLOWN Very many; men and women too. I heard of* one of them no
longer than yesterday, a very honest woman, but something*   250
given to lie,* as a woman should not do but in the way of
honesty;* how she died of the biting of it, what pain she felt.
Truly, she makes a very good report o'* th'worm, but he
that will believe all that they say, shall never be saved by
half that they do.* But this is most falliable,* the worm's an   255
odd worm.
CLEOPATRA Get thee hence, farewell.
CLOWN I wish you all joy of the worm.
                                [*He puts down his basket*
CLEOPATRA Farewell.
CLOWN You must think this, look you, that the worm will do his   260
kind.*
CLEOPATRA Ay, ay; farewell.
CLOWN Look you, the worm is not to be trusted, but in the keeping of
wise people, for indeed there is no goodness in the worm.
CLEOPATRA Take thou no care;* it shall be heeded.*   265
CLOWN Very good. Give it nothing, I pray you, for it is not worth the
feeding.
CLEOPATRA Will it eat me?
CLOWN You must not think I am so simple but* I know the devil
himself will not eat a woman. I know that a woman is a dish*   270
for the gods, if the devil dress* her not. But truly, these same
whoreson* devils do the gods great harm in their women,* for
in every ten that they make, the devils mar five.

275   *forsooth:* certainly.
277   *Immortal longings:* longings for immortality.
279   *Yare:* Quickly.
283   *To excuse their after wrath:* to extenuate their subsequent punishment of men (for being
          arrogant in their undeserved good luck).
284   *Now . . . my title:* May my courage now prove that I am entitled to call you husband.
285   *I am fire and air* – In her elevated mood, Cleopatra feels that she has nothing in her of the
          two baser elements, earth and water. It was believed that man was composed
          of the four elements of earth, water, air and fire.
       Plutarch does not tell us how Iras dies, and the Folio has no stage directions concerning
          the deaths of the three women. It seems likely that she took an asp from the
          basket while Cleopatra was kissing Charmian (line 287). Some editors hold
          that at line 299 Cleopatra takes the asp that had bitten Iras, but that its poison
          had lost its power so that she has to take another from the basket at line 308.
          This works at once (as Iras's had on her), but loses its potency after biting
          Cleopatra, so that it takes longer to kill Charmian. Other editors argue that
          Iras dies of a broken heart, like Enobarbus.
289   *aspic* – i.e. the poison of the asp.
290   *nature:* human life.
293   *thus* – i.e. by quietly taking your life.
295   *Dissolve:* Melt into drops.
296   *This* – i.e. the death of Iras.
297   *curlèd:* carefully barbered. – Cleopatra pictures Antony carefully prepared for her coming,
          just as he was at Cydnus, where, Plutarch tells us, he was 'barbered ten times
          o'er'.
298   *spend . . . my heaven:* expend on her that kiss which is heaven to me.
299   *mortal wretch:* deadly creature. – *Wretch* and *fool* (line 301) could be used as terms of
          affection, as here, where Cleopatra addresses the asp, unable to speak, as her
          baby.
300   *intrinsicate:* intricate.
302   *dispatch:* end it quickly.
303   *Ass/Unpolicied:* A fool, outwitted in his policies.
304   *eastern star* – i.e. Venus, the morning star, and particularly appropriate since Venus was
          the goddess of love.
306   *asleep:* to sleep.
306   *break* – Charmian addresses her heart.

CLEOPATRA Well, get thee gone; farewell.
CLOWN Yes, forsooth.* I wish you joy o' th'worm.   [*Exit* 275

Enter CHARMIAN *and* IRAS *with crown and robes.*

CLEOPATRA Give me my robe, put on my crown; I have
Immortal longings* in me. Now no more
The juice of Egypt's grape shall moist this lip.
Yare, yare,* good Iras, quick. Methinks I hear
Antony call. I see him rouse himself   280
To praise my noble act. I hear him mock
The luck of Caesar, which the gods give men
To excuse their after wrath.* Husband, I come.
Now to that name my courage prove my title!*
I am fire and air;* my other elements   285
I give to baser life. So, have you done?
Come then, and take the last warmth of my lips.
Farewell, kind Charmian, Iras, long farewell.
                    [*She kisses them.* IRAS *falls and dies**
Have I the aspic* in my lips? Dost fall?
If thou and nature* can so gently part,   290
The stroke of death is as a lover's pinch,
Which hurts, and is desired. Dost thou lie still?
If thus* thou vanishest, thou tell'st the world
It is not worth leave-taking.
CHARMIAN Dissolve,* thick cloud, and rain, that I may say   295
The gods themselves do weep!
CLEOPATRA   This* proves me base.
If she first meet the curlèd* Antony,
He'll make demand of her, and spend that kiss
Which is my heaven* to have. Come, thou mortal wretch,*
                    [*To an asp which she applies to her breast*
With thy sharp teeth this knot intrinsicate*   300
Of life at once untie. Poor venomous fool,
Be angry, and dispatch.* O, couldst thou speak,
That I might hear thee call great Caesar 'Ass,
Unpolicied!'*
CHARMIAN   O eastern star!*
CLEOPATRA   Peace, peace!
Dost thou not see my baby at my breast,   305
That sucks the nurse asleep?*
CHARMIAN   O, break!* O, break!

307   *As sweet . . . gentle* – According to Plutarch this was the effect produced by the asp's bite.
309   *What:* Why.
310   *In this wild world* – Charmian completes Cleopatra's unfinished sentence. – *wild:* savage.
311   *in thy possession:* that in your keeping.
312   *Downy windows* – i.e. eyelids as soft as down.
313   *golden Phoebus:* the sun.
314   *Of:* by.
314   *awry:* crooked, on at an angle.
315   *mend it:* put it straight.
315   *and then play* – a moving reference to Cleopatra's earlier words (line 231–2). Charmian has
         now performed her last *chare* for her mistress.
318   *dispatch:* hurry. – She addresses the asp.
319   *beguiled:* deceived.
326   *Touch their effects:* reach their expected results.
327   *performed* – i.e. already performed.
329   *A way:* Make way.
330   *sure an augurer:* accurate a prophet. – Cf. IV.xii.4 and note.
331   *that:* that which, what.
331   *Bravest at the last* – Cleopatra, Caesar says, was braver in her death than ever before.
332   *levelled at:* guessed. – The image is taken from the levelling of a weapon to take aim.

CLEOPATRA As sweet as balm, as soft as air, as gentle.*
　　　　　O Antony! Nay, I will take thee too.
　　　　　　　　　　　　　　[*Applying another asp to her arm*
　　　　　What* should I stay –　　　　　　　　　[*She dies*
CHARMIAN In this wild world?* So, fare thee well.　　　　310
　　　　　Now boast thee, death, in thy possession* lies
　　　　　A lass unparalleled. Downy windows,* close;
　　　　　　　　　　　　　　[*She closes* CLEOPATRA'S *eyes*
　　　　　And golden Phoebus* never be beheld
　　　　　Of* eyes again so royal! Your crown's awry;*
　　　　　I'll mend it,* and then play* –　　　　　315

　　　　　Enter the GUARD *rushing in.*

FIRST GUARD Where's the Queen?
CHARMIAN 　　　　　　　　Speak softly, wake her not.
FIRST GUARD Caesar hath sent –
CHARMIAN 　　　　　　　　Too slow a messenger.
　　　　　　　　　　　　　　　　[*She applies an asp*
　　　　　O, come apace, dispatch!* I partly feel thee.
FIRST GUARD Approach ho! All's not well. Caesar's beguiled.*
SECOND GUARD There's Dolabella sent from Caesar; call him.　320
FIRST GUARD What work is here, Charmian? Is this well done?
CHARMIAN It is well done, and fitting for a princess
　　　　　Descended of so many royal kings.
　　　　　Ah, soldier!　　　　　　　　　　[*She dies*

　　　　　Enter DOLABELLA.

DOLABELLA How goes it here?
SECOND GUARD 　　　　　　　All dead.
DOLABELLA 　　　　　　　　　　　Caesar, thy thoughts　325
　　　　　Touch their effects* in this: thyself art coming
　　　　　To see performed* the dreaded act which thou
　　　　　So sought'st to hinder.

　　　　　Enter CAESAR *and all his Train.*

ALL A way* there, a way for Caesar!
DOLABELLA O sir, you are too sure an augurer:*　　　　330
　　　　　That* you did fear is done.
CAESAR 　　　　　　　　Bravest at the last,*
　　　　　She levelled at* our purposes, and being royal
　　　　　Took her own way. The manner of their deaths?
　　　　　I do not see them bleed.
DOLABELLA 　　　　　　　　Who was last with them?

337	*lived but now:* was alive a moment ago.
338	*trimming up the diadem:* setting the crown straight.
343	*As she would:* as if she wished to.
344	*her strong toil of grace:* the powerful snare of her beauty.
345	*vent:* discharge.
345	*and something blown:* and (her breast is) somewhat swollen.
346	*like:* same.
351	*conclusions infinite:* innumerable experiments.
355	*clip:* embrace.
356	*High events . . . them:* Great events such as these deeply afflict those who cause them.
357	*their story . . . lamented –* This could mean (a) the story of these events merits as much pity as he who caused the lamentation for them deserves glory, i.e. referring to Antony; or (b) the story of Antony and Cleopatra deserves as much pity as he who caused them to be the objects of pity deserves glory, i.e. referring to himself. Caesar ends on a characteristically ambiguous note, having it both ways.
361	*see . . . great solemnity:* see that this solemn funeral is carried out with fitting dignity.

FIRST GUARD	A simple countryman, that brought her figs. 335
	This was his basket.
CAESAR	Poisoned then.
FIRST GUARD	O Caesar,

This Charmian lived but now;* she stood and spake.
I found her trimming up the diadem*
On her dead mistress; tremblingly she stood,
And on the sudden dropped.

CAESAR   O noble weakness!   340
If they had swallowed poison, 'twould appear
By external swelling; but she looks like sleep,
As she would* catch another Antony
In her strong toil of grace.*

DOLABELLA   Here on her breast
There is a vent* of blood, and something blown;*   345
The like* is on her arm.

FIRST GUARD This is an aspic's trail; and these fig-leaves
Have slime upon them, such as th' aspic leaves
Upon the caves of Nile.

CAESAR   Most probable
That so she died, for her physician tells me   350
She hath pursued conclusions infinite*
Of easy ways to die. Take up her bed,
And bear her women from the monument.
She shall be buried by her Antony.
No grave upon earth shall clip* in it   355
A pair so famous. High events as these
Strike those that make them;* and their story is
No less in pity than his glory which
Brought them to be lamented.* Our army shall
In solemn show attend this funeral,   360
And then to Rome. Come, Dolabella, see
High order in this great solemnity.*

                                        [*Exeunt*

Glossary

(S.D. = Stage direction)

A

'a, he II.vii.83, 127, III.xiii.132
abhorring, a loathsome state v.ii.60
abide, stay I.iii.102, II.ii.248
abode, staying I.ii.163
abominations, disgusting actions III.vi.95
about, near II.ii.165
absolute, perfect I.ii.2, III.vii.42
  certain IV.iii.9
abstract, essence I.iv.9
  short cut (or) something withdrawn III.vi.61
abused, wronged III.vi.87, III.xiii.108
abysm, abyss III.xiii.147
accumulation, winning III.i.19
adieu, farewell I.iii.77, III.ii.21 etc
admiral, flagship III.x.2
admitted, included v.ii.140
Aeneas, a Trojan prince. See note IV.xiv.53
afeard, afraid II.iii.22, III.iii.1
affect, be inclined, prefer I.iii.71
affection, passion I.v.12, 17, II.vi.125 etc
after, (adj.) subsequent v.ii.283
Ajax, a hero in Greek mythology. See notes IV.xiii.2, IV.xiv.38
alack, alas I.ii.136, III.x.23
alarum, a call to arms, or warning of imminent action S. D. III.x., etc
Alcides, Hercules, son of Alceus IV.xii.44. See under *Hercules*
allay, take away from II.v.50
almanacs, books published annually forecasting events I.ii.139
alms-drink, dregs or remains of drink II.vii.4
amorous, loving I.v.28, II.i.33, II.ii.200
anchor, fix I.v.33
and, if II.vii.93
angel, guardian angel II.iii.21
angle, fishing rod II.v.10
annexed, attached IV.xiv.17
anon, a little later II.vii.34
answer, obey III.xii.33
  accept an invitation to fight III.xiii.27, 36
  be held responsible for v.ii.178
answering, corresponding v.ii.102
anticked, made fools of II.vii.118
apace, quickly I.iii.50, IV.vii.6 etc
appeal, accusation III.v.10
apply, accede v.ii.126

appointment, appearance, equipment IV.x.8
approof, proof III.ii.27
approves, proves true I.i.61
Arabian bird, the phoenix III.ii.12
argument, proof III.xii.3
arm-gaunt, worn in battle (?), hungry or ready for battle (?) I.v.48
art, skill in magic II.iii.32
article, exact terms II.ii.86, 91
as, as if I.ii.90, III.xiii.85, IV.i.1, v.ii.343
  that v.ii.20
  although I.iv.22
  when II.ii.57
aspect, gaze I.v.33
aspic, asp (a small poisonous snake) v.ii.289, 347, 348
assurance, certain success III.vii.46
Atlas, a Titan in Greek mythology. See note I.v.23
atone, reconcile II.ii.106
attend, look at II.ii.64
  wait for III.x.31
audience, interview II.ii.78, III.xii.21
aught, anything I.v.10
augmented, increased III.vi.55
augurer, Roman religious official who foretold events IV.xii.4, v.ii.330
auguring, foretelling II.i.10
author, cause II.vi.124
authority, power of officers of law II.vi.96
avaunt, go away! A term used to dismiss witches and evil spirits IV.xii.30
avoid, withdraw, go away v.ii.242
awaked, stirred up I.iii.61
awry, crooked, at an angle v.ii.315
ay, yes I.ii.82 etc
ay me, ah, alas III.vi.77

B

bacchanals, rites in honour of Bacchus II.vii.97
Bacchus, the Greek god of wine II.vii.107
ballad, compose ballads v.ii.216
band, bond, promise III.ii.26
bands, bodies of troops III.xii.25
banquet, light refreshment of fruit and wine I.ii.10, II.vii.S.D.
bards, poets III.ii.16

barked, stripped of bark IV.xii.23
baseness, humiliation IV.xiv.77
battery, bombardment II.vii.102, IV.xiv.39
battle, line of battle III.ix.2
bear, have in mind I.iii.67, III.iii.29
　　carry (a burden) I.iii.94, I.iv.24
　　sing the chorus of a song II.vii.104
beastly, by a beast I.v.50
beaten, hammered II.ii.195
beck, beckoning gesture III.xi.60
　　command with a look IV.xii.26
become, suit, befit I.i.49, I.iii.84, I.iv.21 etc
becomings, fitting feelings and behaviour
　　I.iii.96
before, ahead V.ii.202
beguiled, deceived III.vii.77, IV.xii.29, V.ii.319
belike, it is likely I.ii.33,
　　probably IV.iii.5
beloving, loving others I.ii.21
bench-holes, latrines IV.vii.9
bend, divert I.i.4
bends, graceful movements II.ii.211
bent, curve I.iii.36
bereave, deprive V.ii.130
bestrid, straddled V.ii.82
betimes, early IV.iv.20, 27
betray, deceive II.v.11
betwixt, between III.vi.78
bidding, command III.xi.60
blasted, destroyed (as by blight) III.x.4
　　withered III.xiii.105
blest, fortunate I.ii.143
bliss, heavenly joy I.iii.36
blood, courage I.ii.178
blow, deposit eggs on V.ii.60
blown, (of a flower) that has finished
　　blooming III.xiii.39
　　swollen V.ii.345
blows, swells to bursting IV.vi.33
boggler, waverer III.xiii.111
bolts up, locks up V.ii.6
bond, duty I.iv.84
bondman, slave III.xiii.149
boot, (v.) reward II.v.71
　　(n.) advantage IV.i.9
bound, joined in marriage II.v.58
　　obliged II.v.111
bourn, limit I.i.16
boy, (referring to boy actors) play a part
　　V.ii.220
branchless, lopped (of honour) III.iv.24
branded, marked conspicuously IV.xiv.76
brave, defy IV.iv.5
bravely, proudly I.v.22
brazen, (a) brassy (b) bold IV.viii. 36
break, tell I.ii.165
　　split IV.xiv.31
breaking, (a) destruction (b) report V.i.14
breaking forth, showing anger III.vi.80
breath, breathing space IV.i.8
breather, a person III.iii.21
breathing, speech I.iii.14

breeze, (a) horsefly (b) wind III.x.14
brief, summary list V.ii.138
briefly, soon IV.iv.10
brine, salt II.v.65
broached, set in motion I.ii.159, 161
broad-fronted, having a broad forehead I.v.29
brooched, adorned (as with a brooch) IV.xv.25
browsed, fed on I.iv.66
bruised, dented IV.xiv.42
buffet, a blow I.iv.20
builded, intact III.ii.30
burgonet, light steel helmet I.v.24
burnished, polished II.ii.194
burnt, flushed with drink II.vii.116
but, only I.i.11, I.v.54, II.ii.75, II.vi.19 etc
　　unless I.i.43, III.xi.47, IV.xi.1
　　except III.iii.4
but that, if it were not that I.iii. 91
but was, that was not I.iii.37
by, according to II.vii.5, III.iii.39

C

call from, withdraw III.vi.21
call on, make (someone) pay I.iv.28
cantle, segment of a sphere III.x.6
captain, commander I.i.6 etc
captainship, leadership III.xiii.8
car, chariot IV.viii.29
carbuncled, jewelled IV.viii.28
carouse, (v.) drink deeply IV.xii.12
　　(n.) deep drinking IV.viii.34
carriage, performance I.iii. 85
carries, propels forward III.vii.75
case, (a) situation (b) garment I.ii.155
　　body IV.xiv.41, IV.xv.89
　　situation III.xiii.54
cast, (a) throw (b) add up II.vi.54
　　add up III.ii.17
castaway, discarded III.vi.40
celebrate, consecrate, make sacred II.vii.98
celerity, speed I.ii.134, III.vii.24
chafe, (n.) anger I.iii.85
chance, (n.) luck II.iii.35
　　fortunes III.x.35, V.ii.174
　　(v.) happen III.iv.13
chaps, jaws III.v.12
chare, chore, dreary task IV.xv.75, V.ii.231
charge, (n.) expense III.vii.16
　　message IV.iv.19
　　(v.) command IV.v.13, IV.vi.8
　　(v.) load I.ii.4
charm, magic spell II.i.20
　　enchantress IV.xii.16, 25
check, (n.) rebuke IV.iv.31
chid, reproved I.iv.30
chronicle, history book III.xiii.175
chuck, chick (a term of endearment) IV.iv.2
cinders, living fire V.ii.173
circle, crown III.xii.18
cistern, pond II.v.95

design, enterprise v.i.43
despatch, conclude II.ii.170
despiteful, malicious II.vi.22
determine, come to an end III.xiii.161: decide
    IV.iii.2, IV.iv.37
determined, predestined III.vi.85
devised, invented II.ii.191
    diadem, crown v.ii.338
Dido, Queen of Carthage. See note IV.xiv.53
difference, quarrel II.i.49, II.ii.21
diminution, lessening III.xiii.197
diminutives, small people, hence, the common
    people IV.xii.37
disaster, (v.) ruin II.vii.14
discandy, melt III.xiii.165, IV.xii.22
discontents, (n.) discontented men I.iv.39
discretion, judgement II.vii.8
disgested, settled II.ii.180
disguise, drunken revelry II.vii.117
dish, appetising food, hence, lover II.vi.122,
    v.ii.270
dislimns, effaces the shape of IV.xiv.10
dismission, dismissal I.i.26
dispatch, hurry III.xii.26, IV.iv.15, IV.v.17
    (a) hurry (b) finish off v.ii.230, 302
    (a) settle matters (b) finish off III.ii.2
    kill quickly IV.xiv.104
disponge, drop (as from a sponge) IV.ix.13
disposed, made an agreement IV.xiv.122
disposition, character I.v.53, II.vii.5
disquiet, trouble II.ii.74
dissembling, imitation I.iii.79
dissuade, persuade IV.vi.13
distract, divide, confuse III.vii.43
distraction, detachment of troops III.vii.76
    mad rage IV.i.9
divine, predict II.vi.113
division, quarrel II.i.48, III.iv.13
do his kind, act according to its nature
    v.ii.260, 262
doctrine, lesson v.ii.31
dodge, be shifty III.xi.62
dolorous, mournful IV.ii.39
dolts, fools IV.xii.37
domestic, internal I.iii.47
donned, put on II.i.33
dotage, infatuation I.i.1, I.i.108
doting, (adj.) infatuated III.x.19
    (n.) infatuation III.xi.15
doughty-handed, brave in action IV.viii.5
downy, soft as down v.ii.312
dragonish, shaped like a dragon IV.xiv.2
drave, drove I.ii.85
dread, greatly feared III.iii.8
drench, soak (in blood) II.vi.18
dress, prepare v.ii.271
drink, inhale v.ii.213
drives/O'er, forces upon III.vi.83
droven, driven IV.vii.5
drums, (v.) summons I.iv.29
dryness, aching I.iv.27
dumbed, silenced I.v.50

dungy, dirty, earthy I.i.35
duty, respect III.xiii.82
dwarfish, short in stature III.iii.16

E

ear, plough I.iv.49
earing, ploughing I.ii.102
easy, easily II.ii.68
eat, ate II.ii.229
ebbed, at the lowest point I.iv.43
edge, end II.ii.119
    sword II.vi.38
edict, decree III.xii.32
e'en for *even,* only IV.xv.73, just II.iv.3
effects, results v.ii.326
elements, life-principle II.vii.39
    the world, made up of the four elements,
    earth, water, air and fire III.ii.40
embattle, draw up in line of battle IV.ix.3
embossed, foaming at the mouth IV.xiii.3
embraced, accepted II.vi.33
enclouded, enveloped v.ii.212
enforce, emphasize II.ii.103, v.ii.125
enfranched, set free III.xiii.149
enfranchise, set free I.i.23
engender, produce III.xiii.159
enlarge, set free III.v.10
enow, enough I.iv.11
entangled, ensnared, deceived I.iii.30
enter, introduce favourably IV.xiv.112
entertain, receive II.i.46
    accept II.vii.59
entertainment, reception III.xiii.141
    employment IV.vi.17
envy, malice v.ii.164
epicure, one devoted to pleasure II.vii.47
epicurean, one who caters for pleasure
    seekers II.i.24
ere, before II.ii.79, 170 etc
estate, situation, condition v.ii.152
estridge, goshawk (a member of the falcon
    family) III.xiii.196
eunuch, castrated man S.D. I.i.10, S.D. I.ii,
    etc
ever, always III.i.16
excellent, exceptional I.i.40
exigent, moment of urgent need to IV.xiv.63
expectation, expectant people III.vi.47
expedience, (a) haste (b) expedition I.ii.166
extemporally, without previous thought or
    preparation v.ii.217
extended, seized I.ii.92
eye, (v.) appear I.iii.97
    (n.) sight III.ix.2
eyne, eyes II.vii.107

F

faction, party strife I.iii.48
factors, agents II.vi.10

fair, good II.vi.66
  beautiful II.vi.99
  fine IV.iv.24
fairer, (a) more beautiful (b) more fortunate
  I.ii.15
fairy, enchantress IV.viii.12
fall, faint I.iii.15
  befall III.vii.39
  let fall III.xi.69
fall to, to cut II.vii.68
falling, death IV.i.8
falliable, a malapropism for *infallible,* certain
  V.ii.255
false-played, lost through cheating IV.xiv.19
fame, rumour II.ii.168, III.xiii.119
  highest praise II.vi.64
fancy, imagination II.ii.204, V.ii.99
farthest, utmost III.ii.26
fast and loose, a game of deception IV.xii.28
fats, vats II.vii.108
favour, facial expression II.v.38
  leniency III.xiii.133
favouring, gracious IV.viii.23
fear, frighten II.vi.24
feature, appearance II.v.112
feeders, servants III.xiii.109
fell away, deserted IV.vi.17
fell upon, burst in upon II.ii.79
fervency, eagerness II.v.18
fetch in, capture IV.i.14
fever, (v.) throw into a fever III.xiii.138
fie, shame on you I.i.48, II.v.51, III.xi.31
fiery, shining brightly I.iv.13
figures, rhetorical devices used to adorn
  speech III.ii.16
files, ranks I.i.3, IV.i.12
filth, evil inclinations III.xiii.113
firm, constant I.v.43
  certain III.vii.48
flag, reed I.iv.45
flaw, cracked fortunes III.xii.34
fleet, (v.) float III.xiii.171
fleeting, rushing away I.iii.104
  inconstant V.ii.240
flies, hastens away I.iii.102
flourish, trumpet blast S.D. I.i.10
  S.D. II.ii.27, etc
flow, depth of water II.vii.15
flush, hot-blooded I.iv.52
fly off, desert II.ii.157
foils, disgraceful actions I.iv.24
foison, plenty II.vii.18
fool, (a) lover, (b) hired entertainer I.i.13;
  term of endearment V.ii.301
foot, infantry IV.x.4
footmen, infantrymen III.vii.44
for, as for II.ii.200, III.xii.19, V.ii.66
  as if III.vii.18
forbear, withdraw, leave alone I.ii.112,
  II.vii.34, 91, V.ii.175
  refrain (from) I.iii.11
forborne, refrained from III.xiii.107

forked, with two or more peaks IV.xiv.5
formal, ordinary II.v.41
forsake, leave II.vii.32
forsooth, certainly V.ii.275
forspoke, spoken against III.vii.3
fortune, give a fortune I.ii.66
foul, ugly I.ii.65
found, proved true IV.xiv.121
frame, perform II.ii.214
  adapt V.i.55
freely, in abundance IV.vi.7
fretted, (a) decayed, (b) chequered IV.xii.8
friend, lover III.xii.22
from, against III.xi.60
front, (n.) face I.i.6
  (v.) confront face I.iv.79
fronted, opposed II.ii.65
frustrate, defeated V.i.2
fugitive, deserter IV.ix.22
full, (adv.) exceedingly I.i.59
  (adj.) whole I.iii.43
fullest, most complete in character and
  fortunes III.xiii.87
fuming, fuddled with alcohol II.i.24
furnished, in a position, situation I.iv.77
further, (v.) support II.ii.151
Fury, one of the ancient Greek goddesses of
  vengeance II.v.40

G

gait, manner of walking III.iii.17
garboils, noisy commotions I iii 61, II.ii.71
gaudy, festive III.xiii.182
gaze, stare in wonder III.xiii.12, IV.xiv.52
general tongue, what everyone is saying I.ii.96
gests, deeds IV.viii.2
ghosted, haunted II.vi.13
gibbet, gallows V.ii.61
gibe, mock at II.ii.78
gilded, covered with yellow scum I.iv.62
  made golden I.v.37
give off, end IV.iii.21
glow, to make glow II.ii.207
go, (a) bear children (b) walk I.ii.58
go on wheels, run quickly and easily II.vii.86
go to, very well II.ii.114, II.v.36
  nonsense III.iii.2
going off, leaving IV.xiii.6
Gorgon, in Greek mythology, Medusa who
  turned those who looked at her to stone
  II.v.116
got upon, taken precedence over IV.xiv.98
grace, (n.) (a) divine favour, (b) rue, a herb
  IV.ii.38
  (v.) do a favour to IV.xiv.135
  favour V.ii.28
graceful, favourable II.ii.64
graces, good qualities II.ii.134
gracious, pleasing II.v.86
grates, irritates I.i.18

grave, deadly IV.xii.25
graveless, unburied III.xiii.166
'greed, agreed II.vi.37
green, inexperienced I.v.74
green-sickness, anæmia III.ii.6
griefs, grievances II.ii.104
grossly, unpleasantly clearly III.x.28
grow to, increase II.ii.25

H

habiliments, dress III.vi.17
halt, limp IV.vii.16
haltered, with a rope around the neck
  III.xiii.130
hap, chance II.iii.32
haply, perhaps III.xiii.48, IV.ii.26
happiness, good fortune III.xiii.30
happy, fortunate IV.v.1,
hardly, reluctantly I.iv.7, V.i.74
harness, armour IV.viii.15
harried, treated harshly III.iii.39
ha't, have it II.vii.65, 98
haunt, (*n.*) (a) company, (b) place where
  ghosts resort IV.xiv.54
hautboy, a wood-wind instrument (the
  modern oboe) S.D. IV.iii.11
haven, harbour IV.x.7
hazard, chance III.vii.47
hazarded to, dependent on III.xii.19
head, promontory, headland III.vii.51
heads, officers IV.i.10
health, toast II.vi.128, II.vii.27
healthful, in good health II.v.38
heave, throw II.vii.11
heaviness, (a) weight, (b) sorrow IV.xv.33
Hector, a great Trojan prince and warrior
  IV.viii.7
heighth, height III.x.20
helm, helmet II.i.33
Herculean, like Hercules, a hero in Greek
  mythology I.iii.84
hereditary, inherited I.iv.13
Herod, a King of the Jews I.ii.26, III.iii.3
hid, filled to the brim II.vii.82
hie, go quickly II.iii.13, V.ii.194
high, loudly I.v.49, IV.xv.43
  great V.ii.356
high-battled, commanding great armies
  III.xiii.29
high-coloured, flushed with wine II.vii.3
hint, opportunity III.iv.9
hold, follow I.iii.7
  command III.vii.58
  stop V.ii.39
holding, chorus of a song II.vii.104
homager, dutiful servant I.i.31
home, bluntly I.ii.96
honest, chaste I.v.16
honesty, frankness II.ii.96
  honour III.xiii.41
  (a) truthfulness, (b) chastity V.ii.251

honourable, honourably V.i.58
hoop, bond (literally the iron band round a
  barrel) II.ii.119
horse, cavalry III.vii.59, 71, III.x.33
hot, fierce I.iv.50
hotter, more sensual III.xiii.119
how, what! I.i.24, III.ii.11
  what is I.ii.104
how now, what are you saying? I.iii.39
  what is it? II.i.27, III.v.i, IV.iii.17
huswife, hussy, strumpet IV.xv.44

I

idleness, frivolity I.iii.92, 93
ignorance, stupidity III.x.7
ill, badly II.vi.79, III.iii.34, IV.xiv.105
  evil IV.vi.18
ill-rooted, insecure II.vii.1
ills, faults I.ii.101
  evils I.ii.120
ill-uttering, evil-speaking II.v.35
immoment, unimportant V.ii.166
immortal, malapropism for *mortal* V.ii.246
impediment, objection II.ii.150
imperious, imperial IV.xv.23
import, (*n.*) gravity III.iv.3
  (*v.*) carry II.ii.137
importeth, concerns I.ii.112
importune, beg IV.xv.19
impress, forced conscription III.vii.36
in, (a) in drink, drunk, (b) in the game
  II.vii.29
  on III.xiii.161
inches, height I.iii.40
inclination, disposition II.v.113
inclips, embraces II.vii.64
infinite, innumerable V.ii.351
ingrossed, assembled III.vii.36
inhooped, enclosed in a hoop II.iii.38
inroads, raids I.iv.50
intent, meaning II.ii.45
  plan V.ii.126, 226
intrinsicate, (a) intricate, (b) essential V.ii.300
iron, armour IV.iv.3
Isis, Egyptian goddess of the earth, moon and
  fertility I.ii.58, 62 etc
issue, success I.ii.84
  offspring III.vi.7
it, its II.vii.38, 42
itch, craving III.xiii.7

J

Jack, rascal III.xiii.93, 103
jaded, driven exhausted (like an overworked
  horse) III.i.34
jealousies, suspicions II.ii.136
Jewry, Judaea I.ii.26 etc
jointing, joining I.ii.83

Jove, Jupiter, a sky deity, the chief god of the Romans I.ii.140, II.vii.63 etc
joy, be happy IV.vi.20
jump, (n.) venture III.viii.6
Juno, chief Roman goddess III.xi.28
Jupiter, II.ii.6, III.ii.9, 10. See under *Jove*

K

keels, ships I.iv.50
keep the turn, drink round for round I.iv.19
keeps, guards II.iii.19
kind, nature v.ii.261
kindly, of gentle nature II.v.78
kite, bird of prey of hawk family III.xiii.89
knave, servant IV.xiv.12, 14, v.ii.3
    rascal I.ii.65, I.iv.21, II.v.102
know, learn I.iv.81
    recognize II.vi.71
knowing, intelligent III.iii.23
known, met before II.vi.84

L

la, an exclamation to add emphasis IV.iv.8
labour, birth pains III.vii.80
lack, fail to understand II.ii.61
lack blood, turn pale I.iv.52
lacked, absent, missed I.iv.44
lackeying, following like a lackey or servant I.iv.46
lady, feminine v.ii.165
lamps (of night), stars I.iv.5
landsmen, troops IV.iii.10
languish, lingering disease v.ii.42
lanked, grew thin I.iv.71
large, unrestrained III.vi.94
lascivious, indecent I.iv.56
lated, belated, overtaken by darkness III.xi.3
laugh away, throw away II.vi.103
launch, to lance v.i.36
lawful, legitimate III.xiii.108
lay on me, have me blamed for v.ii.129
laying, imputing II.ii.59
leaner, of less importance II.ii.19
legion, Roman military division III.vii.58 etc.
length, continuance of life IV.xiv.46
lessons, teachers a lesson III.xii.13
Lethe, a river in the Hades whose waters produced forgetfulness II.i.27, II.vii.101
levelled, guessed v.ii.332
levity, frivolity III.vii.13
levy, enrol III.vi.67
liberal, hearty II.vi.47
libertine, one given to immoral pleasures II.i.23
licence, freedom I.ii.99
Lichas, a figure in Greek mythology. See note IV.xii.45
lictors, Roman officials v.ii.214

lie (upon), remain unsold II.v.105
    depend on III.viii.5–6
lief, soon, willingly II.vii.10
lieutenantry, subordinate officers III.xi.39
light, frivolous I.ii.164
    (a) bright, (b) merry II.ii.183
lightness, levity I.iv.25
like, likely I.i.25, II.vi.72
lingering, long-lasting, slow II.v.66
lipped, kissed II.v.30
list, listen IV.ii.11
    listen to IV.ix.6
livery, uniform, colours v.ii.90
loathness, unwillingness III.xi.18
lodge, impale IV.xii.45
loofed, (a) with ship's head turned close to the wind, (b) departed III.x.17
look for, expect II.vi.105
loose-wived, married to an unfaithful wife I.ii.64
lottery, prize II.ii.246
loud, loudly II.ii.21
low-voiced, quiet III.iii.13
lowness, low level II.vii.17
    low fortunes III.xi.63
lust-wearied, exhausted by pleasure II.i.38
lustre, brilliance II.iii.27
luxuriously, lustfully III.xiii.120

M

made, counted for II.vi.115
main, greatest I.ii.179
make battery, bombard II.vii.102
make prize, haggle, bargain v.ii.183
malefactor, criminal II.v.53
maliciously, fiercely III.xiii.178
mallard, wild drake III.x.19
mandragora, sleep-producing juice of the mandrake plant I.v.3
mangled, mutilated IV.ii.27
manlike, manly I.iv.5
mantles, cloaks II.v.22
marble-constant, unchanging as marble v.ii.240
maritime, near the sea I.iv.51
mark, target (in archery), hence 'limit' III.vi.88
Mars, the Roman god of war I.i.4, I.v.18 etc
master-leaver, runaway servant IV.ix.22
masters, friends IV.iii.17, 19
maul, beat IV.vii.14
mean, midway position II.vii.17
    intermediary III.ii.32
    means IV.vi.34
measure, limit I.i.2
    amount II.vi.37, III.iv.8, III.xiii.35
mechanic, vulgar, of the working class IV.iv.32, v.ii.209
medicine, philosopher's stone, alchemist's elixir of life I.v.36

meet, fitting II.vi.2
meeter, more appropriate V.i.49
meetly, quite good I.iii.81
members, people I.ii.153
memory, memorials, i.e. children III.xiii.166
mend, amend, improve I.ii.56, I.v.45
  improve I.iii.82
  put right V.ii.315
Mercury, the messenger of the gods in Roman mythology IV.xv.35
mered, whole III.xiii.10
merely, completely III.vii.8, 47, III.xiii.62
merit, deserving service II.vii.50
  deserts (whether reward, as here, or punishment) V.ii.178
methinks, it seems to me I.iii.6, III.iii.39
mettle, ardent spirit I.ii.133
mince, soften I.ii.96
mingle, (*n*.) mixture I.v.59, IV.viii.37
  (*v*.) exchange III.xiii.156
mingled, interwoven IV.xiv.24
minister, agent III.vi.89, III.xiii.23, V.i.20, V.ii.4
mirth, joke, or (possibly) entertainment I.iv.18
misdoubt, distrust III.vii.62
mislike, dislike III.xiii.147
missive, messenger II.ii.78
misthought, misjudged V.ii.176
mocks, makes ridiculous V.i.2
modern, ordinary V.ii.167
modesty, moderation II.v.72
moe, more IV.xiv.18
moiety, half V.i.19
monstrous, astounding II.ii.187
  unnatural II.vii.92
moody, melancholy II.v.1
mortal, deadly V.ii.299
motion, intuition II.iii.13
motive, cause II.ii.100
mouth-made, spoken I.iii.30
move, (a) act, (b) circle like a planet II.vii.12
  incite II.i.42
  anger II.ii.4
muleters, mule-drivers II.vii.35
mused of, thought about II.xiii.83
muss, a scrambling game III.xiii.91
musters, assembled troops I.i.3
mutiny, quarrel III.xi.13
mutual, equally loving I.i.37

N

nag, a term applied to an immoral woman (literally, a small horse), III.x.10
name, reputation I.ii.177, I.iv.54
Narcissus, a mythological Greek who fell in love with his own beauty II.v.96
narrow, small III.iv.8
nature, natural feelings V.i.29

naught, unimportant III.v.21
  ruined, reduced to nothing III.x.1
  nothing IV.xv.78
ne'er touched, chaste III.xii.31
Neptune, Roman god of the sea II.vii.125, IV.xiv.58
Nereides, the fifty daughters of Nereus the sea-god II.ii.209
nerves, muscles IV.viii.21
Nessus, the Centaur in Greek mythology. See note IV.xii.43
nice, luxurious III.xiii.179
nicked, (a) got the better of, (b) cut a piece out of, hence, maimed III.xiii.8
noble, nobly II.ii.102
nod, beckon with a nod III.vi.66
  bow IV.xiv.6
noise, rumour I.iii.131
noises, raises a tumult III.vi.97
nonpareil, one without an equal III.ii.11
nor . . . nor, neither . . . nor I.v.52
note, importance IV.ix.31
nothing (*ill*), not at all (badly) II.vi.79
  no one III.vi.87
nothing of, no part of II.ii.84
novice, inexperienced youth IV.xii.14
number, write verse III.ii.17

O

O, circle V.ii.81
oblivion, forgetfulness I.iii.90
observance, powers of observation III.iii.22
occasion, expedience II.vi.126
occupation, profession IV.iv.17
odds, chances in favour of II.iii.27
  distinction between great and small IV.xv.66
o'ercount, outnumber II.vi.26
  cheat II.vi.27
o'er-picturing, surpassing the picture II.ii.203
of, for I.i.62
  out of I.v.12
  by II.i.15, II.ii.163, V.ii.34
  because of II.iii.26, V.ii.212
  over II.iii.36
  about II.vi.113
  from IV.xv.46
office, service I.i.5, III.xii.10
  task II.ii.214
  duties of state II.iii.1
  duty IV.vi.27
oily, sweaty, moist I.ii.47
olive, olive-branch, symbol of peace IV.vi.7
onion-eyed, tearful IV.ii.35
on't, about it III.vii.23
  of it III.vii.69
operation, working power II.vii.25, IV.xv.26
opinion, view of oneself II.i.36
oppression, pressure IV.vii.2
opulent, rich I.v.46

or . . . or, either . . . or IV.ii.5–6
orb, sphere in which planets and stars were
thought to revolve III.xiii.146
the earth V.ii.85
ordinary, public meal in a tavern II.ii.228
orient, (a) eastern, (b) shining I.v.41
ostentation, public display III.vi.52
out, away with you! I.ii.37
fall out II.vii.28
outgo, go faster than III.ii.61
outstrike, strike faster than IV.vi.35
outwork, exceed II.ii.204
overplus, excess III.vii.50
in addition IV.vi.22
overtake, attain V.ii.103
overtopped, exceeded in height IV.xii.24
owe, own IV.viii.31

P

pace, keep (a horse) under control II.ii.68
packed, cheated in dealing IV.xiv.19
pageant, show, dramatic performance
IV.xiv.8
palate, (n.) sense of taste I.iv.63
palates, (v.) tastes V.ii.7
pales, encloses II.vii.64
palled, decayed II.vii.77
palter, equivocate, use trickery III.xi.63
paragon, (v.) compare I.v.71
parcel, (n.) of the same nature as III.xiii.32
(v.) make up the total V.ii.163
pardon, (n.) permission III.vi.60
(v.) excuse from performing an action
IV.xiv.80
part, (v.) depart I.ii.167, II.vi.38, II.vii.114
III.ii.1, 4 etc
divided III.vi.78
particular, personal concern I.iii.54, IV.ix.20
partisan, broad-headed, long-handled spear
II.vii.10
parts, (n.) personal features or qualities
II.ii.56, 60
sides, parties III.ii.32, III.iv.14
pass, (v.) stake, pledge III.ii.27
passion, disturbing emotion III.x.5, v.i.63
patch, make up out of odds and ends
II.ii.56, 60
pauses, delays V.i.3
pavilion, tent, awning, II.ii.202
pawn, exchange I.iv.32
pays, suffers I.i.31
peep, show itself III.xiii.190
peerless, without equal I.i.40
pelleted, consisting of falling hailstones
III.xiii.165
pendant, overhanging IV.xiv.4
penetrative, penetrating deeply IV.xiv.75
perchance, perhaps I.i.20, 25, IV.ii.27
perforce, of necessity III.iv.6, v.i.37
period, end IV.ii.25, IV.xiv.107
perjure, make corrupt III.xii.30

persisted, (adj.) persisted in V.i.30
pestilence, plague II.v.61, III.x.9
pestilent, destructive to life III.xiii.193
petition, beg I.ii.171
petty, trivial I.v.45, II.i.34, 49
insignificant III.xii.8
Phoebus, the sun-god in Greek mythology
I.v.28
pickle, pickling solution II.v.66
piece, (n.) masterpiece I.ii.142, III.ii.28, v.ii.99
(v.) (a) add to, (b) mend I.v.45
pinch, find fault with II.vii.5
pinion, feather III.xii.4
pinioned, (of a bird) having its wings clipped
V.ii.53
pink, (of eyes) (a) small, half-closed, (b) red
with drinking II.vii.107
placed, immovably fixed V.ii.237
plainness, plain speaking II.vi.78
plant, (v.) place IV.vi.9
plants, (a) feet (from Latin *planta*, sole of the
foot), (b) things 'planted' by the triumvirs,
like their new friendship II.vii.1
plated, covered in armour I.i.4
plates, silver coins V.ii.92
pleached, folded IV.xiv.73
pleasure, will I.ii.122, I.v.8 etc.
intention I.ii.182
plebeians, common people IV.xii.34
pledge, (v.) drink in answer to a toast II.vii.80
plighter, one who promises III.xiii.126
plucked, stripped of power III.xii.3
plumpy, plump II.vii.107
pocket up, put away (unread) II.ii.77
points, laces or tags for fastening clothes
III.xii.157
pole, (a) maypole, (b) pole star, (c) military
standard or flag IV.xv.65
policy, prudence in political affairs II.ii.73,
II.vi.115
poop, ship's stern II.ii.195
populous, numerous III.vi.50
port, city gate I.iii,46, IV.iv.23
bearing, behaviour IV.xiv.52
portends, foretells III.xiii.155
portentous, boding evil — not present
posits, — not present
possess, control, II.vii.95
put in possession of III.xi.21
posts, messengers I.v.61
posture, representation V.ii.221
potent, powerful III.vi.96
power, army III.vii.57, 76
bodily faculty III.xii.36
practise, (v.) plot II.ii.43, 44
pray in aid, beg assistance (a legal term)
V.ii.27
pray ye, what did you say? II.vi.110
precedence, what has gone before II.v.51
precedent, going before IV.xiv.83
pregnant, obvious II.i.45
presages, indicates I.ii.43, 45
prescience, fortune-telling I.ii.19
prescript, written instructions III.viii.5

presence, distinguished company II.ii.113
present, sudden II.ii.143
presently, immediately II.ii.163, III.iv.15,
    III.v.7, 20
president, sovereign ruler III.vii.17
prevail, be victorious III.xiii.23
primal, primeval I.iv.41
principalities, regions ruled over by a prince
    III.xiii.19
prithee, please, I beg you (literally 'I pray
    thee') I.ii.33, I.iii.76, 83 etc
privy to, having knowledge of I.ii.38
prize, contest, haggling V.ii.183
prized, valued I.i.56
process, legal summons I.i.28
prognostication, prediction I.ii.47
project, put forward V.ii.121
prompt, ready III.xiii.75
proof, proven impenetrability IV.viii.15
proper, honest III.iii.37
propertied, endowed with distinctive quali-
    ties V.ii.83
property, quality I.i.58
prorogue, put off II.i.26
prosecution, pursuit IV.xiv.65
proud, magnificent II.v.69
proved, experienced I.ii.31
provide, make arrangements for III.iv.36,
    V.ii.195
puppet, (a) actor, (b) doll, (c) contemptuous
    name for a woman V.ii.208
purchased, aquired I.iv.14
purge, cure by blood-letting I.iii.53
    expel IV.xiv.123
purpose, (n.) resolution IV.iii.11
    (v.) intend I.ii.165
purposes, proposals II.vi.4
pursed, put in purse, *i.e.* took possession of
    II.ii.189
put off, out to sea II.vii.68
puzzle, confuse, III.vii.10
pyramides, pyramids V.ii.61

Q

quail, make cower V.ii.85
quails, small birds like partridges II.iii.37
quality, (a) character, (b) occupation I.i.54
    nature III.xiii.33, V.i.63
    manner I.ii.179
quarter, extent of area to be watched by a
    guard IV.iii.20
quartered, divided up IV.xiv.58
queasy, sickened III.vi.20
question, concern II.ii.44
    conversation II.ii.85
    cause of dispute III.xiii.10
quick, piercing I.ii.101
    lively V.ii.216
quicken, give life to I.iii.69
    come to life IV.xv.39

quit, reward III.xiii.124
    repay III.xiii.151

R

race, origin I.iii.37
rack, drifting cloud IV.xiv.10
rail, find fault, reproach I.ii.98, IV.xv.43
ram, battering ram III.ii.30
ranged, widespread I.i.34
ranges, lines (of warships) III.xiii.5
rank, (v.) list IV.ix.21
    (adj.) smelling offensive V.ii.212
rare, splendid II.ii.208, 221
rarely, exceptionally well IV.iv.11
    exceptionally V.ii.158
rate, allot a share III.vi.25
    be worth III.xi.69
rather, more readily II.ii.23
raught, seized IV.ix.29
reconciles, (a) persuades to agree to, (b)
    re-unites II.vii.6
record, chronicle, history book IV.ix.8,
    IV.xiv.99
reel, (v.) stagger drunkenly I.iv.20
reels, (a) revelry, (b) drunken staggering
    II.vii.87
regiment, authority III.vi.96
register, history book, chronicle IV.ix.21
relieved, rescued, V.ii.41
religion, sacred duty V.ii.199
remarkable, to be wondered at IV.xv.67
remembrance, thoughts I.v.57
    memory of kindnesses received
    II.ii.161
rend, divide II.ii.19
render, surrender III.x.32, IV.xiv.33
reneges, casts off, renounces I.i.8
repair, make (their) way I.iv.39
reports, reporters II.ii.51
reputation, good name III.xi.49
require, request III.xii.12, 28, III.xiii.66
rest you, (may God) keep you I.i.62
revel(s), revelry I.iv.5, V.ii.218
revenue, income III.vi.30
revolt, (n.), desertion IV.ix.19
    (v,), desert IV.v.4, IV.vi.9, 12, IV.ix.8
revolution, change produced by the passage
    of time I.ii.116
rheum, watering of the eyes III.ii.57
rhymers, inferior poets V.ii.215
ribaudred, wanton III.x.10
rift, split III.iv.32
rig, prepare for sea II.vi.20, III.v.18
riggish, wanton II.ii.243
right, true IV.xii.28
rightly, truly I.iv.77, IV.ii.11
rioting, revelling II.ii.76
riotous, wild I.iii.29
rivality, equal partnership III.v.7
rive, tear apart IV.xiii.5

rose, rosy bloom III.xiii.20
rudest, coarsest I.iv.64
rule, carpenter's ruler II.iii.7, v.ii.210
rush, straw III.v.16

S

sad, serious I.iii.3
safe, assure the safety of I.iii.55, IV.vi.26
sail(s), ships II.vi.24, III.vii.49
salad, young and inexperienced I.v.73
salt, lustful II.i.21
salt-fish, dried fish II.v.17
sap, life III.xiii.191
saucy, insolent III.xiii.98, IV.xiv.25
  lascivious v.ii.214
savage, bitter III.xiii.128
say, tell I.ii.182
scald, contemptible v.ii.215
scales, graduated marks II.vii.16
scant, restrict IV.ii.21
scantly, grudgingly III.iv.6
scarce, scarcely I.i.21, III.i.29
sceptres, rulers III.vi.76
  ruler's staffs IV.xv.76
score, cut notches in IV.vii.12
scotches, gashes IV.vii.10
scourge, whip, punish II.vi.22
scribes, professional penmen III.ii.16
scroll, paper III.viii.5
scrupulous, distrustful I.iii.48
scutcheons, shields displaying the owners'
  coats-of-arms v.ii.135
sea-like, seaworthy III.xiii.171
seal, ratify by fixing a seal to II.vi.59,
  IV.xiv.49
sealing, affixing seals to III.ii.3
security, safety III.vii.48
seel, stitch up III.xiii.112, v.ii.146
seeming, apparent II.ii.212
self, same v.i.21
semblable, similar III.iv.3
senators, rulers II.vi.9
sennet, music accompanying a procession of
  dignitaries S.D. II.vii.14
sense, senses II.ii.215, II.vii.100
serves, is sufficient IV.vii.11
several, separate I.v.62, 77
shackles, (v.) chains up v.ii.6
shakes off, rejects III.vii.33
shards, wings III.ii.20
sheets, covers like a white sheet I.iv.65
shift, exchange v.ii.152
shifts, tricks III.xi.63
shiny, moonlit IV.ix.3
show, exhibition III.xiii.30, IV.xv.23
show-place, arena III.vi.12
shows (fairly), looks (promising) II.ii.149
  seems to be III.iii.20
shrewd, harmful IV.ix.5

shrewdness, astuteness II.ii.73
shrill-tongued, loud-voiced III.iii.12
shroud, protection III.xiii.71
sickly, feebly III.iv.7
sides, bounds, limits I.iii.180, I.iii.16
signs, signifies IV.iii.13
silvered, plated with silver III.vi.3
sing (after), repeat I.v.73
sir, lord, v.ii.120
  term of address to a woman IV.xv.85
sirrah, term of address to a social inferior
  II.iii.10, II.v.32, or to a woman v.ii.229
slight, slightly I.i.56
slippery, fickle I.ii.173
smarting, stinging II.v.66
smock, a woman's linen petticoat, hence
  used as a term for a woman I.ii.156
snaffle, horse's bridle-bit with no curb
  II.ii.67
so, as I.v.61
  in this way III.ii.20, III.iv.28
  very well III.xiii.52
sober, modest v.ii.54
soberly, in a serious manner I.v.48
soft, pleasant I.i.44
  go carefully II.ii.87
solder, cement III.iv.32
soldiership, skill as a soldier II.i.34
something, somewhat IV.vii.20, v.ii.250
sooth, indeed IV.iv.8
soothsayer, fortune-teller S.D. I.ii., I.ii.2, 5
sorely, severely IV.vi.19
sottish, stupid IV.xv.79
sourest, most bitter, controversial II.ii.24
sovereign, royal I.iii.60
  (a) potent, (b) royal v.i.41
  supreme IV.ix.12
space (my), the amount of earth (I want)
  I.i.34
  distance II.iii.23
space, interval of time II.i.31
spanielled, followed devotedly like a spaniel
  IV.xii.21
speak with, meet (in battle) II.vi.25
speeds, is successful II.iii.35
sphere, one of the seven crystalline concen-
  tric spheres, each containing a planet,
  which, according to Ptolemaic astronomy,
  moved around the earth (IV.xv.10, v.ii.84).
  Hence 'an important position' II.vii.12
splits, speaks indistinctly II.vii.117
spoiled, plundered III.vi.25
sport, amusements I.iv.29
spot, blemish IV.xii.35
spots (of heaven), stars I.iv.12
sprightly, (a) high-spirited, (b) spirit-like
  IV.xiv.52
spring, (a) springtime, (b) stream (of tears)
  III.ii.43
spritely, high-spirited IV.vii.15
spurn, kick II.v.63, III.v.15
squadrons, bodies of troops III.ix.1

square, (*adj.*) faithful II.ii.188
  (*n.*) carpenter's tool for measuring right
  angles, hence a rule for right action II.iii.6
  troops in a square formation III.xi.40 (*v.*)
  quarrel II.i.45, III.xiii.41
squeaking, shrill-voiced V.ii.220
squire, body-servant, valet IV.iv.14
stablishment, possession III.vi.9
stage, bring on the stage III.xiii.30, V.ii.218
stain, (*v.*) eclipse III.iv.27
stale, urine I.iv.62
stall, live V.i.39
stand, endure I.iv.20
  remain motionless III.ii.49
stand up, set up as I.ii.178
  oppose in war II.i.44
  stand firm IV.iii.10
stands upon, depends upon II.i.50, 51
start forth, jump forward III.xiii.91
state, empire I.iv.30
  condition I.iv.41
station, manner of standing III.iii.19
staunch, firmly together II.ii.119
stay by, keep going II.ii.181
stay upon, wait for I.ii.106
steeped, bathed II.vii.100
stewed, pickled II.v.65
stiff, unpleasant I.ii.91
still, (*adj.*) quiet II.vi.119
  inactive IV.xi.1
  silent IV.xv.28
  (*adv.*) continually, always I.i.59, III.ii.60,
  V.i.75
stirred, angered I.i.43
stirring, activity II.i.36
stirs, events I.iv.82
stolen upon, come stealthily III.vi.42
stomach, (*n.*) desire II.ii.54
  (*v.*) resent III.iv.12
stomaching, resentment II.ii.9
store, plenty IV.i.15
straight, at once II.ii.173, IV.xii.3
strange, unusual II.ii.159
stretch, pass I.i.46
strike, damage I.iv.54
  clink (glasses) or open (a cask); the
  meaning is uncertain II.vii.90
  (a) fight, (b) surrender IV.ii.8
  afflict deeply V.ii.357
strings, heartstrings, affections III.xi.57
stripes, whip marks III.xiii.152
stroyed, destroyed III.xi.54
strumpet, prostitute I.i.13, V.ii.215
strut, swagger III.xiii.114
studied, carefully prepared II.ii.143, II.vi.47
study on, consider carefully V.ii.10
stuff, matter, materials V.ii.97
subdue, destroy IV.xii.47
subscribe, sign IV.v.14
success, result (whether good or bad) III.v.5
sudden, suddenly I.iii.5
Sue, beg I.iii.

suffered, obeyed IV.ii.23
sullen, miserable I.iii.13
surfeiter, one given to excess II.i.33
surfeits, sicknesses produced by excess
  I.iv.27
sustain, stand, endure I.iii.17
  support III.xi.45
sway, direct II.ii.153
sweep, smooth III.xi.17
swell, body of water III.ii.49
swerving, transgression III.xi.50
sworder, professional swordsman III.xiii.31
synod, assembly III.x.5

T

tabourines, long, narrow drums IV.viii.37
tackle, a ship's sails, ropes, rigging etc.
  II.ii.212
take, (a) arrest, (b) see II.vi.96
  bewitch IV.ii.37
  catch IV.vii.13
take (*the flow*), measure (the depth) II.vii.15
take in, capture I.i.23, III.vii.23, III.xiii.83
taken, captured I.iv.54
tall, brave II.vi.7
targes, shields II.vi.39
target, shield I.iii.82, IV.viii.31
tart sour II.v.38
tawny, dark-skinned I.i.6
tawny-finned, dark-finned II.v.12
Telamon i.e. Ajax, a Greek prince. See note
  IV.xiii.2
temper, self-control I.i.8
temperance, chastity III.xiii.121
  moderation V.ii.48
tempt, provoke I.iii.11
tend, attend, wait on II.ii.210, IV.ii.24, 32
terrene, earthly III.xiii.153
Thetis, a Nereid (*q.v.*) and daughter of
  Achilles III.vii.60
thick, in quick succession I.v.63
  foul V.ii.211
thickens, grows dim II.iii.27
thought, remorse IV.vi.35, 35
threats, threatens III.v.17
three-nooked, three-cornered IV.vi.6
throws forth, gives birth III.vii.80
Tiber, the river on which Rome stands I.i.33
tie up (sword), cause to sheathe II.vi.6
tight, skilful IV.iv.15
time, present state of affairs III.vi.83
timelier, sooner II.vi.51
tinct, (a) colour, (b) the alchemist's elixir of
  life I.v.37
tippling, drinking too much I.iv.19
tires, head-dresses II.v.22
title, rightful claim V.ii.284
toil, snare, trap V.ii.344
tokened, denoting signs III.x.9

touch (*v.*) discuss II.ii.24
 affect, move II.ii.144, V.i.33
 reach V.ii.326
touches, things that move or concern one
 closely I.ii.168
toward, imminent II.vi.73
toys, trifles V.ii.166
traduced, censured III.vii.13
train, attendants S.D. I.i.10, S.D. I.iv.
transmigrates, passes into another body
 II.vii.40
treaties, peace proposals III.xi.62
treble-sinewed, as strong as three men
 III.xiii.177
trencher, wooden plate III.xiii.117
trespasses, wrongs II.i.40
tribunal, raised platform III.vi.3
tributaries, rulers paying tribute or taxes
 III.xiii.96
trick, unexpected action IV.ii.14
 habit V.ii.75
trim, armour IV.iv.22
trimming up, setting straight V.ii.338
triple, one of three I.i.12
triple-turned, unfaithful three times IV.xii.13
triumph, (a) triumphal march through Rome,
 (b) trump card IV.xiv.20
triumphant, magnificent II.ii.188
triumvirate, a group of three men sharing
 political power III.vi.28
true, (a) honest, (b) a true reflection of character, (c) not altered by cosmetics II.vi.98, 99
trull, prostitute III.vi.96
trumpet, announce II.v.39
try you, test your drinking powers II.vii.119
turpitude, baseness IV.vi.32
twain, pair I.i.38
 two I.iv.73, II.i.35, III.iv.30
'tween, between III.vi.61

U

unbewailed, unlamented III.vi.86
uncuckolded, having a wife who has not been
 unfaithful I.ii.65
uncurbable, uncontrollable II.ii.71
undid, removed, cancelled II.ii.208
undinted, undented II.vi.39
undo, cancel III.iv.17
undoing, destruction V.ii.44
undone, ruined II.v.106
unequal, unjust II.v.101
unexecuted, unused, not put into action
 III.vii.44
unfolded, exposed V.ii.170
unhacked, undamaged II.vi.38
unlawful, illegitimate III.vi.7
unnoble, dishonourable III.xi.50
unpeople, empty of people I.v.78
unpolicied, outwitted in policy V.ii.304
unpurposed, unintentional IV.xiv.84

unqualitied, robbed of self-possession III.xi.44
unreconciliable, unable to be reconciled V.i.47
unregistered, not recorded III.xiii.119
unrestored, not returned III.vi.27
unseminared, castrated, seedless I.v.11
unstate, abdicate III.xiii.30
unto, with regard to II.ii.148
up, shut up, imprisoned III.v.10
upon, in, during I.iii.52
urge, put forward (as a reason for action)
 II.ii.50
use, (*n.*) (a) legal trust, (b) interest (in financial
 sense) I.iii.44
 (*v.*) gratify II.vi.125
 treat III.ii.25
 are accustomed II.v.32
used, been accustomed III.vii.65
useful, usefully IV.xiv.80

V

vacancy, leisure time I.iv.26
 vacuum II.ii.219
vagabond, wandering backwards and for-
 wards I.iv.45
vales, valleys IV.xi.3
vant, van, front part of an army IV.vi.9
vantage, advantage III.vii.33, III.x.12
vapour, mist, cloud IV.xiv.3
 breath V.ii.213
variance, dissension II.vi.125
varletry, rabble V.ii.56
varying, often changing I.iv.46, IV.xv.11
vassal, servant II.vi.56, V.ii.29
vent (*n.*) discharge V.ii.345
vented, uttered III.iv.8
Venus, Roman goddess of love I.v.18, II.ii.203
very, total, complete III.x.7, III.xi.44
 itself IV.xiv.48
vesper, evening IV.xiv.8
vessels, either (a) drinking glasses, or (b)
 wine casks II.vii.90
vestal, priestess of the Roman goddess,
 Vesta, vowed to chastity III.xii.31
vex, annoy I.ii.19
vial, small bottle I.iii.63
viands, food III.xi.74
vie, compete V.ii.98
view, gaze I.i.5
violence, extreme I.v.60
virtue, manly power IV.vii.17
visage, face IV.xii.38
volley, echo, sound II.vii.105
voluptuousness, sensuality I.iv.26
vouchsafe, deign I.iv.8
vouchsafing, condescending V.ii.160
vulgar, of the common people III.xiii.119

W

waged, fought V.i.31
wagered, bet II.v.16

wailed, wept for III.ii.58
waned, withered II.i.21
want, lack II.ii.72, II.vi.11, IV.xiv.53
    urgent need III.xii.30
war-marked, battle-scarred III.vii.44
warrant, assure III.iii.47
wassails, revelry I.iv.56
waste, unnecessary expense IV.i.16
watchmen, sentries IV.iii.16
water, tears I.iii.64
waters, (a) deluges, (b) tears I.ii.137
weet, recognise, know I.i.39
weigh, consider II.vi.32
weight, baggage III.i.36
well-divided, well balanced I.v.53
well met, welcome II.vi.56
well studied, well prepared II.vi.47
wharfs, river banks II.ii.216
what, who I.ii.108, III.xiii.86
    what does it matter II.vii.119
    why V.ii.309
whatsome'er, whatever II.vi.98
wherefore, why II.vi.11, III.xiii.122
    what for V.i.4
which, who III.xii.5
who, whoever II.vii.78
whole, together III.vii.71, 74, III.viii.3
whoreson, a term of abuse, 'son of a whore'
    V.ii.272
wild, (a) mad, (b) wanton I.ii.46
    savage V.ii.310
will, desire, lust III.xiii.3
window, shutter, hence eyelid V.ii.312
windowed, placed in a window IV.xiv.72

winds, (a) winds, (b) signs I.ii.137
witch, a magician (male or female) I.ii.37,
    IV.xii.47
withal, with it I.ii.143, III.vi.59, V.ii.167
without doors, out of doors II.i.13
woo't, will you IV.ii.7, IV.xv.59
word, theme, motto II.ii.48, III.i.31
words, (v.) tries to deceive by words V.ii.191
wore, spent V.i.8
work, trouble IV.vii.2
workman, craftsman IV.iv.18
worky-day, ordinary (like a working day)
    I.ii.48
worm, snake V.ii.243 etc
worser, worse II.v.90
worthiest, most heroic IV.xii.47
wot, know I.v.22
wound, cut through I.iv.49
wrangle, quarrel II.ii.109
wrangling, argumentative I.i.48
wrestle, compete with III.ii.62
wretch, creature (a term of endearment)
    V.ii.299
wrong, wrongly III.vi.81

Y

yare, (*adj.*) nimble, quick III.vii.38, III.xiii,131
    (*adv.*) quickly V.ii.279
yarely, promptly II.ii.214
yield, (*v.*) report II.v.28
    reward IV.ii.33
yond, that (over there) III.ix.1, IV.xii.1